MOON HANDBOOKS

GLACIER NATIONAL PARK

BECKY LOMAX

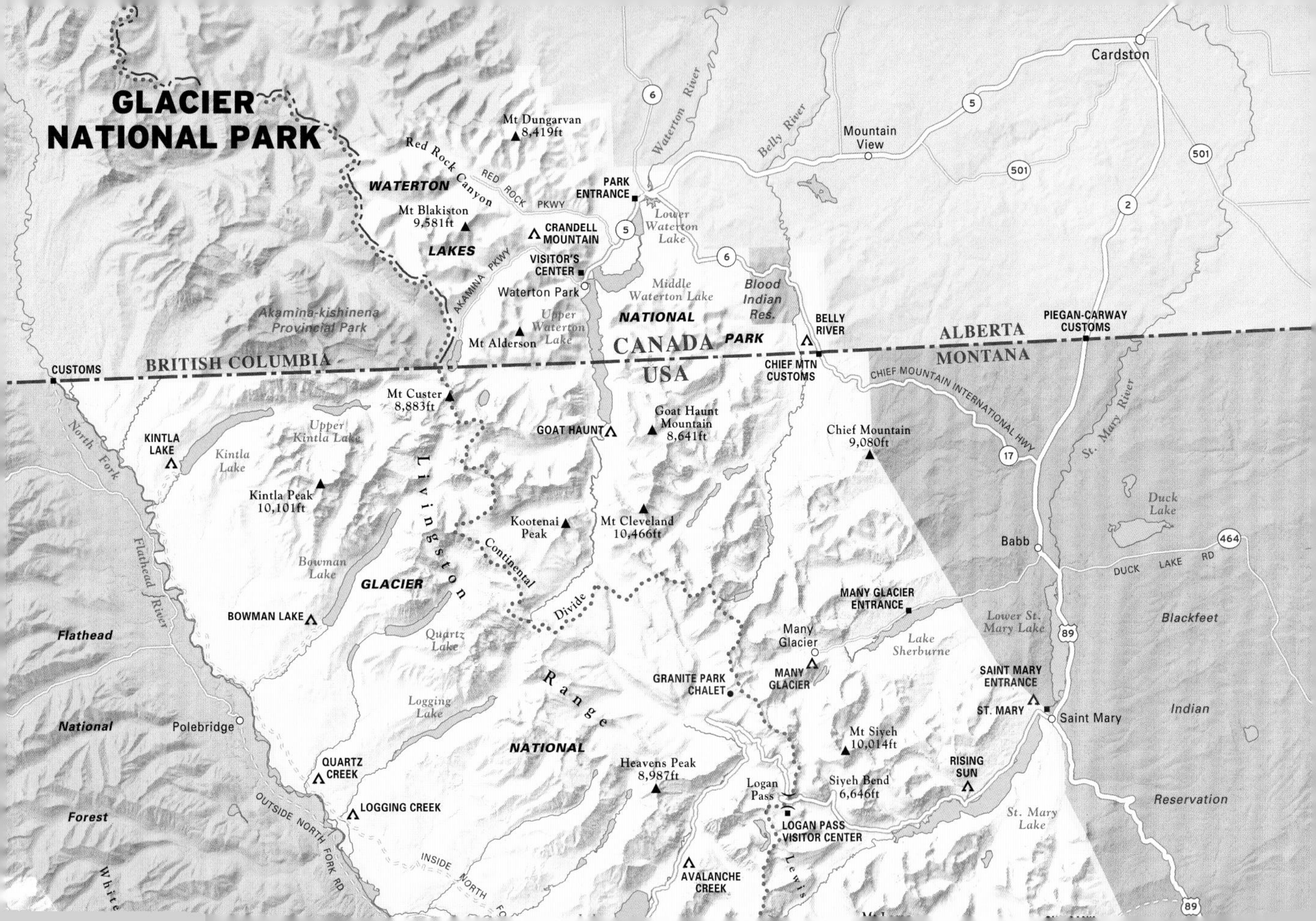
GLACIER NATIONAL PARK
Cardston
Mountain View
Waterton River
Belly River
Mt Dungarvan 8,419ft
Red Rock Canyon
RED ROCK PKWY
WATERTON
LAKES
Mt Blakiston 9,581ft
PARK ENTRANCE
CRANDELL MOUNTAIN
VISITOR'S CENTER
Waterton Park
AKAMINA PKWY
Lower Waterton Lake
Middle Waterton Lake
Upper Waterton Lake
Blood Indian Res.
NATIONAL
PARK
Akamina-kishinena Provincial Park
Mt Alderson
CANADA
USA
BELLY RIVER
PIEGAN-CARWAY CUSTOMS
ALBERTA
MONTANA
BRITISH COLUMBIA
CUSTOMS
CHIEF MTN CUSTOMS
CHIEF MOUNTAIN INTERNATIONAL HWY
Mt Custer 8,883ft
Goat Haunt Mountain 8,641ft
GOAT HAUNT
Chief Mountain 9,080ft
St. Mary River
KINTLA LAKE
Kintla Lake
Upper Kintla Lake
Kintla Peak 10,101ft
Livingston
Kootenai Peak
Mt Cleveland 10,466ft
Continental
Divide
Duck Lake
Babb
DUCK LAKE RD
Bowman Lake
GLACIER
BOWMAN LAKE
North Fork
Flathead River
Flathead
National
Forest
White
MANY GLACIER ENTRANCE
Lower St. Mary Lake
Blackfeet
Indian
Reservation
Many Glacier
Lake Sherburne
MANY GLACIER
Quartz Lake
GRANITE PARK CHALET
SAINT MARY ENTRANCE
ST. MARY
Saint Mary
Range
Logging Lake
Polebridge
NATIONAL
Mt Siyeh 10,014ft
QUARTZ CREEK
Heavens Peak 8,987ft
Logan Pass
Siyeh Bend 6,646ft
RISING SUN
LOGGING CREEK
LOGAN PASS VISITOR CENTER
St. Mary Lake
OUTSIDE NORTH FORK RD
INSIDE NORTH
AVALANCHE CREEK
Lewis
2
5
6
17
89
464
501

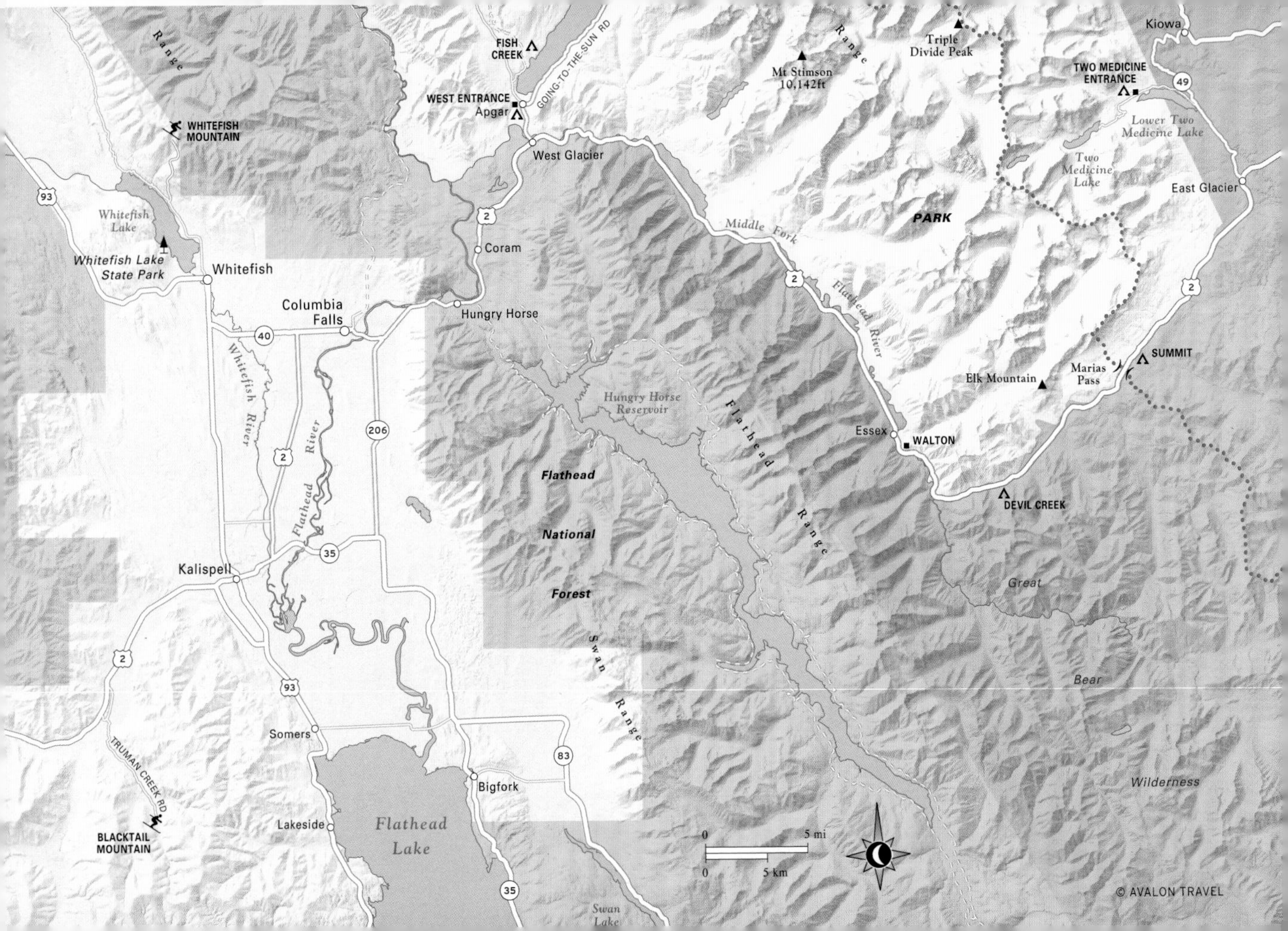
Range
FISH CREEK
GOING-TO-THE-SUN RD
WEST ENTRANCE
Apgar
WHITEFISH MOUNTAIN
Mt Stimson 10,142ft
Range
Triple Divide Peak
Kiowa
TWO MEDICINE ENTRANCE
49
Lower Two Medicine Lake
Two Medicine Lake
East Glacier
West Glacier
93
Whitefish Lake
Whitefish Lake State Park
Whitefish
2
Coram
Middle Fork
PARK
Flathead River
Columbia Falls
Hungry Horse
40
Whitefish River
206
Flathead River
Hungry Horse Reservoir
Flathead Range
Marias Pass
SUMMIT
Elk Mountain
Essex
WALTON
DEVIL CREEK
Flathead National Forest
35
Kalispell
Great Bear Wilderness
Swan Range
93
Somers
83
Bigfork
TRUMAN CREEK RD
BLACKTAIL MOUNTAIN
Lakeside
Flathead Lake
0 5 mi
0 5 km
35
Swan Lake
© AVALON TRAVEL

Contents

Discover
Glacier National Park

Glacier National Park is the undisputed "Crown of the Continent." Its glaciers acsend steep arêtes where mountain goats walk like acrobats. Acres of lush green parkland plunge down jagged red pinnacles, exposing some of the world's oldest stones. Waterfalls roar, ice cracks, and rockfall echoes in scenery still under the paintbrush of change.

In this rugged one million acres, indigenous grizzly bears and wolves top the food chain. Wolverines romp in high glacial cirques. Bighorn sheep graze in alpine meadows while pikas shriek nearby. Only two animals present in Lewis and Clark's day are missing: woodland caribou and bison.

The Continental Divide splits Glacier into the west side and the east side—both different in character, yet wrought from the same geologic building blocks scraping the sky. Two Wild and Scenic Rivers splash along park boundaries, converging at 3,150 feet in elevation while six peaks surpass 10,000 feet. Mount Cleveland is the tallest, its north face one of the highest vertical walls in the United States.

Slicing through the park's heart, the historic Going-to-the-Sun Road twists and turns on a narrow cliff climb. Tunnels, arches, and bridges lead sightseers over precipices where seemingly no road could go. Visitors

overlook glacially scooped ice-abraded valleys, thundering cascades, mammoth lakes, and serrated peaks.

More than 700 miles of trails wind through Glacier's remote wilderness. Hikers walk up verdant valleys, beneath frigid waterfalls, and over high passes. Peak panoramas and blue-green lakes are strung like pearls along trails in places of solitude.

Designated a Biosphere Reserve and World Heritage Site by UNESCO, Glacier hosts a rich diversity of wildlife and a wealth of natural attributes. The park not only has ancient geological heritage; for centuries it was sacred land for Native Americans. Combined with Canada's Waterton Lakes National Park, Glacier is the world's first International Peace Park.

As the Crown of the Continent, the park's glaciers fuel North America's major rivers, with water from here tumbling to Hudson Bay, the Gulf of Mexico, and the Pacific. But as the park celebrated its centennial in 2010, ecologists moved up the predicted end of the glaciers to the next decade—a change that will repaint the scenery once again.

Glacier preserves some of the nation's wildest country. Welcome to this rugged slice of nature's best.

Planning Your Trip

▸ WHERE TO GO

West Glacier and Apgar

West Glacier and Apgar form the park's western portal. Divided by a nationally designated Wild and Scenic River, the area whips into a summer frenzy with white-water rafting, trail riding, fishing, kayaking, boating, hiking, and backpacking. Apgar houses the largest campgrounds on the park's largest lake—Lake McDonald.

North Fork

For those looking to escape the crowds, the remote North Fork on Glacier's west side has real rusticity, not just the look of it. Without electricity, Polebridge Mercantile and Home Ranch Store attract travelers who relish bumpy dirt roads, solitude at Bowman and Kintla Lakes, and wolf serenades.

Going-to-the-Sun Road

As the park's biggest attraction and the only road bisecting the park, Going-to-the-Sun Road leads drivers on a skinny cliff shimmy into the craggy alpine. The National Historic Landmark crosses the Continental Divide at Logan Pass, a wildflower wonderland dancing with glaciers, waterfalls, mountain goats, and top-of-the-world trails.

St. Mary and Many Glacier

Small seasonal St. Mary bustles as a hub of campgrounds, lodges, cabins, cafes, shops, and Going-to-the-Sun Road's eastern portal. In Many Glacier, glimmering sapphire lakes attract hikers. The historic Many Glacier Hotel is in the center of this grizzly-bear haven.

hoary marmot

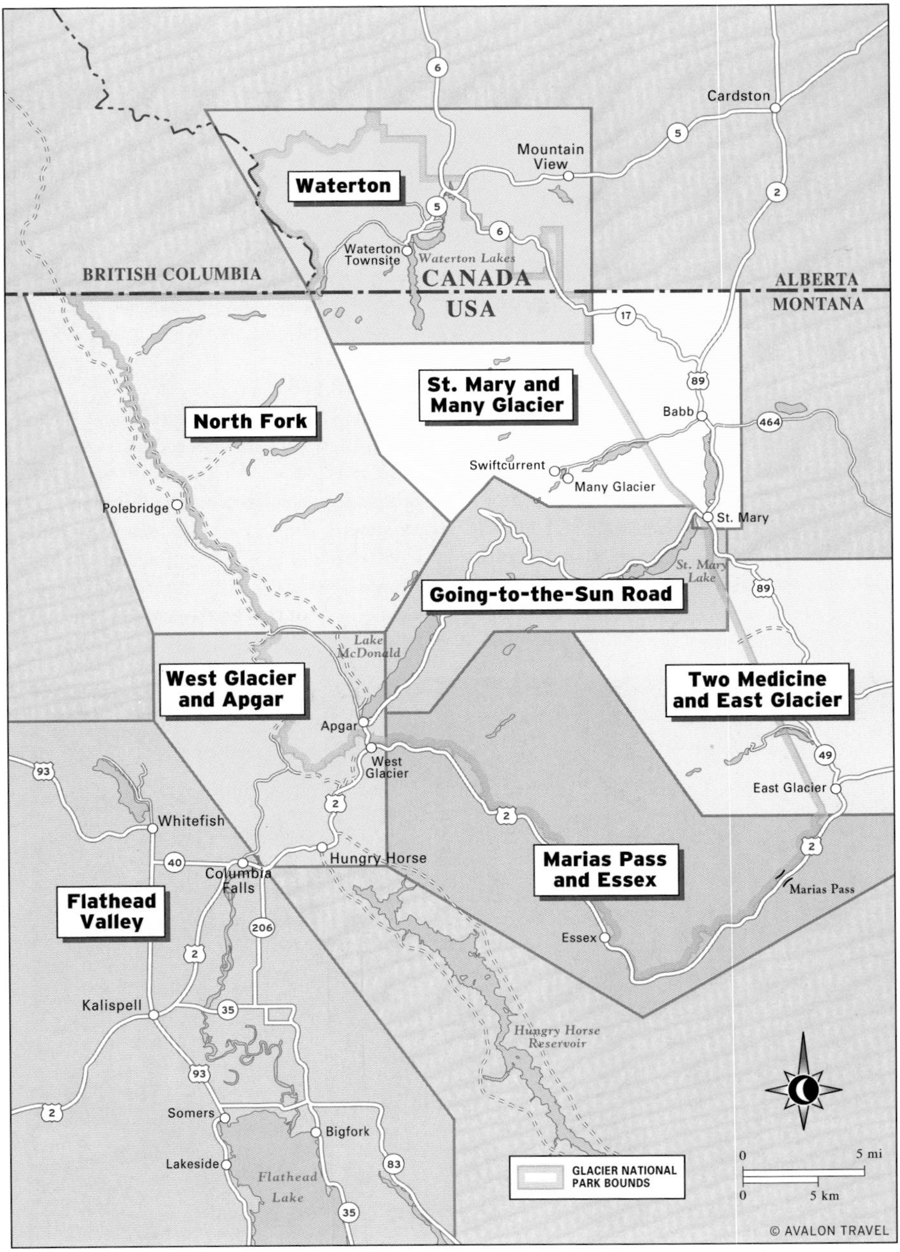
Waterton
North Fork
St. Mary and Many Glacier
Going-to-the-Sun Road
West Glacier and Apgar
Two Medicine and East Glacier
Flathead Valley
Marias Pass and Essex
BRITISH COLUMBIA
CANADA
USA
ALBERTA
MONTANA
Cardston
Mountain View
Waterton Townsite
Waterton Lakes
Babb
Swiftcurrent
Many Glacier
St. Mary
St. Mary Lake
Polebridge
Lake McDonald
Apgar
West Glacier
Whitefish
Columbia Falls
Hungry Horse
Essex
East Glacier
Marias Pass
Kalispell
Hungry Horse Reservoir
Somers
Bigfork
Lakeside
Flathead Lake
GLACIER NATIONAL PARK BOUNDS
0
5 mi
0
5 km
© AVALON TRAVEL

IF YOU HAVE . . .

- **ONE DAY:** Drive over Going-to-the-Sun Road.
- **THREE DAYS:** Visit Many Glacier.
- **ONE WEEK:** Explore West Glacier, Waterton, and Two Medicine.
- **TWO WEEKS:** Add the North Fork, U.S. 2, and Flathead Valley.

Two Medicine and East Glacier

In Glacier's southeast corner, the park's historic headliner hotel, Glacier Park Lodge, greets travelers with its flowered walkway and huge lobby. It buzzes with golfers, swimmers, and trail riders. But Two Medicine Lake yields a quiet contrast for hikers, boaters, anglers, wildlife-watchers, and campers.

Marias Pass and Essex

Pale next to Going-to-the-Sun Road's drama, U.S. 2 crosses mile-high Marias Pass in the fastest route over the Continental Divide along Glacier's southern end. The scenic drive squeezes between Glacier and the Bob Marshall Wilderness, passing the Goat Lick, historic Izaak Walton Inn, and a Wild and Scenic River.

Waterton

In Canada, Waterton Lakes National Park, Glacier's sister park, provides access to Glacier's remote north end. Visitors on Waterton Lake travel by boat to cross the international boundary to Goat Haunt, USA, and walk to the International Peace Park Pavilion. Below the historic Prince of Wales Hotel, Waterton Townsite is a nucleus for boat tours, hiking, shopping, bicycling, dining, and camping.

Two Medicine Lake

Continental Divide at Piegan Pass

Flathead Valley

More than Glacier's western gateway, Flathead Valley is an attraction in itself, with Kalispell, Whitefish, Bigfork, and Columbia Falls drawing visitors for their unique personalities. The valley lives up to its outdoor reputation with boating, fishing, rafting, camping, biking, golf, swimming, hiking, and skiing.

▶ WHEN TO GO

Summer attracts hordes when lodges, campgrounds, and trails are open. Barring deep snows, Going-to-the-Sun Road is open mid-June–mid-September, with peak visitation crammed into four weeks during midsummer. Snow buries some trails into July, when moderate weather rides in. Mosquitoes descend with a vengeance in early summer, wildflowers peak in late July, and huckleberries ripen in August.

Although saddled with unpredictable weather, off-season offers less-hectic visits. Low-elevation trails are usually snow-free in late spring and early fall, but few commercial services are open. While Going-to-the-Sun Road is closed to vehicles, bikers and hikers tour it without cars in spring and fall. In spring, May–June rains intersperse with cobalt-blue skies. In fall, warm bug-free days and cool nights usher in the larch and aspen turning gold and peak-top snows by September's end. In winter, snow closes most park roads, which become snowshoeing and cross-country ski trails.

Paddle the Flathead River.

▸ BEFORE YOU GO

Nondriving travelers usually fly into Glacier Park International Airport in Flathead Valley—the closest airport—or hop the Seattle-Chicago Amtrak train that stops daily in East Glacier and West Glacier. Once at Glacier, shuttles aid travel, but only in summer and only to certain locations. Summer travelers should reserve rental cars in advance. Visitors heading to Waterton will need appropriate documentation to cross the international border.

Northwest Montanans have a saying: "Wait five minutes...the weather will change." Because snow can fall in August, dress in layers—lightweight wicking synthetics, fleeces, and breathable waterproof or water-resistant fabrics. Bring gloves, a warm hat, and rain gear for cold snaps and a hat, sunscreen, and sunglasses for sun. Sturdy walking shoes or hiking boots work best on the rugged trails.

In Montana, dressing for dinner means putting on a clean shirt. Casual attire is the restaurant norm, as are hiking boots and river sandals. Cool weather brings out fleece rather than cashmere. Despite the Wild West heritage, cowboy hats and boots are only for wranglers.

For hiking, bring a pack, a water bottle, and binoculars for wildlife-watching; buy pepper spray for bears. Don't forget the camera, as Glacier's scenery creates foolproof photo opportunities.

Explore Glacier National Park

▸ BEST OF GLACIER NATIONAL PARK

While Glacier adventures can fill a lifetime, you can taste the best of its wild side in a week. Camp throughout the park to carry your adventure from the sun waking you up to sunset with roasting marshmallows on a fire and even beyond with dark skies affording a star-filled night. If camping isn't your thing, you can also enjoy this week of outdoor fun by staying in motels or park lodges.

Day 1

Launch your week of adventures early by selecting a campsite in Two Medicine. Settle in, and put on the hiking boots to climb 3.1 miles to Scenic Point, a hike that will put you on top of the world with east views of the plains and countless mountains to the west. You'll see marmots and perhaps bighorn sheep. After returning to camp, cool down with a swim in Pray Lake. Spend the evening with binoculars watching bears, mountain goats, or bighorn sheep on Rising Wolf's slopes, and enjoy the extreme quiet at night.

Day 2

In the morning, hike 5.2 miles to Cobalt Lake. You'll cross a swinging bridge and see a waterfall en route, and those with extra gumption can climb to Two Medicine Pass for far-reaching views. You can cool off once again in the lake before driving north to St. Mary

backpackers on the Red Eagle Lake trail near St. Mary

Campground or St. Mary KOA, where you made reservations for three nights.

Day 3

Get an early start for Many Glacier. Head 4.5 miles to Iceberg Lake for the novelty of seeing an ice-laden lake in August. Picnic at the lake while watching mountain goats on the surrounding cliffs. Swim with the icebergs, if you dare. Before departing, stop by the spotting scope in the Swiftcurrent parking lot to see bears.

Day 4

Drive to Canada for a lighter day of fun in Waterton Lakes National Park. Look for wildlife on the Akamina Parkway en route to Cameron Lake for a paddling adventure. Rent a canoe or kayak for an hour to paddle to the south end of the lake on the U.S.-Canadian border and a good place to spot grizzlies. Return to the Waterton Townsite and rent surrey bikes for an hour to pedal to Cameron Falls. Before departing, drive through the bison paddock to see the animals that once populated the area.

Day 5

Head up Going-to-the-Sun Road early to Siyeh Bend to hike 12.8 miles over Piegan Pass to Many Glacier. Marmots, pikas, ptarmigan, bighorn sheep, and bears are frequently seen. From Many Glacier, catch shuttles back to Siyeh Bend. (For a shorter nine-mile hike, go just to Piegan Pass and back). Drive west over Logan Pass to Lake McDonald, where you have reservations at Fish Creek for three nights.

Day 6

Saddle up for a full day trail ride from Lake McDonald Lodge to Sperry Chalet. Tour the forest on horseback as the trail winds around Mount Edwards and climbs through avalanches swaths to reach your destination for lunch and fresh-baked pie. When you return to camp, a dip in the lake will wash the dust off.

Rafting is the perfect ending to a week of wild adventures.

Day 7

Go rafting. A full-day trip with any of the raft companies in West Glacier will start you off with a relaxing float on the Middle Fork of the Flathead River. After lunch at Lincoln Creek, you'll hit the white water for a splash-bang ending to your trip, while a photographer captures your paddling through Bonecrusher Rapids.

▶ STEPPING IN HISTORIC FOOTPRINTS

The Great Northern Railway built many of Glacier's lodges to attract train riders. Starting in 2013, several of the historic lodges will be celebrating centennials in successive summers. This tour takes you into these old park lodges, most of them National Historic Landmarks, which have changed little in the past 100 years. Ride Amtrak to get to Glacier in historic style, but then rent a car from Glacier Heli Tours on your first day in West Glacier. History buffs will enjoy this tour with a copy of *Glacier's Historic Hotels and Chalets: View with a Room* in hand.

Day 1

Arrive in West Glacier to stay at the Belton Chalet in a room facing Apgar Mountain. Built in 1910, concurrent with the birth of Glacier National Park, this small hotel provides the perfect leap back in time as well as a start to exploring the park.

Day 2

Drive to East Glacier following the historic Great Northern Railway line as it parallels the highway. From the train station in East Glacier, saunter up the flowered walkway to Glacier Park Lodge, which opened in 1913 as the headliner hotel, and peruse the historic display in the lobby. Take a short drive to Two Medicine Lake to see what remains of the chalet colony built 1911-1915. Enjoy the views from the tour boat up-lake and walk three miles back along the north shore.

Glacier Park Lodge

FUN FOR KIDS

A young hiker puts on her boots after wading.

The trick with kids in Glacier is to be prepared on hikes and adventures. Take along layers to don in case the weather sours. Have kids, even little ones, carry their own packs—even if they only tote a snack. Bring water and snacks; places to fuel kids up are few and far between.

- Stop at a ranger station or visitors center to pick up the Junior Ranger booklet, and complete five activities to receive a badge.
- Visit the Discovery Cabin in Apgar for hands-on learning about wildlife and rocks in Glacier.
- Take a trail ride on horseback in Apgar, West Glacier, East Glacier, Many Glacier, and at Lake McDonald.
- Hike 1.5 miles from Logan Pass to Hidden Lake Overlook to walk across the Continental Divide. Sturdy hikers can add another 1.5 miles to swim in Hidden Lake, but you will need to also hike three miles for the return.
- Hop the double boat ride across Swiftcurrent and Josephine Lakes in Many Glacier to hike one mile to Grinnell Lake, crossing a river on a swinging bridge.
- Hike to Avalanche Lake for wading at its foot or fishing at its head.
- Rent a canoe or kayak for paddle fun on Lake McDonald, Swiftcurrent Lake in Many Glacier, Two Medicine Lake, or at Cameron Lake in Waterton.
- Pedal through the Waterton Townsite on a two-person surrey bike.
- Gaze at wildlife through the ranger spotting scope in the Swiftcurrent Parking Lot at Many Glacier.
- Drive through the Bison Paddock in Waterton to see buffalo that used to populate the plains.
- Raft the Middle Fork of the Flathead River with one of the companies in West Glacier. Do a float trip with young children; older kids will love the white water.
- Reward good hikers with ice cream at Many Glacier Hotel, St. Mary Lodge, Two Medicine Campstore, or Eddie's Snack Bar in Apgar.

Many Glacier Hotel

Day 3

Head north to Many Glacier Hotel via Browning and the Blackfeet Reservation. En route, stop at the Museum of the Plains Indians for the history of how the railroad impacted the Blackfeet. In the afternoon at Many Glacier, take a guided tour of the historic Many Glacier Hotel, built in 1915, and dine in the scenic Ptarmigan Dining Room, now restored to its 1920s look. You can also glean historical tidbits from the display in the lobby.

Day 4

To get a feel for old-time travel in Glacier, take a two-hour trail ride with Swan Mountain Outfitters to Cracker Flats, the site of a mining boomtown in the late 1900s. In the afternoon, enjoy Swiftcurrent Lake by renting a canoe to paddle its waters or taking the double tour boats to the head of Josephine Lake.

Day 5

Drive to St. Mary, stopping at the visitors center to see the Native American displays. Head up Going-to-the-Sun Road, a National Historic Landmark that opened in 1932. At Sun Point, walk out to the site for the Sun Point Chalets, built in 1912 and razed after World War II. The once popular chalets commanded a postcard view of St. Mary Lake. At Logan Pass, tour the visitors center, walk some of the short paved loop trails and a portion of the boardwalk, and photograph yourself at the Continental Divide sign. Descend to Lake McDonald Lodge for the night.

Day 6

Before departing Lake McDonald Lodge, tour the grounds, the lake shore, and the main lodge, which opened in 1914. Drive to Avalanche to walk the one-mile Trail of the Cedars or hike two miles to Avalanche Lake, as early park visitors did. As you depart Glacier, you'll drive the full length of Lake McDonald, stopping at a pullout or two to relish the lake's clear water to return to your starting point in West Glacier.

▸ THE GEOLOGIC LANDSCAPE

With some of North America's oldest exposed rock, a landscape created from moving earth and the carving action of glaciers, Glacier is a naturalist's playground. Put this exploration trip together by staying in park lodges, motels, or campgrounds. Novice geologists will enjoy this tour with the books *Geology Along Going-to-the-Sun Road* and *Glacier: The Story Behind the Scenery* to aid in the discovery.

Day 1

Discover Glacier's ancient shallow inland Belt Sea origins by driving Going-to-the-Sun Road to Logan Pass. Hike 1.5 miles to Hidden Lake Overlook, stopping at the huge red rocks adjacent to the boardwalk. You'll see ripple marks and mud cracks, evidence of the sea. The surrounding peaks also show multicolored layers from different sediments that solidified 1.6 billion years ago. Spend the next three nights in Many Glacier or St. Mary.

Day 2

Head to Many Glacier to join the park naturalist guided hike to Grinnell Glacier. You'll take a boat ride and climb 3.9 miles into the glacial basin. You'll learn the difference between ancient Pleistocene glaciers that carved the giant valleys and today's alpine glaciers, plus see first-hand the glacier melting into a lake.

Day 3

To hike through a mountain, climb five miles to Ptarmigan Tunnel. You'll see folds in rock layers above the switchbacks, the result of pressure from moving plates. Rich colorful layers of sentiments border the tunnel, and red explodes from the oxidized argillite when you exit the tunnel's north side.

Day 4

Take a relaxing drive to Marias Pass on U.S. 2 to see where geologists first discovered

colorful layers of sedimentary Belt Sea strata

GLACIERS: UP CLOSE AND PERSONAL

mountain goat at Sperry Glacier

Sadly, the park's namesake glaciers are expected to melt away completely within the next 8-18 years. See them up close while you still can. Trails lead to the edge of several glaciers, but without proper gear and safety training, stay off the ice. Crevasses, ice bridges, and underground streams make them deadly.

SPERRY GLACIER

Hike or ride horseback six miles from Lake McDonald to Sperry Chalet. Spend two nights among mountain goats at the backcountry campsite or the chalet and climb four miles up through the rock-hewn stairway at Comeau Pass into the scoured basin that houses Sperry Glacier. Follow rock cairns to the overlook of the ice—now reduced to about 200 acres.

PIEGAN AND SEXTON GLACIERS

Catch a morning shuttle to Siyeh Bend to hike the 10.3-mile Siyeh Pass Trail. The route offers views of the 62-acre Piegan Glacier while climbing to the pass and Sexton Glacier while descending to Sunrift Gorge. A spur trail leads closer to the 68-acre glacier hugging Going-to-the-Sun Mountain.

GRINNELL GLACIER

From Many Glacier Hotel, hop the early hiker shuttle across Swiftcurrent and Josephine Lakes; then climb four miles to Grinnell Glacier. Sit on the shore of the 152-acre glacier that is melting into a frigid iceberg-filled lake. The 42-acre Salamander Glacier clings in the cliffs above the lake while Gem Glacier, a mound perched on Mount Gould, no longer has the required size to qualify as a glacier.

BLACKFOOT AND JACKSON GLACIERS

You can see these glaciers from Going-to-the-Sun Road at Jackson Overlook and the next two pullouts east. Use binoculars to scope out the 688 acres of Blackfoot and Jackson Glaciers. An eight-mile hike leads to Jackson Glacier, but it still requires an off-trail scramble to get to the ice.

Highline Trail from Going-to-the-Sun Road

the Lewis Overthrust. An interpretive sign explains the huge movement of the older Pacific Plate shoving atop the younger Continental Plate, and you can see the line separating the two on Summit Mountain. Farther west, stop at the Goat Lick, where river erosion exposed minerals that attract the white creatures. Follow the river-carved Stevens Canyon and the Middle Fork of the Flathead River to West Glacier, Apgar, or Lake McDonald for overnighting.

Day 5

Return to Logan Pass to culminate your geological explorations with the Highline Trail. Hike along the Continental Divide to see U-shaped valleys, distant glaciers, hanging valleys, and ancient fossils. In the basin before Haystack Saddle, examine the large gray boulders for swirling shapes—stromatolites, the only fossils from the Belt Sea. Turn around at the saddle for a 7-mile hike or continue to Granite Park Chalet and The Loop for an 11-mile hike.

Grinnell Glacier is melting into a lake.

WILDLIFE-WATCHING HOT SPOTS

bighorn sheep

With 60 mammal species and more than 260 species of birds, wildlife watchers keep busy in Glacier.

GOAT LICK

On U.S. 2, the natural mineral lick attracts mountain goats in early summer.

INSIDE NORTH FORK ROAD

Spot elusive gray wolves on this uncrowded dirt road at dawn or dusk.

MCGEE MEADOWS

The North Fork Valley houses 196 bird species, half which are nesters. McGee Meadows bustles with snipes, soras, and red-tailed hawks.

LOGAN PASS

Mountain goats and bighorn sheep wander through the parking lot at Logan Pass and frequent the Hidden Lake Overlook trail.

AVALANCHE CHUTES

In early spring, grizzly bears prowl for carcasses in avalanche slopes on Mount Cannon and the Glacier Wall on Going-to-the-Sun Road.

ST. MARY AND VIRGINIA FALLS

These two waterfalls create perfect habitat for dark, bobbing American dippers.

HENKEL AND ALTYN

Grizzly and black bears feed on huckleberries on these two peaks in Many Glacier in late summer.

SWIFTCURRENT TRAIL

A gentle hike runs through moose country to Red Rocks and Bullhead Lakes. The valley also teems with birds: white-crowned sparrows, loons, Clark's nutcrackers, and golden eagles.

TWO DOG FLATS

In spring and late fall, elk feed in early morning at Two Dog Flats near Rising Sun while aspens attract woodpeckers, flickers, and owls.

BISON PADDOCK

The Waterton bison paddock houses a small herd of shaggy bovines that once roamed wild.

WATERTON LAKES

Waterton's Maskinonge and Linnet Lakes wetlands abound with ospreys, swans, and kingfishers.

KOOTENAI LAKES

Hop the Waterton tour boat and hike to Glacier's Kootenai Lakes to see moose and trumpeter swans.

▸ LAKES, RIVERS, AND WATERFALLS

Glacier National Park is more than mountains; it fills with water—spewing from mountainsides in waterfalls, coursing down frothy rivers, and spilling into long finger lakes. Follow this tour of impressive water features in the Crown of the Continent watersheds. For the best conditions, plan to complete the tour in July after spring runoff leaves waters crystal clear but while snowmelt still feeds the waterfalls.

Day 1

Begin in Waterton Lakes National Park, hopping aboard the *International* for a ride down Waterton Lake, a narrow fjord-like waterway tucked below high peaks and shared by Canada and the United States. After debarking at Goat Haunt, hike 2.8 miles through old-growth forest to Kootenai Lakes, where you can often spot moose and trumpeter swans.

Day 2

Drive to Many Glacier to stay for three nights. From the Swiftcurrent Parking Lot, walk 1.8 miles up to Red Rocks Falls for a dazzling display of color, frothy white against the red argillite, as the water tumbles into Red Rocks Lake. You can continue walking up valley to add on Bullhead Lake and waterfalls plunging over the headwall below South Swiftcurrent Glacier.

Day 3

From the Swiftcurrent Picnic Area, hike 5.6 miles to Grinnell Glacier to see the newest lake forming in the park. As the glacier melts, Upper Grinnell Lake grows bigger. You can chop off mileage by taking the boat over Swiftcurrent and Josephine Lakes. En route you'll look down on turquoise Grinnell Lake and Grinnell Falls. On your return, you'll get a view down the valley of the string of lakes left as footprints of ancient ice-age glaciers.

kayaker on Lake McDonald

TOP 10 DAY HIKES

The Iceberg Trail runs below the dramatic Iceberg Wall.

Glacier is a hiker's park, with more than 700 miles of trails. Shuttles running July-Labor Day help accommodate point-to-point hiking over Going-to-the-Sun Road.

APGAR LOOKOUT

Located at Lake McDonald's foot, the lookout requires a 3.6-mile climb to attain the big view rewards. Glacier's far-reaching panorama stretches from Canada to the Bob Marshall Wilderness.

AVALANCHE LAKE

In the McDonald Creek Valley, a two-mile trail heads up a red rock side canyon to the idyllic lake. Fed by Sperry Glacier above, waterfalls spew thousands of feet down the cliffs rimming the lake.

HIGHLINE TRAIL

Beginning at Logan Pass, the stunning 11.6-mile point-to-point goat walk tiptoes through high wildflower meadows along the Garden Wall arête to historic Granite Park Chalet.

SIYEH PASS

At Siyeh Bend on Going-to-the-Sun Road, this point-to-point trail circles 10.5 miles around Going-to-the-Sun Mountain with views of several glaciers. Preston Park blazes with purple wildflowers.

SCENIC POINT

Above Two Medicine Lake, this three-mile yields huge plains and mountain views.

DAWSON-PITAMAKIN LOOP

In a hike that includes a boat ride across Two Medicine Lake, the 16-mile loop actually crosses three passes: Dawson, Cutbank, and Pitamakin on a narrow top-of-the-world path.

ICEBERG LAKE

To see icebergs in August, a 4.5-mile ascent in Many Glacier leads to a lake where chunks of white ice float in deep blue waters.

GRINNELL GLACIER

The 5.5-mile path delights with wildflowers, bighorn sheep, grizzly bears, waterfalls, and stunning turquoise Grinnell Lake.

CARTHEW-ALDERSON

Beginning at Cameron Lake in Waterton, the nearly 12-mile Carthew-Alderson trail climbs into windswept alpine tundra with panoramic views extending to Glacier. Its descent drops past gleaming tarns to the Waterton Townsite.

CRYPT LAKE

Requiring boat access across Waterton Lake, the trail throws a unique twist with a ladder, tunnel, and cliff walk in its five miles.

A short walk leads to St. Mary Falls.

Day 4

Take a day trip south along Glacier's eastern front to Two Medicine Lake, the highest lake you can drive to in the park. Hop on the *Sinopah* tour boat across the lake for a 2.2-mile walk to Twin Falls and Upper Two Medicine Lake, both fed by snowmelt; no active glaciers remain in Two Medicine.

Day 5

Get ready for waterfalls, big rivers, and huge lakes on this Continental Divide-crossing day. Drive to St. Mary to tour Going-to-the-Sun Road, a 52-mile route that links Glacier's two largest lakes, St. Mary Lake and Lake McDonald. Hike 1.5 miles to gushing St. Mary Falls and misting Virginia Falls, whose waters rush toward Hudson Bay. After summiting Logan Pass, drive down the west side to get your car doused by the Weeping Wall and see the 492-foot-tall Bird Woman Falls with water heading toward the Pacific Ocean. Below Avalanche, stop to enjoy McDonald Creek Falls on the longest river in Glacier before reaching Lake McDonald, lodging or camping for two nights at the lake or in Apgar.

Day 6

Spend the day enjoying Lake McDonald, the park's largest lake, filled with multicolored rocks. For a short stroll, walk the Lake McDonald Trail one mile to Rocky Point. For a longer hike, climb 3.6 miles Apgar Lookout for an eagle's eye view of the entire lake valley. In the afternoon, rent a kayak to paddle the shoreline or take the tour boat from Lake McDonald Lodge. Finish your last evening with a sunset picnic and a swim at Apgar Picnic Area.

WEST GLACIER AND APGAR

Sitting just two miles apart, the communities of West Glacier and Apgar span Glacier Park's southwestern boundary—the Middle Fork of the Flathead River. While West Glacier sprouted up outside the park along the Great Northern Railway's line, early trapper and logger homesteads dug in a foothold at Apgar on Lake McDonald—the port to the park's wild interior before Going-to-the-Sun Road was built. Connected by the "new bridge," the park entrance road, and a two-mile paved bicycling and walking pathway, the pair are doorways for exploring Glacier's western wilderness. As such, they throng with cars and visitors in summer; 60 percent of visitors access the park via this west entrance. The communities also launch sightseers in two different directions: to the untrammeled North Fork Valley and to Glacier's crowning highway, Going-to-the-Sun Road.

Today, many concessionaires are headquartered in West Glacier, just outside the national park boundaries. The tiny town has evolved into a seasonal mecca for rafting, guided hiking and backpacking, guided fishing trips, trail rides, and helicopter tours. Along with the train station, campgrounds, restaurants, motels, shops, and even an espresso stand, West Glacier is a place to gas up the car one last time before seeking the park's interior. On Lake McDonald's shores and inside the park, Apgar is calm in comparison. Although its restaurant, lodging, camping, shopping, boat ramp, and

HIGHLIGHTS

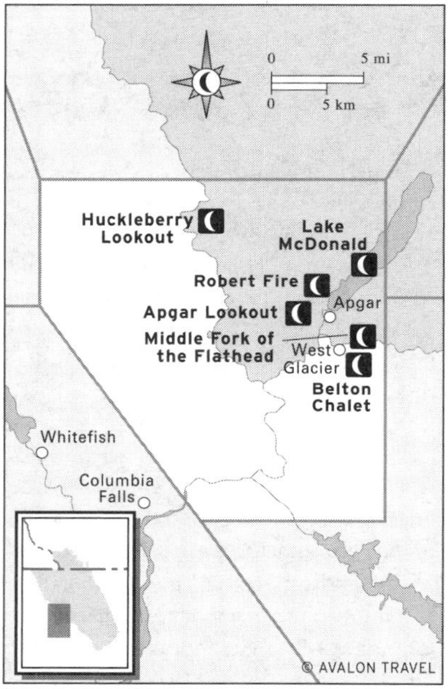

LOOK FOR TO FIND RECOMMENDED SIGHTS, ACTIVITIES, DINING, AND LODGING.

Belton Chalet: Enjoy a tribute to a bygone era of tourism in a chalet as old as the park. On chillier days, cuddle up at the stone fireplace; on warmer days, lounge at sunset on the deck with a local brew (page 33).

Robert Fire: See a forest renewing itself after the 2003 fire on Apgar Mountain and Howe Ridge. The fire forced the evacuation of West Glacier, Apgar, and the McDonald Valley (page 34).

Lake McDonald: Leap into the park's largest lake for a refreshing swim, or paddle its shoreline in a kayak or canoe. The clear waters lure boaters, anglers, scuba divers, photographers, and rock skippers (page 35).

Apgar Lookout: Climb to where you can look down at Lake McDonald, West Glacier, and the North Fork. You'll see a huge panorama of peaks from Canada to the park's southern tip (page 36).

Huckleberry Lookout: Traipse along a top-of-the-world ridge walk where views stretch from Flathead Lake to Canada on this 12-mile round-trip hike (page 36).

Middle Fork of the Flathead: Crash through white water on a raft. This Wild and Scenic River drops through rapids such as Screaming Right Turn, Bonecrusher, Jaws, and Could Be Trouble (page 41).

petite west-side visitors center swarm in high season, miles of lake sprawl with blue waters and enough shoreline to find a niche for solitude.

HISTORY

Native Americans

For the Ksanka or Standing Arrow people, known today as the Salish and Kootenai, whose lands are at Flathead Lake's south end, Glacier's Lake McDonald area held special significance. Ten thousand generations ago, legend says, the Ksanka were first given a ceremonial dance by the spirits at their winter camp near Apgar. Originally called the Blacktail Deer Dance, the ceremony became an annual event for Ksanka, and the area became known as "the place where people dance." Today, the annual dance—now called the Jump Dance—takes place on the Flathead Reservation, but rapids on McDonald Creek still hold the original name, Sacred Dancing Cascade.

Early Tourism

When the Great Northern Railway completed its westbound track in 1891, early visitors jumped off the train in Belton (now West Glacier) to see the area. With no bridge across the Middle Fork of the Flathead, visitors rowed

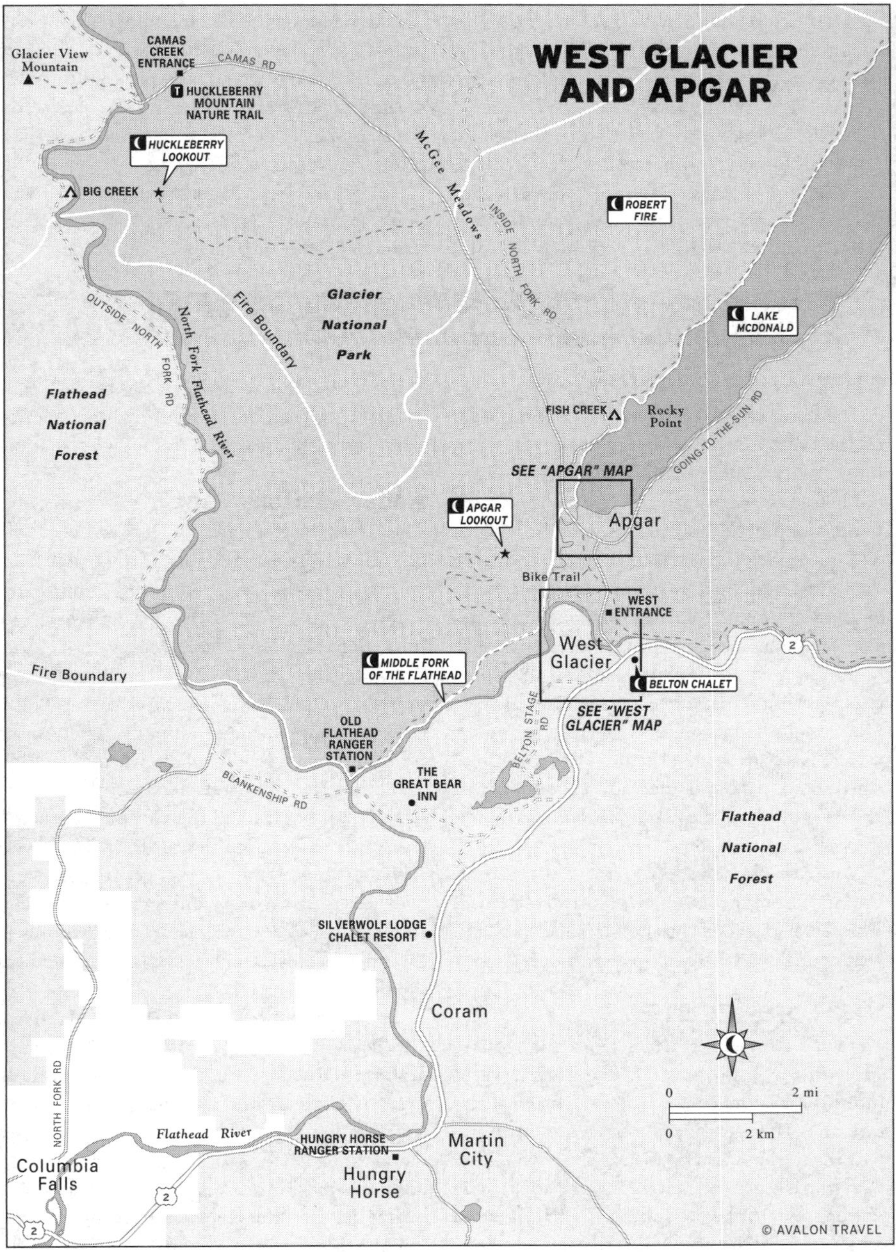
WEST GLACIER AND APGAR
Glacier View Mountain
CAMAS CREEK ENTRANCE
CAMAS RD
HUCKLEBERRY MOUNTAIN NATURE TRAIL
HUCKLEBERRY LOOKOUT
BIG CREEK
McGee Meadows
INSIDE NORTH FORK RD
ROBERT FIRE
Glacier National Park
Fire Boundary
OUTSIDE NORTH FORK RD
North Fork Flathead River
LAKE MCDONALD
Flathead National Forest
FISH CREEK
Rocky Point
GOING-TO-THE-SUN RD
SEE "APGAR" MAP
APGAR LOOKOUT
Apgar
Bike Trail
WEST ENTRANCE
West Glacier
2
MIDDLE FORK OF THE FLATHEAD
BELTON CHALET
Fire Boundary
SEE "WEST GLACIER" MAP
BELTON STAGE RD
OLD FLATHEAD RANGER STATION
BLANKENSHIP RD
THE GREAT BEAR INN
Flathead National Forest
SILVERWOLF LODGE CHALET RESORT
Coram
NORTH FORK RD
0
2 mi
0
2 km
Flathead River
HUNGRY HORSE RANGER STATION
Martin City
Columbia Falls
Hungry Horse
2
2
© AVALON TRAVEL

across the river and then saddled up for a horseback ride to Apgar. Finally, in 1895 a rough dirt road eased the two-mile journey, followed two years later by a bridge across the river.

As the railroad dropped visitors in Belton, Lake McDonald homesteaders leaped into the tourism business, offering cabins, meals, pack trips, boat rides, and guided tours. After Glacier became a national park in 1910, local landowners along the lake retained their property as inholdings. While private summer homes still exist within the park boundaries, to the envy of everyone, when sellers are ready, the National Park Service can purchase these properties at fair market value.

To coincide with Glacier's first summer as a national park, the Great Northern Railway opened Belton Chalet in 1910 across from the depot.

Exploring West Glacier and Apgar

ENTRANCE STATION

Crossing the Middle Fork of the Flathead River on the West Glacier Bridge officially takes you into Glacier National Park. There's even a pullout before the park entrance sign for those who photo-document their travels with park signs. The park entrance is usually staffed during daylight hours during summer and on weekends off-season. If you miss someone in the station, you can use the self-pay cash-only kiosk to purchase a pass. If you don't have an annual pass, seven-day passes cost $25 per vehicle or $12 for individuals on foot, bicycles, or motorcycles. Rates drop to $15 and $10 November-April. Also, pick up a map and the summer or winter edition of the *Waterton-Glacier Guide,* the park's newspaper.

You can also enter Apgar via the Camas Entrance from the rough dirt North Fork Road. There is an unstaffed entrance station at its northwest end, along with a self-pay cash-only kiosk.

VISITORS CENTERS

Glacier's west side suffers from inadequate space in the visitors center. Plans are afoot to move the visitors center from its current location in a tiny cramped house with minimal parking to the Apgar Transit Center, which has a large parking area. However, the move may not happen until after summer 2013. The two locations in Apgar are about a two-minute drive or a seven-minute walk apart. Either way, when the park service does move the visitors center, signage should direct you to the right location.

Apgar Visitors Center

The Apgar Visitors Center (Apgar Loop Rd., 0.2 miles from Camas Rd. or 0.9 miles from Going-to-the-Sun Rd., 406/888-7800, 8am-6pm daily July-Aug., 9am-5pm daily May-late June and early Sept.-late Oct., 9am-4:30pm Sat.-Sun. Nov.-Apr.) has been crammed into a tiny two-room house where more than 190,000 visitors tromp through annually. The visitors center houses a few displays, an information desk, and the small Glacier Natural History Association bookstore. You can pick up maps, naturalist activity guides, and *Junior Ranger Activity Guides.* You can also get the latest updates on trails, roads, campgrounds, fishing, and boating. When the visitors center moves to the Apgar Transit Center, displays and services should expand.

The **Backcountry Permit Office** (May-Nov. 406/888-7859, Dec.-Apr. 406/888-7800, 7am-4:30pm daily May-Sept., 8am-3:30pm daily Oct.) is opposite the old red schoolhouse in Apgar rather than in the visitors center. This is the main office for acquiring permits for overnight backpacking or boating trips. Rush hour is the first 2-3 hours of each morning.

For some free, fun, hands-on activities for

© BECKY LOMAX

Kids can enjoy hands-on learning at the Discovery Cabin in Apgar.

kids, stop by the **Discovery Cabin** in the woods across the street from Eddie's. With the help of interpretive rangers, learning stations teach about wildlife, geology, and natural history. The limited hours vary; consult the visitors center for the current schedule and walking directions to the cabin.

Apgar Transit Center

The transit center is the place to catch shuttles heading up Going-to-the-Sun Road and may house the visitors center in the near future. By car, enter its enlarged parking lot from the junction of Camas Road and Going-to-the-Sun Road, or walk on a trail from the Apgar Visitors Center or Apgar Campground. The transit center, constructed in 2007, reflects high green building standards: restrooms with low-flow toilets, automatic lights, and indigenous flora landscaping. Outdoor signage highlights interpretive information for all major regions of the park. Large parking stalls accommodate RVs.

Alberta Visitor Information Center

Located in West Glacier, the Alberta Visitor Information Center (125 Going-to-the-Sun Rd., 800/252-3782, www.travelalberta.com, 8am-7pm daily late May-early Sept., 8am-5pm daily late Sept.) is a building-size advertisement for Alberta, complete with dinosaur bones. For those heading over the border to Waterton, the center is worth a stop to help with travel planning. The staff has plenty of brochures and maps to give away. You'll also find big clean public restrooms.

SHUTTLES AND TOURS

Shuttles

Free shuttle buses (7am-7pm July 1-Labor Day) link Apgar Campground, Apgar Village, and Apgar Transit Center with stops on Going-to-the-Sun Road. Shuttles circulate every 15-30 minutes. Look for the interpretive signs marking the shuttle stops. From the transit center, you can catch shuttles heading up

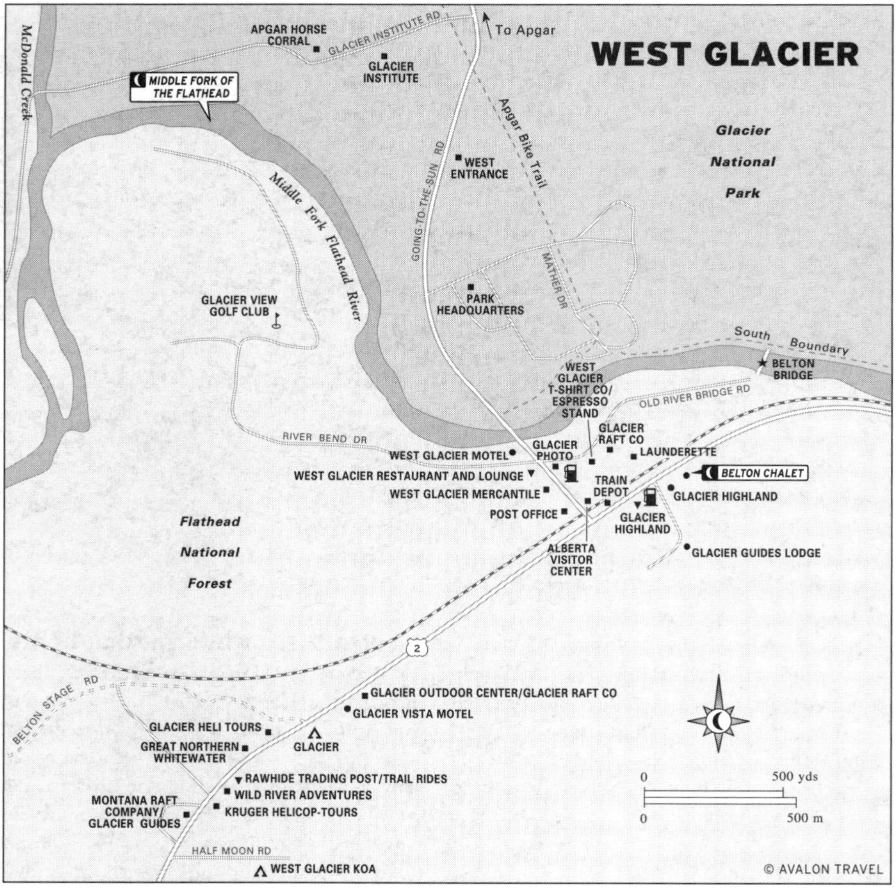

Going-to-the-Sun Road toward McDonald Lodge, Avalanche, several trailheads, and Logan Pass, where you can transfer to the St. Mary shuttle. The no-reservations, no-tickets shuttles are popular, so you may have to wait for a seat during the peak season. Designed for hikers, the shuttles do not come with interpretive guides. If you are heading toward Logan Pass, be sure to take a day pack with water, snacks, and extra clothing for fast-changing weather.

Running late May-late September, **Glacier Park Inc.** (406/892-2525, www.glacierparkinc.com) shuttles rail passengers between West Glacier's Belton Depot and Apgar Village Inn (adults $6, children $3) or Lake McDonald Lodge (adults $10, children $5). Reservations are mandatory, and the shuttle does not stop at campgrounds, but there are campgrounds within a 10-minute walk of the inn or the lodge.

Flathead-Glacier Transportation (406/892-3390 or 800/829-7039, www.glaciertransportation.com) runs shuttle buses by reservation between Glacier International Airport and West Glacier ($40 one-way) or Apgar ($45 one-way). Rates are for the first passenger, with each additional passenger costing $3.

Bus Tours

For those with oversize vehicles not permitted on Going-to-the-Sun Road, two companies offer the easiest way to tour Logan Pass when it is open.

Glacier Park's fleet of **Red Buses** (406/892-2525, www.glacierparkinc.com, late May-Sept., adults $40-85, children $20-43) are the best way to tour in historic style, with roll-back tops allowing for unobstructed peak views and au naturel air-conditioning. Make reservations a day in advance, especially in midsummer. Half-day, full-day, and evening tours are run from Lake McDonald Lodge but have pickups at West Glacier KOA, Village Inn in Apgar, and Apgar Transit Center. When Logan Pass is closed (mid-Sept.-mid-June), the red buses tour around Huckleberry Mountain. Rates do not include park entrance fees, meals, or driver tips.

With a pickup at the Alberta Visitor Information Center, **Sun Tours** (406/226-9220 or 800/786-9220, www.glaciersuntours.com, call for times and days, adults $40, under age 13 $20, park entrance fees not included) departs for four-hour tours to Logan Pass and back. The air-conditioned 25-passenger coaches are extremely comfortable, with extra-big windows enhancing the views. Native American guides give insight into the park's rich Native American heritage—from the days of the buffalo to modern spirituality.

Helicopters

Two helicopter tour companies—both less than one mile west of the train depot—fly half-hour and one-hour tours over Glacier Park daily mid-May-September. Rates range $120-970 pp, based on the number of passengers and flight duration. Since tours are weather dependent, storms may force rescheduling. Make reservations a few days in advance, especially if you want to keep the cost down by sharing the ride with other passengers. **Glacier Heli Tours** (11950 U.S. 2 E., 406/387-4141 or 800/879-9310) flies two helicopters, seating four or six passengers. **Kruger Helicop-Tours** (11892 U.S. 2 E., 406/387-4565 or 800/220-6565, www.krugerhelicopters.com) carries four passengers per flight.

SERVICES

Gasoline is not available inside the park, on Going-to-the-Sun Road, or on U.S. 2 until East Glacier. The last chance for gas is West Glacier, where gas is available year-round with a credit card at **Glacier Highland** (across from the train depot) or in summer at **West Glacier MRC Gasoline** (across from the Mercantile).

The **West Glacier Laundromat** (8am-10pm daily mid-May-mid-Sept.) is behind the Alberta Visitor Information Center. If it is packed, both the West Glacier KOA and West Glacier Campground have launderettes. You can also get a hot shower ($5) at both campgrounds.

The post office is in West Glacier opposite the Alberta Visitor Center. ATMs are located in Apgar at Eddie's and in West Glacier near the MRC gas station.

Glacier Heli Tours (11950 U.S. 2 E., 406/387-4141 or 800/879-9310, www.glacierhelitours.com) rents a selection of sedans, minivans, and SUVs.

Cell Phones and Internet

Cell phone service is available in West Glacier and Apgar, but it is intermittent in adjacent canyons. Only a few hotels and private campgrounds between West Glacier and Hungry Horse provide Internet access.

Shopping

West Glacier and Apgar each have several small gift shops with souvenirs, T-shirts, and books. In Apgar, stop by **Montana House of Gifts** (Apgar Rd., next to the visitors center, 406/888-5393, year-round) for its locally made pottery, weaving, jewelry, crafts, and arts—some by Native Americans. In West Glacier,

Glacier Outdoor Center (11957 U.S. 2 E., 406/888-5454 or 800/235-6781, daily May-Oct.) carries outdoor gear for hiking, rafting, and fishing. Also in West Glacier next to the MRC gas station, **Glacier Photolabs Inc.** (205 Going-to-the-Sun Rd., 406/212-6497, www.glacierphoto.com, late May-Sept.) carries cameras and photography gear. The shop also leads photography workshops and rents camera lenses for wildlife photography.

Located in the historic Belton Railway Station in West Glacier, the **Glacier National Park Conservancy** (GNPC, 406/888-5756, www.glaciernationalparkconservancy.org, year-round) headquarters sells books, posters, and maps of Glacier. This is the place to go for all reference, natural history, centennial, hiking, and picture books on the park. GNPC also runs a small bookstore in the Apgar Visitors Center and at six other park locations. You can also order products from the GNPC website.

Newspapers and Magazines

Look for three daily newspapers: Kalispell's *Daily Interlake, The Missoulian* from Missoula, and the *Great Falls Tribune.* For the scoop on park news, the weekly *Hungry Horse News* gives a good inside look. You can also find the free weekly *Flathead Beacon* (www.flatheadbeacon.com), covering Flathead Valley and park news.

Emergencies

For emergencies within park boundaries, contact a ranger or call 406/888-7800. Outside park boundaries, call 911. A seasonal urgent-care clinic operates in West Glacier (100 Rea Rd., 406/888-9224, 9am-4pm daily, Memorial Day-Labor Day). The nearest hospitals are in the Flathead Valley: **Kalispell Regional Hospital** (406/752-5111) and **North Valley Hospital** (406/863-3500 or 888/815-5528) in Whitefish.

The nearest ranger station inside the park is **Glacier National Park Headquarters** (406/888-7800), on Going-to-the-Sun Road just west of the park entrance station. Turn onto the well-signed side road and take the first right into the parking lot for the headquarters building. You can also get assistance at the Apgar Visitors Center.

For concerns with the Flathead River system or in Flathead National Forest, stop in **Hungry Horse Ranger Station** (10 Hungry Horse Dr., Hungry Horse, 406/387-3800, www.fs.fed.us/r1/flathead). Find it just off U.S. 2 at milepost 143.1.

DRIVING TOUR

Camas Road

Outside Apgar, the 11.3-mile summer-only Camas Road runs north across Lower McDonald Creek toward the North Fork of the Flathead River. Climbing along the base of the Apgar Range, the road traverses through the **2003 Robert Fire** and the **2001 Moose Fire,** which offer a contrast in forest succession after burns. Several pullouts en route are worth a stop: If you can stand the mosquitoes, grab binoculars to peruse **McGee Meadows** (at 5.5 miles) for moose, deer, and bear. Just west of the Camas entrance station, at 11.1 miles, a turnoff leads to **Huckleberry Mountain Nature Trail,** a 0.9-mile self-guided loop with views of the remote Livingston Range. After crossing the park boundary—the North Fork River—the Camas Road terminates at North Fork Road. When bears frequent the Camas Road, you may see rangers hazing them away from the roadway. They are trying to condition the bears to steer clear of trafficked areas for their own safety.

SIGHTS

While most visitors head straight to Lake McDonald, the biggest attraction in the area, there's plenty more to see in West Glacier and Apgar.

West Glacier

The town of West Glacier, originally known as Belton, was historically centered around the

Belton Train Depot and Belton Chalet. Today, U.S. 2 divides the two, and West Glacier now has recreational concessions such as rafting, backpacking, hiking, helicopter tours, and fishing. To leave the highway bustle, drive through the railroad tunnel and enter a historic world preserved by the Lundgren family, operators for over 50 years of the West Glacier Mercantile Company. The vintage brown 1938 buildings house a bar, a restaurant, gift shops, a grocery, and a motel. Fall finds birch leaves covering the ground as shops board their windows, leaving the town's 224 year-round residents to themselves.

Belton Chalet

In 1910, Glacier became a national park, and the Belton Chalet opened its doors to guests arriving via the Great Northern Railway. The first in a series of Swiss-themed railroad-company chalets built in the park, the Belton served as the park gateway. Milkmaid-attired hostesses and flowered walkways greeted guests. In the Taproom, you can see its original look in the photo that includes the trellised walkway from the train depot to the chalet. Over the years, the chalet changed hands, serving as housing for Civilian Conservation Corps crews building Going-to-the-Sun Road as well as a pizza parlor and a bakery. After heavy snows destroyed roofs and floors in the late 1990s, owners from Bigfork restored the lodge and cabins to the tune of $1 million. In 2000, Belton Chalet was added to the National Register of Historic Places.

© BECKY LOMAX

Belton Chalet is a National Historic Landmark.

Historic Belton Bridge

Belton Bridge opened in 1920, allowing park visitors to drive across to the Flathead River instead of rowing a boat. Ironically, this wood and cement bridge remained standing during the 1964 flood while torrents of water destroyed the new bridge downstream. For a time, this bridge was used again while the new bridge was being repaired. The National Park Service recently fixed up the "old bridge," as locals call it, open now for foot traffic only. It accesses the Boundary Trail, Middle Fork fishing spots, and calm but deep chilly pools for swimming. To find it, turn right in West Glacier on Old Bridge Road, and drive to the end.

Middle Fork of the Flathead

The Middle Fork of the Flathead River collects its waters from deep within the Bob Marshall Wilderness Complex and Glacier National Park. Its north shore high-water mark denotes the national park boundary. Designated a Wild and Scenic River, the Middle Fork—the shortened moniker most people use for the river—vacillates between raging rapids and mesmerizing meanders. Anglers and swimmers gravitate to its blue-green pools. Rafters and kayakers splash through rapids known as Bonecrusher and Jaws. Hikers tootle along its Boundary Trail.

WILDFIRES

In an average summer, 13 wildfires burn in Glacier, altering 5,000 acres of forest landscape. Most are caused by lightning, with more than 80 percent of strikes hitting the park's heavily timbered west side. Some are small and unseen while others send huge smoke plumes thousands of feet in the air.

Two large fire seasons have ripped through Glacier since 2000. In 2001 the Moose Fire burned 71,000 acres in the North Fork area, including Flathead National Forest. In 2003 an onslaught of lightning strikes burned nearly 150,000 acres in several separate fires, creating one of the largest fire seasons in the park's history. You can see the evidence from Going-to-the-Sun Road across Lake McDonald and at The Loop. In 2006 the Red Eagle fire ate up 32,000 acres outside St. Mary. But even in these recent fire zones, plants and forests are already regenerating.

As flames eat up wood, ash falls to the ground, releasing nutrients. Similar to putting good fertilizer on a garden, the ash fosters energetic plant growth, especially with the open tree canopy permitting more sunlight to reach the ground. As a natural succession of greenery takes over, wildlife dependent on plant foraging finds improved habitat. In short, fires help maintain a natural balance. They also remove deadfall and insect infestations that can kill trees. Fires reduce the power of future fires and create forests that are more resistant to drought and nonnative plant invasions. Fire isn't the end of a forest, but an ongoing process of succession in an ever-changing landscape.

Larch and ponderosa, with thick resinless bark and minimal low branches, survive fires. Some species even rely on fires for reproduction: The lodgepole pine's serotinous cones require high heat to release their fast-growing seeds from the sticky resin. Ceanothus, hollyhock, and morel mushrooms flourish after fires.

Until 1968, federal policy suppressed all fires—resulting in excessive fuel buildup, bug infestations, and elimination of some floral species. Today, the National Park Service manages each fire individually. If fires threaten human life or structures, they are suppressed, but lightning fires ranging in the wilds are often just monitored, allowing for a natural cycle. Sometimes, park crews set intentional fires to reduce fuel buildup or protect a resource, such as a prairie, from invasion by other species.

Glacier's wildfires used to be monitored from 17 different lookouts. Today, satellite and airplane surveys have reduced the need for staffed lookouts to Huckleberry, Scalplock, Numa, and Swiftcurrent.

Apgar

Two miles from West Glacier, Apgar is on the shore of the park's largest body of water, Lake McDonald. With Apgar Campground within walking distance and Fish Creek Campground a couple of miles away, Apgar is crowded in summer but still quiet compared to the West Glacier highway hubbub. It's the quintessential national park community. The tiny west-side visitors center, a restaurant, a camp store, two inns, Lake McDonald's only boat ramp, swimming beaches, and picnic areas all cluster here at Lake McDonald's foot. One local gift shop is in Apgar's historic red schoolhouse. Like West Glacier, most of Apgar shuts down by October and opens again in May.

Robert Fire

Summer 2003 unleashed some of the biggest fires in Glacier Park's history. Raging winds shoved the Robert Fire over Apgar Mountain, burning 7,000 acres in four hours. Campers, motel guests, and park headquarters personnel evacuated from West Glacier and Apgar while helicopters doused the fire with water scooped from Lake McDonald. The fire burned 39,000 acres, 29 percent of the park's forests. See postfire forest regeneration on the Camas Road, the Lake McDonald Trail

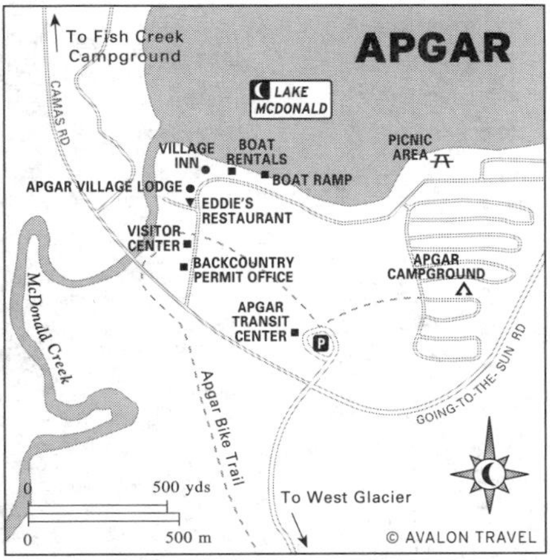

starting at Fish Creek Campground, or from Apgar Lookout. Fast-growing new vegetation thriving on the fire's ash and nutrient-rich soils prompted prolific flower blooms, like pink fireweed, and some tree species requiring fire to sprout are growing again.

Lake McDonald

Catching water from Glacier's longest river, Lake McDonald is 10 miles long and 1.5 miles wide—the largest lake in Glacier National Park. Squeezed between Mount Brown and Stanton Peak at its head, the lake is up to 472 feet deep—the deepest waters in the park. Resting in an ice-scoured trough, the 6,823-acre lake is buffered by larch forests that turn gold in fall. On the lake, visitors fish, boat, and swim in its quiet cold blue; Jet Skis are not allowed. Even waterskiing attracts a few wet-suited diehards. Access the lake's shores via Fish Creek or Apgar Picnic Area, the Apgar boat ramp, or the many pullouts along Going-to-the-Sun Road.

Recreation

If Glacier has a recreation center, it's West Glacier and Apgar. The communities offer hiking, biking, rafting, horseback riding, kayaking, boating, fishing, swimming, and golfing. West Glacier is the unofficial park headquarters for white-water rafting, with two Wild and Scenic Rivers (nationally designated rivers protected for their wilderness and beauty) a short step from the back door.

HIKING

Hiking in Apgar improved substantially with the 2003 Robert Fire. Flames opened up views amid once thick dark forests, and nutrient-enriched ash soils sprouted lush growth. Wildflowers now run amok on slopes that once had meager color. This also is the only park area where a trail permits dogs: The two-mile paved Apgar Bike Trail connecting West Glacier and Apgar is open to walkers, leashed dogs, and bicyclists.

Rocky Point

- Distance: 2 miles round-trip
- Duration: 1 hour
- Elevation gain: none
- Effort: easy
- Trailhead: Fish Creek Campground by Apgar

Rocky Point is a short interpretive romp along Lake McDonald through the 2003 Robert Fire and looping around a promontory on Lake McDonald's north shore. Places of heavy burn with slow regrowth alternate with lighter burn clogged now with lush greenery. Don't forget your camera: The view from Rocky Point looks up the lake toward the Continental Divide and grabs grand shots of Mount Jackson and Mount Edwards to the south. If the lake is calm, you'll get some stunning reflection photos. Snow leaves early and comes late to this trail, making it good for spring and fall hiking. The loop trail connects to the Lake McDonald Trail.

The hike to Huckleberry Lookout yields a panorama of Glacier's peaks.

Apgar Lookout

- Distance: 7.2 miles round-trip
- Duration: 4 hours
- Elevation gain: 1,868 feet
- Effort: moderate
- Trailhead: end of Glacier Institute Road, 1.9 miles from Going-to-the-Sun Road
- Directions: Take the first left after the West Entrance Station at the Glacier Institute sign. At the first fork, follow the sign to the horse barn and veer left, crossing over Quarter Circle Bridge. Drive to the road's terminus at the trailhead.

Beginning with a gentle walk along an old dirt road, Apgar Lookout Trail soon climbs steeply uphill toward the first of three long switchbacks. As the trail ascends, large burned sentinels stand as relics from the 2003 Robert Fire. In 2010 more than 300 of the burned trees blew down, opening up the views of the Middle Fork drainage, Rubideau Basin, the railroad line, and West Glacier. Following the third switchback, the trail traverses the ridge—which has snow in June—to the rebuilt lookout. A panoramic view unfolds from Canada to the park's southern sector, and you can see all six of the park's peaks that are higher than 10,000 feet.

From this 5,236-foot aerie, you can see the path of the Robert Fire where it burned 7,000 acres in four hours. Prior to the fire, heavy timber and brush occluded views, but Apgar Lookout now ranks as one of the park's most scenic hikes. While fire and blowdown improved the views, trees no longer shade the southwest-facing slope; hike in the morning on hot days. Park communication radio antennas clutter the summit, but at least they are clustered in one location at the lookout instead of spread out.

Huckleberry Lookout

- Distance: 12 miles round-trip
- Duration: 5-6 hours

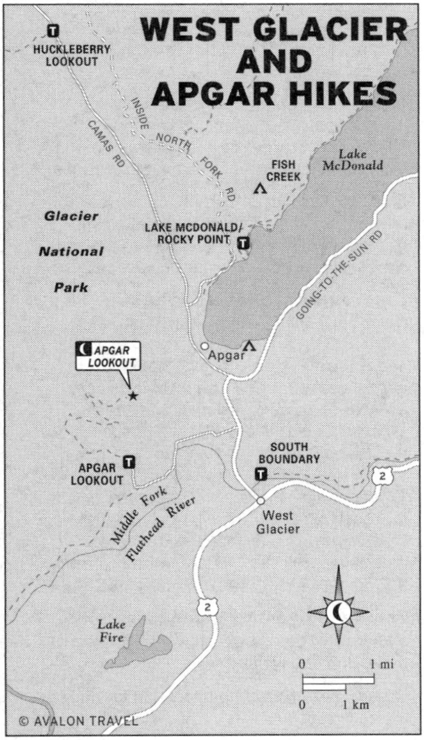

- Elevation gain: 2,725 feet
- Effort: strenuous
- Trailhead: six miles up Camas Road from Apgar, just past McGee Meadows

Huckleberry Lookout trail is aptly named, for huckleberries do abound in this area. During certain times of the season, usually late summer-early fall, the trail closes due to bear activity. The heavy concentration of huckleberries attracts a significant bruin population looking to bulk up for the winter. Check with the park service for the current status. When the trail is closed, clear closure signs are posted at the trailhead.

The trail begins with a gentle walk through lodgepole forest. Soon the path climbs, steadily gaining elevation among larches until it emerges on steep-sloped meadows and reaches a saddle at 4.5 miles. In a short reprieve from the climb, the trail traverses a wide bowl until it crests the Apgar Range for the final ascent to the lookout at 6,593 feet. A spectacular view of the North Fork Valley and the park's Livingston Range unfolds. During fire season, the lookout is staffed. Evidence of the 2001 Moose Fire clings to Huckleberry Mountain as well as Demers Ridge below and the North Fork Valley. Snow often packs the upper trail until mid-July.

Lake McDonald West Shore Trail

- Distance: 7 miles one-way
- Duration: 3.5 hours
- Elevation gain: none
- Effort: easy
- Trailhead: Fish Creek Campground or North McDonald Road

While this year-round trail (use skis or snowshoes in winter) wanders mostly back in the trees along the north shore of Lake McDonald, you can garner views of the peak-flanked lake when it pops out to the shoreline. The brushy trail also offers a study of postfire forest succession. Burned by the 2003 Robert Fire, the trail passes through lush new growth and stands of black or gray trunks. Most hikers opt to saunter out for a few miles to the backcountry campsite, perhaps drop a fishing line into the lake, and turn around again. With a car shuttle, you can hike the full length.

South Boundary Trail

- Distance: 10.6 miles round-trip to Lincoln Creek
- Duration: 5 hours
- Elevation gain: 400 feet
- Effort: easy
- Trailhead: behind park headquarters on Mather Drive's south end, or the old bridge in West Glacier

After parking at headquarters, walk through the headquarters housing area to the trailhead.

HIKING ESSENTIALS

Hiking in Glacier demands preparedness. Unpredictable fast-changing weather can mutate a warm summer day into wintry conditions in hours. Different elevations vary in temperature, wind, and visibility: Sun on the shore of Two Medicine Lake may hide knock-over winds barreling over Dawson Pass six miles away. Hot valley temperatures may give way at Grinnell Lake to chilly breezes blowing down from the Continental Divide across the ice. To be prepared in Glacier's backcountry, take the following:

- **Extra clothing:** Rain pants and jackets can double as wind protection, while gloves and a lightweight warm hat will save fingers and ears. Carry at least one extra water-wicking layer for warmth. Avoid cotton fabrics, which stay soggy and fail to retain body heat.
- **Extra food and water:** Depending on the hike's length, take a lunch and snacks, like compact high-energy food bars. Low-odor foods will not attract animals. Always carry extra water: Heat, wind, and elevation lead quickly to dehydration, and most visitors find they drink more than they do at home. Avoid drinking directly from streams or lakes. Due to the possibility of giardia and illness-inducing bacteria, always filter or treat water sources before drinking.
- **Map and compass or GPS device:** Although Glacier's trails are extremely well signed, a map can be handy for ascertaining distance traveled and location. A compass or GPS device will also help, but only if you know how to use it. In deep, heavily forested valleys, a GPS receiver may not pick up the satellites.
- **Flashlight:** Carry a small flashlight or headlamp for after-dark emergencies. Take extra batteries too.
- **First-aid kit:** Two bandages may not be enough. Carry a fully equipped standard first-aid kit with blister remedies. Many outdoor stores sell suitably prepared kits for hiking. Don't forget to add personal items like bee-sting kits and allergy medications.
- **Sun protection:** Altitude, snow, ice, and lakes all increase ultraviolet radiation. Protect yourself with SPF 30 sunscreen, sunglasses, and a sun hat or baseball cap.
- **Emergency toilet supplies:** Not every hike conveniently places a pit toilet at its destination. To accommodate an alfresco toilet stop, carry a small trowel, plastic baggies, and toilet paper, and move at least 200 feet away from water sources. For urinating, aim for a durable surface, such as rocks, logs, gravel, or snow. "Watering" fragile plants, campsites, or trails attracts mineral-starved animals that dig up the area. Bury feces 6-8 inches deep in soil. Do not bury toilet paper; use a baggie to pack it out.
- **Feminine hygiene:** Carry heavy-duty zippered baggies and pack out tampons, pads, and everything else.
- **Insect repellent:** Summer can be abuzz at any elevation with mosquitoes and blackflies. Insect repellents that contain 50 percent DEET work best. Purchase applications that rub or spray at close range rather than aerosols that go airborne onto other people, plants, and animals.
- **Pepper spray:** If you want to carry pepper spray, purchase an eight-ounce can, as nothing smaller will be effective; however, do not bother unless you know how to use it and what influences its effectiveness. Do not use it like bug repellent.
- **Miscellaneous:** A knife may come in handy, as can a few feet of nylon cord and a bit of duct tape (wrap a few feet around something small like a flashlight handle or water bottle). Many hikers have repaired boots and packs with duct tape and a little ingenuity.

© BECKY LOMAX
Lake McDonald has flat rocks for skipping.

Follow the old Glacier Park Entrance Road to the historic Belton Bridge, where a trail continues upstream. You can also access this trail via the Belton Bridge, but the trailhead here does not have as much parking. With gentle ascents and descents, the path hugs the north-shore hillside above the Wild and Scenic Middle Fork of the Flathead River.

This year-round trail won't feel like wilderness: Noise from the railroad and highway competes with the river's roaring white water. But it's a great place to watch rafters shoot rapids, swim in deep pools, or fish. The trail descends to a fine rocky beach at Lincoln Creek, a stopping point for rafters before they hit the white water. From here, backpackers can opt to continue another 15 miles upriver to Coal Creek or turn 9.4 miles up Lincoln Creek to Lincoln Lake.

Guided Hikes

National Park Service naturalists guide hikes and walks around Apgar mid-June-mid-September. Days and times vary, and the hikes range from easy to strenuous. In winter, the National Park Service offers guided snowshoe trips to look for animal tracks. Grab a current copy of *Ranger-led Activities* at visitors centers to check the schedule. These guided hikes are the best price of all: free.

Glacier Guides (11970 U.S. 2 E., West Glacier, 406/387-5555 or 800/521-7238, www.glacierguides.com, mid-May-Sept.) leads day hikes, backpacking, and overnight chalet trips, but most destinations are outside the West Glacier-Apgar area. For day hiking, hiring a guide costs $390-470 for up to five people. Reservations are required, and rates include the guide service, a deli lunch, and transportation to the trailhead. Solo travelers can hook up with the Tuesday Hikes (July-Aug., $80 pp). Backpacking trips depart every week for 3-6-day adventures; rates run around $155 per day and include the guide service, transportation to and from the trailhead, meals, and snacks. Overnight hikes to backcountry chalets run multiple times each summer for three days ($730) or six days ($1,900). Customized trips are available and cost more. Plan to tip your guide at least 15 percent for day hikes and 20 percent for overnights.

Rentals

Two companies in West Glacier offer rental gear for hikers, backpackers, and campers. **Glacier Outdoor Center** (11957 U.S. 2 E., 406/888-5454 or 800/235-6781, www.glacierraftco.com) carries the most extensive line of rental gear: day packs, backpacks, trekking poles, tents, child carrier packs, ice axes, tents, sleeping bags, sleeping pads, cook stoves, and water purifiers. Each item rents for $3-10 per day. They also rent a full car camping setup for four people ($60 per day). **Glacier Guides** (11970 U.S. 2 E., 406/387-5555 or 800/521-7238, www.glacierguides.com) rents tents, backpacks, or sleeping bags and pads for $8-10 per item.

CYCLING

Bicycling Glacier National Park is not for everyone. Narrow, shoulderless roads are packed with curves, and most trails prohibit bikes. However, the West Glacier-Apgar area does provide off-road options. Pick up rentals in Flathead Valley before coming to the park, as none are available here.

Cycling Trails

A level, paved bicycle trail connects West Glacier with Apgar. Approximately 2.6 miles long, the **Apgar Bike Trail** begins on the north side of the West Glacier Bridge. After dropping through the woods, it crosses through the National Park Service employee housing area before entering the forest again, where it continues on to Apgar, connecting finally with the campground. Be cautious at two road crossings en route. The short dirt **Fish Creek** bike trail provides a shortcut between Apgar and Fish Creek. Bike trails permit dogs on leashes, and they are good flat riding for kids.

The 10-mile round-trip **Old Flathead Ranger Station** ride tours a combination of dirt road and trail that was once a road. It terminates at the confluence of the Flathead River's North and Middle Forks. Access the route from midway between West Glacier and Apgar on the Apgar Bike Trail, turning west on the dirt Glacier Institute Road. At the first junction, follow the sign to the horse barn; at the second, hang a left toward Quarter Circle Bridge. About 0.5 miles past the bridge, the Old Flathead Ranger Station Trail begins. Turn left, biking 3.7 miles to the confluence.

Bicycle Road Tours

Several roads offer bike-tour options. From Apgar, you can climb up the paved Camas Road or explore the dirt Inside Road in the North Fork Valley.

For a longer mountain-bike tour (about 37 miles, 4 hours) on a mix of dirt and paved roads, the **Apgar Mountain Loop** starts in West Glacier and heads west over Belton Stage and Blankenship Roads to connect with North Fork Road. From here, ride north, parallel with the North Fork River to the Camas Road entrance and back into the park. Follow the rolling paved Camas Road back to the Apgar Bike Trail. The scenic loop is well worth a ride, especially in late spring before Going-to-the-Sun Road is open, but be prepared to suck serious dust on the dirt sections during dry spells and to battle mosquitoes and dodge bears along Camas Road.

Apgar is also the launch point for those cycling Going-to-the-Sun Road.

TRAIL RIDING

Swan Mountain Outfitters (406/387-4405 or 877/888-5557, www.swanmountainoutfitters.com, late May-early Sept.) operates two corral locations: one in Apgar and one in West Glacier. Located on Glacier Institute Road northeast of the park entrance station, the **Apgar Corral** (summer 406/888-5010, $40-110) leads daily trail rides to three destinations in Glacier. An easy one-hour saunter to McDonald Meadows and a popular two-hour ride along the C. M. Russell Trail depart several times each day. The half-day ride to Apgar Lookout, which requires a minimum of four people, departs at 7:45am.

Located behind the Rawhide Restaurant, the **West Glacier Corral** (12000 U.S. 2 E., 406/387-5005, $35-155) offers horseback tours through the lodgepole foothills of Flathead National Forest. One- and two-hour tours amble through the forest while the half-day and full-day rides climb to viewpoints. Overnight trips as well as combination saddle-paddles or ride-and-dine trips extend the horseback riding experience.

For trail riding, be sure to wear long pants; you'll be a lot less sore afterward. For safety, wear sturdy shoes or hiking boots, not sandals. Reservations are strongly advised. Swan Mountain Outfitters does not take children under age seven nor riders weighing over 250 pounds.

© BECKY LOMAX

Swan Mountain Outfitters runs trail rides from Apgar and West Glacier.

RAFTING

Two Wild and Scenic-designated rivers form the west and southwest boundaries of Glacier National Park. The Middle Fork and North Fork of the Flathead River offer scenery, wilderness, float sections, and white water. Together the rivers provide 219 miles of recreation. The rafting season runs May-September, with high water usually peaking in late May. Rafters should purchase the *Three Forks of the Flathead Float Guide* ($13), available through Glacier National Park Conservancy (406/888-5756, www.glaciernationalparkconservancy.org) for locations of rapids and public lands for camping. Flathead National Forest manages both rivers; consult the Hungry Horse Ranger Station (10 Hungry Horse Dr., Hungry Horse, 406/387-3800), nine miles west of West Glacier, for assistance in planning a self-guided overnight trip. Toilet systems and fire pans are required for overnight trips.

Middle Fork of the Flathead

Bordering Glacier's southern boundary, the Middle Fork of the Flathead has scenic float sections interrupted by raging white water. The river's headwaters are deep within the Bob Marshall Wilderness Complex, and it drains Glacier's immense southern valleys.

While the white water here cannot compete with the Grand Canyon's monster rapids, the Middle Fork is a fun, splashy place with rapids such as Screaming Right Turn, Jaws, and Pinball. It's easy enough for kids and good introductory fun for a first-time river trip. Whitewater trips begin at Moccasin Creek and end in West Glacier; scenic float trips begin in West Glacier and end at Blankenship.

The Middle Fork offers several put-ins and takeouts easily accessed along U.S. 2. Different sections are appropriate for overnights, day trips, fishing, and short floats. While a few rapids at certain water levels are rated Class IV, the river along Glacier's boundary is primarily Class II and III. No permits are required. However, all camping must be done on the south shore; no camping is permitted on Glacier's shoreline. Since private property abuts some of the south shore, you'll need to be knowledgeable about where you can camp.

North Fork of the Flathead

From Canada, the North Fork of the Flathead flows 59 miles through the remote North Fork Valley. As the river enters the United States, it forms the western boundary of Glacier. Accessed via the bumpy dirt Outside North Fork Road, the Class II-III river provides multiday float trips, day rafting, and fishing. Those looking for tamer water can take out at Big Creek before the Upper Fool Hen Rapids. Put-ins and takeouts are found up and down North Fork Road. No permits are required, but campsites must all be set up on the western shore; no camping is permitted on Glacier's bank except at Round Prairie. The river ends

West Glacier is the rafting capital of the park.

at the confluence with the Middle Fork at the Blankenship River Access, 10 minutes' drive west of West Glacier.

Guides

The commercial rafting season runs May-September, with high water usually peaking in late May-early June. Four West Glacier rafting companies lead half-day and full-day trips on the Middle Fork as well as scenic, dinner, barbecue, and evening floats. They also do saddle-paddle combinations that put you on a horse and a boat the same day. Each company launches 4-5 half-day raft trips daily through the white-water section and guides overnight and multiday trips. Children should be at least six years old for white water.

If you're comparing rates among companies (they're all very similar in cost), be sure to ask if the 7 percent service fee is included in the rate or added on. Also, ask about the size of the raft and the number of people it carries. Smaller rafts have a more exciting ride. Expect to pay (not including service fees) around $50 per adult for a half-day raft trip or $85 for a full day; kids run about $10-25 cheaper. For more fun, tackle the white water in a small sport raft with more kick or on an inflatable kayak, otherwise known as a rubber ducky. Both run around $65-75 pp for a half-day trip; rates include helmets. Paddles and life jackets are included in all rates, but some companies charge additional fees for wetsuits and booties. Clarify the costs when you make your reservation. Plan on tipping the guide about 15 percent.

Overnight rafting trips range 2-5 days; longer trips are usually paired with hiking, horseback riding, or backpacking. Expect to pay around $170 per adult per day for an overnight rafting trip and $140 for children. Specialty trips with cabin stays, horseback riding, or flights will cost more. Plan to tip your guide 20 percent. When making reservations, clarify what you'll need to bring for your overnight.

© BECKY LOMAX

Historic Belton Bridge accesses the Middle Fork River and Trail.

The companies can provide tents, sleeping bags, sleeping pads, and dry bags for your gear.

Glacier Raft Company (6 Going-to-the-Sun Rd., West Glacier, 406/888-5454 or 800/235-6781, www.glacierraftco.com) is right in West Glacier village adjacent to the river—close enough to the takeout that white-water rafters debark at the Middle Fork Bridge to walk two blocks back to the office. Specialty combo packages include half-day white-water rafting with half-day horseback riding or fly-fishing. The company offers 2-4-day overnights and is the only local company permitted to guide trips on the Class III-IV Upper Middle Fork of the Flathead River in the Great Bear Wilderness. Access requires a flight to a remote put-in near the headwaters for the four-day trip ($1,500).

Located one mile west of downtown West Glacier, **Great Northern Whitewater** (12127 U.S. 2 E., 406/387-5340 or 800/735-7897, www.greatnorthernresort.com) is the one company that offers river instruction through Glacier River School courses. The company also runs 2-3-day custom floats on the Middle Fork.

Just off the highway 1.5 miles west of West Glacier, **Montana Raft Company** (11970 U.S. 2 E., 406/387-5555 or 800/521-7238, www.glacierguides.com) is the only company that can combine guided hiking in Glacier National Park with raft trips. An extensive menu of hike-raft or backpack-raft combos can fill a day or a week. The overnight river trips float the Middle Fork or the North Fork of the Flathead River. One series of North Fork overnight trips includes cabin stays.

Also located 1.5 miles west of West Glacier, **Wild River Adventures** (11900 U.S. 2 E., 406/387-9453 or 800/700-7056, www.riverwild.com) offers the unique leisurely Boat and Float trip, which combines a half day of scenic floating on the Middle Fork with a Lake McDonald boat tour. For the more adventurous, the paddle-saddle combo trips include a four-day campout adventure.

Rentals and Shuttles

Got the river savvy to guide yourself? If so, you can do a self-guided raft or inflatable-kayak trip with rentals available in West Glacier. **Glacier Raft Company** (11957 U.S. 2 E., West Glacier, 406/888-5454 or 800/235-6781, www.glacierraftco.com) will outfit you up with the raft, paddles, helmets, life jackets, and a bit of instruction from an experienced guide for a trip from West Glacier down 10 miles of Class I-II river ($105-200). The guide will also help set up your shuttle. The company also offers shuttles for all locations on the Middle and North Forks of the Flathead River using your vehicle or in their rigs ($30-360, depending on locations). Rafts and inflatable kayaks ($40-140) are available and include paddles and life jackets. Individual items such as dry bags, toilet systems, and wetsuits range $3-12. **Montana Raft Company** (11970 U.S. 2 E., West Glacier, 406/387-5555 or 800/521-7238, www.glacierguides.com) also rents rafts, inflatable kayaks, and toilet systems for comparable rates.

WHITE-WATER KAYAKING

White-water kayakers drop into the **Middle Fork of the Flathead River,** which churns up Class II-III rapids. Kayakers play in the froth between Moccasin Creek and West Glacier, surfing the rapids on Tunnel Rapid. Some eliminate the flat water before and after the rapids by using railroad accesses. To locate rapids and ascertain their difficulty, consult *Three Forks of the Flathead Float Guide* ($13), available through the Glacier Natural History Association (406/888-5756, www.glacierassociation.org). Bring your own kayak with you, as no rentals are available in West Glacier.

Glacier Kayak School (12127 U.S. 2 E., West Glacier, 406/387-5340 or 800/735-7897, www.greatnorthernresort.com, $100-250) teaches white-water kayaking to introduce beginners to paddling fundamentals and rolling. Experienced kayakers can hire a guide to lead them down the lines of the Middle Fork.

BOATING

With its vast water acreage, Lake McDonald attracts boaters, but it's never crowded—usually just a few quiet anglers in the early morning followed by a few die-hard water-skiers, sightseers, and kayakers touring the shoreline. Because the frigid waters inhibit most water-skiers and Jet Skis are not permitted, the lake never has a frenzied hubbub of noise. In fact, national park regulations enforce a maximum noise level of 82 decibels. Similar to many of the park's lakes, you'll rarely see a sailboat or sailboard: unpredictable swirling winds on Lake McDonald make other lakes outside the park more appealing. Located adjacent to Village Inn, Apgar's boat ramp provides the lake's only public ramp access.

Boaters must get free permits and show that their boats have been cleaned, drained, and dried to avoid bringing aquatic invasive species into park lakes. Permits for up to 14 days are available at the Backcountry Office or park headquarters, as directed by the orange sign at the west-side entrance station.

Rentals

For boating and fishing on Lake McDonald, **Glacier Park Boat Company** (406/257-2426, www.glacierparkboats.com) rents rowboats, canoes, kayaks, and 8-hp motorboats for $18-25 per hour from the Apgar boat dock next to Village Inn. Paddles, life jackets, and fishing regulations are included in the rates.

Regulations

Two shoreline closures affect boaters: from the Apgar boat ramp north to the lake's outlet, and between the Apgar Amphitheater and Going-to-the-Sun Road. To protect swimmers, boaters must stay 300 feet off the shoreline and are not permitted to beach. Watch for additional temporary wildlife closures marked with buoys, especially where bald eagles nest at the lake's east end.

While any craft over 12 feet must be registered in Montana, temporary use of out-of-state boats is permitted without registration. On Glacier's waters, federal boating regulations and water travel etiquette apply. For a complete list of boating regulations, check with visitors centers or Glacier's website (www.nps.gov/glac).

CANOEING AND KAYAKING

With its monstrous shoreline, **Lake McDonald** is a treat for canoeing and kayaking, but watch for winds whipping up large whitecaps. When glassy calm waters prevail, you'd be hard-pressed to beat it at sunrise or sunset. Touring the shoreline, you may encounter wildlife closures, especially for nesting bald eagles at the lake's head. Paddlers must pick up free permits to launch on any park lake. Get them at the Backcountry Office or park headquarters, as directed by the orange sign near the west-side entrance station. Paddlers can also camp overnight at the Lake McDonald backcountry campground, a five-mile paddle from Apgar that is only accessible by trail or water. An overnight permit is required, just like for backpackers.

Two rivers offer options for flat-water paddlers. The **Middle Fork of the Flathead River** is gentle enough for canoeing and kayaking from West Glacier downriver to Blankenship, but the section includes one challenging rapid that can be portaged. A one-hour paddle, the scenic **Lower McDonald Creek** starts north of the Apgar boat launch on Lake McDonald and floats past beaver dams to Quarter Circle Bridge.

At the Apgar boat dock next to Village Inn, **Glacier Park Boat Company** (406/257-2426, www.glacierparkboats.com) rents canoes and plastic double kayaks ($18 per hour, cash only). Boats come with paddles and life jackets.

FISHING

Lake McDonald, the park's biggest lake, has a reputation for mediocre fishing. Boats work best to troll for lake trout. For catch-and-release fly-fishing, **Lower McDonald Creek** from the lake to Quarter Circle Bridge works, but it's

© BECKY LOMAX

Lake McDonald is great for paddling.

also heavily fished because of its easy access. For several miles in both directions from West Glacier, the **Middle Fork of the Flathead** presents good fishing, but be ready to contend with rafters and fishing outfitters. Because of the concentration of visitors in the West Glacier-Apgar area during high season, you may not feel like you're off in the wilderness when you toss in a line, but you just might pull in native trout. Good fishing usually starts near the end of June when the water clears.

Park Regulations

Fishing inside Glacier Park does not require a license, but waters here have some restrictions, such as a ban on lead lures. Lake McDonald has no limit on lake trout or whitefish, but westslope cutthroat are catch-and-release only. Lower McDonald Creek from the lake outlet to Quarter Circle Bridge has been catch-and-release only, but check with the rangers as nonnative-species rules may change. Despite its name,

FISHING IN GLACIER

With 27,023 acres of lakes, 563 streams, and 22 species of fish, Glacier is a place where no angler should sit with a slack line. Only a scant 10 percent of park visitors fish, so those who do typically enjoy calm vistas and a few native trout. While weather and skill variables influence success, a few tips for Glacier's waters can help.

FISHING TIPS

- Avoid a long hike to a remote lake to fish—unless you go for the sake of the journey. While many anglers find more success in waters away from roads, remoteness doesn't mean good fishing. Waterfalls prevent fish from reaching some streams and lakes.
- Since arrival at a high mountain lake will most likely be midday, when fishing is lackluster, stay overnight in the backcountry or at a nearby lodge. Then fish in the morning or evening, when fish feed, for best results. Overcast days also produce better fishing than sunny days.
- During early summer runoff, when river waters cloud with sediments, fish hang out on the bottom to feed; try lures that mimic insect larvae. Alternately, fish in lakes instead.
- When streams run clear, fly-fishing is the most productive. Try to match a prominent hatch, but traditional high-floating attractor patterns will also move fish.
- At lakes, look for inlets and outlets to fish, but be considerate of heavily trafficked areas.
- Trolling from a motorboat (where allowed) or canoe is the most effective way to fish for lake trout.

FISHING IN BEAR COUNTRY

- Bears pose special considerations. Since smells attract bears that travel waterways, lessen your bear encounter chances by keeping fishy scents away from clothing. Catch-and-release fishing minimizes attracting bears.
- For cleaning fish in the front country, dispose of the entrails in bear-resistant garbage cans. In the backcountry, do not bury or burn the innards, as that may attract bears. Instead, go at least 200 feet away from a campsite or trail, puncture the air bladder, and throw the entrails into deep water. Keep only what you can eat, and eat it as soon as you can.

NATIVE SPECIES

Glacier Park's fishing regulations enforce protection of native species through selected area closures and limits on taking native species. The park service no longer stocks fish, as many of the introduced species took a toll on native fish through competition for food and predation. Until 1972, an estimated 45-55 million fish and eggs were planted in Glacier's waters, introducing arctic grayling, rainbow trout, kokanee salmon, brook trout, and Yellowstone cutthroat trout. Lake trout and lake whitefish also invaded the park's west-side water systems through stocking in Flathead Lake.

Of Glacier's 10 sport fish and 12 nonsport fish, the **bull trout** is listed as a threatened species under the Endangered Species Act. In Montana, this predatory fish, which can grow to two feet long, now inhabits less than half of its original streams due to a number of factors, including habitat degradation. No fishing for bull trout is allowed; immediately release any that are caught incidentally. Look on the dorsal fin: no black, put it back.

Glacier is also one of the few remaining strongholds for **westslope cutthroat trout,** which now inhabit only 2.5 percent of their original range. Threatened by interbreeding with rainbow trout, genetically pure populations of cutthroat remain in 15-19 park lakes. Conscientious anglers release them after catching them.

While the law protects bull trout, anglers need to help preserve the park's native fishery. Learn to identify native and nonnative species. Follow park guidelines for harvesting or releasing fish. In general, release native fish; keep only your limit of nonnative species.

For the best fishing recommendations, grab a copy of Russ Schneider's *Fishing Glacier National Park.*

Fish Creek is closed to fishing. Lake McDonald is open to fishing all year, but stream fishing in and outside the park runs from the third Saturday in May through November 30.

Licenses and Rentals

Fishing outside Glacier on Flathead River drainages requires a Montana fishing license. You can pick one up at **Glacier Outdoor Center** (11957 U.S. 2 E., West Glacier, 406/888-5454 or 800/235-6781, www.glacierraftco.com). The center also sells fishing gear and rents rods ($12-15 per day), waders, and float tubes. Montana Fishing Licenses come in several forms. Montana residents can buy two-day ($13) or full-season ($26) licenses. Nonresidents can get two-day ($25), 10-day ($54), or full-season ($70) licenses. Kids under age 12 fish free. Teens ages 12-14 and Montana seniors can buy licenses for $8. You can also order licenses online (www.fwp.mt.gov).

Guides

Four fly-fishing companies in West Glacier guide trips daily in drift boats on Glacier's boundary waters on the Middle Fork and the North Fork of the Flathead River, but none guide fishing adventures inside Glacier Park. For beginners, they offer fly-fishing schools ($450 for 2 people) to teach the basics of casting, mending, and catch-and-release. Reservations are mandatory. The companies begin fishing trips in late June-early July when the waters clear and then run through mid-September.

Half-day ($350), full-day ($450), and overnight ($400-900) guided fishing trips for 1-2 people are available. Plan on tipping the guides about 15 percent. Tip higher if you catch lots of fish or for overnights. It's pricey, but the guides usually get you to the good fishing holes. Rates include all equipment, such as life jackets, rods, and flies. As with rafting trips, a 7 percent service fee is added to all fishing trips, but some companies include it in the price. You'll also need to buy your own fishing license.

All West Glacier fishing companies offer half-day, full-day, and multiday trips as well as fishing schools. These are licensed with the state: **Glacier Guides** (11970 U.S. 2 E., 406/387-5555 or 800/521-7238, www.glacierguides.com), **Montana Fly-fishing Guides** (Great Northern Resort, 12127 U.S. 2 E., 406/387-5340 or 800/735-7897, www.greatnorthernresort.com), **Wild River Fishing Guides** (11900 U.S. 2 E., 406/387-9453 or 800/700-7056, www.riverwild.com), and **Glacier Anglers** (Glacier Outdoor Center, 11957 U.S. 2 E., 406/888-5454 or 800/235-6781, www.glacierraftco.com), which adds on their specialty 4-7-day Great Bear Wilderness fishing trips ($700 pp per day), half-day private pond fishing ($236), and a one-hour casting clinic ($45).

GOLF

Glacier View Golf Club (640 River Bend Dr., West Glacier, 406/888-5471, wwww.glacierviewgolf.com, daily Apr.-Oct., snow permitting, 18 holes $30) may tax your concentration as you tee off. Moose, elk, bears, and deer wander across the fairways, and the mountain views are hard to ignore. The 18-hole course has a pro shop, a restaurant, a practice green, a driving range, lessons, cart rentals ($26), and club rentals ($12). To locate the golf course in West Glacier, turn west onto River Bend Drive and follow signs to the clubhouse. The club has RV hookups ($30).

CROSS-COUNTRY SKIING AND SNOWSHOEING

Winter converts the roads and trails around Apgar into easy cross-country ski and snowshoe paths late November-April. Quiet and scenic, road skiing makes for easy route finding with little avalanche danger at lower elevations. Roads are plowed into Apgar and up Lake McDonald's south shore. Beyond plowing, popular ski tours follow roads and trails to **Fish Creek Campground, Rocky Point, McGee Meadows,** and the **Old Flathead**

Ranger Station near the Middle Fork and North Fork confluence. Those with stamina and skiing expertise climb to **Apgar Lookout.** For route descriptions, pick up *Skiing and Snowshoeing* in the visitors centers or online (www.nps.gov/glac). Skiers and snowshoers should be well equipped and versed in winter travel safety before venturing out, even on snow-covered roads.

Guides

The National Park Service guides free weekend snowshoe tours from Apgar Visitors Center (406/888-7939) January-mid-March. Call for departure times for the two-hour walks. Interpretive rangers point out how flora and fauna adapt to harsh winters, and they point out tracks. Hikers should wear winter footwear, dress in layers, and bring water. Snowshoes rent for $2.

Guided snowshoe and ski tours are available through **Glacier Adventure Guides** (406/892-2173 or 877/735-9514, www.glacieradventureguides.com). Expect to pay $255 per day for solo travelers, or with a minimum of two people, $180 pp. Plan on tipping the guide 15 percent. Ski tours can be cross-country, telemarking, or alpine touring. If you're a solo traveler, it's the best way to get accompanied into the backcountry with avalanche-certified guides to find pristine powder stashes. Lunch, snacks, park entrance fees, and equipment are included. Multiday trips are also available.

ENTERTAINMENT

Most park visitors take advantage of the long daylight hours (dark doesn't descend until almost 11pm in June) to explore everything they can instead of seeking nightlife. If you're looking to party, you can hang out at the West Glacier bar shooting pool with the river rats.

Park Naturalist Evening Programs

Fish Creek Campground Amphitheater and **Apgar Campground Amphitheater** host free park naturalist evening programs (usually mid-June-mid-Sept.) on wildlife, fires, and natural phenomena. Check a current copy of *Ranger-led Activities* for subjects, times, and dates for these 45-minute programs. Schedules are posted in campgrounds, hotels, and at the visitors center.

Accommodations

On Lake McDonald's shore, the limited lodging at Apgar is extremely popular, so West Glacier options often serve as backup. But given that the communities are only two miles apart and are connected by a bike path, they are equally convenient to each other and their outdoor activities. Additional lodging is found in Coram and Hungry Horse. You can also find private cabins and vacation homes to rent at **VRBO** (www.vrbo.com). Montana tacks on a 7 percent bed tax, so your bill will be higher than the quoted room rate. Most of the facilities are smoke-free.

APGAR

Reservations are a must at the two adjacent lodges in Apgar tucked at Lake McDonald's foot. To preserve their get-away-from-it-all ambience, neither have air-conditioning, Internet access, in-room phones, or TVs. Pay phones can be found outside the lobbies. Both share a block with Eddie's Restaurant and Grocery, the visitors center, the boat dock, rental boats, several gift shops, shuttle stops, and the beginning of the Apgar Bike Trail. Although the area is a busy hive during the day, at night it's quiet.

On Lake McDonald's beach, every one

of the 36 guest rooms in the **Village Inn** (Apgar Loop Rd., 0.3 miles from Camas Rd. or 0.8 miles from Going-to-the-Sun Rd., 406/892-2525, front desk 406/888-5632, www.glacierparkinc.com, late May-mid-Sept., $140-250) wakes up to a striking view up-lake toward the Continental Divide. Some guest rooms include kitchenettes and can sleep up to six. No elevator is available for the second floor. Although the inn has been redecorated, not much else has changed since it was built in 1956. Despite the nondescript guest rooms, the views are stunning.

Set back in huge old-growth cedars along McDonald Creek, **Apgar Village Lodge** (Apgar Loop Rd., 0.3 miles from Camas Rd. or 0.8 miles from Going-to-the-Sun Rd., 406/888-5484, www.westglacier.com, late May-Sept., $142-260) is a cluster of 20 small motel rooms and 28 rustic cabins—most with kitchens—within a few steps of the lake. The creek cabins (6, 7, and 8) are particularly serene—mixed with a wonderful ambience of wildlife and the sound of the stream. Although older, the cabins have all been upgraded since the mid-1990s. All baths contain shower stalls. Some cabins require a two-night minimum stay. Ask about early-season discounts.

WEST GLACIER

Lodging in West Glacier is convenient for hopping on the train, going river rafting or fishing, and heading off on guided backpacking trips. It's also such a quick jaunt to Lake McDonald that if park lodging is full, West Glacier options work as an easy backup. Be prepared, however, for nightly noise—not from people, who are tired from packing in so much activity during the long days, but from trains on the BNSF Railway line. Bring earplugs if you're a light sleeper. During midsummer, most West Glacier lodging options fill nightly; reservations are advised.

Apgar's Village Inn sits right on Lake McDonald.

Glacier Guides Lodge is the newest place to stay in West Glacier.

Lodges

Located across from Belton Train Depot, the National Historic Landmark **Belton Chalet** (12575 U.S. 2 E., 406/888-5000 or 888/235-8665, www.beltonchalet.com) saw a $1 million restoration in 2000. Centered around a large stone fireplace, the cozy lobby contains a piano and stuffed rockers. Stay in the main lodge rooms (late May-Sept., $125-180) or private year-round cottages ($325-350 summer, $99-250 winter), both of which are discounted in spring and fall. Simple guest rooms are a slice of history: original wainscoting and wood floors, push-button lights, twig tables, and historic photos, but no phones, Internet access, TVs, or alarm clocks. Original closets were converted into in-room baths with showers. Stay in one of the nine balcony rooms to sit in wicker rockers with a glass of wine as the sun sets over the Apgar Range. Remedies Day Spa massages are available on-site. The chalet's restaurant serves outstanding dinners.

Glacier Guides Lodge (120 Highline Blvd., 406/387-5555 or 800/521-7238, May-mid-Oct., $175), owned by Glacier Guides-Montana Raft Company, is the newest lodging in West Glacier. The ecofriendly lodge, which opened in 2010, has 12 guest rooms with wireless Internet access, TVs, and air-conditioning. Continental breakfast is included with stays, and two lounge areas provide places to relax outside the guest rooms. Its location back in the woods tucked under mossy cliffs makes it one of the quietest places in the area. Guest rooms are discounted in shoulder seasons.

Cabins

Two cabin complexes are less than one mile west of West Glacier's shops and restaurants. They are operated by raft companies, making rafting convenient while staying here. Both come with fully equipped kitchens, wireless Internet access, TVs, and gas grills. **Glacier Outdoor Center** (11957 U.S. 2 E., 406/888-5454 or 800/235-6781, www.glacierraftco.com, Apr.-Oct., $315-550) has 1-3-bedroom log cabins that sleep 6-14 people. Set back from the highway amid birch trees around a trout pond, the cabins include log furniture, decks, and gas fireplaces. The deluxe cabin has a washer, dryer, and hot tub. Discounts are given for multiple-night stays and shoulder seasons.

Part of the Great Northern Resort, with the rafting, fishing, and kayaking company located on-site, **Great Northern Chalets** (12127 U.S. 2 E., 406/387-5340 or 800/735-7897, www.greatnorthernresort.com, year-round, $295-415 summer, $99-335 off-season) rents two small six-person and three large eight-person log chalets. Set around a landscaped garden pond but in view of the highway, the cozy two-story chalets are decorated in Glacier outdoor themes, and several have sweeping views of Glacier's peaks. A three-night minimum stay is required in summer.

Motels

For basic guest rooms, two motels in West Glacier are within walking distance of shopping, rafting, restaurants, the park entrance, and the train depot. Guest rooms have thin walls and come without in-room phones, air-conditioning, or Internet access. Early- and late-season discounts are available. Located on the Middle Fork, **West Glacier Motel** (200 Going-to-the-Sun Rd., 406/888-5662, www.westglacier.com, late May-mid-Sept.) has 32 motel units ($90-110) and three cabins (2-night minimum, $170-270) without TVs. Across from the Belton Train Depot, the **Glacier Highland** (12555 U.S. 2 E., 406/888-5427 or 800/766-0811, www.glacierhighlandresort.com, mid-May-mid-Oct., $115-170) has 33 rooms with TVs.

About 0.5 miles west of the Belton Train Depot, **Glacier Vista Motel** (12340 U.S. 2 E., 406/888-5311 or 877/888-5311, www.glaciervistamotel.com, mid-May-mid-Sept., $90-165) perches on a hill with Glacier views. The family-run 1950s motel attracts visitors for its outdoor heated swimming pool. Guest rooms come with wireless Internet access and a light continental breakfast but no TVs.

OUTSIDE WEST GLACIER

When lodging facilities in West Glacier and Apgar book up for July-August, you can find alternatives lining the nine miles of U.S. 2 from West Glacier to Hungry Horse. In some locations, be prepared for trains rumbling by at night.

Lodges

Secluded in the woods 10 minutes outside West Glacier, **The Great Bear Inn** (5672 Blankenship Rd., 406/250-4577, http://thegreatbearinn.com, year-round, $245-385 d) offers the most upscale lodging in West Glacier. There are several types of large lodge rooms, with the high-end guest rooms including king beds, rock fireplaces, and a daybed. Two loft cabins offer more privacy. Rates include a light continental breakfast and a three-course dinner, but you can opt out of the dinners when making reservations. Dinner menus are on a nine-day rotating schedule. The owner's pets roam the property.

Cabins

Two modern cabin complexes feature log furniture, wireless Internet access, and satellite TV. **Glaciers Mountain Resort** (1385 Old U.S. 2 E., 406/387-5712 or 877/213-8001, www.glaciersmountainresort.com, year-round, $120-250) has five air-conditioned one-bedroom knotty pine cabins with distant Glacier views. Sleeping four, the cabins come with fully equipped kitchens and gas grills. Off-season rates drop 25-50 percent, and a two-night minimum stay is required. **Silverwolf Log Chalet Resort** (Gladys Glenn Rd. and U.S. 2 E., 406/387-4448, www.silverwolfchalets.com, mid-May-mid-Oct., $140-180) has 10 two-person log chalets on a landscaped lawn under lodgepole pines behind a privacy fence. Chalets include gas fireplaces, microwaves, coffeemakers, and mini fridges. The resort is an adults-only place. Discounts are available for multiple-night stays and shoulder seasons.

Built in 1907, the **Tamarack Lodge** (9549 U.S. 2 E., 406/387-4420 or 877/387-4420, www.historictamaracklodge.com, year-round, $150-320) offers a renovated log-beam guest room in the historic lodge, knotty pine cabins, and several larger modern cabins with kitchens. Rates drop substantially fall-spring.

Budget Motels

Located seven miles west of the park, the **Evergreen Motel** (10159 U.S. 2, Coram, 406/387-5365, www.evergreenmotelglacier.com, May-Oct., $65-95) offers budget lodging in small cabins or guest rooms. Hungry Horse, nine miles from West Glacier, also has several basic motels.

Bed-and-Breakfasts

Two B&Bs offer year-round lodging on the outskirts of West Glacier. Overlooking the

Flathead River, **Glacier Park Inn** (9128 U.S. 2 E., 406/387-5099, www.glacierparkinn.com, $100-150) has five guest rooms in an octagonal home with a giant wraparound deck. The inn, which has wireless Internet access, gets rave reviews for its location, breakfast, and the owners—avid hikers who can recommend trails for appropriate seasons.

Located about 15 minutes outside West Glacier with a remote feel, the ecofriendly three-story **Moss Mountain Inn** (4655 North Fork Rd., 406/387-4605, www.mossmountaininn.com, $175-195) has four guest rooms, a 300-square-foot solarium, and wireless Internet access. The inn serves up creative gourmet organic breakfasts with fresh fruit and daily entrees that you can try yourself at home with the owner's cookbook.

CAMPING

Lake McDonald is the big attraction for camping at Apgar, but if you require hookups and showers, you'll need to stay in commercial campgrounds in or near West Glacier.

Apgar

In Apgar, two National Park Service-operated campgrounds sit amid thick forests with easy access to Lake McDonald. Rustic and without hookups, both have flush toilets, fire rings with grills, disposal stations, shared hiker-biker sites (Apgar $5, Fish Creek $8), amphitheaters for evening naturalist talks, and sites that accommodate large RVs. Due to the location inside the park, away from highway and railroad noise, they are popular. Bring your own firewood, as collecting wood is prohibited.

Fish Creek (end of Fish Creek Rd., 406/888-7800, June-early Sept., $23), one of two campgrounds in the park that can be reserved through the National Park Reservation System (877/444-6777, www.recreation.gov), is one of the larger park campgrounds, with 178 sites tucked under cedars, lodgepole pines, and larches. Loops C and D have the best sites, adjacent to the lake, although Loop B has some larger, more level sites. A few lukewarm token-operated showers are available. Eighteen campsites accommodate RVs up to 35 feet long; 62 sites fit RVs up to 27 feet. To find Fish Creek, drive 1.25 miles north from Apgar on Camas Road and turn right, dropping one mile down to the campground. Lake McDonald Trail departs from the campground.

Apgar Campground (Apgar Loop Rd., 0.4 miles from Going-to-the-Sun Rd., 406/888-7800, Apr.-Nov., $20) is within a short walking distance of Apgar Village, Lake McDonald, and the shuttles. The campground has 194 sites, making it the park's largest, with group campsites and 25 sites accommodating RVs up to 40 feet. A paved trail connects it to the Apgar Transit Center, Apgar Bike Trail, and Apgar Village, which includes a restaurant, gift shops, the visitors center, and a boat dock. Primitive camping (Apr. and mid-Oct.-Nov., $10) has pit toilets available but no running water. In winter, you can camp free at the Apgar Picnic Area, but it's just a plowed lot with a pit toilet.

West Glacier

Commercial campgrounds in the West Glacier vicinity are convenient for rafting, fishing, biking, and trail rides, but they are located outside the park. If you require hookups, this is where you'll need to be. Standard amenities in these campgrounds include flush toilets, laundries, hot showers, camp stores, picnic tables, fire rings with grills, firewood, propane, disposal stations, playgrounds, hookups, and wired or wireless Internet access. Also, these campgrounds can handle the big RV rigs. If you're a light sleeper, bring earplugs; many of the campgrounds are near the rumble and screech of passing trains.

Although most commercial campgrounds lean toward serving RVers and car campers,

© BECKY LOMAX

Apgar Campground offers camping under large cottonwoods and firs.

bikers and backpackers should ask about special rates in shared area sites, which run around $10 pp. Many of the campgrounds offer rustic camping cabins or yurts, which have no kitchens or baths; bring your own sleeping bags or pay extra for clean linens, blankets, and towels ($10-15 pp). Commercial campgrounds tack on a 7 percent Montana bed tax to their rates. When you make your reservations, check for deals; many give discounts for Internet registration, seniors, staying early or late in the season, and Good Sam, AAA, or military members. For July-August, make reservations, especially for big rigs requiring large sites.

On 40 timbered acres 0.5 miles from West Glacier, **Glacier Campground** (12070 U.S. 2 E., 406/387-5689 or 888/387-5689, www.glaciercampground.com, May-Sept., $20-30) is one mile west of the park entrance. Lush undergrowth surrounds private sites separated by birch and fir trees. Several cabins ($35-55) share a covered outdoor cooking area with gas burners and a barbecue. Leashed pets are welcome. With the campground set back from the road, trees reduce highway and railroad noise. For evening entertainment, the campground sponsors Forest Service presentations.

Removed one mile from U.S. 2 and 2.5 miles west of the park entrance, **West Glacier KOA** (355 Half Moon Flats Rd., 406/387-5341 or 800/562-3313, www.westglacierkoa.com, mid-May-Sept., $32-90) is the only campground with a heated swimming pool (June-mid-Sept.) and a couple of hot tubs (all season). It also has evening programs, cabins ($80-300), horseshoes, and summer barbecue dinners and pancake breakfasts. Due to its location away from the highway and railroad, this is one of the quieter campgrounds.

Outside West Glacier

Seven commercial campgrounds ($25-41) sprawl along U.S. 2 in the nine miles between West Glacier and Hungry Horse. Four offer distinctive features: **San-Suz-Ed RV Park** (11505 U.S. 2 E., 406/387-5280 or 800/630-2623, www.sansuzedrvpark.com, May-Oct.) runs a nightly community campfire pit (bring your own marshmallows) where you can glean tidbits from other Glacier travelers. For those needing open space for clear satellite reception, **North American RV Park and Campground** (10784 U.S. 2 E., 406/387-5800 or 800/704-4266, www.northamericanrvpark.com, mid-Apr.-Oct.) is in a big grassy area with shorter trees. **Canyon RV and Campground** (9540 U.S. 2 E., 406/387-9393, www.montana-campground.com) is the only one bordering the Flathead River, accessible by a trail. One of the quietest campgrounds, **Mountain Meadows RV Park** (9125 U.S. 2 E., 406/387-9125, www.mmrvpark.com, May-Sept.) spans 77 acres of forested hillside with a stocked catch-and-release rainbow trout pond.

Backcountry Campsites

Lake McDonald has one prime backcountry campsite on the north shore. Perched on a point with huge views up and down the lake, the campsite can be accessed only by trail or by water. It has a communal cooking site, a fire pit, a pebble beach, and two large tent sites that can sleep four people each. Overnight permits are required (adults $5 pp per night, $2.50 ages 8-15, under age 8 free). Pick up permits at the Apgar Backcountry Office (406/888-7900) 24 hours in advance of your trip. You can apply for advance reservations ($30) online (www.nps.gov/glac).

Food

Glacier is a place for good home-style cooking, where tasty fresh-baked fruit pies are still the rage, rather than upscale or international fare. Seasonal restaurants cater to summer visitors; hours can shorten in spring or fall, and only a few remain open in winter. Many of the restaurants can pack lunches to go for travelers.

RESTAURANTS

Apgar

Now under the same ownership as Izaak Walton Inn, **Eddie's Restaurant** (Apgar Loop Rd., across from the visitors center, 406/888-5361, www.eddiescafegifts.com, 7am-9pm daily late May-mid-Sept.) is the only game in town, but it has good family-friendly breakfasts and lunches ($6-12), including hiker lunches to go. Dinner ($12-20) features entree salads, grilled trout, broasted chicken, and buffalo meat loaf and burgers. With large waiting lines in midsummer, takeout can be quicker; walk a few steps away to Lake McDonald's shore to picnic. Montana microbrews and wine can accompany dinner, and the huckleberry desserts are a must.

West Glacier

At the historic **Belton Chalet** (12575 U.S. 2 E., 406/888-5000 or 888/235-8665, www.beltonchalet.com, late May-early Oct.) you can dine in the intimate Belton Grill (5pm-10pm daily), by the fireplace in the Taproom (3pm-midnight daily), or on the deck watching trains and the sunset over Apgar Mountain. The Belton's restoration to its 1910 grandeur converted the lodge's old boiler into the kitchen's outdoor grill. Fine-dining flavors, some with Asian flair, are made with fresh local ingredients. Entrees ($20-34) like the flavorful Montana meat loaf—buffalo wrapped in hickory-smoked bacon with roasted-tomato gravy—pair well with Taproom wines and Montana microbrews. The dessert tray changes nightly, but if available, try the huckleberry crisp or cheesecake with sauce made with cherries from the owners' Bigfork orchard. Lighter

Taproom meals ($9-14) feature hors d'oeuvres, sandwiches, and salads. Box lunches are available to go. In winter (Dec.-Mar.), the Belton serves sandwiches and comfort-food entrees (3pm-9pm Fri.-Sat.) and Sunday brunch (10am-2pm Sun.).

Two West Glacier Restaurants offer good places for family dining with breakfasts and lunches running $7-12 and dinners $10-20. The **West Glacier Restaurant and Lounge** (200 Going-to-the-Sun Rd., 406/888-5359, 7am-10pm daily mid-May-late Sept.) is located between the park entrance bridge and the railroad tunnel. The restaurant has waiting lines in midsummer because of its blueberry pancakes and fresh-baked pies. Ironically, the best thing to sate a hungry hiker's stomach—the Glacier Monster Cheeseburger—is listed under "Lighter Appetites," but it is huge, with bacon and cheese atop a half-pound hamburger, served with fries. The burger-and-beer crowd heads to the adjacent bar—locally known as Frieda's—to order from the restaurant menu. Across from the Belton Train Depot, the **Glacier Highland** (12555 U.S. 2 E., 406/888-5427, www.glacierhighland.com, 7am-10pm daily mid-Apr.-mid-Oct.) bakes large huckleberry muffins, cinnamon rolls, and fruit pies. A large menu of sandwiches, burgers, fish, and steaks can pacify a variety of eaters.

© BECKY LOMAX

The West Glacier Mercantile supplies campers and travelers during summer.

Meat lovers will want to head to the **Rawhide Trading Post Restaurant and Steakhouse** (12000 U.S. 2 E., 406/387-5999, www.glacier-rawhide.com, 6am-10pm daily mid-May-mid-Oct.) The restaurant serves breakfast and lunch ($7-10), and dinner ($14-26) features the house specialty, mesquite-grilled prime rib—a 10-ounce cowgirl, 12-ounce cowboy, or the one-pound Wayne's Cut. The restaurant also does kids' meals and takeout for easy campfire dinners.

Outside West Glacier

In Coram, 5.5 miles west of West Glacier, locals head to **Glacier Grill and Pizza** (10026 U.S. 2 E., Coram, 406/387-4223, 7am-10pm daily year-round) for any meal of the day. Cafe fare ($7-12) includes breakfast, soups, large salads, sandwiches, and nachos, but the main reason to eat here is the inexpensive beer and pizza ($12-19). The Mediterranean special with feta cheese is baked with a delightful twist on spices.

CAFFEINE

Several summer-only espresso stands provide a caffeine fix. Hours vary at each, depending on the season. **Eddie's Snack Bar** in Apgar serves espresso drinks and ice cream, but if you are particular about your espresso order, head to the **Glacier Espresso** near the Alberta Visitor Information Center in West Glacier.

GROCERIES

Groceries (food, beer, and wine) and camping items (ice, firewood, and stove gas) can be purchased in West Glacier, Apgar, and

Coram at three seasonal stores, usually open daily May-September. In Apgar, get supplies at **Eddie's Cafe and Gifts** (Apgar Loop Rd., across from the visitors center, 406/888-5361). In West Glacier, the **West Glacier Mercantile** (0.1 miles west of U.S. 2-Going-to-the-Sun Rd. junction, 406/888-5362) has the bigger selection of meats, fresh veggies, and fruits. Convenience-store items are also available at **Glacier Highland** (U.S. 2, across from the Belton Train Depot), with cheaper beer and wine prices. In Coram, the **Glacier General Store** (10630 U.S. 2 E., 406/871-3746) carries convenience-store and camping items.

In summer, the farmers market comes to West Glacier, adjacent to the mercantile on Friday afternoons. The nearest year-round grocery store is in Hungry Horse, on U.S. 2 nine miles west of the park entrance. Look for the "Supermarket" sign. You'll have to drive 30 minutes into Flathead Valley to hit the mega-stores that carry huge brand selections.

PICNIC AREAS

Two picnic areas, both with beach access, rim Lake McDonald's western shores. **Apgar Picnic Area** is just off Going-to-the-Sun Road on the lake's southwest corner, with a beautiful up-lake view to the Continental Divide. **Fish Creek Picnic Area** is next to Fish Creek Campground, where a one-mile hike leads out to Rocky Point for more views. Both have picnic tables, flush toilets, and fire rings with grills, but firewood is not provided, and gathering it is prohibited; purchase firewood in Apgar or West Glacier.

NORTH FORK

It's remote. It's wild. It's not for everyone. The North Fork Valley defines rustic: Not rustic as in cute and comfortable, but really backwoods. No flush toilets, no electricity, and no cell-phone service. But for those who want to get away from the mayhem, it's the place to go. A visit to the North Fork transports you back in time. The pace of life slows with the ambience of the Polebridge Mercantile and Northern Lights Saloon.

For the average traveler, the North Fork's nasty dirt roads alone deter interest. Brutal potholes, jarring washboards, and clouds of dust launch vehement debates about paving the North Fork Road, but pavement into this remote enclave would alter its nature forever.

The North Fork Valley spans diverse habitats from grassland prairies to alpine glaciers. It's home to an immense range of wildlife—huge grizzly bears to tiny pygmy shrews. Spruce trees 300 years old root the valley in deep history. Surrounded by thick subalpine fir forests, Bowman and Kintla Lakes have miles of empty shoreline dotted with only boats of anglers or a few kayaks. Trails from the North Fork see only a few people, even in high season. Wildlife watchers can find animals and birds at the northernmost and southernmost fringes of their habitats. Nothing chills the soul quite like the wild call of wolves in the dead of night.

HIGHLIGHTS

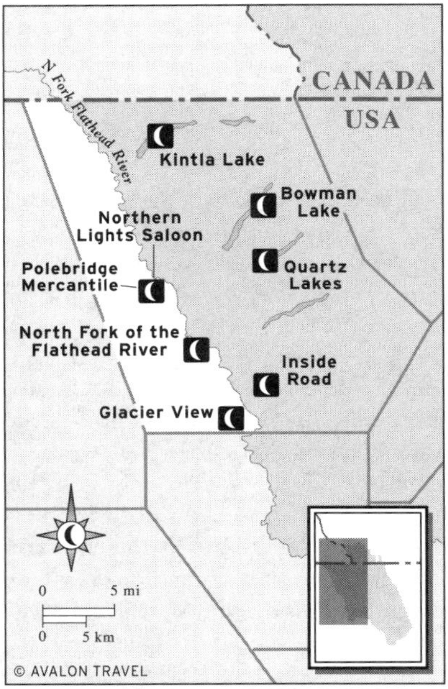

LOOK FOR ☾ TO FIND RECOMMENDED SIGHTS, ACTIVITIES, DINING, AND LODGING.

☾ **Inside Road:** Survive this rough road: This 28-mile scenic byway presents a real challenge for vehicles and mountain bikes, with close encounters with wildlife and potholes (page 63).

☾ **Polebridge Mercantile:** Smell freshly baked cookies and breads when you walk into this historic hub of the North Fork Valley. An old-fashioned cash register clangs to ring up your groceries (page 64).

☾ **Northern Lights Saloon:** Order a microbrew and sit outside to enjoy the view or just soak up the chatter from the locals inside. In spite of its remote location, the saloon attracts diners for its tiny log cabin historic charm (page 64).

☾ **North Fork of the Flathead River:** Throw your watch away to let river time take over as you float this scenic river. Forming the park's western boundary, the river courses through prime habitat where grizzly bears and wolves hunt prey (page 64).

☾ **Bowman Lake:** Look down the lake; you're looking straight into wild country. Rainbow Peak juts 4,500 feet straight up from the lakeshore, while Thunderbird Mountain scrapes the sky behind nesting bald eagles (page 65).

☾ **Kintla Lake:** Get far away from civilization at this remote lake. Although it may have been the site for oil drilling a century ago, today it's a mean 42 miles from pavement and launches into some of the park's most isolated backpacking terrain (page 65).

☾ **Quartz Lakes:** Hike to three lakes lined up like pearls on a necklace. The lakes lure anglers for native westslope cutthroat trout–but pack insect repellent, as the lakes are havens for mosquito as well (page 66).

☾ **Glacier View:** Climb up a short grunt with scenery galore. The route may tax the lungs, but you'll smell wild roses, and your eyes will relish Glacier's panorama from the top (page 70).

HISTORY

In the late 1800s, handfuls of homesteaders, loggers, hunters, and trappers eked out a living in the North Fork Valley, connected to each other only by a network of trails. In 1900, a Butte businessman, on a quest for oil at Kintla Lake, built the Inside North Fork Road—a 65-mile wagon track riddled with ruts, bogs, and stumps. It was sufficient for hauling drilling equipment from Belton (now West Glacier) to Kintla Lake, where sleds skidded supplies across the frozen lake to drill Montana's first oil well in 1901. The road attracted more homesteaders, but there was already talk of Glacier becoming a national park—a change the homesteaders disliked because the park

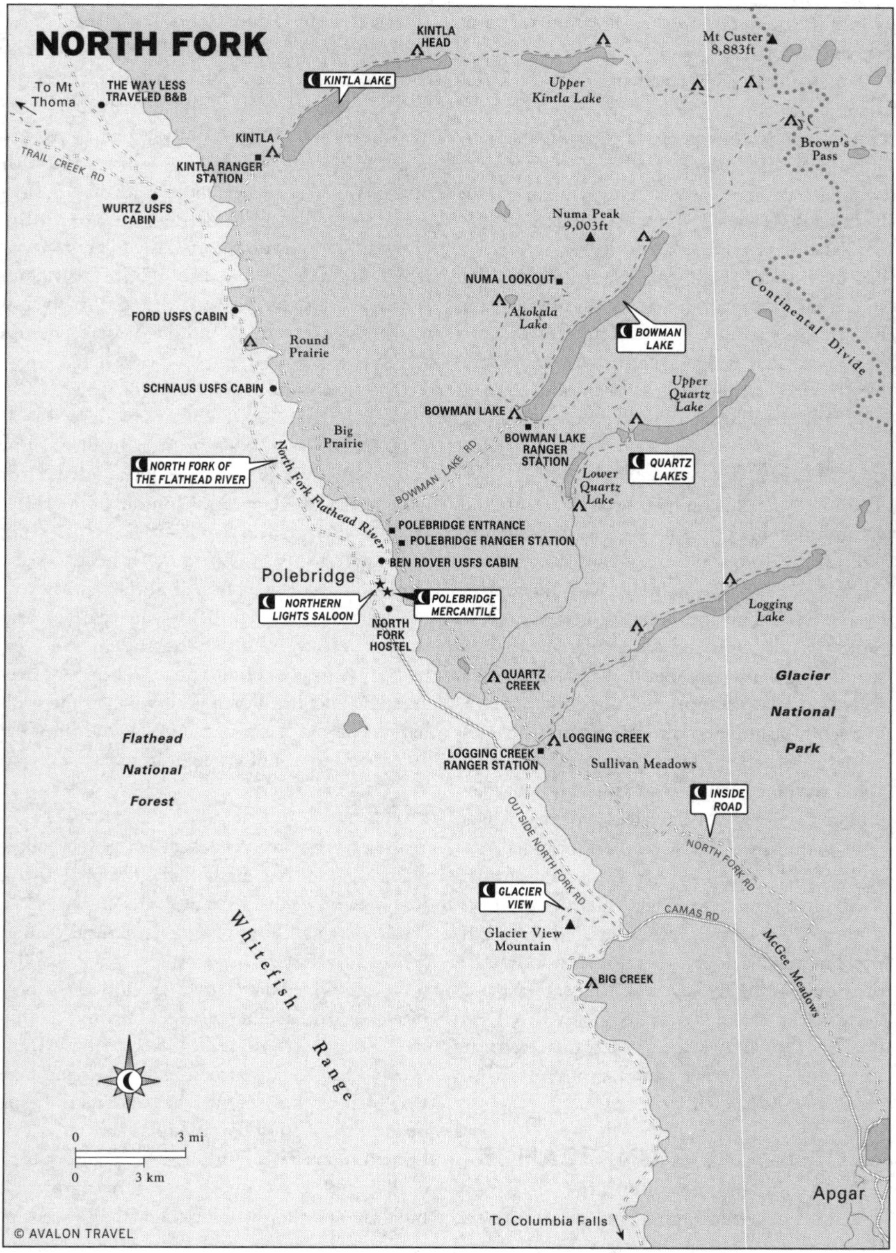
NORTH FORK
KINTLA HEAD
KINTLA LAKE
Upper Kintla Lake
Mt Custer 8,883ft
To Mt Thoma
THE WAY LESS TRAVELED B&B
KINTLA
KINTLA RANGER STATION
TRAIL CREEK RD
Brown's Pass
WURTZ USFS CABIN
Numa Peak 9,003ft
NUMA LOOKOUT
Continental Divide
Akokala Lake
FORD USFS CABIN
BOWMAN LAKE
Round Prairie
SCHNAUS USFS CABIN
Upper Quartz Lake
BOWMAN LAKE
BOWMAN LAKE RANGER STATION
Big Prairie
BOWMAN LAKE RD
NORTH FORK OF THE FLATHEAD RIVER
North Fork Flathead River
QUARTZ LAKES
Lower Quartz Lake
POLEBRIDGE ENTRANCE
POLEBRIDGE RANGER STATION
BEN ROVER USFS CABIN
Polebridge
NORTHERN LIGHTS SALOON
POLEBRIDGE MERCANTILE
NORTH FORK HOSTEL
Logging Lake
QUARTZ CREEK
Glacier National Park
Flathead National Forest
LOGGING CREEK
LOGGING CREEK RANGER STATION
Sullivan Meadows
INSIDE ROAD
OUTSIDE NORTH FORK RD
NORTH FORK RD
GLACIER VIEW
Glacier View Mountain
CAMAS RD
McGee Meadows
Whitefish Range
BIG CREEK
0 3 mi
0 3 km
Apgar
To Columbia Falls
© AVALON TRAVEL

would mean an end to their hunting and timber livelihoods.

When Glacier achieved national park status in 1910, construction of the rough Outside North Fork Road two years later prompted many of the 35 homesteading families within the park boundaries to move across the North Fork of the Flathead River, outside the park boundary. In 1914 near Hay Creek one resident, Bill Adair, built a new mercantile—a two-story plank building. The "merc," as locals call it, is listed on the National Register of Historic Places. The area today is known as Polebridge—named for the funky North Fork River bridge, a one-lane lodgepole affair that burned in the 1988 Red Bench Fire.

CULTURE

The North Fork is unique. It's a small intimate community that prides itself on its rustic nature. Not L.L.Bean squeaky-clean cookie-cutter rustic, but real bucolic earthiness with no electricity and few phone lines. Generators and propane tanks provide lights and power, along with some solar energy. The population of the four-mile-wide floodplain comprises year-round residents living off the grid and summer cabins. Most residents roll their eyes at visitors who complain about the North Fork Road's dust and potholes; talk of paving raises the hackles of many, who don't want to see the North Fork changed.

The hub of valley life is the Polebridge Mercantile, where residents catch up on news, sometimes not much differentiated from gossip. The town's dogs run amok and lounge on the front porch. However, visiting canines must be leashed. Hand-painted signs will tell you so: "Local dogs at large." One of the warning signs on the Northern Lights Saloon claims, "Unleashed dogs will be eaten."

ECOLOGICAL SIGNIFICANCE

The North Fork area contains all five of Glacier's ecosystems: grassland prairies, aspen parklands, montane forests, subalpine, and alpine tundra. Rich floodplains teem with wildflowers, berries, shrubs, and trees. Fens abound with orchids, bladderworts, sundews, mosses, sedges, ferns, and bulrushes. McGee Meadows, which is actually a fen, houses at least 50 species of flora. The valley is rife with grizzly and black bears, moose, coyotes, mountain lions, and elk—all manner of wildlife down to its tiniest mammal, the pygmy shrew, which preys on 25 species of bugs, insects, and snails. Birders have documented 196 species of woodpeckers, owls, raptors, waterfowl, and songbirds, over half of which nest here.

With the natural migration of wolves from Canada in the 1980s, Glacier saw its first wolf pack in 50 years, with its first litter of pups in 1986. Numbers have since rebounded. Now wolf packs range across Montana, which has prompted controversy over their status as an endangered species. But don't expect to see a wolf around every tree; their numbers vary year to year, they roam up to 300 square miles, and they are elusive. But you may hear them—especially at night. High concentrations of deer and elk make the North Fork Valley prime wolf habitat; to maintain its health, a wolf must eat 10 percent of its body weight in meat every day.

FIRES

Years of fire suppression policies led to thick lodgepole stands and bug infestations. The 38,000-acre Red Bench Fire in 1988 saw policy change when the fire was allowed to run its natural course. Silver sentinels stand as a reminder that Polebridge was nearly wiped off the map. In 2001, the Moose Fire shot over Demers Ridge, burning 71,000 acres, over one-third inside Glacier. In 2003, the Wedge Canyon Fire burned 53,315 acres, jumping the North Fork River into the park and traveling up the side of Parke Peak, while the Robert Fire burned the valley's south end. Evidence of each of these fires is obvious, but swift new growth is building a new forest blooming with fireweed, arrowleaf balsamroot, and lupine.

Exploring North Fork

ENTRANCE STATIONS

The North Fork River is the boundary between national forest and national park. From the North Fork Valley, two roads cross the river into the park. On the south end, the paved **Camas Road** enters from the dirt North Fork Road, with an unstaffed entrance station and a self-pay cash-only kiosk. A mile northeast of Polebridge, the **Polebridge entrance station** is staffed during summer only, but a self-pay cash-only kiosk is also available.

TOURS AND SHUTTLES

The closest thing to guided tours in the North Fork is guided outdoor recreation: river rafting or backpacking. However, the companies that guide these trips are based in West Glacier. You can also hook up with a **Glacier Institute** (406/755-1211, www.glacierinstitute.org) course that might be wildlife-watching in the area.

Routine bus service does not visit the North Fork; however, **Flathead-Glacier Transportation** (406/892-3390 or 800/829-7039) provides a shuttle on demand between Glacier International Airport and Polebridge (call for rates); reservations are required.

SERVICES

You won't find strip malls or services up the North Fork. You can get gas at the Polebridge Mercantile or Home Ranch Store, but it's pricey. Forget the ATMs, post office, television, visitors centers, and shopping. You'll find mostly outhouses and vault toilets—very few flushers. Phone lines run only as far as Polebridge. The **Polebridge Mercantile** (265 Polebridge Loop) has a pay phone on its front deck. **Home Ranch Bottoms** (8855 North Fork Rd.) has hot showers ($7). It's pricey due to the power source—a generator.

Cell Phones and Internet

Cell-phone reception is spotty to nonexistent. Those who can't cut the technological umbilical cord head to Home Ranch Bottoms. When the store is open, you can get some cell service via their booster. Wireless Internet access is available at the Polebridge Mercantile.

Emergencies

For emergencies within park boundaries, contact a ranger or call 406/888-7800. Outside park boundaries, call 911. A seasonal urgent-care clinic operates in West Glacier (100 Rea Rd., 406/888-9224, 9am-4pm daily Memorial Day-Labor Day). The nearest hospitals are in the Flathead Valley: Kalispell Regional Medical Center (310 Sunny View Lane, Kalispell, 406/752-5111) and North Valley Hospital (1600 Hospital Way, Whitefish, 406/863-3500).

The **Polebridge Ranger Station** (406/888-7800, year-round) sits one mile from Polebridge across the North Fork River at the park entrance; backcountry camping permits are available when someone is available to write one. During summer, Logging Creek Ranger Station on the Inside North Fork Road is staffed, as are stations at Bowman and Kintla Lakes; however, these seasonal rangers may be out patrolling miles of backcountry trails.

DRIVING TOURS

Outside North Fork Road

Open year-round, the Outside North Fork Road is the easier drive of the two dirt and gravel access roads. Although the road running from Columbia Falls to Canada is wide enough for two cars to pass, be prepared for washboards, potholes, ruts, dust in summer, slush in fall or spring, and ice in winter. In 2012, the section between Camas Road and

NORTH FORK WONDERS

TINY FAUNA

The North Fork Valley is home to the rare **northern bog lemming,** a small, brown-backed, gray-bellied rodent that seeks mats of thick wet sphagnum moss for habitat. Weighing only one ounce (the same as one heaping tablespoon of sugar) but growing up to six inches long, the tiny cousin of the Arctic lemming is a relic of the Pleistocene ice age, which began two million years ago. Although it's rarely seen, look for small neat piles of clipped grass it leaves along the mossy thoroughfares en route to underground nests. One study found that bog lemmings make up 2 percent of the pine marten's diet.

Glacier's smallest predator, the **pygmy shrew,** inhabits floodplains in the North Fork Valley. This tiny carnivore is one of North America's rarest mammals. Shorter than 2.5 inches in length and weighing less than a quarter ounce, this shrew's voracious appetite for insects, slugs, snails, and carrion puts larger shrews to shame. One study watched a female eat three times her own body weight daily for 10 days. Their high metabolism echoes their respiration rate—25 times more frequent than humans—and their hearts beat up to 1,320 times per minute when excited. To feed their high metabolic rates, pygmy shrews eat every couple of hours 24-7 year-round.

PLANTS

Carnivorous plants inhabit North Fork fens. The **sundew** attracts insects to its sparkling droplets, which look like morning dew. Sitting atop hairs lining its leaves, the sticky droplets, like wet cement, trap unsuspecting visitors. Slowly, the leaves curl around the victim as digestive juices work their magic. The **bladderwort** has also refined trapping. Buoyant bladders trap anything that swims by—from mosquito larvae to fish fry. When the prey passes, it brushes hairs that open a trapdoor that sucks water in along with the naive prey. Digestive enzymes make short work of the meal, with the trap reset in 15 minutes to two hours.

BIRDS

Birders find a feast for the eyes and ears in the North Fork. With 196 species of birds documented—at least 112 nesters—the valley teems with avian activity. Migratory birds stop on their flight highways to wintering ranges or summer nesting. To help with identification of Glacier's birds, pick up a bird list from visitors centers or on the park's website.

Raptors: Birds of prey find abundant food in the North Fork Valley. Numerous rodents, ground squirrels, songbirds, and carrion feed their appetites. The valley's forests attract sharp-shinned and Cooper's hawks. Bald eagles nest on Kintla and Bowman Lakes. Northern harriers, red-tailed hawks, goshawks, and American kestrels prowl above the prairies. At night, the hoots of large great-horned and pygmy owls haunt the air.

Waterfowl: With the Flathead River, many large lakes, swamps, and wetlands, waterfowl have no shortage of suitable habitat. Herons, ducks, grebes, geese, loons, and swans migrate through or nest in the plentiful waters.

Songbirds: The North Fork could be considered downright noisy at times—not from auto traffic, but from the scads of songbirds flitting among its trees and cattails. American redstarts, warbling vireos, kinglets, nuthatches, crossbills, sparrows, and warblers are just a few of the neotropical songbirds that migrate annually into the valley. In winter, you'll spot tree sparrows and redpolls.

Woodpeckers: After fires, dead standing timber attracted the three-toed woodpecker, picking away for bugs. Watch also for the large red-headed pileated woodpecker looking for a favorite food—carpenter ants.

© BECKY LOMAX

The Outside North Fork Road links to the Inside Road through Polebridge.

Home Ranch Bottoms saw improvements with grading, gravel, and dust inhibitors.

Locals refer to this road as simply the North Fork, dropping the "Outside," for it is the valley's main gateway. Every few years, clamor arises about paving the North Fork, which many locals oppose because pavement would change the valley's nature. The North Fork Road is intermittently plowed in winter as far as the Canadian border, but do not attempt it without good snow tires and a 4WD vehicle. Carry chains and emergency supplies in the car.

From Columbia Falls, the North Fork Road leaves pavement just past Blankenship Road and follows the North Fork River for 13 miles. After a junction with the paved Camas Road, an alternate access from Apgar, the road passes a few small bucolic ranches whose pastures provide browse for cows and wild elk herds. Six miles of rough pavement reappears at Home Ranch Bottoms, where cattle walk the road; drive with caution. At 32 miles and a little over one hour's drive, the road meets Polebridge Loop—the cutoff to the Merc, the Inside North Fork Road, and **Bowman** and **Kintla Lakes.** Hand-painted signs used to warn drivers entering town: "Slow Down, People Breathing." Respect residents; speed kicks up a tremendous amount of dust in summer.

From the Polebridge junction, the road continues 22 more miles north toward Canada—another hour's drive. It accesses the upper Whitefish Range, the North Fork River, and Forest Service cabins. Although drivers used to cross into Canada, the Canadian government no longer opens the Trail Creek port of entry.

Inside Road

Not for everyone, the summer-only (May-Oct.) dirt Inside North Fork Road throws precipitous drops, curves, and climbs at drivers. Monster potholes and washboards are commonplace;

spaces wide enough for two vehicles to pass are rare. You're definitely off the beaten path on this bumpy trek, where speeds top out at 20 mph. Marked as Glacier Route 7 on some maps and known as simply the "Inside Road" to locals, the road is the rougher of the two choices and requires high-clearance vehicles. Big RV rigs have trouble, and it's a rough ride for a trailer. Although it's only 29 miles to Polebridge, the drive will take two hours. Many link with Outside North Fork and Camas Roads for a 53-mile scenic loop drive.

From the south, the Inside Road begins at Fish Creek Campground and climbs through the 2003 Robert Fire. Atop the ridge, look for peek-a-boo views of **McGee Meadows,** a good wildlife-watching spot if you can squeeze your vehicle off the road and tolerate swarms of mosquitoes. Then compare fire reqrowth as you drive through the 2001 Moose Fire. After dropping down steep Anaconda Hill (12.5 miles from Fish Creek) and crossing the creek, the road bisects Sullivan Meadows, famous for Glacier's wolves, before passing two small campgrounds—Logging Creek (17.5 miles) and Quartz Creek (20 miles). At 28 miles, the road intersects with the Polebridge park entrance. From here, cross the North Fork River, drive one mile to **Polebridge** to connect with Outside North Fork Road.

You can also continue up the Inside Road to **Bowman** and **Kintla Lakes.** A few minutes north of the Polebridge Ranger Station, the curvy Bowman Lake road turns off, a six-mile (25-minute) snakelike drive eastward up the valley. Continuing northward toward Kintla, the Inside Road crosses **Big Prairie,** the largest of the North Fork's unique grasslands. **Round Prairie** follows at one-third the size. The road reenters the forest and passes through the 2003 Wedge Canyon Fire zone before dead-ending at Kintla Lake, 14 miles north of the North Fork entrance station.

SIGHTS

Polebridge Mercantile

The red-planked "Merc" is the hub of the North Fork. The Polebridge Mercantile, listed on the National Register of Historic Places, was built in 1914. It is more than a place to buy a forgotten can of pork and beans for camping. It sells local handmade jewelry and not-to-be-missed bakery goods fresh from the oven. While the smell of cookies and pastries fills the small room, an old-fashioned cash register clangs up sales. Flannery Coats and Stuart Reiswig, who consider themselves "caretakers" rather than owners, have kept the Merc's flavor, but swapped the old diesel generator for solar power.

Northern Lights Saloon

Next door to the Merc, the tiny Northern Lights Saloon (dinner daily in summer) looks like a ramshackle log cabin but packs in diners, extras spilling outside onto picnic tables. Hikers celebrate their adventures here with whatever Montana microbrew is currently on tap and lounge outside, staring at Rainbow Peak.

North Fork of the Flathead River

Forming the western boundary of Glacier National Park, the North Fork of the Flathead River rises in Canada and ends near West Glacier at its confluence with the Middle Fork. Fifty-nine miles of the river flow through private, state, and federal lands while descending the North Fork Valley's diverse habitats. Designated as a Wild and Scenic River, the Class II river with six accesses is great for multiday float trips, day rafting, fishing, and scenic floating.

McGee Meadows

Between Camas Road and the Inside Road, McGee Meadows is a wildlife-watching spot, but during spring and early summer, the fen is too wet to walk due to its soggy nature. It is also a mosquito haven. As a fen, its low-oxygen

The North Fork of the Flathead River attracts anglers looking for trout.

waters build up dead plant matter, but nutrients feed it via precipitation and ground water, making it fertile ground for diverse vegetation. The meadow is home to rare plants and over 50 species of flora—bulrushes, bladderworts, sphagnum moss, sundews, and orchids. Wildlife sightings can include bears, moose, deer, and a host of birds. Cross-country skiers tour the meadows in winter.

Bowman Lake

Seven miles northeast of Polebridge, Bowman Lake sits in a narrow glacier-scoured trough on a dirt road with a bouncing ride. The lake's six miles sprawl toward nesting bald eagles and Thunderbird Peak; its 0.5-mile width squeezes in between the hulks of Numa Peak and Rainbow Peak, the latter rising 4,500 feet straight up from the south lakeshore. In summer, lake waters offer solitude: Drop in a canoe to tour its shoreline. In winter, the icy expanse and snow-laden crags call to cross-country skiers, who ski in on the road pockmarked with wolf and elk tracks.

Big Prairie

Located 30 miles up the Inside North Fork Road, just two miles past the Bowman Lake turnoff and three miles from Polebridge, Big Prairie is the largest of four Palouse prairies in the North Fork. At one mile wide and four miles long, the prairie is a grassland with wheatgrass, fescues, oat-grass, and sagebrush. Because the Whitefish Range causes a rain shadow, the North Fork receives only 20 inches of precipitation per year, which fosters this drier flora.

Kintla Lake

Kintla Lake is a place to go only on purpose. Fifteen miles of washboarded, rutted road links Polebridge with the remote lake. Its tiny campground tucked deep in the trees offers quiet, a place to decompress. Cowering between Starvation and Parke Ridges, the 0.5-mile-wide lake curves a little over five miles up valley, a prelude to Upper Kintla Lake. Only one trail starts along the north shore and runs toward the isolated Kintla-Kinnerly peak complex and Boulder Pass. Haul a canoe or kayak to Kintla Lake for unbeatable secluded paddling.

Recreation

HIKING

Hiking in the North Fork leads to stunning vistas, but be prepared for tromping through long, mosquito-ridden, thick-forested valleys to earn your views. While day hikers trek to lakes and lookouts, backpackers gain altitude into rugged glaciated alpine bowls above the tree line. In this undeveloped area, you're on your own to get to trailheads; no shuttle service runs up the North Fork. On opposite sides of the valley, hikes depart into Glacier and the Whitefish Range in Flathead National Forest. Those looking for hikes for the pooch should head to the national forest.

Backpackers going overnight in Glacier need permits (adults $5 pp per night, ages 8-15 $2.50, under age 8 free). Pick them up 24 hours in advance in person at the Polebridge Ranger Station (406/888-7800), but call ahead to ensure someone will be available; or the Apgar Backcountry Permit Office (406/888-7900). You can apply for advance reservations ($30) online via the Backcountry Camping Application (www.nps.gov/glac). No permits are needed in Flathead National Forest for overnight trips.

While trails in Glacier Park are well signed, Flathead National Forest trails are less so. Trail signs may consist of just a number with no distances, destinations, or directions. For that reason alone, always hike with a topographic map in Flathead National Forest, and know how to read it. National forest trails are maintained less frequently; expect to encounter deadfall and downed trees as well as brushy routes. For hiking maps of Flathead National Forest, contact the Glacier View Ranger District (406/387-3800) in Hungry Horse. Topographic quad maps of the Whitefish Range can be purchased at outdoor sporting-goods stores in Flathead Valley. For hiking Glacier's trails, take along a topographic map, available through Glacier National Park Conservancy (406/888-5756, www.glaciernationalparkconservancy.org).

Quartz Lakes

- Distance: 12.4-mile loop
- Duration: 6 hours
- Elevation gain: 1,430 feet to Upper Quartz, 927 feet on return over the ridge
- Effort: moderate
- Trailhead: backcountry parking area at Bowman Lake in Glacier Park

In June, early parts of the trail burst with calypso orchids while the path crossing Cerulean Ridge is still buried under snow. Less than 0.5 miles up the trail, the path splits. You'll return to this junction at the end of the loop. Take the left fork, heading to Quartz Lake. With peek-a-boo views of Numa Peak, the trail climbs through thick spruce and fir forests until it crests Cerulean ridge. As the trail drops 1,000 feet to Quartz Lake, it enters the 1988 Red Bench burn, where open meadows afford views of Vulture Peak's steep north face and the lake.

At Quartz Lake, the trail cuts through the backcountry campsite and rounds the lake through boardwalk bogs, passing Middle Quartz Lake. Even as the trail moves away from water, mosquitoes swarm. The trail drops to a backcountry campsite at Lower Quartz Lake's

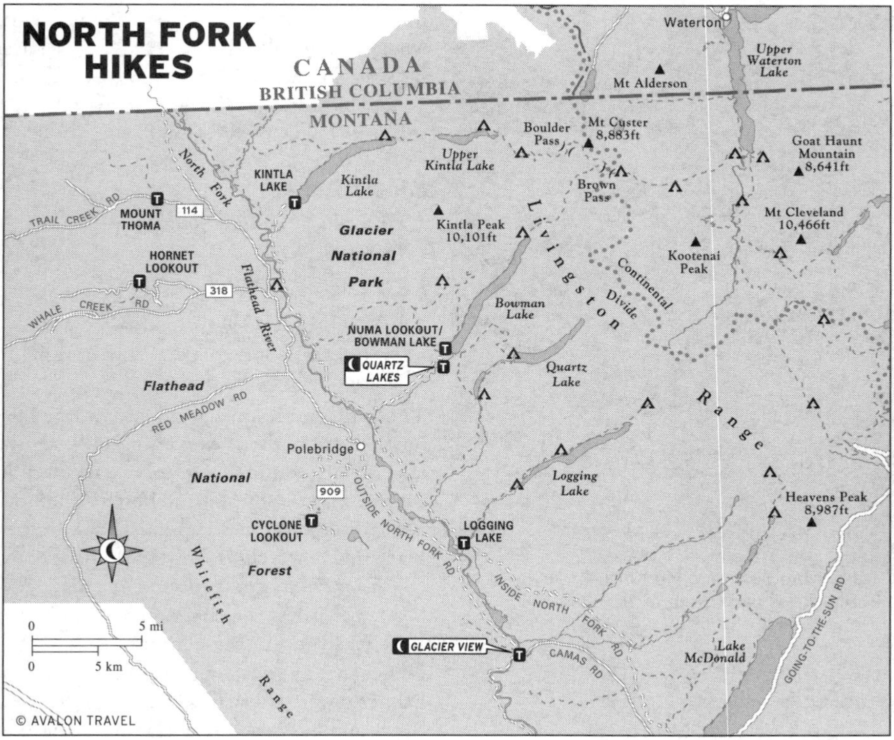

outlet. From here, it climbs 1.5 miles with good views to the top of Cerulean Ridge before dropping back to the junction. For families with kids, an out-and-back excursion just to Lower Quartz Lake may be easier, at seven miles round-trip.

Numa Lookout

- Distance: 11.2 miles round-trip
- Duration: 5.5 hours
- Elevation gain: 2,931 feet
- Effort: moderately strenuous
- Trailhead: Bowman Lake Campground in Glacier National Park

Although the bulk of the trail crawls through deep forest, the view from Numa Lookout is well worth the climb. Following the northwest shore of Bowman Lake, the trail winds 0.7 miles through damp cedars to a junction. Take the left fork. The trail climbs steadily uphill to a saddle with a small boggy pond. During mosquito season, hike fast to get past the swarms.

After the trail switchbacks up the final climb within eyesight of the lookout, the treed slope breaks into dry open meadows. At 6,960 feet high, the lookout, which is staffed during fire season, has views across Bowman Lake at the steep massif of Square, Rainbow, and Carter Peaks.

Bowman Lake

- Distance: 14.2 miles round-trip to the head of the lake

Trails from Bowman and Kintla Lakes lead to Boulder Pass and Hole-in-the-Wall.

- Duration: 6 hours
- Elevation gain: none
- Effort: easy, but long
- Trailhead: Bowman Lake Campground in Glacier National Park

This easy-walking trail wanders the forested northeast shoreline of Bowman Lake. For a stroll, walk it as far as you want, and then turn around. The trail nears the shore close enough for beach access only a few times when June water levels flood beaches. Intermittent views of the Square, Rainbow, and Carter massif poke out from the trees.

At the head of the lake, a backcountry campground with a marvelous pebble beach is a great place to have lunch, but eat near the community cooking site rather than in or near the backcountry sleeping sites. Bring binoculars, because bald eagles nest at the lake's head. For backpackers, the trail continues on, climbing to Brown's Pass atop the Continental Divide, where it splits, dropping east to Goat Haunt on Waterton Lake (23 miles total) or climbing around Hole-in-the-Wall and over Boulder Pass to Kintla Lake (37 miles total).

Kintla Lake

- Distance: 12.4 miles round-trip
- Duration: 6 hours
- Elevation gain: 200 feet
- Effort: easy, but long
- Trailhead: Kintla Lake Campground in Glacier National Park

The gentle trail cruises along Kintla Lake's north shore with an expanding view up the lake before its midsection tours back deep in the trees. Look for woodland flowers: trilliums, twisted stalk, queen's cup, fairybells, bunchberry, and bog orchids. Toward the head of the lake, the trail returns to a shoreline tour.

At 6.3 miles, the trail reaches the Kintla Lake backcountry campground. Pull out the binoculars, as you might see moose, bear, or bald eagles from its shoreline. Eat lunch near the community cooking site rather than in or near backcountry sleeping sites. The trail continues on through the 2003 Wedge Fire, growing with prolific pink fireweed, and past the dramatic Long Knife Waterfall to Upper Kintla Lake, 2.9 miles from Kintla Head Backcountry Campsites. At the head of Upper Kintla, it begins a substantial climb to Boulder Pass, where it drops through Hole-in-the-Wall cirque to Brown's Pass on the Continental Divide and then splits, dropping east to Goat Haunt on Waterton Lake (32 miles total) or down to Bowman Lake (37 miles total).

Logging Lake

- Distance: 8.8 miles round-trip
- Duration: 4 hours
- Elevation gain: 380 feet

The lookout from Mount Thoma yields broad views of the North Fork and Kintla area.

- Effort: easy
- Trailhead: Logging Creek Campground on the Inside North Fork Road in Glacier National Park

With expansive views en route, the trail attracts mostly anglers fishing for cutthroat, some with gumption enough to haul in float tubes to get away from the brushy shoreline. Above Logging Creek, the trail climbs quickly at the start but then levels out across a timbered ridgeline that offers a glimpse or two of the creek canyon. At the lake, far beyond its opposite shoreline eight miles away, you can spot Mount Geduhn and Anaconda Mountain.

Mount Thoma

- Distance: 10 miles round-trip
- Duration: 5 hours
- Elevation gain: 2,913 feet
- Effort: strenuous
- Trailhead: north side 3 miles up Trail Creek Road in Flathead National Forest
- Directions: Drive north of Polebridge on the Outside North Fork Road approximately 13 miles to Trail Creek, 6 miles from the Canadian border. Turn left and drive 3 miles to the trailhead.

The forested trail starts off gently but soon pitches into an uphill grunt. Brushy and rarely maintained, the trail frequently has downed trees barring the path, requiring climbing and worming through branches. But soon it breaks out into a high ridgeline meadow with bluebells. At the end of the ridge, it climbs a series of switchbacks to the summit.

The summit is well worth the hike. Glacier's peaks sprawl to the southeast. The swath along the border between Canada and the United States slices an unnaturally straight line across the valley. In Canada, a mosaic of clear-cuts leads up to Akamina-Kishinena Provincial Park bordering Waterton National Park. To the south, the Whitefish Range layers off peak after peak as far as the eye can see.

Hornet Lookout

- Distance: 2 miles round-trip
- Duration: 1 hour
- Elevation gain: 746 feet
- Effort: easy
- Trailhead: Hornet Road's terminus in Flathead National Forest
- Directions: 10 miles north of Polebridge, turn west on Whale Creek Road (Forest Rd. 318) for 4 miles, then turn north, climbing on narrow Hornet Road (Forest Rd. 9805) for 5.2 miles.

A short climb uphill through huckleberry, fireweed, and bear grass slopes leads to a small lookout with great views of Glacier's skyline and the North Fork Valley. Silvered trees remain from the 2003 Wedge Fire; you'll get a good look at the full scope of the burn. While the drive may take longer than the hike, the lookout makes a great kid destination with rewarding views for adults. You can rent the U.S. Forest Service lookout for 1-2 people to spend the night.

Cyclone Lookout

- Distance: 5.6 miles round-trip
- Duration: 3 hours
- Elevation gain: 1,034 feet
- Effort: moderate
- Trailhead: on the North Fork Road between Home Ranch and Polebridge, turn west into Flathead National Forest onto Forest Road 376 for 1.25 miles. Turn south onto Forest Road 909 for 4.2 miles.

The trail begins on an old road but soon narrows into a path that switchbacks up through a lodgepole forest. During huckleberry season, you may find a good crop of berries. At the summit, the lookout provides views of the Whitefish Range and straight across the North Fork Valley into the Bowman Lake region of Glacier National Park. The lookout is staffed in summer.

Glacier View

- Distance: 4.5 miles round-trip
- Duration: 4.5 hours
- Elevation gain: 2,725 feet
- Effort: strenuous
- Trailhead: junction of Camas and North Fork Roads in Flathead National Forest; the trail sign says "Demers Ridge"

A steep climb up the side of Demers Ridge leads to Glacier View. Its name says it all: Views from the top span the park's peaks. You'll even see Flathead Lake in the distance. The trail passes through the 2001 Moose Fire zone, with charred stumps and silver toothpick trees. In the valley below, you can see the fire's mosaic as it burned with different intensities and leaped

© BECKY LOMAX

A steep climb leads to Glacier View, a panorama of peaks stretching from the Canadian border to the Bob Marshall Wilderness.

TIPS FOR WILDLIFE-WATCHING

- Safety is important when watching wildlife—safety for you and safety for the wildlife. For spying wildlife up close, use a good pair of binoculars.
- Do not approach wildlife. Although our inclinations tell us to scoot in for a closer look, crowding wildlife puts you at risk and endangers the animal, often scaring it off. Sometimes simply the presence of people can habituate an animal to hanging around people; with bears, this can lead to more aggressive behavior.
- Let the animal's or bird's behavior guide your behavior. If the animal appears twitchy, nervous, or points eyes and ears directly at you, back off: You're too close. The goal is to watch wild animals go about their normal business, rather than to see how they react to disruption. If you behave like a predator stalking an animal, the creature will assume you are one. Use binoculars and telephoto lenses for moving in close rather than approaching an animal.
- Most animals tend to be more active in morning and evening. These are also optimum times for photographing animals in better lighting.
- Blend in with your surroundings. Rather than wearing loud colors, wear muted clothing that matches the environment.
- Relax. Animals sense excitement. Move slowly around them because abrupt, jerky movements can startle them. Look down, rather than staring animals directly in the eye.
- Don't get carried away watching big showy megafauna like bears and moose only to miss a small carnivore like a short-tailed weasel.
- Use field guides to help with identification and understanding the animal's behavior.
- If you see wildlife along a road, use pullouts or broad shoulders to drive completely off the road. Do not block the middle of the road. Use the car as a blind to watch wildlife, but keep pets inside. If you see a bear, you're better off just driving by slowly. Bear jams tend to condition the bruin to become accustomed to vehicles, one step toward getting into more trouble.

tree glades. In June, wild roses scent the air amid a botanical dream of wildflower species.

Right from the start, the trail makes no bones about going uphill: There are no flats to catch your breath and no warm-up for the legs. But with a decent pair of lungs, the steep ascent is not bad. Just adopt a slow steady pace, and you'll reach the top, where meadows afford a scenic top-of-the-world place to lunch, with Glacier's peaks from its southern border to Canada spread across the skyline. The fire removed shade from the slopes, so the trail bakes in the August heat. In winter, snowshoers trek up.

Guides

Glacier Guides (406/387-5555 or 800/521-7238, West Glacier, www.glacierguides.com) has the sole guiding concession for Glacier Park. Most of its day-hiking trips head elsewhere, but many of its multiday backpacking trips begin or finish at the Bowman and Kintla trailheads. No companies run guiding services for hiking in the Whitefish Range of Flathead National Forest.

BIKING

With the North Fork's rough gravel roads, mountain biking is the only way to go; road bikes won't cut it. You can rent mountain bikes in Polebridge from North Fork Recreational Rentals (80 Beaver Dr., Polebridge, 406/888-9985, http://northforkrecmt.com, $30 per day). Reservations are strongly advised.

Mountain bikers ride a 54-mile loop from Apgar up the Inside North Fork Road, overnight in Polebridge, and cycle down the Outside

North Fork and Camas Roads. The Inside Road has serious elevation gain as it climbs and drops through five creek drainages. A good two-day ride, the loop requires carrying only minimal supplies: Stay at the North Fork Hostel, dine at the Northern Lights Saloon, and breakfast on baked goodies at the Merc. Just carry your lunch, the day's water, emergency supplies, and, of course, insect repellent. In June, when moisture still clings to the gravel, the ride is less dusty, but you'll eat your share of mosquitoes.

RIVER RAFTING, KAYAKING, AND CANOEING

Floating the Wild and Scenic **North Fork of the Flathead River** decompresses life to river pace on Class II waters. Despite the lazy ambiance, log jams pose hazards, and between Big Creek and Glacier Rim, the Class III Upper Fool Hen rapids can flip the unwary. Paddlers can avoid this stretch by taking out at Big Creek. Seven river put-ins stagger down the river's 59 miles from the Canadian border to its confluence with the Middle Fork: the border, Ford, Polebridge, Coal Creek, Big Creek, Glacier Rim, and Blankenship. Flows peak in late May, with low water in August. In July, the average float time from the border to Blankenship is 16 hours, which most floaters tend to break into three days.

Three Forks of the Flathead Float Guide ($13), available through Glacier National Park Conservancy (406/888-5756, www.glaciernationalparkconservancy.org), provides details on camping, rapids, and navigation. Solid human waste containment is required; take a toilet system, groover, or disposable biodegradable waste bags. Fire pans to prevent fire scarring are recommended.

Respect the rights of private-property owners along the river. Signage at river accesses identifies land ownership en route. For questions regarding rafting on the North Fork, call Glacier View Ranger District (406/387-3800).

Overnights

No permits are required for floating, but all camps must be set up on the western shore rather than Glacier National Park's eastern shoreline. Camping—first-come, first-served only—is free in Flathead National Forest and on state lands. Round Prairie, on Glacier's bank, is the one exception; this backcountry campground requires a permit.

Guides

Several river rafting companies lead overnight trips down the North Fork; however, none base their operations in the North Fork Valley. All commercial outfitters begin their trips in West Glacier. Due to the Class II nature of the river, the float trips are great for families and kids.

Rentals and Shuttles

In Polebridge, catarafts, canoes, and inflatable kayaks are available for rent from North Fork Recreational Rentals (80 Beaver Dr., Polebridge, 406/888-9985, http://northforkrecmt.com, $60 per day). Rates include paddles and life jackets. The gear is in demand, so make reservations. Rubber rafts are available to rent in West Glacier from **Glacier Guides/Montana Raft Company** (406/387-5555 or 800/521-7238) or **Glacier Outdoor Center** (406/888-5454 or 800/235-6781), which also offers vehicle shuttle services ($60-355) in your vehicle or theirs.

BOATING

All types of unpowered boats and sail craft are allowed on **Bowman** and **Kintla Lakes,** but constrictive mountains create swirly winds that make sailing and sailboarding almost impossible. Seasonal wildlife closures at the lakes' heads, marked with orange buoys, protect nesting bald eagles. While Kintla does not permit motorized boats, Bowman allows motors of 10 horsepower or less. Both lakes are closed to Jet Skis and waterskiing. No boat rentals are available in the North

© BECKY LOMAX

River-rafters float the North Fork of the Flathead River along Glacier's western boundary.

Fork Valley; bring rentals from Flathead Valley. You can rent stand-up paddleboards ($50 per day) in Polebridge from **North Fork Recreational Rentals** (80 Beaver Dr., Polebridge, 406/888-9985, http://northforkrecmt.com).

All boats must pick up free permits. Boats must be cleaned, drained, and dried to avoid bringing Aquatic Invasive Species into park lakes. The permits are available at the Polebridge Entrance Station.

LAKE KAYAKING AND CANOEING

The quiet waters of **Bowman** and **Kintla Lakes** appeal to kayakers and canoers. Kintla is a paddling paradise due to its ban on motorized watercraft. While both lakes make for stellar paddling on calm days, their waters kick up with lusty winds in minutes. Wildlife closures are marked with orange buoys at the head of each lake, where bald eagles nest. Free boating permits are available at the Polebridge Ranger Station. By permit, paddlers can camp overnight in the backcountry campgrounds at the heads of Kintla and Bowman Lakes.

You can rent kayaks and canoes ($60-80 per day) in Polebridge from **North Fork Recreational Rentals** (80 Beaver Dr., Polebridge, 406/888-9985, http://northforkrecmt.com). Rates include paddles and life jackets; reservations are recommended.

FISHING

Anglers are attracted to the North Fork for its native fish: westslope cutthroat and bull trout. Be able to identify each, as they are catch-and-release only. Bull trout have spots on their sides that are pink or orange, and they lack black on their backs; cutthroats have a red slash under their jaw.

Kintla and **Bowman Lakes** are the main lakes accessible by car for fishing. Shorelines near their campgrounds are rimmed with trails. For those willing to hike, the three **Quartz Lakes** hop with native trout and whitefish.

Along the Inside North Fork Road, most of the western creek drainages provide some fishing, with various degrees of accessibility. Fishing closures in the area include Upper Kintla Lake and Kintla Creek between the two Kintla Lakes, Bowman Creek above the lake, and Logging Creek between Logging and Grace Lakes.

The most popular North Fork Valley fishing is on the **North Fork River** itself, where seven river accesses (Canadian border, Ford, Polebridge, Coal Creek, Big Creek, Glacier Rim, and Blankenship) allow for raft or boat launching and fishing. Anglers also fish around the Camas Bridge.

Several commercial outfitters guide overnight fishing trips on the North Fork River; all fishing outfitters base their operations out of West Glacier. Rental gear is also available in West Glacier.

Licenses and Regulations

The North Fork River's high water line on the eastern shore is Glacier National Park's western boundary. Inside the park, fishing licenses or permits are not required, but outside the park, anglers must possess a Montana State Fishing License. When fishing the North Fork River from the east bank, park regulations apply; when fishing from the west bank, state regulations apply. Purchase a Montana fishing license in West Glacier or Flathead Valley before you come up the North Fork; they are not sold in Polebridge. Find fishing-license information and how to order in advance online (www.fwp.mt.gov).

HUNTING

Hunting is illegal in Glacier National Park. But in the North Fork, Flathead National Forest holds popular deer, elk, and bird hunting grounds. Get the regulations, seasons, and license info from Montana Fish, Wildlife, and Parks (406/444-2535, www.fwp.mt.gov).

CROSS-COUNTRY SKIING

Roads in the North Fork Valley convert to easy avalanche-free cross-country ski and snowshoe trails in winter. But don't expect pristine smooth snows: The North Fork thrives as a winter habitat for moose, wolves, deer, elk, snowshoe hares, coyotes, and bobcats, whose tracks pockmark the roads. Grab a track identification book to help in deciphering the footprints. Bring gear, as none is available for rent. The nearest ski and snowshoe rentals are in Flathead Valley.

Park at the Polebridge entrance station to ski to **Bowman Lake,** touring 0.5 miles north on the Inside Road before climbing six miles up to Bowman Lake's frozen shores. **Big Prairie, Inside Road,** and **Hidden Meadows** all provide other routes starting from the same point. For route descriptions, pick up a free brochure on *Skiing and Snowshoeing* online (www.nps.gov/glac) or from visitors centers or ranger stations.

For an overnight in Flathead National Forest, skiers traverse 12 miles up Whale Creek Road to stay in Ninko Cabin on the flanks of Thompson-Seton Mountain. For information on this trip, call Glacier View Ranger Station (406/387-3800).

SNOWMOBILING

While snowmobiles are not permitted in Glacier, they are allowed in Flathead National Forest in the Whitefish Range, where snowfall piles up 6-12 feet. December-April, snowmobilers ride unplowed roads heading west off the North Fork Road. The Flathead Snowmobile Association (www.flatheadsnowmobiler.com) grooms a few routes. Glacier View Ranger Station (406/387-3800) regulates snowmobile use, seasons, and closures, and it has maps; check for current conditions and restrictions. The nearest rentals are in Flathead Valley.

ENTERTAINMENT

Instead of red, white, and blue marching bands, witness cross-dressers, beer-can draggers, bicycles, the 1956 Polebridge fire truck, and rafts in Polebridge's annual **Fourth of**

July Parade—the more slightly off-kilter, the better. Hundreds of people line the dirt main street for the noon parade that's really not a parade. Parking is a nightmare, and it's a two-for-one show as the parade goes up the street and then back down the same street. Enter for free; watch for free. Who's in charge? No one knows.

Accommodations and Food

North Fork lodging is off the grid. With no electricity, generators or solar panels provide power, lights are propane, woodstoves provide heat, and phone lines only reach Polebridge. However, despite the rusticity, the state of Montana still charges its 7 percent bed tax.

LODGING

Bed-and-Breakfast

For those looking to get away from it all, **The Way Less Traveled Bed and Breakfast** (16485 North Fork Rd., 406/261-5880, www.thewaylesstraveled.com, year-round) is about as far away as you can get and still have the comforts of civilization. Proprietors Paul and Nancy Winkler encourage guests to forget about the world. Located 17 miles north of Polebridge near the Canadian border, the smoke-free, alcohol-free bed-and-breakfast has three themed guest rooms. Two of the rooms ($95) share a bath, but the Lewis and Clark room ($115) has a private bath and a deck. The dining room, where the full breakfast features goodies like cinnamon-raisin-vanilla french toast, is surrounded by wildlife-watching windows; in summer, breakfast on the deck is accompanied by loons singing on a nearby lake. A generator powers lights, hot water, a satellite TV for those who just cannot live without it, and wireless Internet access.

Hostel and Cabins

Located 0.25 miles south of the Merc and Northern Lights Saloon, the **North Fork Hostel and Inn** (80 Beaver Dr., Polebridge, 406/888-5241, www.nfhostel.com, open year-round) offers a mix of hostel rooms, cabins, and unique accommodations. Reservations are required in winter and strongly advised in summer. The hostel may be off the electric grid, but you don't "rough it": A huge storage battery powers phone, fax, and wireless Internet access. Propane powers lights, a cooking stove, and a refrigerator, with a few kerosene lights added in. Wood heats up the cedar hot tub. The hostel has a shared living room, fully equipped kitchen, outhouses, and baths with hot showers. Lodging options include mixed dorm bunks ($20 pp) and private guest rooms ($45-50). An assortment of tepees, cabins, and a 1950s trailer called the Green Zucchini add summer options ($40-50). Bring food, towels, and sleeping bags, or rent linens ($5-10).

Nearby at **Square Peg Ranch,** the hostel also rents two log homes (3-night minimum, $80)—one a 1918 homestead. Kitchens are equipped with propane lights, a fridge, and cooking ranges, and the buildings are heated with wood. Cold running water, solar-heated showers, and outhouses complete the rustic stay. Bring sleeping bags or sheets, food, towels, and containers to haul fresh drinking water from the hostel. Each home sleeps four adults and two children.

Cabins

Private cabins are sprinkled up and down the North Fork, and some owners rent them out. Find options such as rustic one-roomers and log homes online at **VRBO** (www.vrbo.com) under "Polebridge."

Home Ranch Bottoms recently added the newest cabins in the North Fork adjacent to the store and pub. The **Polebridge Ranch Cabins** (8950 North Fork Rd., 406/662-1552, www.polebridgemontana.com, May-Oct.) offer two types of lodging. The nicer cabins, named for the North Fork lakes of Bowman and Kintla, have private baths with showers and porches. The Bowman (3-night minimum, $160) includes a fully equipped kitchen, while The Kintla (2-night minimum, $125) is more like a hotel cabin without a kitchen. The "Bunkottages" ($50) can sleep four people on two bunk beds, and guests use separate shared toilet and shower facilities. Electricity for all the cabins comes from a generator.

Flathead National Forest (Glacier View Ranger District, Hungry Horse, 406/387-3800, www.fs.fed.us/r1/flathead) maintains six rental cabins scattered throughout the North Fork. With a three-night maximum stay, the cabins ($20-65) have beds, outdoor vault toilets, kitchens equipped with propane cook stoves, outdoor fire pits, and firewood. Bring water, bedding, and food. The nonsmoking cabins do not permit pets, tents, or RVs. Reservations are mandatory (877/444-6777, www.recreation.gov). After confirmation, you'll get the cabin combination. You must clean up at the end of your stay and pack garbage out with you. Four cabins are available year-round. In a rather drafty tiny 1922 building perched atop a mountain, **Hornet Lookout,** which sleeps two, is a one-mile hike in summer or 11-mile ski or snowmobile trek in winter. The lookout has a small cupola with spectacular views of Glacier. The deck at **Schnaus** yields sweeping views of Glacier's Livingston Range, making it a local favorite for its sunrises and sunset alpenglow. The cabin, which sleeps 12, has vehicle access right up to the front door and is less than one mile from the North Fork

© BECKY LOMAX

Wurtz Cabin is a homestead dating back to 1913.

River. Located on the North Fork River, **Ben Rover,** which sleeps eight and has drive-up access, is popular for skiing to Bowman Lake in winter, walking to Polebridge in summer, and fishing right out the front door. The farthest north, **Wurtz Cabin,** which sleeps 12, is an old 1913 homestead with a large yard on the west side of the North Fork Road. The river is within a 15-minute walk. Two small cabins offer seasonal lodging. **Ninko** (Dec.-Mar.), which sleeps seven, requires a 12-mile ski or snowmobile trek to reach its remote forested setting. **Ford** (late May-mid-Mar.), which was built in 1922 as part of the ranger station, sleeps eight. It has drive-up access and is adjacent to a river access site.

CAMPING

Rustic national park or national forest campgrounds—all first come, first served—are the norm, with a sprinkling of small private options. If you require hookups and disposal stations, go to West Glacier and Columbia Falls.

Glacier National Park Campgrounds

Glacier's seasonal North Fork campgrounds (406/888-7800, www.nps.gov/glac) are only accessible via rough dirt roads. Between rugged roads and smaller sites, these campgrounds don't accommodate huge RVs or large trailer combinations. But that's precisely their attraction: Fewer people equals solitude and quiet. They have pit toilets, fire rings, and picnic tables. While the park prohibits firewood collecting in most places, including the campgrounds, you can collect dry, downed firewood on the Bowman Lake Road and the Inside Road from one mile north of Fish Creek Campground to Kintla Lake. Cutting live timber is not permitted. After fall closures, Bowman and Kintla campgrounds permit primitive camping ($10). You can haul cooking water from lakes and streams to boil or purify. The four campgrounds are buggy in June, serene in August, and closed in winter when the roads are buried in snow.

At the foot of Kintla Lake, **Kintla Lake Campground** (late May-mid-Sept., $15) is 15 miles north of Polebridge. The tiny 13-site campground is tucked under large trees, with hand-pumped water and small sites. One hiking trail leads up-lake and beyond to Upper Kintla Lake and Boulder Pass. If you don't have reservations, plan to arrive early enough that if all the campsites are full, you can still drive back toward Bowman Lake.

At the foot of Bowman Lake, **Bowman Lake Campground** (late May-mid-Sept., $15) is seven miles from Polebridge. Its 48 sites, the largest of the North Fork's campgrounds, spread out under a mixed conifer forest. It has running water, and a short five-minute walk leads to the lakeshore and the boat ramp. Trails connect to Quartz Lakes, Numa Lookout, Akokala Lake, and up Bowman Lake to Brown's Pass.

Two tiny campgrounds flank the Inside Road in the woods midway between Apgar and Polebridge. They are best for tent campers who can drive the rugged road. No running water is available, so bring your own or plan to purify stream water. Arrive by midafternoon to allow plenty of time to go elsewhere if the campground is full. **Quartz Creek Campground** (July-Nov., $10), a tiny seven-site campground six miles southeast of Polebridge, is adjacent to Quartz Creek. From the campground, a 6.8-mile rough trail with infrequent maintenance follows the creek up to Lower Quartz Lake. Located 8.3 miles southeast of Polebridge, **Logging Creek Campground** (July-Sept., $10), adjacent to Logging Creek Ranger Station, has only seven sites. This is a popular site for anglers heading to Logging Lake.

Glacier Backcountry Camping

North Fork trails lead to some of the park's most coveted backcountry campsites in the

© BECKY LOMAX

Kintla Lake Campground has sites overlooking Kintla Creek.

high country between Bowman and Kintla Lakes. Spectacular **Boulder Pass, Brown's Pass,** and **Hole-in-the-Wall** campsites are snow-free late July-early September. Low-elevation campsites are snow-free at the heads of **Bowman** and **Kintla Lakes** May-October, providing prized canoe and sea-kayak destinations. Anglers head to **Quartz Lakes** and **Logging Lake.** River floaters can stay at **Round Meadows** on the banks of the North Fork of the Flathead, and paddlers can camp at the heads of **Bowman** and **Kintla Lakes.**

Permits (adults $5 pp per night, ages 8-15 $2.50, under age 8 free) are required for all overnight backcountry camping in Glacier. Pick them up 24 hours in advance in person at the Polebridge Ranger Station (406/888-7800), but call ahead to ensure someone will be available; or the Apgar Backcountry Permit Office (406/888-7900). You can apply for advance reservations ($30) online via the Backcountry Camping Application (www.nps.gov/glac).

Flathead National Forest Campground

Located 20 miles north of Columbia Falls and 13 miles from Apgar on North Fork Road, **Big Creek Campground** (Glacier View Ranger District, 406/387-3800, mid-May-mid-Oct., $13) is in Flathead National Forest. It can be accessed via a five-minute drive on a gravel road from the Camas Road park entrance. Several of the campground's 22 sites can accommodate 40-foot RVs and trailers among its large cottonwoods and dog-hair firs. Drinking water is available, along with vault toilets. Prime campsites line the North Fork of the Flathead River, with easy fishing access. You can collect firewood here, but by August the surrounding woods are scoured.

Private Campgrounds

Camping is also available at two small North Fork private campgrounds. The **North Fork Hostel** (80 Beaver Dr., Polebridge,

© BECKY LOMAX

Northern Lights Saloon and Cafe serves up beer and dinner.

406/888-5241, www.nfhostel.com) accommodates tenters ($14). Cyclists can stay for $7. **Home Ranch Bottoms** (8855 North Fork Rd., Polebridge, 406/888-5572, www.homeranchbottoms.com) charges $20 for up to six people in one vehicle; showers are extra.

FOOD

A rustic off-the-grid restaurant in a tiny funky old log cabin built in 1912, the **Northern Lights Saloon and Cafe** (255 Polebridge Loop, Polebridge, 406/888-9963, www.northernlightssaloon.net, 4pm-9pm daily late May-Sept., entrees $7-20) is where hikers stop to celebrate with a beer and then linger over a meal. The ever-changing menu with homemade goodies features seasonal specialties, vegetarian dishes, elk burgers, and steaks. Freshly baked fruit pies finish off the meal. New owners in 2010 overhauled the restaurant interior and equipment and got the liquor license reinstated in 2011. Waiting lines attest to its unique backwoods ambience and slower pace; don't expect to dine and dash. Some people even drive up the North Fork just to go to the historic restaurant.

For limited groceries, camping stove fuel, propane, fishing tackle, and beer, stop at the **Polebridge Mercantile** (265 Polebridge Loop, Polebridge, 406/888-5105, www.polebridgemercantile.com, 8am-6pm daily May-Nov.). You can pick up forgotten camping items, but don't expect a broad selection of choices. The bakery has fresh pastries, cookies, lunch breads, and cinnamon rolls fresh from the oven daily.

Home Ranch Bottoms (8855 North Fork Rd., Polebridge, 406/888-5572, www.homeranchbottoms.com, 9am-9pm daily late May-early Sept.), run by Beth and Greg Puckett, is worth a stop to see the evidence preserved in the clawed floor of when a grizzly tore up the building. Signed with hand-painted advertising, the small store sells convenience-type groceries, beer, coffee, soda pop, T-shirts, firewood, and ice. A large log bar—**The Bottoms**

Tavern—stays open later than 9pm if people hang around. The tavern serves pizza, burgers, cold beer, and a daily $1-2 beer special. Try one of the signature drink specials: the Moose Dropping (Montana version of an Irish Car Bomb) or the North Fork Margarita. The woodstove is fired up on chilly days, and folks lounge on the deck when it's warm. Music jams happen spontaneously, with a guitar and banjo kept on hand.

GOING-TO-THE-SUN ROAD

Historic Going-to-the-Sun Road is a testament to human ingenuity and nature's wonders. Tunnels, switchbacks, arches, and a narrow two-lane highway cutting across precipitous slopes reveal the feats of engineering—marvels in themselves. Yet in the road's 52 miles, an incomparable diversity unfolds, with surprises around each corner. Cedar rainforests give way to windblown subalpine firs, broad lake valleys lead into glacial corridors, 1,000-foot cliff walls abut wildflower gardens, and waterfalls spew from every pore. Defying gravity, ragged peaks rake the sky, crowning all.

This National Historic Landmark is a place to savor every nook and cranny. Oohs and aahs punctuate every sweep in the road as stunning scenery unfolds. Stopping at myriad pullouts along the road, many sightseers burn through their digital pixels only halfway up the alpine section. The sheer immensity of the glacier-chewed landscape leaves visitors gasping, "I can't fit it all in my camera."

To stretch your legs, well-signed short paths guide hikers through a dripping rainforest, along a glacial moraine, amid mountain goats, and beside a roaring waterfall. Those ready to put miles on their boots should tackle at least one of the longer high alpine trails, where you'll feel you've reached the apex of the world, sending your spirit soaring.

The Sun Road, as locals call it, is one place

HIGHLIGHTS

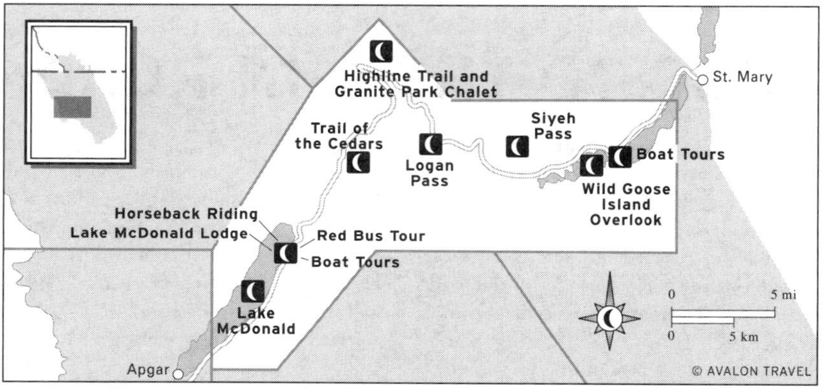

LOOK FOR TO FIND RECOMMENDED SIGHTS, ACTIVITIES, DINING, AND LODGING.

Red Bus Tour: Ride over Logan Pass in historic style. The 1937 vintage touring sedans, designed especially for national parks, roll their canvas tops back for superb views and perhaps dousing from the Weeping Wall (page 86).

Boat Tours: Hop aboard *Little Chief* for the best way to see St. Mary Lake, or aboard the *DeSmet* to see Lake McDonald—the park's two largest lakes (page 87).

Lake McDonald: Stop to see Glacier's largest lake, which fills a monstrous valley gouged by an ancient ice age glacier. Rent a boat to fish, or swim from any of the pullouts on Going-to-the-Sun Road (page 92).

Lake McDonald Lodge: Sit on the back porch of the historic lodge gracing Lake McDonald. The lodge's rustic hunting motif harks back to a pre-national park era when the region served as a hunting preserve (page 93).

Logan Pass: Touch the Continental Divide, where waters stream toward both the Pacific and the Gulf of Mexico. The apex of Going-to-the-Sun Road sprawls with broad alpine meadows teeming with wildflowers and mountain goats (page 96).

Wild Goose Island Overlook: Bring the camera: Hands down the most photographed spot in the park, tiny Wild Goose Island cowers in St. Mary Lake below the Continental Divide's rugged skyline (page 98).

Trail of the Cedars: Walk through the easternmost Pacific rainforest in the United States. The boardwalk and paved pathway circles under a shady tree canopy that keeps temperatures cool, even in midsummer (page 102).

Highline Trail and Granite Park Chalet: Hike a wildflower-packed trail clinging high on cliffs along the Garden Wall to a historic backcountry chalet where bear-watching is a worthy pastime (page 103).

Siyeh Pass: Climb over one of the most scenic and diverse trails in Glacier. The path wanders wildflower parks and descends colorful sedimentary strata—perhaps touching on every color in the rainbow (page 104).

Horseback Riding: Saddle up with Swan Mountain Outfitters for a ride to Sperry Chalet, where you can lunch in the historic dining room and smack your lips over freshly baked pie (page 108).

GOING-TO-THE-SUN ROAD

you won't want to miss. Its rugged beauty leaves a lasting impression.

HISTORY

Early Development

By 1895, Lake McDonald boomed with tourism brought by the railroad's arrival in West Glacier. Hauling a 40-foot steamboat up from Flathead Lake, George Snyder shuttled guests from Apgar to his 12-room hotel, where Lake McDonald Lodge currently sits. With Sperry Glacier's discovery in 1896, Snyder's guests had a popular horse trip destination above his lodge. Funded by the Great Northern Railway, Dr. Lyman Sperry and 15 of his students built the Gunsight Pass and Sperry spur trail to accommodate travel between St. Mary and Lake McDonald. While the west side surged with turn-of-the-20th-century tourism, on the east side, Roes Creek (Rose Creek at Rising Sun) boomed as a short-lived mining town that was vacated with the Alaska gold rush.

Lodges and Chalets

Under dubious circumstances—perhaps a poker game—ownership of Snyder's hotel went to John and Olive Lewis in 1906, who moved the old hotel and built a cedar and stone lodge facing Lake McDonald. Opening in 1914, Lewis's Glacier Hotel imitated the Swiss theme of the Great Northern Railway's hotels and chalets springing up park-wide. Lewis promoted Going-to-the-Sun Road, spending his own money to cut part of the route along the lake, grade the road, and build bridges. From West Glacier, the road reached his hotel in 1922, increasing the number of hotel visitors with the growing popularity of the automobile.

Because of Lewis's foothold in McDonald Valley, the Great Northern Railway ignored the area around the park's largest lake, instead frenetically erecting chalets between 1912 and 1914 at Sun Point, Gunsight Lake, and Sperry and using Sperry's trail over Gunsight Pass to link the three. A year later and quite behind schedule, Granite Park Chalet was finally completed as a destination from Many Glacier Hotel and Sun Point. With packed bunk-bed dorms and canvas tents outside, Granite and Sperry could house 144 and 152 guests, nearly four times the number that each can sleep today. Their popularity increased in the 1920s as wealthy Easterners spent an average of 21 days in the park touring on horseback with Park Saddle Company. However, Gunsight Chalet lasted only five years, wiped out by an avalanche.

In 1930 the Great Northern Railway purchased Lewis's hotel, adding it to its lodge arsenal. When ownership changed, so did the name—to Lake McDonald Lodge. Two years later the lodge was sold to the National Park Service.

Ironically, along with the Great Depression and increased auto travel, Going-to-the-Sun Road, which was completed in 1932, hastened the demise of the chalets. Visitors who took horse trips dropped from 26 percent to 3 percent. Natty automobile drivers sought more affordable places to stay. In 1940 the railroad company built East Glacier Auto Cabins (now Rising Sun Motor Inn), where two people could rent a cabin without a shower for $1.75. Finally, World War II park closures, deteriorating buildings, and increased costs of supplying the chalets taxed the railroad company to the point where it razed Going-to-the-Sun Chalets and sold Sperry and Granite Park to the National Park Service for $1.

Building the Road

Nearly 20 years of planning and construction went into building Going-to-the-Sun Road, fueled by burgeoning excitement over the automobile. While proponents proposed various passes for the "Transmountain Highway," its original name, in 1918 Logan Pass was selected by the National Park Service. The plan called for 15 switchbacks up the west side, later replaced with

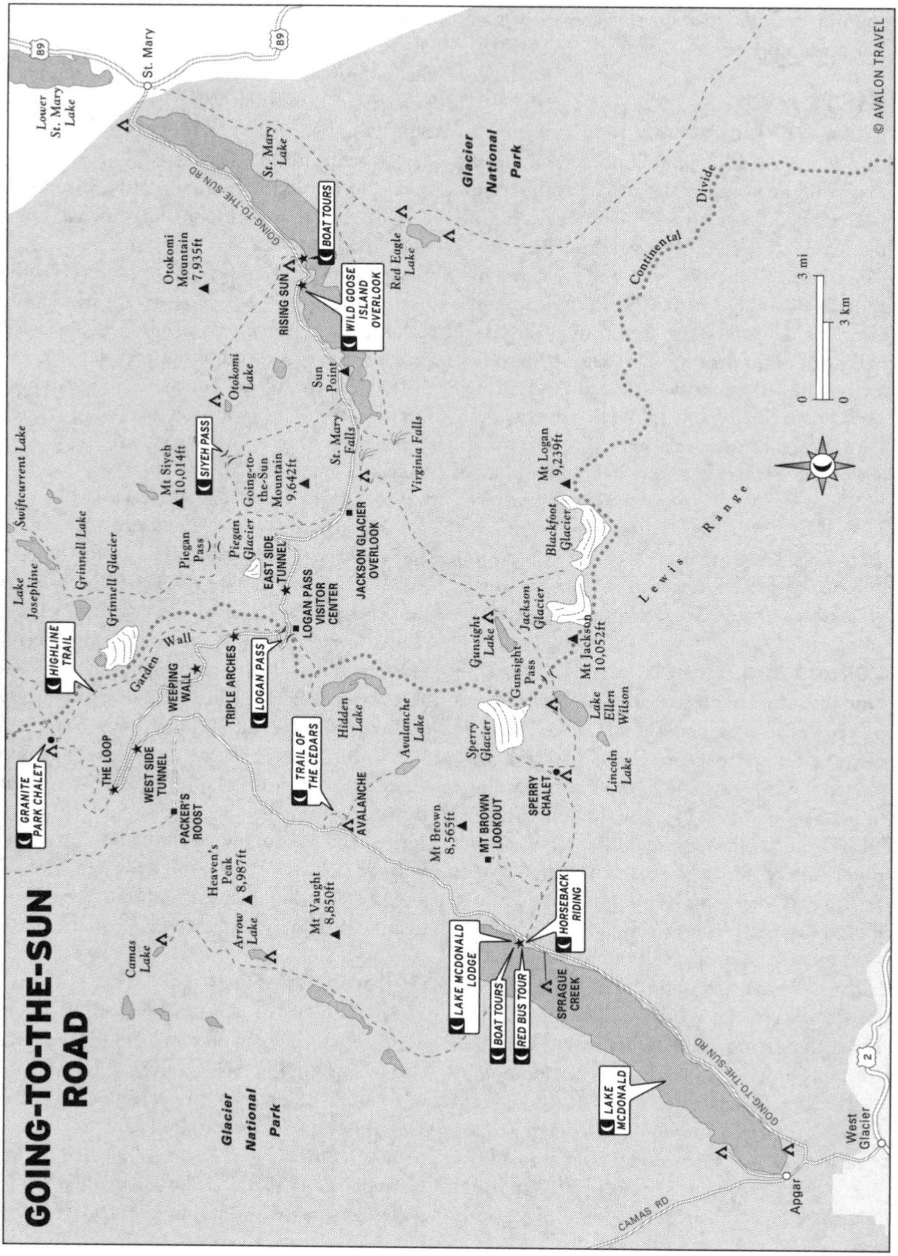
GOING-TO-THE-SUN ROAD
Glacier National Park
Glacier National Park
Lower St. Mary Lake
St. Mary
89
89
St. Mary Lake
GOING-TO-THE-SUN RD
BOAT TOURS
RISING SUN
WILD GOOSE ISLAND OVERLOOK
Red Eagle Lake
Otokomi Mountain 7,935ft
Otokomi Lake
Sun Point
St. Mary Falls
Virginia Falls
Continental Divide
Swiftcurrent Lake
Mt Siyeh 10,014ft
SIYEH PASS
Going-to-the-Sun Mountain 9,642ft
Mt Logan 9,239ft
Grinnell Lake
Lake Josephine
Grinnell Glacier
Piegan Pass
Piegan Glacier
EAST SIDE TUNNEL
JACKSON GLACIER OVERLOOK
Blackfoot Glacier
LOGAN PASS VISITOR CENTER
Lewis Range
HIGHLINE TRAIL
Garden Wall
WEEPING WALL
TRIPLE ARCHES
LOGAN PASS
Gunsight Lake
Jackson Glacier
Mt Jackson 10,052ft
Gunsight Pass
Hidden Lake
Lake Ellen Wilson
GRANITE PARK CHALET
THE LOOP
WEST SIDE TUNNEL
PACKER'S ROOST
TRAIL OF THE CEDARS
Avalanche Lake
Sperry Glacier
Lincoln Lake
SPERRY CHALET
AVALANCHE
Mt Brown 8,565ft
MT BROWN LOOKOUT
Heaven's Peak 8,987ft
Mt Vaught 8,850ft
Arrow Lake
Camas Lake
HORSEBACK RIDING
LAKE MCDONALD LODGE
BOAT TOURS
RED BUS TOUR
SPRAGUE CREEK
LAKE MCDONALD
GOING-TO-THE-SUN RD
2
West Glacier
Apgar
CAMAS RD
0
3 mi
0
3 km
© AVALON TRAVEL

one long switchback. Over several years, Congress appropriated $2 million for its construction.

Surveying the route required the tenacity to hang by ropes over cliffs and tiptoe along skinny ledges—perhaps causing the 300 percent crew turnover in three months. Over six seasons, three companies excavated rock using only small blast explosives and minimal power tools to create tunnels, bridges, the Triple Arches, and guard walls. With power equipment unable to reach the East Side Tunnel, crews cleared its 405-foot length by hand boring 5.33 feet per day.

In 1932, during late fall, the first automobile chugged over Logan Pass. The following July, over 4,000 people attended dedication ceremonies at the pass, celebrating the road's completion and ending with a peace ceremomy for the Blackfeet, Kootenai, and Flathead people.

Although guardrails, surfacing, and grading were not completed until 1935, nearly 40,000 visitors flocked to the road in its first year despite its rough tread and the Great Depression. Until the late 1930s, crushed rock covered its surface. Finally, in 1938, the National Park Service embarked on a 14-year project to pave the scenic highway—completed at last in 1952.

Exploring Going-to-the-Sun Road

Going-to-the-Sun Road connects West Glacier and St. Mary with 52 miles of one of the most scenic highways in the United States. The road links two immense glacier-carved valleys—McDonald and St. Mary—via Logan Pass. It crosses the Continental Divide at 6,646 feet. From Lake McDonald, the road ascends up 3,400 feet to the pass; from St. Mary, it rises about 2,200 feet. Given the road's extreme elevations, it takes rash punishment from brutal weather.

ENTRANCE STATIONS

Both ends of Going-to-the-Sun Road have entrance stations: one at West Glacier, the other at St. Mary. Staffed during daylight hours in summer and on weekends only fall-spring, the stations hand out national park maps and the *Waterton-Glacier Guide,* the park's newspaper, updated twice annually. If you miss working hours, you can use the self-pay cash-only kiosks, on the right just beyond the booths. If you don't have an annual pass, get a seven-day pass ($25 per vehicle, $12 pedestrians, bicyclists, and motorcyclists May-Oct.; $15 per vehicle, $10 pedestrians, bicyclists, and motorcyclists Nov.-Apr.).

VISITORS CENTER

The one place everyone wants to go is Logan Pass, but its visitors center is small, and the parking lot is cramped on sunny days. We all put up with the hassle because no one wants more pavement and a larger building impinging the meadows. Unprepared visitors arrive expecting a resort atmosphere at **Logan Pass Visitors Center** (406/888-7800, 9am-7pm daily mid-June-Labor Day, 9:30am-4:30pm daily Labor Day-Sept.). It's a seasonal outpost with a tiny Glacier National Park Conservancy Bookstore (406/888-5756, www.glaciernataionalparkconservancy.org), an information desk, and a few displays. Set your hand in the cast of a grizzly paw to marvel at the size difference.

While a fireplace crackles upstairs on cold days, one bench allows only a few to snuggle up to its heat. Restrooms are available downstairs or near the parking lot. No food or beverages are sold here, not even coffee and candy bars. Due to the elevation, expect harsher weather—wind, rain, and snow even in August. Don't be surprised if you left the lowlands in sunny summer only to arrive at Logan Pass in winter.

© BECKY LOMAX

Logan Pass Visitors Center is only open for a few months in summer.

SHUTTLES AND TOURS

Shuttles

To avoid Logan Pass parking-lot hassles, shuttles are the way to go. Better yet, shuttles enable point-to-point hiking on some of Glacier's most spectacular trails. The **free shuttle service** (406/888-7800, www.nps.gov/glac) helps eliminate congestion on Going-to-the-Sun Road during construction. These shuttles are extremely popular: In midsummer, you may find yourself waiting in lines to get on or see full shuttles bypass a stop. But going car-free to trailheads is still worth it compared to struggling for a parking spot.

The Going-to-the-Sun Road free shuttles run July 1-Labor Day, stopping at 17 locations. Get on or off at any of the stops denoted by interpretive signs, each one featuring a different animal print. No tickets are needed, and no reservations are taken. Both east-side and west-side shuttles begin running up the road at 7am; the last shuttles depart Logan Pass at 7pm.

On the west side, shuttles depart every 15-30 minutes, with stops at the Apgar Transit Center, Sprague Creek Campground, Lake McDonald Lodge, Avalanche Creek, The Loop, and Logan Pass. The 32-mile ride from the Apgar Transit Center to Logan Pass takes 90 minutes or more. Shuttles visit several different destinations on the west side: Confirm your destination when boarding to be sure you catch the right bus.

On the east side, free shuttles depart every 30 minutes from St. Mary Visitors Center. The 18-mile ride to Logan Pass takes one hour, with stops at Rising Sun, Sun Point, Sunrift Gorge, St. Mary Falls, Gunsight Pass Trailhead, and Siyeh Bend. At St. Mary, for a fee you can connect with the daily van service run by **Glacier Park Inc.** (GPI, 406/892-2525, www.glacierparkinc.com, no reservations, early June-late Sept., adults one-way $10-50, under age 12 $5-25), linking St. Mary with East Glacier, Two Medicine, Many Glacier, and Waterton. For hikers on The Highline or Piegan Pass trails that drop to Many Glacier, GPI runs an afternoon shuttle from Many Glacier to St. Mary (4:45pm daily July-Labor Day, $10).

For those arriving by Amtrak with reservations at Lake McDonald Lodge, GPI runs a shuttle (daily late May-late Sept., adults $10, children $5) to or from the Belton Depot in West Glacier; reservations are mandatory.

Flathead-Glacier Transportation (406/892-3390 or 800/829-7039) runs shuttles by reservation between Glacier International Airport and Lake McDonald Lodge (one-way $55 for 1 person, $3 each additional person).

Red Bus Tour

In historic style, red jammer buses tour visitors over Going-to-the-Sun Road in vintage 1930s White Motor Company sedans operated by **Glacier Park Inc.** (406/892-2525, www.glacierparkinc.com, mid-June-mid-Sept., adults $40-85, under age 12 $20-43, meals and park entrance fees not included). On good-weather

© BECKY LOMAX

Tops roll back on red buses for unlimited peak views.

days, the jammers (tour bus drivers known for their storytelling) roll the canvas tops back for spectacular views of the Continental Divide. Without a roof, it's one of the most scenic ways to feel the expanse of the glacier-carved terrain. From Lake McDonald Lodge, tours depart daily to explore Going-to-the-Sun Road: The eight-hour Crown of the Continent tour departs at 9am, and three-hour Logan Pass tours depart several times daily. You can make reservations by phone or at hotel activity desks. Evening tours are available in July-August.

For those staying at Rising Sun Motor Inn, daily tours originating at Many Glacier Hotel or Glacier Park Lodge will stop to pick up riders. Inquire at the motel's front desk.

Native American Tour

A Blackfeet-led tour provides a different perspective, with emphasis on Native American cultural and natural history. **Sun Tours** (406/226-9220 or 800/786-9220, www.glaciersuntours.com, June-Sept., adults $35-75, children $20-25, meals and park entrance fees not included) drives comfortable air-conditioned 25-passenger coaches with extra-big windows for taking in the massive mountains on Going-to-the-Sun Road. You can catch four-hour Logan Pass tours daily from St. Mary (9am) with a Rising Sun pickup shortly after. The tours actually originate at 8am in East Glacier. You'll drive up the east side of Going-to-the-Sun Road, explore Logan Pass, and drive down the west side to Big Bend to see the Weeping Wall before returning. Make reservations at least one day in advance. Call for the west side schedule from Apgar Visitors Center.

Boat Tours

Lake McDonald and St. Mary, the park's largest lakes, dominate the lowlands here, and **Glacier Park Boat Company** (406/257-2426, www.glacierparkboats.com) runs boat tours on both. Buy tickets at the boat docks or make reservations by phone with a credit card. In

RED BUSES

Red buses are a Glacier icon. Built by Ohio's White Motor Company specifically for national park touring, the red buses became a symbol of the nation's Western parks. Yosemite, Yellowstone, Zion, Mount Rainier, Grand Canyon, and Bryce had their own fleets, and so did Glacier. Nearly 500 red buses toured visitors around Glacier, Yosemite, and Yellowstone alone.

Although red bus fleets disappeared from the other parks in the 1950s, Glacier steadfastly held on to its 33 scarlet prizes, upgrading parts as necessary. The canvas tops rolled back to create an open-air touring car, so guests rode in historic style over Going-to-the-Sun Road, covering up with blankets if temperatures chilled down. Nicknamed "jammers" or "gear jammers" for the tremendous noise their gears made while shifting, the vintage 25-foot-long 17-passenger vehicles first drove Glacier's curvy roads in 1936 as the park's second generation of touring sedans. Decades later, as automatic transmissions replaced the manual transmissions and power steering eased driving Going-to-the-Sun Road's curves, jammers continued to tour folks through Glacier until 1999, when safety concerns sidelined the red rigs.

Glacier Park Inc., operator of the historic park lodges, owned the jammers but donated the fleet to the National Park Foundation. Ford Motor Company rehabilitated the vehicles, keeping the historic appearance, but converting them to run on gasoline or propane. New wiring, interiors, and paint jobs completed the project. Check out a jammer up close: You'll see both White and Ford logos. Thirty-two of the red buses are back in service and owned now by Glacier National Park; one was kept intact for historical purposes.

Red bus tours are operated daily by Glacier Park Inc. (406/892-2525, www.glacierparkinc.com), with departures from Lake McDonald Lodge, Glacier Park Lodge, St. Mary Lodge, Many Glacier Hotel, and Prince of Wales. Pickups are also available at other Glacier environs locations.

midsummer, purchase tickets at least a few hours in advance; midday, cocktail, and sunset cruises fill up. Check *Ranger-led Activities,* available at visitors centers, for launches that have ranger naturalists aboard.

At the boat dock behind Lake McDonald Lodge, hop on the historic *DeSmet* (adults $16, children $8) for a one-hour tour around the lake. Tours depart at 11am, 1:30pm, 3pm, 5:30pm (after July 1), and 7pm daily late May-late September, although the first and last cruise end in early September. With a 90-passenger capacity, the 1930s-vintage 57-foot wooden boat motors to the lake's core, where surrounding snow-clad peaks pop into sight. Go for a prime seat on the top deck, even in marginal weather—just bring along a jacket.

At the Rising Sun boat dock on St. Mary Lake, catch a ride on *Little Chief* (adults $24, children $12) as it braves the lake's choppy waters. Views of Sexton Glacier and Wild Goose Island can't be beat, but be ready for some healthy wind. Daily departures launch for 90-minute cruises at 10am, noon, 2pm, 4pm, and 6:30pm daily mid-June-early September. See Baring Falls at a stop, or take a guided two-hour hike to St. Mary Falls.

SERVICES

Be prepared for driving Going-to-the-Sun Road, because no services exist at Logan Pass. The closest gas stations are outside the park at St. Mary and West Glacier. With no food services available at the pass, you'll enjoy your time better and in less of a rush if you pack a lunch.

Restrooms are few and far between on this historic highway. Flush toilets are available at Lake McDonald Lodge, Logan Pass Visitors Center, and Rising Sun. Vault toilets are available at Avalanche Picnic Area, Logan Creek, The Loop, Jackson Glacier Overlook, and Sun Point. Only the campgrounds and lodges have running water for washing your hands.

Hot showers (one token for 7 minutes $3) are available at Rising Sun. For laundry, you'll have to go to West Glacier or St. Mary.

Find ATM machines at Lake McDonald Lodge and Rising Sun Motor Inn. The Lake McDonald Lodge area also has a small seasonal post office across from the camp store; the current hours are posted on the door.

Find local newspapers in gift shops and camp stores at Lake McDonald Lodge and Rising Sun. They carry the *Great Falls Tribune* and Flathead Valley's *Daily Interlake.*

Cell Phones and Internet

While some cell phones pick up service at Logan Pass and high elevations, most do not work throughout the road's length due to the high surrounding peaks and narrow valleys. No service is available in McDonald Valley except around Apgar; St. Mary Valley gets service only in St. Mary. Granite Park Chalet has cell service, but be aware that many visitors go there to get away from that, so be discreet in your phone use on trails. Public pay phones are at Lake McDonald Lodge, Rising Sun, and Avalanche Campground. You can purchase calling cards for them at the Rising Sun and Lake McDonald stores. The Sun Road is a place to break the technological umbilical cord: No Internet access is available anywhere.

Shopping

Find gift shops in Lake McDonald Lodge, Two Dog Flats Grill at Rising Sun, and camp stores in both locations. They carry a good selection of guidebooks, coffee-table photo books, maps, and natural-history books, along with gifts, T-shirts, postcards, and jewelry. The Logan Pass Visitors Center has a small bookstore.

Emergencies

If you have an emergency on Going-to-the-Sun Road, contact the National Park Service (406/888-7800). If you cannot leave the scene to make a phone call, flag down a vehicle heading up or down the pass to notify the nearest ranger (usually at Logan Pass, St. Mary Visitors Center, or by phone from Lake McDonald Lodge). On the west side of the Sun Road, a seasonal **Urgent Care Clinic** (100 Rea Rd., West Glacier, 406/888-9224, 9am-4pm daily Memorial Day-Labor Day) operates, but the nearest hospitals are in Flathead Valley: **North Valley Hospital** (1600 Hospital Way, Whitefish, 406/863-3500) and **Kalispell Regional Medical Center** (310 Sunny View Lane, Kalispell, 406/752-5111). On the east side, the Blackfeet Reservation houses the **Blackfeet Community Hospital** (760 Government Square, Browning, 406/338-6154).

DRIVING TOUR

Of all the driving tours in Glacier National Park, **Going-to-the-Sun Road,** the 52-mile historic transmountain highway bisecting Glacier's heart, stands in a class by itself. For some, scary tight curves that hug cliff walls produce white-knuckle driving. But for most, its beauty, diversity, color, flora, fauna, and raw wildness will leave an impression like no other. For that reason, many park visitors drive it more than once during their stay.

In July-August, expect crowds, especially around Logan Pass. To avoid the hordes, drive in early morning or early evening, when lighting is often better for photography and wildlife is more active. In midsummer, Logan Pass parking lot fills by 11am. Signs at the entrance will indicate this and include the estimated wait time for a parking space, usually 30-60 minutes or more. If the parking lot is full, forgo Logan Pass for the time being and return later in the day. While pullouts are 0.5 miles east and west of the pass, the shoulderless road does not afford safe walking to the pass, and tromping across the fragile alpine Oberlin meadows is taboo. Parking lots at Avalanche, The Loop, and St. Mary Falls also fill.

DRIVING TIPS: GOING-TO-THE-SUN ROAD

FOUR SIGNS OF A ROOKIE GOING-TO-THE-SUN ROAD DRIVER

- **A burning brake smell.** Hint: Use second gear to slow your speed on descents rather than riding the brakes down the mountain.
- **A dangling extension mirror.** Hint: Retract or remove those extension mirrors for fifth-wheels or trailers before driving the narrow west side below Logan Pass.
- **A center-line hugger.** Hint: Stay in your own lane. You're more apt to scrape another vehicle on the skinny road than drive off the cliff. Acrophobes should let someone else drive.
- **A traffic slug.** Hint: Rather than holding up traffic by slowing to a stop in the road to take pictures, pull off into one of the many pullouts.

OTHER TIPS

- Follow posted speed limits, and turn on your headlights.
- During high season (mid-July-mid-Aug.), Logan Pass parking lot fills up by 10:30am, with long waits for parking spaces. Get an early start for touring Going-to-the-Sun Road.
- Take lunch, snacks, and drinks. Between Lake McDonald Lodge and Rising Sun, no food or drinks are sold.
- Watch for bicyclists. Although bicycle restrictions are in effect during July-August on Going-to-the-Sun Road's west side, the narrow roadway, lack of shoulders, and curves squeeze cyclists. Show them courtesy by slowing down to ease around them.
- Expect construction delays. Reconstruction work usually reduces traffic to a single lane controlled by construction personnel. When workers are not present, timed traffic lights control flow. Obey both, as the single lanes allow for no pullover room for passing.
- Check for summer closures. Heavy rains, snowstorms, fires, and accidents may close portions of the road—even in July-August. Entrance and ranger stations as well as lodges have current updates of the road status available.
- Be prepared for all types of weather. Sunny skies may prevail in the valleys while visitors at Logan Pass creep along slowly in a dense fog on icy pavement.
- Passengers with a fear of heights should sit on the driver's side of the car for ascending the west side and descending the east. This will put you farthest from the cliff edges.
- Cell phones get little or no service the Sun Road. Turn it off and enjoy the views.
- For updates on Going-to-the-Sun Road status, call 406/888-7800 or check www.nps.gov/glac.

Although you can drive its 52 miles in less than two hours with no stops, most visitors take all day. Construction, sightseeing, and traffic slow travel. Don't be anxious with it; just sit back and enjoy the view. Pack drinking water, snacks, and a lunch to avoid frustration over lack of food services. Most restaurants around Glacier sell box or sack lunches; order them the day before you want them. The road passes through a wonderland whose development has been kept in check; no one wants to see that changed to accommodate hunger.

Season and Hours

Going-to-the-Sun Road is open 24 hours daily mid-June-mid-September...usually. Weather, construction, and snow can affect the open hours. The roadway is undergoing a decade of federally funded reconstruction to repair its aging, ailing infrastructure. Shoulder seasons are used to accelerate construction while keeping the entire road open in summer for sightseers, provided that snow conditions allow for a mid-June opening. In years with heavy snow and stormy springs, Logan Pass has opened as late as July 13. During summer the road may close temporarily for snowstorms, washouts, or accidents. The park regularly updates road status reports (406/888-7800 or www.nps.gov/glac).

Starting in 2013 fall operations will change on the Sun Road. The west side to Logan Pass will remain open until late October, pending snow conditions. Through 2015 the east side to Logan Pass will close in mid-September for construction. When parts of the Sun Road are closed to vehicles for construction, sometimes bicyclists and hikers can tour the road, especially on weekends when crews may not be working. Call the park first, as work schedules changes daily.

Snow buries the Sun Road in winter. The usual vehicle closure runs from Lake McDonald Lodge to St. Mary late October-spring, but cross-country skiers and snowshoers trek the lowland corridors where avalanche danger is minimal.

Vehicle Restrictions

Large vehicles are restricted on Going-to-the-Sun Road between Avalanche Campground and Rising Sun. Because the road is narrow and has overhangs, vehicles must be less than 21 feet in length, 10 feet high, and 8 feet wide. These dimensions include side mirrors, bumpers, towed units, and bike racks. Remember to pull in side extension mirrors; you'll see broken ones in the gutter claimed by the cliff wall. Even though smaller truck-camper units may be allowed, drivers will feel pinched on the skinny road.

Road Construction

Maintenance is interminable on Going-to-the-Sun Road. Avalanches, torrential downpours, and snows constantly wreak havoc. Summer snowstorms and heavy rains cause washouts that require annual repairs. Road construction is a fact of life, but it's also a unique chance to watch how workers cling to the side of thousand-foot cliffs.

Since 2007 Going-to-the-Sun Road has been undergoing a decade-long $270 million rehabilitation project. The critical state of the road requires repairs for weather damage and wear and tear from the 475,000 vehicles that travel the road annually. Because heavy snows constrict repairs to 4-6 months, summer means construction. The work has improved road safety, pavement, parking, guardrails, drainage, cracks, and deteriorating road beds—all while maintaining the historic character, fabric, and width of the road. Most significant, it's done without closing the road during the peak visitor season.

Mid-June-mid-September, construction may reduce driving to one skinny lane in places. Traffic delays are scheduled for a maximum of 30 minutes total while crossing the road. Usually this is true; longer delays are scheduled for early morning, evening, and night. During fall and spring, some sections of the road close completely to speed up construction. Starting in 2013, Logan Pass should be accessible in fall from the west side in late October, but the east side access will close for construction in mid-September annually through 2015.

While road construction elicits complaints and moans, repairing this road is not like repaving a normal highway. You can watch state-of-the-art road technology at work in a cliff-ridden environment: Cranes and bobcats jockey for position along one narrow lane, somewhat akin to working on a tightrope. Anyone with a mild interest in engineering will be blown away, and you get a feel for the immensity of building the original road.

Plowing Going-to-the-Sun Road

Every April, snowplows take to Going-to-the-Sun Road to heave more than 100,000 cubic yards of snow off the pavement. It's a big deal. Avalanche piles range 30-50 feet thick from The Loop to Logan Pass. Just east of the pass, a 50-80-foot-deep snowdrift, the Big Drift,

© BECKY LOMAX

Parts of the Sun Road's two lanes narrow to just 16 feet wide.

clings to a 40-degree slope; no wonder the job takes several months. For the duration, 25-30 equipment operators, mechanics, and snow specialists dig in with more than 20 different machines—excavators, bulldozers, sweepers, loaders, and rotary blowers.

More than 60 avalanche swaths between The Loop and Siyeh Bend smash snow onto the road. Sometimes crews replow the same pavement over and over, or plow themselves out at night. Heavy rains, fog, and whiteouts also hamper progress.

When spring snows prohibit the road opening in mid-June, everyone gets nervous, from local businesses to the governor of Montana. The opening of the road is tied to the local economy. Glacier Park's website tracks plow progress with daily reports (www.nps.gov/glac), and the park's communications center (406/888-7800) posts updates.

SIGHTS

Going-to-the-Sun Road is a sight to behold. The following sights are listed as visitors see them driving from Lake McDonald to St. Mary. Mileage designations are hard to follow on the road, and the road has no mileage markers to help out. GPS coordinates are listed parenthetically.

Lake McDonald

The largest lake in the park, Lake McDonald (48.529423°, -113.975854° to 48.611131°, -113.881939°) fills a valley hollowed out by a monstrous several-thousand-foot-deep glacier. Lining both sides, Howe and Snyder Ridges are lateral moraines left from that ice age bulldozer. At 10 miles long and 1.5 miles wide, the lake is big enough to plummet to a frigid depth of 472 feet. Its deep waters collect from melting glaciers and snow fields high atop the Continental Divide. Kayakers and boaters tour the shoreline, anglers pull trout from its pool, and a few water-skiers brave the cold. The road hugs its southeastern shore, with frequent pullouts for access. If rare glassy waters reflect Stanton Peak, snag a photo.

© BECKY LOMAX

The Sun Road follows McDonald Creek for seven miles with several opportunities for viewing what was known once as Sacred Dancing Cascade.

Lake McDonald Lodge

At Lake McDonald's east end, the historic Lake McDonald Lodge (48.617299°, -113.878551°) was designed to resemble a hunting lodge. A taxidermist's delight or an animal-rights activist's nightmare, the tall, stately cedar-log lobby is cluttered with stuffed goats and mounted heads of bighorn sheep, deer, elk, and moose. Look for the woodland caribou—still represented among the furry creatures here, even though it no longer exists in the park. Because the lodge was built prior to the road, the front door actually opens on the lakeside, facing the original boat approach. In 1976, the lodge was listed on the National Register of Historic Places. Explore the lobby, take a boat tour, or sit a spell in a log rocker on the back porch.

McDonald Creek

Originating near the Continental Divide, McDonald Creek (48.641473°, -113.856666°) is the longest river in the park at 25.8 miles and definitely more than a creek, but we won't quibble about nomenclature. The Sun Road follows the river path until it begins its ascent to Logan Pass. In the seven miles where the road borders the river, several tumbling rapids and waterfalls are worth a stop. But be extremely cautious of hazardous slippery rocks. Unseen algae, mosses, and swift cold waters have been lethal for the unwary. At **Upper McDonald Creek Falls** (48.655885°, -113.840193°), waters roil through scoured rock; wooden stairs take you down to a convenient observation platform right over the falls.

Trail of the Cedars

Trail of the Cedars (48.680204°, -113.819108°) runs through a rainforest, the easternmost in the country. On a 0.7-mile wheelchair-accessible boardwalk and pavement, the shaded trail passes water-carved Avalanche Gorge. Several-hundred-year-old western red cedars, hemlocks, and towering black cottonwoods form a dense canopy that cools the forest floor, where mosses, lichens, Pacific yew, and devil's club grow in the rich duff. Fire has bypassed this small ecosystem, leaving gigantic old grandfather trees—some toppling from heavy rains, snows, and winds.

Avalanche Paths

As the road sneaks through a slim corridor between the Glacier Wall and Mount Cannon (48.706329°, -113.803757°), look for avalanche paths. Snow, set in motion thousands of feet above, roars down gullies, uprooting trees and snapping them like toothpicks. In early summer, scour the slope for remnants of avalanches—ice, snow, and rock rubble piled up. Grizzly and black bears forage for carcasses along these avalanche paths in hopes of stumbling across some unfortunate mountain goat. Bring binoculars or spotting scopes to aid in bear-watching from a safe distance.

© BECKY LOMAX

A bridge of native rock crosses Haystack Creek.

West Side Tunnel

An engineering marvel, the West Side Tunnel (48.751062°, -113.788763°) is 192 feet long, with two stunning alcoves framing Heavens Peak. Early in the season, the alcoves drip with thin-sheeted waterfalls, but hop through the spray to reach the dry rock-hewn guardrails. Photographers especially will enjoy working the alcoves into framing pictures of Heavens Peak. To walk into the tunnel, park below in the pullouts; above the tunnel, the road narrows, making walking hazardous. Early in the season, a waterfall on the tunnel's uphill side splatters car windshields, unpleasant in a convertible with the top down.

The Loop

Going-to-the-Sun Road has one massive hairpin turn known as The Loop (48.754694°, -113.800147°). With parking lots both below and above the switchback, it's a popular stop for views and the trailhead to Granite Park Chalet. Across the valley, the 8,987-foot **Heavens Peak** makes a stunning backdrop for a family photo. Early in the season, it will be snow-covered; by late August, only a few snow fields remain. In 2003 the **Trapper Fire** blew through The Loop; evidence of the burn lingers in skeletal trees.

Bird Woman and Haystack Falls

About two miles past The Loop, look for the sign marking **Bird Woman Falls** (48.739259°, -113.749213°). Many travelers assume the sign denotes the cascade crossing under the road. That stair-step waterfall is **Haystack Creek,** whose ledges evolved from eroding layers of Belt Sea sedimentary rock created between 800 million and 1.6 billion years ago. To see Bird Woman Falls, look across the valley for waters tumbling nearly 500 feet from a hanging valley, carved by a glacier in the last 6,000 years and lounging like a hammock in between Mount Oberlin, Mount Cannon, and Clements Peak. Early summer runoff pumps both falls full of water that dwindles to late-August trickles.

Glaciation

On one of the viewpoints between Haystack Falls and the Weeping Wall, peek down McDonald Valley. Once filled with several-thousand-foot-thick ice, the valley's U shape shows the gouging, scouring, and carving of the behemoth glacier as it chugged around the Glacier Wall approximately two million years ago. Through the trough, McDonald Creek courses 26 miles and ends at Lake McDonald. Test your vertigo by gazing 2,500 feet below; you'll see Going-to-the-Sun Road, with cars looking tiny like ants as they drive the narrow corridor.

Weeping Wall and Big Bend

As its name implies, the Weeping Wall (48.727042°, -113.727292°) does weep, but it's a moody thing. In early summer the wall wails profusely, enough to douse cars driving

THE CONTINENTAL DIVIDE

At Logan Pass, you can take your photo next to a sign that says you're atop the Continental Divide. But what is it?

The Continental Divide runs the length of North America from Alaska and Yukon to Mexico. Along the Rocky Mountains, it is the highest point in the land, dividing stream runoff in two directions: the Pacific and the Gulf of Mexico. In Glacier Park, the Continental Divide runs along the tops of the Livingston Range from Canada south to Trapper Ridge and West Flattop, where it leaps to the Lewis Range.

To cross the Continental Divide, drive over Logan or Marias Pass. You can hike across the divide on several passes: Brown's, Swiftcurrent, Hidden Lake, Gunsight, Cut Bank, Dawson, Two Medicine, and Firebrand. Beginning in New Mexico, the 3,100-mile Continental Divide Trail ends here, with its last 110 miles in Glacier National Park.

Glacier's Continental Divide also stands in a class by itself, for it houses a tri-oceanic divide—the only one in the United States. (Western Canada's Mount Columbia is the continent's other significant three-way oceanic divide.) Not particularly high by Glacier Park standards, Triple Divide Peak stands at only 7,397 feet above sea level. But its placement on the Continental Divide with connecting ridge spurs splits waters in three directions: Hudson Bay Creek, Atlantic Creek, and Pacific Creek. Their names cite their eventual destinations in the continent's major watersheds of the Saskatchewan, Missouri, and Columbia.

On the southeast corner of St. Mary Lake, Divide Mountain with St. Mary Ridge forms the division between waters flowing to Hudson Bay and the Gulf of Mexico. To drive over this unmarked divide, head from St. Mary south on U.S. 89.

the inside lane. Roll up your windows unless you want a shower. In August, drips slow to a trickle. At the Weeping Wall, the road affords no room to pull over; instead, drive ahead into the bowl named Big Bend (48.726904°, -113.724307°) to find ample parking on both sides of the road. Here, where avalanches careen from Mount Gould into the bowl, snow often remains until mid-July.

Triple Arches

One of the most striking engineering marvels on Going-to-the-Sun Road, Triple Arches (48.716994°, -113.718789°) requires a slow drive to see, for no pullouts offer a good view. You can see this feature only driving uphill, as it is behind downhill traffic. Approximately 1.5 miles past Big Bend, you'll come upon the arches abruptly. Start watching for them as you enter a very narrow curvy part of the road. You'll see them at several sharp S turns. As you drive over the arches, don't think about the stonework repairs hanging over hundreds of feet of air.

Garden Wall

In the three miles from Big Bend to Logan Pass, the peaks above the road form an arête, a wall carved by glaciers on two sides. Below its top cliffs, wildflower meadows bloom with every color of the rainbow: white cow parsnip, pink spirea, yellow columbine, purple nodding onion, and blue gentian. In a short 0.5 miles, you may pass more than 30 varieties of plants. For this reason, this wild botanical wonderland has been dubbed the Garden Wall. For the best look at the Garden Wall, hike the Highline Trail from Logan Pass.

Oberlin Bend Overlook

As Going-to-the-Sun climbs its final mile to Logan Pass, it sweeps around a large curve below Mount Oberlin. Park on the uphill lane side for the wheelchair-accessible walk to Oberlin Bend Overlook (48.699452°, -113.725173°). Mountain goats wander in the subalpine fir thickets; look for newborns with only nubbins for horns. The overlook provides the best spot

© BECKY LOMAX

The Weeping Wall sheds prolific water in June.

for photographing the road's west-side climb as well as viewing the Continental Divide and peaks marching toward Canada. Look far north for Mount Cleveland, the park's highest peak.

Logan Pass

Logan Pass (48.696380°, -113.717674°) sits atop the Continental Divide at 6,646 feet. With its altitude and location between mountainous hulks, weather can be chilly even in midsummer. For evidence, look at the gnarled trees, growing low in krummholz or thick mats for protection against the elements. Explore the visitors center and scan surrounding slopes for goats, bighorn sheep, and bears. In June skiers and snowboarders hike the flanks of Mount Clements for turns. In late July, the wildflowers reach their prime—pink alpine laurel, paintbrush, and monkeyflower. Logan Pass is designated an Important Plant Area, with more than 30 rare plants and mosses. Meadows at this elevation are fragile with short-lived flora, so stick to the paths. Two must-do trails depart from Logan Pass: Hidden Lake and the Highline Trail to Granite Park Chalet. Two nights in July-August are set aside for stargazing 9pm-midnight; tickets are required but they're free.

Big Drift

Those driving over Logan Pass when it first opens get a treat: Big Drift (48.696927°, -113.711990°) towers on both sides of the road, making a thin corridor bounded by immense snow walls. Winds deposit heavy snows in this zone just east of Logan Pass. At a record 98 feet thick, Big Drift remains the last obstacle for spring road clearing. By August, snow piles disappear.

Lunch Creek

Spilling from a cirque between Piegan and Pollock peaks, Lunch Creek (48.699799°, -113.703624°) makes for a scenic stop at the first bend east of Logan Pass. Sans picnic tables, the pullout's rock guard wall serves as a good impromptu lunch counter. Drag out your binoculars; often bighorn sheep cruise the slopes above, but they're hard to see with their camouflage tan matching the rocks. Fed by a glacier melting into an underground stream, waterfalls spew from the side of Piegan Mountain.

East Side Tunnel

The largest tunnel, the East Side Tunnel (48.697173°, -113.696044°), was excavated entirely by hand—all 408 feet of it. For safety, flip your headlights on as you drive through this tunnel. To stop for photos, drive through to the downhill side to find pullouts, which are also good stops for spotting bighorn sheep. Photograph the large peak looming ahead—**Going-to-the-Sun Mountain**—from which the road acquired its name.

Siyeh Bend

Three miles below Logan Pass, the road

© BECKY LOMAX
East Side Tunnel

swoops through Siyeh Bend (48.701407°, -113.667600°), with ample parking above and below the curve. The trailhead leads to Piegan and Siyeh Passes via Preston Park, a meadowland of fuchsia paintbrush and purple fleabane. For a short stroll, walk up the creek crossing under the road to the junction of two creeks. The city-block-long walk passes gorgeous wildflower blooms in late July. From Siyeh Bend (*Siyeh* means "mad wolf"), named for the 10,014-foot barren peak towering above, you can see Blackfoot Glacier toward the south.

Jackson Glacier Overlook

This is the best view of a glacier on Going-to-the-Sun Road, but binoculars are handy to aid vision. Although trees are beginning to occlude the view from Jackson Glacier Overlook (48.678309°, -113.653986°), you can still spot Jackson Glacier six miles away. One of the six highest peaks in the park, Jackson Peak rises to the west. Jackson Glacier joined its neighboring Blackfoot Glacier in the early 1900s, but the two glaciers melted into separate ice fields by 1939. A trail departs here for Gunsight Lake and Pass. More views are available in the next pullouts east.

Sunrift Gorge

A narrow canyon, Sunrift Gorge (48.678545°, -113.595420°) requires a short 75-foot uphill stroll to see it. Baring Creek cascades through the dark gorge like a knife slicing cake. The dank rock walls create a perfect grotto for ferns and mosses. Parking on both sides of the road is cramped, and it is a trailhead for Siyeh Pass, although most hikers opt to start at Siyeh Bend instead.

Sun Point

The often windy Sun Point (48.676049°, -113.579532°) on St. Mary Lake marks the site of the park's most popular early chalet colony: Going-to-the-Sun Chalets. Accessed via boat from St. Mary, the chalet launched visitors into Glacier's interior. For the best views, walk five minutes on the nature trail from the parking lot to the top of the rock promontory, where you'll see Going-to-the-Sun Peak, Fusillade, and the Continental Divide. A trail leads 0.6 miles to Baring Falls and connects to the St. Mary Falls Trail.

St. Mary Lake

The second-largest lake in the park, St. Mary Lake (48.688712°, -113.557326°) fills a much narrower valley than its larger counterpart, Lake McDonald. At nine miles long and 292 feet deep, it forms a blue platform out of which several stunning red argillite peaks rise. Its width shrinks in The Narrows to less than 0.5 miles, where buff-colored Altyn limestone resisted erosion—the most ancient exposed rock sediments in the park. While its waters attract boaters, anglers, water-skiers, and sailboarders launching from Rising Sun, frequent high winds whip up wicked whitecaps in minutes.

© BECKY LOMAX

Sun Point offers a dramatic view of the Continental Divide's peaks.

Wild Goose Island Overlook

One of the most photographed spots in Glacier Park, tiny Wild Goose Island (48.691747°, -113.531285°) is dwarfed in St. Mary Lake's blue waters. Locate parking on both sides of the road from the signed viewpoint and walk the few steps to the overlook. The Continental Divide serves as the backdrop for the tiny island, with Fusillade Mountain as the prominent central pyramid. For the best lighting, visit this spot in early morning or at sunset. Take a photo, and then check the nearest gift shop for the same photo—you'll find it on postcards, on calendars, and in books.

Rising Sun

Rising Sun on St. Mary Lake is not really a scenic stop so much as one for necessities and services. A picnic area, campground, boat dock and ramp, camp store, restaurant, and cabins make up the area's amenities. It's also a jumping-off spot for hiking to Otokomi Lake and touring St. Mary Lake on the *Little Chief.* To walk along the beach, head to the picnic area (48.694461°, -113.516501°), but hold on to your hat, as winds often rage.

Two Dog Flats

A series of grassland meadows interspersed by aspen groves lines the road from Rising Sun to St. Mary. Known as Two Dog Flats (48.729423°, -113.465250°), the meadows can be good areas for watching elk, coyotes, bears, and birds in early morning or late evening. From here you can see two hydrological wonders to the south—Triple Divide Peak and Divide Mountain. Triple Divide Peak sits atop the Continental Divide, and its waters head toward three coasts—the Pacific Ocean, Hudson Bay, and the Gulf of Mexico. Divide Peak, along with the sweeping moraine heading east, marks the division between the huge Saskatchewan and Missouri watersheds.

TWO CHALETS: GETTING AWAY FROM IT ALL

To sample a few of Glacier Park's top trails and historic charm, head to the backcountry chalets. You'll get away from the hubbub of modern life—no phones, no TVs, no electricity, no hot running water, and no flush toilets. Load up day packs with a few extras like toothbrushes; you'll relish backpacker advantages without lugging huge heavy packs. Solitude, sunrises, and sunsets are prime amenities at the two rustic chalets, reached only by hiking trail. Plan a five-night lodging itinerary that includes two nights each at Granite Park and Sperry Chalets. Between the two chalet stays, treat yourself to a night at Lake McDonald Lodge for a shower. Make chalet reservations early, as high season (July-Aug.) often books up by March.

Trails to the chalets usually open in early July, although in years with heavy snow, some high-elevation access routes don't open until mid-July. Open until mid-September, the chalets often have guest rooms available at the last minute midweek in early fall. With the park's hiker shuttles, you can hike in one trail and out another.

The two historic chalets still stand as enclaves of comfort in the backcountry and as tributes to a bygone era of horse tours. Their stone and log edifices are set in spectacular surroundings, and each offers different amenities. Don't forget earplugs, as the noise from heavy snorers travels between rooms.

SPERRY CHALET

Start from Lake McDonald Lodge for a slog up 6.5 miles on a horse manure-laden trail that climbs 3,500 feet in elevation to the chalet. Set in a cirque, the full-service Sperry Chalet provides everything, including mountain goats clomping on the walkways. With the package that includes meals—dinner, breakfast, and dining room or sack lunch—and guest rooms complete with fresh linens and bedding, you need to carry only your water, clothes, and a few snacks. If you can handle the weight in your pack, throw in a bottle of your favorite beverage for evening sipping.

On your second day at Sperry, grab your lunch and head for **Sperry Glacier.** The eight-mile round-trip trail climbs past bedrock tarns before it squeezes up a narrow stairway through a cliff into the ice-scoured basin housing the glacier, moraines, and crevasses. To exit Sperry on your final day, hike the long 14-mile route over two passes. As the trail crosses the Continental Divide at **Gunsight Pass,** it drops roughly 3,500 feet to Jackson Overlook. Catch shuttles over Logan Pass back to **Lake McDonald Lodge,** where hot showers await.

GRANITE PARK CHALET

Hop an early shuttle to Logan Pass. Walking with the goats, hike the **Highline Trail,** heading north along the Garden Wall. With only an 800-foot climb, the 7.6-mile trail heads out to a knoll with a 360-degree view of surrounding peaks and glaciers.

Granite Park Chalet functions as a hiker hostel: You bring and cook your own food in a fully equipped kitchen or purchase packaged meals on-site to cook yourself. Either tote your sleeping bag or order linen service. In the evening, bring your binoculars outside to watch bears foraging in the valley below; at sunset, walk to the chalet's northwestern side as orange and pink hues spread across the sky.

On your second day, pack in two half-day hikes: one to **Swiftcurrent Lookout** for views of the park from end to end, and the other to **Grinnell Glacier Overlook** to see the melting glacier from the crest of the Continental Divide. Together, the hikes total eight miles.

To depart on your last day at Granite, either drop four miles downhill to The Loop to catch the shuttle, or cross over Swiftcurrent Pass. The 7.6-mile Swiftcurrent Trail descends through a spectacular cliff wall dripping with waterfalls before leveling out for an easy walk past moose browsing in lakes along the valley floor. From Swiftcurrent, grab a GPI shuttle to St. Mary to connect to the Sun Road shuttle back to your car.

Recreation

HIKING

Hikes off Going-to-the-Sun Road are topnotch. Around Lake McDonald, trails all begin in the forest, but several climb to incredible heights. At Logan Pass and eastward, most trails provide quicker access to alpine meadows and spectacular glacially carved scenery. Shorter trails are crowded in midsummer; you may feel like you're walking in a parade to St. Mary Falls or Hidden Lake Overlook. If you want to get away from the masses, head for longer hikes that will take you farther into the backcountry: Granite Park Chalet, Siyeh Pass, Piegan Pass, or Gunsight Lake. The hikes described here are in order of their trailheads from west to east—all serviced by shuttle stops.

Mount Brown Lookout

- Distance: 10.8 miles round-trip
- Duration: 6 hours
- Elevation gain: 4,258 feet
- Effort: strenuous
- Trailhead: Sperry Trailhead, across from Lake McDonald Lodge parking lot

One word describes this hike: *steep*. While the trail starts out climbing through moderate switchbacks, once you turn off the Sperry Trail at

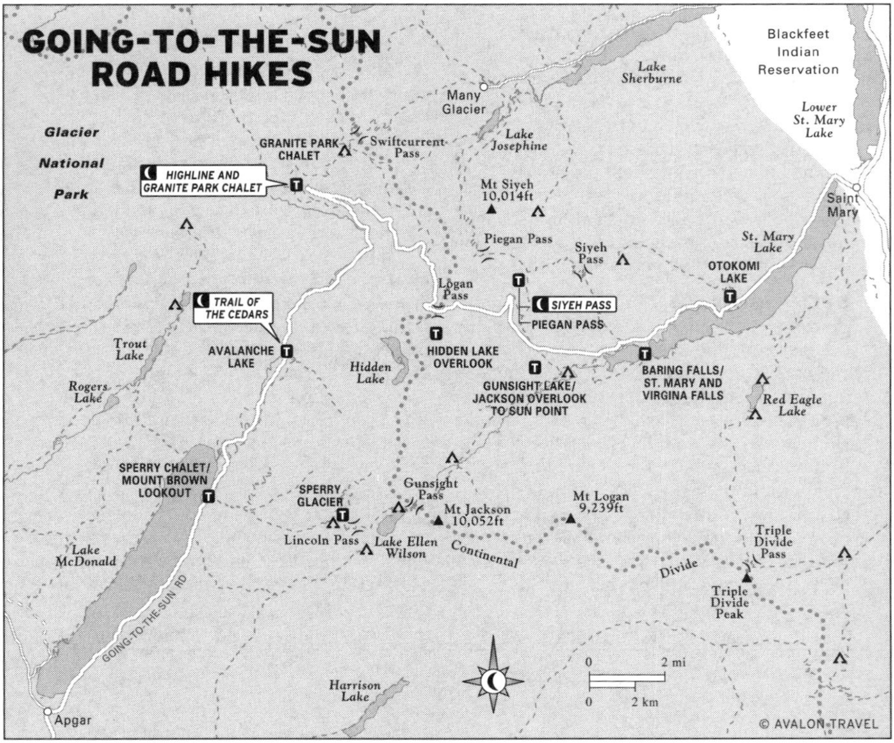

1.8 miles, the next five switchbacks are lung-busters. After these, the remaining 20-some switchbacks level out into a more reasonable ascent.

While trees preclude views for most of this trail, snippets of Mount Edwards poke through now and then. Toward the top, alpine meadows bloom with bear grass and huckleberry patches as the trail works its way along the ridge to the renovated lookout. From this false summit (Mount Brown is higher to the east), you'll get dizzy peering down to Lake McDonald and the lodge. While you zoom binoculars in on Granite Park Chalet, Swiftcurrent Lookout, and the Continental Divide, protect your lunch from the overly curious mountain goats.

Sperry Chalet

- Distance: 12.8 miles round-trip
- Duration: 6.5 hours
- Elevation gain: 3,325 feet
- Effort: strenuous
- Trailhead: Sperry Trailhead, across from Lake McDonald Lodge parking lot

The historic chalet is an attraction in itself, serving lunch and homemade desserts to hikers, but many overnight at the chalet, especially to access Sperry Glacier. The climb begins with moderate switchbacks through a hemlock forest. After crossing Snyder Creek at two miles, the trail takes a long traverse around Mount Edwards, slowly easing up in elevation before switchbacking again up alder-strewn avalanche slopes. Because of the mule and horse trips using this same route, the trail sometimes smells like a barnyard and can be miserable as you dodge equine droppings buzzing with blackflies.

With more than one mile still to climb, you'll spot the chalet clinging to a cliff top high above. The trail crosses Sperry Creek before ascending its final switchbacks, passing the turnoff to Sperry Glacier en route. If mountain goats don't stand in your way, you'll arrive at the dining hall's door, ready for lunch and home-baked pie served inside 11:30am-5pm daily. To spend the night, you'll need a reservation.

© BECKY LOMAX

The Sperry Glacier trail climbs up through an alpine lake basin to Comeau Pass.

Sperry Glacier

- Distance: 8 miles round-trip
- Duration: 4 hours
- Elevation gain: 1,545 feet
- Effort: strenuous
- Trailhead: Sperry Chalet

From the chalet, drop down several switchbacks to the Sperry Glacier trail sign. From here, the trail wraps upward around a glacial cirque below waterfalls and immense cliffs. It switchbacks up past alpine tarns, flower gardens, snow fields lingering into August, and glacially carved rock ledges before it seemingly disappears into a cliff. But voilá: A steep stairway leads through the cliff into the basin above.

In the Sperry Glacier basin, a different world awaits. Snow fields, moraines, and ice mark this environment, with very sparse trees and flowers. From here, follow vertical markers across the snow-covered trail to the glacier overlook. Do not walk out on the glacier, which has hidden crevasses and waterways. Seasoned hikers can do a 21-mile round-trip Sperry Glacier hike in one day from Lake McDonald Lodge: It's a 10-hour-plus day with a 5,000-foot climb followed by a knee-pounding descent.

Trail of the Cedars

- Distance: 0.7-mile loop
- Duration: 30 minutes
- Elevation gain: none
- Effort: easy
- Trailhead: adjacent to Avalanche Campground and Picnic Area

A boardwalk guides hikers through the lush rainforest with interpretive signs. Here, fallen cedars become nurse logs, fertile habitat for hemlocks and tiny foamflowers. Immense black cottonwoods furrow with deep-cut bark. Huge western red cedars dominate the forest. At the boardwalk's end, the trail crosses Avalanche Creek, spitting from its narrow gorge. To make a loop, continue on the paved walkway past large burled cedars to return to the trailhead.

Avalanche Lake

- Distance: 4 miles round-trip
- Duration: 2-3 hours
- Elevation gain: 506 feet
- Effort: easy-moderate
- Trailhead: use Trail of the Cedars, adjacent to Avalanche Campground

One of the most popular hikes, Avalanche Lake is the easiest-to-reach subalpine lake on the west side. Sitting in a cirque with steep-cliffs and tumbling with waterfalls, the lake attracts anglers and hikers alike. High season sees an endless stream of people, some incredibly ill prepared, with no drinking water and inappropriate footwear like flip-flops or heels. Avoid midday crowds by hiking this trail earlier or later in the day, but not at dawn or dusk.

When Trail of the Cedars crosses Avalanche Creek, turn uphill onto the lake's trail. A short grunt leads above the carved gorge. Be extremely careful: Far too many people have had fatal accidents here. From the gorge, the trail climbs steadily through woods littered with glacial erratics—large boulders strewn when the ice receded. Some still retain scratch marks left from the ice abrading the surface. At the lakeshore, enjoy watching waterfalls, mountain goats, and bears.

Granite Park Chalet via The Loop Trail

- Distance: 8 miles round-trip
- Duration: 4 hours
- Elevation gain: 2,420 feet
- Effort: moderate-strenuous
- Trailhead: The Loop

The Loop trail is mostly used by hikers exiting the Highline Trail; when the Highline Trail has too much snow, this trail makes a worthy hike with Granite Park Chalet as a scenic destination. Since the 2003 Trapper Fire, views have improved, but the lack of shade means there is little relief from the sun's blazing heat.

At its beginning, the trail crosses a tumbling creek before joining up with the Packer's Roost trail at 0.6 miles. Note this junction: You do not want to miss it when hiking back down. From here, the trail climbs two long switchbacks before it crests into the upper basin to the chalet. In June you'll have snow in the last mile. Open July-mid-September, the chalet has no running water but does sell candy bars. Bring cash to purchase bottled water, carry your own, or filter water from the campground stream just below the chalet.

© BECKY LOMAX

The Highline Trail trips along the Continental Divide from Logan Pass to Canada.

Highline Trail and Granite Park Chalet

- Distance: 7.6 miles to Granite Park Chalet, 11.6 miles to The Loop
- Duration: 5-6 hours
- Elevation gain: 830 feet
- Effort: moderate
- Trailhead: across Going-to-the-Sun Road from Logan Pass parking lot

Many first-time hikers stop every 10 feet to take photos on this hike, which scares severe acrophobes with its exposed thousand-foot drop-offs. The trail drops from Logan Pass through a cliff walk above the highway before crossing a flower land that gave the Garden Wall arête its name. At three miles, nearly all of the elevation gain is packed into one climb: Haystack Saddle appears to be the top, but it is only halfway. After the high point, the trail drops and swings through several large bowls before passing Bear Valley to reach Granite Park Chalet atop a knoll at 6,680 feet.

En route, side trails lead to Grinnell Glacier Overlook (1.6 steep miles round-trip) and Swiftcurrent Lookout (4.6 miles round-trip). To exit the area, some hikers opt to hike out over Swiftcurrent Pass to Many Glacier (7.6 miles) and catch the Glacier Park Inc. shuttle; backpackers continue on to Fifty Mountain (11.9 miles farther) and Goat Haunt (22.5 miles farther). Most day hikers head down The Loop trail (4 miles) to catch the hiker shuttle.

The chalet (July-mid-Sept.) does not have running water. Plan on purchasing bottled water here, carrying your own, or filtering water from the campground stream below the chalet. Day hikers may also use the outdoor picnic tables or chalet dining room but do not have access to the kitchen. On a rainy day, a warm fire offers respite from the bluster and a chance to dry out. Soda pop and candy bars are also sold.

Hidden Lake Overlook

- Distance: 3 miles round-trip
- Duration: 2 hours
- Elevation gain: 526 feet
- Effort: moderate
- Trailhead: behind Logan Pass Visitors Center

Regardless of crowds, Hidden Lake Overlook is a spectacular hike. The trail is often buried under feet of snow until mid-July or later, but tall poles mark the route. Once the trail melts out, a boardwalk climbs the first half through alpine meadows where fragile shooting stars and alpine laurel dot the landscape with pink. The trail ascends through argillite: Look for evidence of mud-cracked and ripple-marked rocks from the ancient Belt Sea.

The upper trail climbs past moraines, waterfalls, mountain goats, and bighorn sheep. At Hidden Pass, the trail reaches the overlook, with views down to Hidden Lake's blue waters. For ambitious hikers or anglers, the trail continues 1.5 miles down to the lake. Just remember: What drops 675 feet must come back up.

Piegan Pass

- Distance: 9 miles round-trip, 12.8 miles to Many Glacier
- Duration: 4-5 hours
- Elevation gain: 1,736 feet
- Effort: moderate
- Trailhead: Siyeh Bend

Piegan Pass, named for the Pikuni or Piegan people of the Blackfeet nation, is a reasonably unpopulated trail. After climbing two miles through subalpine forest and turning north at the first trail junction, the trail breaks out into Preston Park, bursting with purple fleabane, blue gentians, white valerian, and fuchsia paintbrush. As the trail gains altitude, Piegan Glacier is visible above. A signed trail junction splits the Piegan Pass trail from the Siyeh Pass trail.

Shortly after the junction, the Piegan Pass trail heads into the seemingly barren alpine zone as it crosses the base of Siyeh Peak. But look carefully, for all kinds of miniature flowers bloom—food for pikas. In a long traverse, the trail sweeps around a large bowl to Piegan Pass, tucked under the Continental Divide. Rather than returning to Siyeh Bend, some hikers opt for continuing another 8.3 miles to Many Glacier Hotel, where they can link in with Glacier Park Inc.'s east-side shuttle.

Siyeh Pass

- Distance: 10.3 miles
- Duration: 6 hours
- Elevation gain: 2,254 feet
- Effort: strenuous
- Trailhead: Siyeh Bend

Siyeh Pass trail crosses through such different ecosystems that the entire trail nearly captures the park's diversity in one 10-mile segment. The trail begins with a two-mile climb through subalpine forest broken by meadows, where it passes two well-signed junctions; go left at the first, right at the second. The trail leads through Preston Park, one of the best flower meadows, with purple fleabane and fuchsia paintbrush, before switchbacks ascend above the tree line.

The switchbacks appear to lead to a saddle—a false summit. Eight more turns climb above the saddle before swinging through a cliff to the pass. Be wary of your lunch—there are aggressive golden-mantled ground squirrels here. Due to the elevation, snow can bury switchbacks south of the pass until mid-July. The trail descends past goats, bighorn sheep, and a multicolored cliff band before traversing the flanks of Goat Mountain and dropping to Going-to-the-Sun Road.

Gunsight Lake

- Distance: 12.4 miles round-trip
- Duration: 6 hours

- Elevation gain: 712 feet
- Effort: moderate
- Trailhead: Jackson Glacier Overlook

Gunsight Lake is a tantalizer. For those who hike in for the day, more high country lures them beyond it. The trail begins with a one-mile drop down to Reynolds Creek before gently climbing through a forest of boggy moose ponds that breed mosquitoes. After passing a spur trail leading to Florence Falls, the trail breaks out into flower meadows, climbing along the flanks of Fusillade Mountain. Incomparable views of the wild Blackfoot and Jackson Glaciers sprawl across the scoured basin.

Surrounded by avalanche corridors, the lake sits at the base of Jackson Peak (10,064 feet), one of the six highest peaks in the park. From here, a two-mile spur trail wanders back into Jackson Glacier basin before disappearing in meadow seeps. Another trail climbs to Gunsight Pass (3 miles farther) and on to Sperry Chalet (7.8 miles farther) before descending to Lake McDonald Lodge (20 miles total). Seasoned hikers can do the entire trail over Gunsight Pass to Lake McDonald Lodge in one day.

Jackson Overlook to Sun Point via St. Mary and Virginia Falls

- Distance: 7.5 miles one-way
- Duration: 2 hours
- Elevation gain: 288 feet
- Effort: easy
- Trailhead: Jackson Glacier Overlook

With shuttles, you can do a point-to-point hike from Jackson Overlook to Sun Point, with side trips to St. Mary and Virginia Falls. From Jackson Overlook, drop to Reynolds Creek, where the trail forks eastward along the river. At the falls junction, turn right to explore mesmerizing blue-green St. Mary Falls and climb several switchbacks to misty Virginia Falls, less than one mile farther.

© BECKY LOMAX

St. Mary Falls rages with spring runoff in June.

Return to the junction to continue east over bluffs blooming with stonecrop overlooking St. Mary Lake. (Ignore two signs for Going-to-the-Sun Road parking lot spurs.) Tally up your third waterfall—Baring Falls—just before the trail climbs to Sun Point.

St. Mary and Virginia Falls

- Distance: 3.6 miles round-trip
- Duration: 2 hours
- Elevation gain: 288 feet
- Effort: easy
- Trailhead: St. Mary Falls Trailhead

In midsummer, the trail sees a constant stream of people, but the two falls are still gorgeous. The trail drops through two well-signed junctions en route to St. Mary Falls, where a wooden bridge crosses blue-green pools. From here, the trail switchbacks up to Virginia Falls, a broad waterfall whose waters spew mist. A

0.2-mile spur climbs to the base of Virginia Falls. Be wary of slippery rocks and strong, cold currents at both falls. Also, spot water ouzels, or American dippers, dark gray birds recognized by their dipping action, up to 40 bends per minute, that nest near waterfalls.

Baring Falls

- Distance: 1.2 miles round-trip
- Duration: 1 hour
- Elevation gain: 100 feet
- Effort: easy
- Trailhead: southeast corner of Sun Point parking lot

Start by popping up to Sun Point, a large promontory in St. Mary Lake, the site of the original Sun Point Chalets. From here, a sign identifies peak names circling the often windy lake. After returning to the trail, follow it around the knoll as it gradually descends to lake level. The trail crosses the creek below Baring Falls (originally named Weasel Eyes by the Blackfeet, meaning "huckleberries").

Otokomi Lake

- Distance: 10.4 miles round-trip
- Duration: 5 hours
- Elevation gain: 2,033 feet
- Effort: moderate
- Trailhead: behind Rising Sun Motor Inn

Otokomi Lake makes a good early- or late-season hike, as its elevation is lower than other area trails. Climbing immediately uphill, the trail soon levels out into a gentle timbered ascent above Rose Creek. Pause for breaks at the scenic sections, where fragile shooting stars grow next to rock slabs sliced by the creek. As the trail leads uphill, it has minimal views until the last mile of open bear-grass meadows and red argillite talus slopes. At the lake, scan the cliffs above for mountain goats, and wade the outlet to get to open lunch spots on the west shore.

Guides

Mid-June-mid-September, park naturalists (406/888-7800, www.nps.gov/glac) guide free hikes at Avalanche, Sun Point, and Logan Pass. Both the Avalanche Lake and Hidden Lake Overlook hikes are extremely popular, so expect to walk in a rather long train of people. They also guide longer hikes, like Siyeh Pass, and hikes with boat tours on St. Mary Lake. Pick up a copy of *Ranger-led Activities* from visitors centers for current destinations and schedules, which are also available online (www.nps.gov/glac).

Glacier Guides (11970 U.S. 2 E., West Glacier, 406/387-5555 or 800/521-7238, www.glacierguides.com) runs the trail guiding concession in the park. The guides lead several types of day-hiking trips. Solo travelers can hook up with their Tuesday Hikes (July-Aug., $80 pp), while families and small groups can arrange for their own guide (mid-May-Sept., $390-470). Many of their favorite haunts use Sun Road trailheads. All hikes require reservations and include guide service, deli lunch, and transportation to the trailhead. The guide service also leads three-day trips to Granite Park Chalet ($730), including all meals, transportation from West Glacier to the trailhead, guide services, linens, and lodging, and a very popular six-day Ultimate Chalet trip ($1,900) that spends two nights at Sperry Chalet, a night at Belton Chalet for a shower, and two nights at Granite Park Chalet; all meals (except one dinner), transportation, and lodging are included. The company also has 3-6-day backpacking trips that depart weekly (June-mid-Sept., $155 per day), some via Sun Road trailheads. Plan to tip your guides 15 percent for day trips and 20 percent for overnights.

CYCLING

Going-to-the-Sun Road is a bicycle trip you won't forget. While the 3,500-foot climb in elevation seems intimidating, it's not steep...just a constant thigh-burning grind. During construction in the 1920s, the road grade stayed at

© BECKY LOMAX

Cycle the Sun Road in spring or fall when it's closed to cars.

6 percent because cars of the era required rigorous shifting at a 7 percent grade.

Locals relish spring and fall riding when the Sun Road is closed to cars; new blacktop on finished construction sections smooths the riding. Cycling begins in early April as soon as snowplows free the pavement while the road remains closed to vehicles on the west side from Lake McDonald Lodge or Avalanche, and closed on the east side from Rising Sun. Riders climb up as far as plowing operations and construction permits. Even tricycles and training wheels hit the west-side flats. In fall, portions of the road close again to vehicles but permit cycling. Call the park (406/888-7800) to check on access, as construction limits cycling some days.

When Logan Pass opens, riders head for the top, some returning the way they came, others continuing on to the other side. Local racers make a 142-mile one-day loop (Going-to-the-Sun Road, U.S. 89, Highway 49, and U.S. 2); tourers ride the loop in two days. Locals also celebrate the full moon with a bone-chilling night ride. It's dangerous (injuries and at least one fatality have occurred), but it's an otherworldly experience.

Restrictions and Safety

Bicycles are restricted on the shoulderless Going-to-the-Sun Road during summer due to heavy midday traffic. Bicycles are not permitted between the Apgar Road junction and Sprague Creek or climbing uphill between Avalanche Campground and Logan Pass 11am-4pm daily June 15-Labor Day. If starting from the west side, head out from Lake McDonald by 6:30am for adequate time to pedal to Logan Pass. In late June and early July, long daylight hours allow for riding after 4pm, when traffic lessens.

While helmets are not mandatory in the law, it's stupid not to wear one here—considering most drivers are gaping at the views rather than paying attention to the road. Wear bright colors for visibility and consider tacking a flag on your bike. At dusk or at night, tail reflectors and a front light are required. Be sure to carry plenty of water: exertion, wind, and altitude can lead to a fast case of dehydration. Before heading out, check your brake pads, as the screaming downhill off the Continental Divide can wear them down to nubbins. Both mountain bikes and road bikes are appropriate here, but with skinny tires, be wary of obstacles: debris, grates, rockfall, and ice. Because shoulderless Going-to-the-Sun Road is so narrow, it is not the place for a family ride—except when the road is closed to cars. Pick up bike rentals in Flathead Valley.

HORSEBACK RIDING

Located across Going-to-the-Sun Road from the Lake McDonald Lodge complex, **Swan Mountain Outfitters** (mile 11.2 or 39.2, 406/387-4405 or 877/888-5557, corral 406/888-5121, www.swanmountainoutfitters.com, early June-Sept., $40-165) departs for the best trail ride in the park. From the horse barn, the all-day ride climbs to Sperry Chalet, where you can lunch in the historic dining hall early July-mid-September. The last two miles of the ride break out of thick trees into avalanche chutes, where you'll have better views of the steep-walled valley. Lunch is not included in the rate, so be sure to bring cash, and plan on ordering fresh homemade pie for dessert. Valley trail rides include a one-hour forest and two-hour McDonald Creek ride that depart several times daily. They tour on a trail through lichen-laden cedars and firs with peek-a-boo views of peaks. Wear long pants and hiking boots or tennis shoes. Kids need to be at least age 7, and age 10 for the Sperry ride.

BOATING

Lake McDonald and St. Mary permit motorized boats, kayaks, sailboards, and canoes on both lakes, but Lake McDonald imposes a 10-horsepower limit on motorboats. As with all lakes in the park, Jet Skis are banned. Due to vehicle length restrictions (21 feet), towed boats may not cross Going-to-the-Sun Road between Avalanche and Sun Point. Pick up free boat permits at St. Mary Visitors Center on the east side or on the west side at park headquarters or the Backcountry Office, as directed by the orange sign near the west side entrance station.

Lake McDonald

Because Lake McDonald has only one boat ramp, you must drive to Apgar to launch anything larger than what you can carry. For hand-carried craft, you can launch from Sprague Creek Picnic Area or several pullouts along the lake. At the Lake McDonald Lodge boat dock, **Glacier Park Boat Company** (dock 406/888-5727 or 406/257-2426, www.glacierparkboats.com) rents rowboats ($18 per hour) and eight-horsepower motorboats ($23 per hour). Paddles, lifejackets, and fishing regulations are included. Find the rentals at the boat dock behind Lake McDonald Lodge.

St. Mary

St. Mary Lake permits motorboats with unlimited horsepower. No boats are available to rent, but launch your own from the boat ramp at Rising Sun. Hand-carried craft can also launch easily from Rising Sun Picnic Area. Be aware: Wild winds whip up quickly on St. Mary Lake; keep alert to conditions.

KAYAKING AND CANOEING

Both sea kayaking and canoeing are popular on Lake McDonald and St. Mary Lake. On calm days, shoreline tours are exceptionally scenic, and evening paddles yield stunning alpenglow. On Lake McDonald, launch from any of the Going-to-the-Sun Road pullouts for shoreline tours or from the Apgar Boat Launch. On St. Mary Lake, launch from Rising Sun boat ramp to paddle to Silver Dollar Beach below Red Eagle Mountain; however, watch the weather, as high winds churn up monstrous waves quickly in the narrow valley. Although river kayakers drool at the rapids on

McDonald Creek, the creek is closed to all boating due to nesting harlequin ducks.

Free permits are required to kayak or canoe on these lakes. Pick them up at St. Mary Visitors Center, park headquarters, or the Backcountry Office.

FISHING

You're on your own for fishing in Glacier as no fishing guide service operates inside the park. No fishing licenses are required either, but use catch-and-release barbless hooks for westslope cutthroat and bull trout. Check with the park for current fishing regulations.

McDonald Valley

Heavily fished, Lake McDonald is a haven for kokanee, lake trout, whitefish, and cutthroat. Lake McDonald has no limit on lake trout or lake whitefish. Use catch-and-release fishing for westslope cutthroat trout. Boat fishing tends to produce better results than shore fishing, but you'll see plenty casting from beaches.

Other than Lake McDonald, fishing in McDonald Valley is sporadic at best. Although scads of anglers rim McDonald Creek, the river has a reputation for leaving hooks bare. As for Fish Lake, a three-mile climb from Lake McDonald Lodge accesses the tiny lily-padded shallow lake, where a few westslope cutthroat reside. Snyder Lake, a 4.4-mile climb from Lake McDonald Lodge, also has small cutthroat and is a little more open than Fish Lake's brushy shore. Ignore Avalanche Creek and head instead for Avalanche Lake, where indigenous westslope cutthroat have been kept genetically pure by the gorge's falls. This lake is fished extensively, so drop your line far away from the log-jammed outlet or wade to one of the chilly inlet streams to its south end.

Logan Pass

With a quick three-mile access from Logan Pass, Hidden Lake holds good-size Yellowstone cutthroat trout in spite of its elevation and its reputation as the highest lake in the park with fish. The outlet and the lake near the outlet are closed until July 31.

St. Mary Valley

St. Mary Lake's reputation is similar to Lake McDonald's: beautiful scenery, but not spectacular fishing. It's best fished from boats rather than the shoreline. Upper St. Mary River isn't much better: You often see anglers up and down its reaches, especially around St. Mary Falls, but few catching fish. Gunsight Lake, the best fishing lake, requires a 6.2-mile hike from Jackson Glacier Overlook; expect wind, late snowpack, and brush along the shore.

Gear

Need tackle? The camp stores at Lake McDonald Lodge and Rising Sun sell a few items, like line and flies. The nearest rental location for fishing gear is **Glacier Outdoor Center** (11957 U.S. 2 E., West Glacier, 406/888-5454 or 800/235-6781, www.glacierraftco.com).

WATERSKIING

While both Lake McDonald and St. Mary permit waterskiing (although Lake McDonald has a 10-horsepower limit), you won't find the lakes packed shore to shore with skiers. Frankly, these glacier-fed lakes are frigid. Those who do water-ski wear wetsuits. Precocious winds also whisk up sizable whitecaps—especially on St. Mary Lake. Serious water-skiers head to Flathead Valley's warmer, less whimsical lakes. Flathead Valley also has the nearest ski boat and water-ski rentals.

SAILBOARDING

Of all the park's lakes, St. Mary Lake is the one sailboarders occasionally use. Lake McDonald attracts a few, but inconsistent winds can leave sails slack. On St. Mary Lake, easterlies rage down the valley; however, high mountains and erratic valley confluences create swirly winds on its west end. For that reason, the lake is really not a beginner sailboarding area; experience in self-rescue is paramount. Those who sail these frigid waters usually launch from Rising Sun Picnic Area and wear a wetsuit. No sailboarding equipment is available for rent in the region.

SKIING AND SNOWSHOEING

Since winter buries Going-to-the-Sun Road with snow from Lake McDonald Lodge to St. Mary, the road attracts skiers and snowshoers November-April. They tour up the gated road's lower elevations through relatively avalanche-free zones. The gentle grade makes for good gliding suitable for beginners. For snowshoers, etiquette requires blazing a separate snowshoe trail rather than squishing the parallel ski tracks flat. Some park ski trails are mapped online (www.nps.gov/glac).

In McDonald Valley, ski tours lead past McDonald Creek and Upper McDonald Creek Falls to Avalanche Campground (6 miles). Some skiers cross the bridge at Sacred Dancing Cascade to loop back on the river's north side, but snow coverage is more variable in the trees. A gentle forest ski leads to John's Lake, but as a destination, it's not much. Some skiers head up to Snyder Lakes, but the narrow trail descending through tight trees on the way back down makes for a hair-raising adventure. Blue-sky days attract snowshoers to Mount Brown Lookout.

On the east side, a good six-mile flat ski heads to Rising Sun along Two Dog Flats; however, high winds often strip sections of the roadway bare.

Between Rising Sun and Avalanche Creek, Going-to-the-Sun Road sees significant avalanche activity. Do not attempt to ski any of this section without experience, know-how, and gear—avalanche transceivers, shovels, and probes. Check current conditions at www.flatheadavalanche.org. When Logan Pass opens in June, skiers and snowboarders can hike up the Hidden Lake Overlook trail for turns on the lingering snow pack.

Guides and Rentals

Glacier Adventure Guides (406/892-2173, www.glacieradventureguides.com) leads full-day and overnight ski tours—cross-country touring and backcountry telemark and *randonnèe* skiing. If you're a solo traveler, it's the best way to get accompanied into the backcountry with avalanche-certified guides to find pristine powder stashes. Lunch, snacks, and equipment are included. For deep backcountry, ski in to an igloo to spend the night. Plan on tipping the guide 15-20 percent. Rentals are available in Flathead Valley.

ENTERTAINMENT

Park Naturalists

Lake McDonald Lodge, Avalanche Campground Amphitheater, and Rising Sun Amphitheater offer 45-minute evening park naturalist programs usually starting around 8pm daily. Check for schedules at campground information boards and hotel activity desks, or pick up a copy of *Ranger-led Activities* at visitors centers. Topics range from fires to birds. Best of all, they're free. Once a week at Rising Sun, the program features a Native American speaker, a great way to gain an understanding of the park's rich Native American culture and history.

Jack Gladstone

Grammy-nominated Jack Gladstone, a Blackfeet, presents his ***Buckskin PoetSongs*** (www.jackgladstone.com, adults $5, under age 13 free) usually once a week at the Lake McDonald Lodge auditorium. The show blends storytelling and original music. His highly entertaining show provides insight into Blackfeet history, culture, and animal legends that have sprung from the lands in the area. For showtimes and days, pick up the current copy of *Ranger-led Activities* at visitors centers or check online (www.nps.gov/glac).

Accommodations

Accommodations on Going-to-the-Sun Road are scarce. The west side has Lake McDonald Lodge, 16 miles west of Logan Pass. Twelve miles east of the pass, Rising Sun offers plain cottages and motel units. For those with the feet to carry them, the incomparable Granite Park and Sperry Chalets require hiking and, for Granite Park, the ability to carry your own food. All chalets and inns—all nonsmoking—are listed on the National Register of Historic Places and have limited amenities—no TVs, air-conditioning, or Internet access. Add the 7 percent state bed tax to rates.

LAKE MCDONALD

Historic **Lake McDonald Lodge** (Lake McDonald Lodge Loop, Going-to-the-Sun Rd., 406/892-2525, front desk 406/888-5431, www.glacierparkinc.com, late May-Sept., $133-190) is on the lakeshore, with boating, trail riding, red bus tours, and boat tours. Centered around a massive stone fireplace and its hunting lodge-themed lobby full of trophy specimens hung by John Lewis, the original owner, the complex offers three types of accommodations: main lodge rooms, adjacent cottage rooms, and motel rooms a five-minute walk away. The lodge and cottage exteriors have a quaint cabin look, and the lakeside rooms have views, but the 1950s-style motel is in deep cedars with no views. While all guest rooms are small, cottage rooms tend to be the tiniest, many with space for only two twin beds; the main lodge rooms are the largest. Be prepared for all guest rooms to have petite baths—dinky sinks and skinny elbow-knocking shower stalls—in many cases closets converted into baths. Guest rooms have phones,

© BECKY LOMAX

Lake McDonald Lodge has rooms in the main lodge, as well as cabins and a motel.

but upstairs rooms lack elevator access. This is a place to get out and explore, not sit in your room. Dial back your expectations to the 1940s or 1950s and you'll be delighted with the location and historic ambience. Restaurants, a lounge, a gift shop, and a camp store are in the lodge or within a five-minute walk. Best of all, trails to Mount Brown Lookout, Snyder Lake, Sperry Chalet, and Sperry Glacier start right across the street. Reservations are strongly advised in June and September and are an absolute must in July and August.

RISING SUN

Rising Sun Motor Inn (Rising Sun on Going-to-the-Sun Rd., 406/892-2525, front desk 406/732-5523, www.glacierparkinc.com, mid-June-mid-Sept., $124-141) became the answer for motorists traveling to Glacier during World War II—it was the only facility that stayed open. The inn still retains its old-time feel with a 1940s look and no in-room phones, TVs, or air-conditioning. An outdoor pay phone and fans for guest rooms are available. The compound has cottages and motel units, all with very diminutive private baths; expect to bump your elbows in the shower stalls. The motel also has a restaurant, a store, and a hiker shuttle stop. The trail to Otokomi Lake begins right behind the inn, and access to St. Mary Lake is right across the street, along with the boat tour dock.

While not much has changed at this funky old-time motor inn with its board-and-batten construction, it's hard to beat its location 12 miles from Logan Pass. Although the guest rooms don't have much in the way of amenities, you won't spend your time there anyway, with so much outside to explore. In the evening, go on a gorgeous sunset cruise on St. Mary Lake or drive to look for wildlife on Two Dog Flats between Rising Sun and St. Mary.

BACKCOUNTRY CHALETS

Glacier has two historic gems that remain in the backcountry—part of a series of backcountry chalets built by the Great Northern Railway. Both Sperry and Granite Park Chalets are rustic stone and log buildings owned by the National Park Service and operated by Belton Chalets (406/387-5654 or 888/345-2649, www.sperrychalet.com, www.graniteparkchalet.com, early July-early Sept.). They are set in the scenery-packed territory of mountain goats and grizzly bears. Pack along earplugs, because snores resound through the thin walls. With no electricity or phones, evening entertainment entails quietly watching wildlife and sunsets. Take a flashlight to find the composting vault toilets in the dead of night. No alcohol is sold on the premises or allowed in the dining halls; you can pack along your favorite beverage for your guest room, but pack the containers out with you. To reach the chalets requires hiking 6-14 miles, depending on the route. Reservations are required, and they often fill by March. Hiker shuttles stop at all the Sun Road trailheads for the chalets.

Sperry Chalet offers hikers and horseback riders three meals and a warm bed, which means hauling only a day pack with some extra clothing. Set in a timbered cirque, the chalet has a dining hall, a dorm, and several National Park Service buildings. Seventeen dorm rooms sleep 2-6 people each in bunks or beds with bed linens included ($185 for the first person, $130 for each additional person in the same room). Country meals with roasted turkey sate ravenous hiker appetites, but the menu has maintained culinary sensibilities from the 1950s, with canned fruits and vegetables. Trail lunches packed for you are plain, with a meat sandwich (no lettuce or tomato), candy bars, and fruit leather. However, bakery goods—cookies, freshly baked breads, and pies—are outstanding, using traditional decades-old recipes. To reach Sperry, hike 6.5 miles up from Lake McDonald or 14 miles over two passes from Jackson Glacier Overlook.

Set at the same elevation as Logan Pass,

© BECKY LOMAX

Granite Park Chalet offers 360-degree views from its knoll.

Granite Park Chalet sits atop a knoll, where the 360-degree view alone makes the stay worth it. Granite comprises the main chalet (kitchen, dining room, and guest rooms), a dorm, a National Park Service building, and the composting outhouse. Twelve guest rooms sleep 2-6 people each ($90 for the first person, $73 for each additional person in the same room). This chalet functions somewhat like a hostel: Bring your own sleeping bag, or if you don't want to carry one, purchase linen service ($16 for sheets, a pillow, and blankets). Meals are not supplied; hikers haul their own food to cook in the kitchen. If you don't want to carry food, you can preorder freeze-dried food to be there for you. Candy bars, soda pop, and bottled water are sold on-site. Pots and pans are available for cooking on the huge 12-burner propane stove (it has an oven too), but you'll need to bring your own mugs, plates, bowls, eating utensils, and water filter. (You can purchase environmentally friendly disposable plates and utensils.) Running water is not available; you haul water for cooking and washing from 0.2 miles away. Most hikers reach the chalet from Logan Pass (7.6 miles), The Loop (4 miles), or Swiftcurrent (7.6 miles).

CAMPING

In the 52 miles of Going-to-the-Sun Road, five campgrounds stretch along the corridor, but none sit in the high alpine Logan Pass section. On the west side, Apgar, Sprague Creek, and Avalanche offer more sites than Rising Sun and St. Mary on the east side. In midsummer, the coveted Avalanche, Sprague Creek, and Rising Sun campgrounds can fill by noon; all sites are first come, first served. For all campgrounds on Going-to-the-Sun Road, amenities include shuttle stops, flush toilets, cold running water, picnic tables, and fire rings with grills; bring your own firewood, as collecting is prohibited. For hookups, hit commercial campgrounds outside the park in St. Mary or West Glacier.

For bicyclists, hikers, and motorcyclists, shared hiker-biker sites ($5 pp) with bear-resistant food storage are held until 9pm and are available at all three campgrounds.

If campgrounds are full, oversize RVs must backtrack, because vehicles over 21 feet cannot travel the Sun Road between Avalanche Campground and Sun Point. On the west side, head to Fish Creek and commercial campgrounds in West Glacier. On the east side, aim for commercial campgrounds in St. Mary.

West Side

Sprague Creek Campground (0.9 miles southwest of Lake McDonald Lodge on Going-to-the-Sun Rd., 406/888-7800, mid-May-mid-Sept., $20) is right on Lake McDonald's shore in a timbered setting with shaded sites—a few with prime waterfront. Unfortunately, several sites also abut Going-to-the-Sun Road, with a nice view of cars driving by. After dark, the road noise plummets, so it's not like tenting next to a major highway. As the smallest campground—only 25 sites accessed via a paved road—Sprague Creek does not allow towed units. Most of the parking pads are short and narrow, but a few can fit small RVs up to 21 feet. No hiking trails depart from here, but beach sunsets rank as spectacular. Kayakers and canoers have lakefront access. At 23 miles from Logan Pass, it still has quick access to the high country, and it's five minutes from Lake McDonald Lodge and the camp store.

Set in a cedar-hemlock and fern rainforest, **Avalanche Campground** (at Avalanche on Going-to-the-Sun Rd., 406/888-7800, mid-June-early Sept., $20) opens its 87 sites for a shorter season than Sprague Creek. Six miles east of Lake McDonald Lodge, Avalanche makes the closest west-side base for exploring Logan Pass, 16 miles away, and is convenient for hiking to Avalanche Lake, since the trail departs from the campground's rear. You'll know you're in a rainforest, with its dark overgrown forest canopy allowing little sunlight to hit your picnic table. The moist area sprouts thick patches of thimbleberries and sometimes a good collection of mosquitoes. Half of the sites can fit RVs up to 26 feet. No disposal station is available.

East Side

Located only 12 miles east of Logan Pass and six miles west of St. Mary, **Rising Sun Campground** (Rising Sun on Going-to-the-Sun Rd., 406/888-7800, late May-mid-Sept., $20) is tucked at the base of Otokomi Mountain by St. Mary Lake. The sun drops down early behind Goat Mountain, creating a long twilight at the campground. Adjacent to Rising Sun Motor Inn, the 83-site campground is a few minutes' walk to a restaurant, a camp store, and hot showers. Beach access is across Going-to-the-Sun Road, with a picnic area, a boat ramp, and boat tours. Otokomi Lake trailhead is behind the adjacent inn. The campground has a dump station, and 10 sites can accommodate RVs up to 25 feet.

Backcountry Campsites

Some of the park's most popular trails depart from the Sun Road for backcountry campsites high along the Continental Divide. The Highline Trail connects with **Granite Park** and **Fifty Mountain,** both near wildflower meadows with stunning views. It also makes a loop to Packer's Roost via **Flattop.** The Gunsight Trail has three popular campsites at **Gunsight Lake, Lake Ellen Wilson,** and **Sperry.** From Rising Sun, **Otokomi Lake** also makes a scenic overnight. Pick up permits (adults $5 pp per night; ages 8-15 $2.50, under age 8 free) in person at ranger stations, visitors centers, or the Apgar Permit Office (406/888-7900) 24 hours in advance. Advance reservations ($30) are strongly advised for these popular sites and are available online (www.nps.gov/glac).

Food

No food services—not even vending machines—are available at Logan Pass. The nearest restaurants on the west side are at Lake McDonald Lodge, 21 miles below the pass. On the east side, Rising Sun has the only restaurant, 12 miles from Logan Pass and 6 miles from St. Mary. Most restaurants in and adjacent to the park sell box or sack lunches ($7-10) to accommodate hikers and sightseers spending the day driving the Sun Road.

RESTAURANTS

Lake McDonald

Three distinctly different restaurants are located at Lake McDonald Lodge (Lake McDonald Lodge Loop, Going-to-the-Sun Rd., 406/892-2525, front desk 406/888-5431, late May-Sept.)—all operated by Glacier Park Inc. The headliner dining room inside the lodge is **Russell's Fireside Dining Room,** with woven seats and painted Native American chandeliers. The north windows have a peek-a-boo lake view, but during dinner the blinds usually need to be pulled down as the hot sun blazes in. Breakfast (6:30am-10am daily, $8-15) features a massive buffet spread with fruit, pastries, waffles, eggs, pancakes, french toast, sausage, and bacon. It offers a huge selection and enough to fill big eaters, but entrées will not be steaming hot off the grill. Those looking for something smaller can order á la carte. Lunches (11:30am-2pm daily, $10-15) serve up soups, salads, burgers, wraps, and sandwiches. Dinners (5pm-9:30pm daily, $18-26) include pasta, steak, ribs, chicken, and fish with local ingredients for accents and sides. No reservations are taken, so you may have to wait for a seat. You can order to-go lunches ($9) a day in advance.

For lighter dining, the lodge property has two other options. Drop in to the cozy **Lucke's Lounge** (11:30am-midnight daily, $9-15) adjacent to the lodge's dining room for appetizers and sandwiches, which include the requisite burger and fries. The bar also stocks plenty of local microbrews along with wine and cocktails. The best option for families is **Jammer Joe's Grill and Pizzeria** (11:30am-9:30pm daily late May-early Sept., $9-20) due to the broad spectrum of menu choices and foods with kid appeal. Located across from the lodge, the restaurant serves lunch and dinner in a cafeteria atmosphere with pizza, pasta, sandwiches, burgers, and salads. You can even get pizza with a gluten-free crust.

Rising Sun

Located at Rising Sun Motor Inn, **Two Dog Flats Grill** (milepost 44.7 or 6, Going-to-the-Sun Rd., 406/892-2525, front desk 406/732-5523, mid-June-mid-Sept.) serves breakfast (6:30am-10am daily, $7-12) and an all-day menu (11am-9:30pm daily, $9-17) in its restaurant that's reminiscent of an old coffee shop. Ask for a south window table for views of Red Eagle Peak. Get soups, salads, and sandwiches, and after 5pm full dinners of pork tenderloins, chicken, or fish. It serves Montana microbrews and wine, too. No reservations are taken for the restaurant, which sometimes gets crowded with bus tours. You may have to wait for a table in high season, but if the line is really long, you can go six miles down the road to St. Mary for more dining options; the evening return drive offers good wildlife-watching along Two Dog Flats. The restaurant also has to-go lunches ($9); order them a day in advance.

GROCERIES

You're best off stocking up on groceries before settling for several days along the Sun Road. But for last minute supplies, camp stores (7am-9pm daily mid-June-mid-Sept.) are located at

Lake McDonald Lodge, 21 miles west of Logan Pass (a five-minute walk from Lake McDonald Lodge), and Rising Sun, 12 miles east of the pass. Both camp stores carry limited brand selections, but you can pick up ice, firewood, stove gas, and other camping supplies, as well as convenience-store groceries, beer, wine, gifts, and newspapers. For hikers, both stores are a suitable place to buy trail lunch supplies—crackers, cheese, chips, fruit, and cookies.

PICNICKING

Only four areas accommodate the picnic-basket set on Going-to-the-Sun Road: Sprague Creek, Avalanche Creek, Sun Point, and Rising Sun. All except Sun Point permit fires in the fire rings with grills, but you'll need to bring your own firewood, as gathering wood is prohibited. All four sites have picnic tables. At no time should you leave your picnic gear unattended; there are bears—read the information on fines stapled to the tables. To the right as you drive into the campground, **Sprague Creek Picnic Area** is tucked tightly in the trees between Going-to-the-Sun Road and Lake McDonald, with more road view than scenery; however, short paths access the shoreline. There are flush toilets. **Avalanche Creek Picnic Area** is across the street from the campground and has larger rebuilt vault-toilet restrooms. Picnic sites are under cedar shade adjacent to McDonald Creek. Trailheads for Trail of the Cedars and Avalanche Lake are across the street. **Sun Point Picnic Area** is more or less a parking lot with tables scattered around its perimeter; however, it has great views up St. Mary Valley to the Continental Divide. Its trails access spectacular Sun Point and Baring Falls. Watch the paper plates, as the wind can blow here. It also has vault toilets. **Rising Sun Picnic Area** is adjacent to St. Mary Lake, with open sites slightly buffered from wind by aspen trees. If winds rage, however, hold everything down. Short paths through the trees access the shoreline. It has flush toilets.

Logan Pass has no picnic area, and the National Park Service does not allow coolers outside of vehicles except in picnic areas...although you can eat a sandwich anywhere. If you want to "picnic" up with the views, the best method is to pack a sack lunch to eat on a trail or at one of the many pullouts along the road. Most restaurants in and around the park sell takeout lunches ($7-10) that you can order a day in advance of your trip. Especially scenic and aptly named, Lunch Creek pullout (1.4 miles east of Logan Pass) has a good historic rock wall that makes a great place for a tailgate party, but keep the cooler inside the car. On the west side, many picnic on the rock retaining walls at The Loop or big boulders at Big Bend (2.3 miles west of Logan Pass).

ST. MARY AND MANY GLACIER

On Glacier's east side, mountains graze the sky and drop abruptly to wide open grassland prairies. Below sheer cliffs, elk browse. Aspen leaves chatter in only a hint of breeze. From valley floors, a wild panorama of Glacier's peaks runs across the western skyline, dominated by red sediments and milky-blue sapphire lakes. Ice fields cling for dear life to cliffs as the summer sun makes them smaller each year. It's a place of extravagant color, where pink, purple, white, and yellow wildflowers intoxicate the eyes as much as the tumbling waterfalls.

Due to the Continental Divide, wind is a constant companion. It shapes trees into gnarled bent wonders and whips up whitecaps on lakes in seconds. But every minute yields another view to fill pixels with rugged scenery. No wonder the Blackfeet called Glacier the "Backbone of the World."

While St. Mary is the eastern portal to Glacier's famed Going-to-the-Sun Road, Many Glacier is a setting of dreams: distinctive peaks, idyllic lakes, pastoral meadows. The morning sunrise gleams gold across a rampart of peaks speckled with the most accessible glaciers in the park. Loons call across glassy lakes. Grizzly bears forage on hillsides, clawing at the ground for glacier lily bulbs. By evening, when the trails vacate, the sunset paints royal hues above the Continental Divide. Dark descends, with a multitude of stars. And if you're lucky, the northern lights dance across the sky.

HIGHLIGHTS

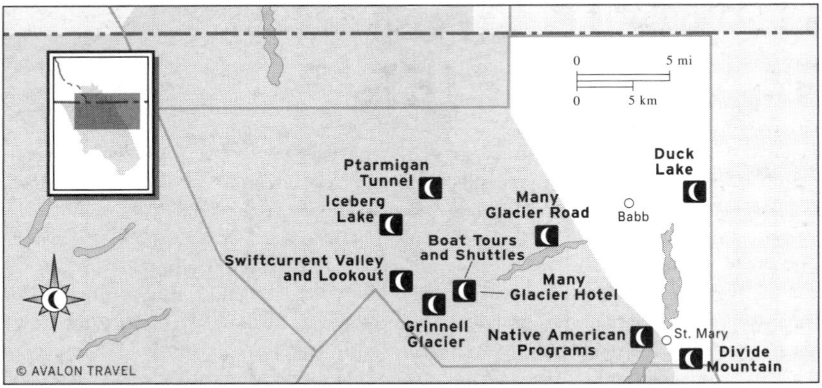

LOOK FOR TO FIND RECOMMENDED SIGHTS, ACTIVITIES, DINING, AND LODGING.

Boat Tours and Shuttles: Jump aboard the Many Glacier boat tour that combines two scenic rides with a short stroll. Launch on Swiftcurrent Lake and walk to Lake Josephine for the second boat—both with unbeatable views (page 123).

Many Glacier Road: Enjoy a scenic evening drive into Many Glacier. Sunsets turn the peaks rosy with alpenglow, and wildlife is frequently afoot. At the end of the road, the National Park Service often sets up a spotting scope for watching wildlife (page 126).

Divide Mountain: Look for a pyramid southwest of St. Mary. This aptly named peak separates water flowing north to the Saskatchewan drainage from that heading south into the Missouri (page 128).

Grinnell Glacier: Hear ice calve off Grinnell Glacier while waterfalls tumble from Salamander Glacier above. Hikers on this trail to the glacier often spot grizzly bears (pages 128 and 135).

Many Glacier Hotel: Visit the grandest of the park's lodges. This historic hotel lives up to its reputation for beauty with its enormous four-story log lobby and two-story floor-to-ceiling dining room windows matching the majesty of its idyllic setting (page 129).

Iceberg Lake: Swim with icebergs! Tucked below goat-studded cliffs, the lake gleams with icebergs floating in its blue waters... even in August. But you have to hike to get here (pages 129 and 135).

Ptarmigan Tunnel: Climb to a hiker's tunnel built in the 1930s (page 130). A walk through its dark corridor spits you out with a burst of color: Red argillite smears across hillsides, with Elizabeth Lake's indigo waters below (page 136).

Swiftcurrent Valley and Lookout: Muster the gumption to climb atop the Continental Divide. You'll survey glaciers and peaks for as far as you can see (page 135).

Duck Lake: Fish the lake, known for its large rainbow trout. The views aren't bad either, with Chief Mountain looming above the blue waters (page 141).

Native American Programs: Gain an understanding of Blackfeet culture and heritage by catching one of these programs, which feature storytellers, singers, and dancers. Popular shows have standing room only (page 142).

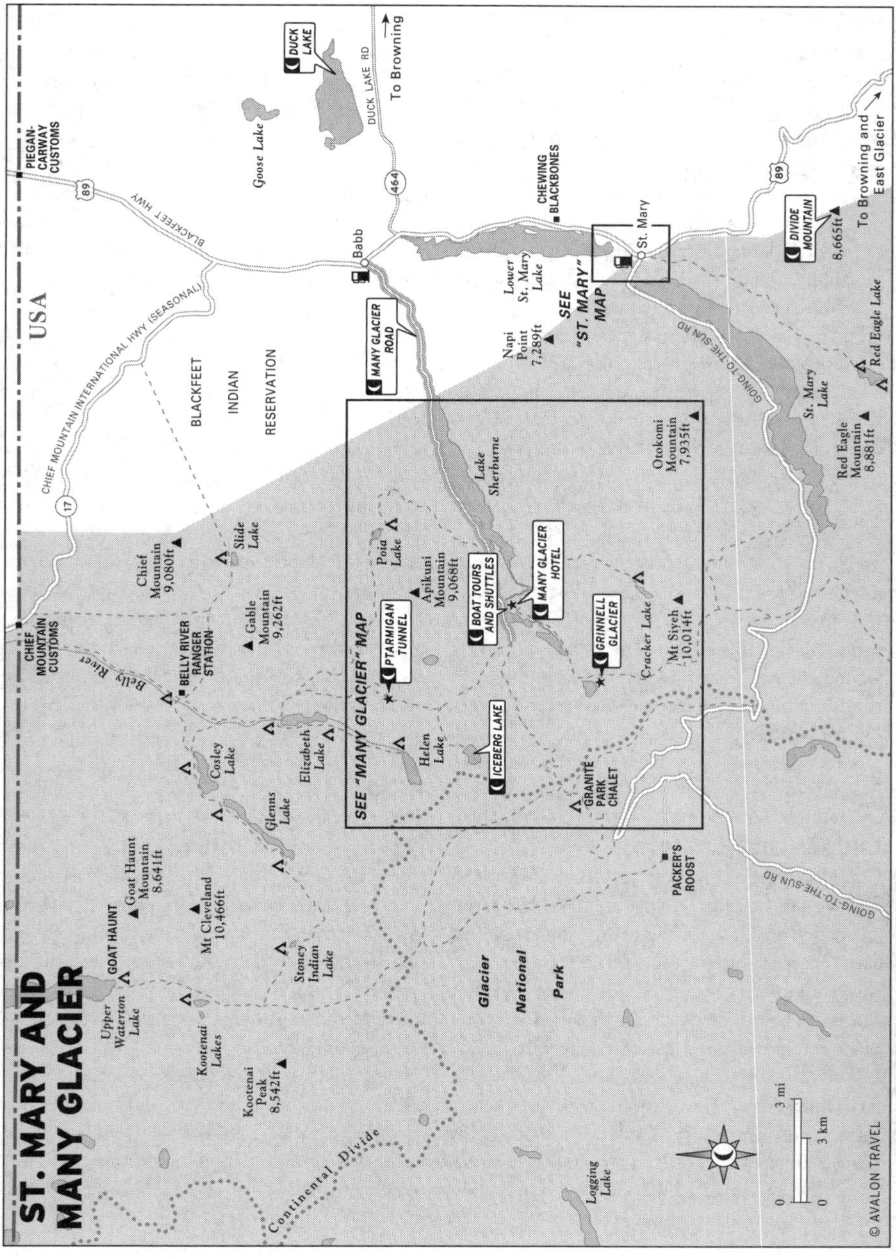

ST. MARY AND MANY GLACIER
USA
BLACKFEET INDIAN RESERVATION
PIEGAN-CARWAY CUSTOMS
CHIEF MOUNTAIN CUSTOMS
CHIEF MOUNTAIN INTERNATIONAL HWY (SEASONAL)
BLACKFEET HWY
DUCK LAKE RD
DUCK LAKE
Goose Lake
To Browning
Babb
CHEWING BLACKBONES
Lower St. Mary Lake
St. Mary
SEE "ST. MARY" MAP
Napi Point 7,289ft
MANY GLACIER ROAD
To Browning and East Glacier
DIVIDE MOUNTAIN
8,665ft
GOING-TO-THE-SUN RD
St. Mary Lake
Red Eagle Lake
Red Eagle Mountain 8,881ft
Otokomi Mountain 7,935ft
Lake Sherburne
SEE "MANY GLACIER" MAP
Poia Lake
Apikuni Mountain 9,068ft
BOAT TOURS AND SHUTTLES
MANY GLACIER HOTEL
PTARMIGAN TUNNEL
GRINNELL GLACIER
Cracker Lake
Mt Siyeh 10,014ft
ICEBERG LAKE
Helen Lake
GRANITE PARK CHALET
PACKER'S ROOST
Chief Mountain 9,080ft
Slide Lake
Gable Mountain 9,262ft
BELLY RIVER RANGER STATION
Belly River
Elizabeth Lake
Cosley Lake
Glenns Lake
Goat Haunt Mountain 8,641ft
GOAT HAUNT
Mt Cleveland 10,466ft
Stoney Indian Lake
Upper Waterton Lake
Kootenai Lakes
Kootenai Peak 8,542ft
Glacier National Park
Continental Divide
Logging Lake
0 3 mi
0 3 km
© AVALON TRAVEL

HISTORY

Parkhood

George Bird Grinnell first set eyes on his namesake glacier in 1887. The editor of *Forest and Stream* magazine, the precursor to *Field and Stream,* made several excursions to Glacier over two decades, during which he lobbied Congress for support for the area's preservation. Congress agreed to purchase lands from the Blackfeet to open to the public, and Grinnell helped negotiate the sale.

After the federal government purchased the land from the Blackfeet, Glacier became a forest reserve, open to prospecting and hunting. The Many Glacier Valley attracted hordes of would-be miners digging for copper, silver, and gold. In 1898 the mining boom gave rise to Altyn, a town site located where Sherburne Reservoir is today. At its peak, the burg housed 800 residents, but by December 1902 it was a ghost town, its yields meager and its inhabitants lured north into the Klondike gold rush.

Grinnell pressed on in his efforts to preserve Glacier. Finally, in 1910, President Taft signed the act creating Glacier National Park, the United States' 12th national park. In recognition of Grinnell's efforts, a glacier, a peak, a point, and two lakes have been named after him, all in Swiftcurrent Valley.

Lodges and Chalets

On old wagon roads, the Great Northern Railway built a dirt road in 1911-1912 from Midvale (now East Glacier) to St. Mary and Swiftcurrent Valley—soon to be the home of the "showplace of the Rockies," Many Glacier Hotel. When dry, the road was drivable; when rains fell, it mutated into treacherous muck. In the hustle to create guest lodging for train passengers, the train company threw up Many Glacier and St. Mary Chalets in 1912-1913. Guests rode the 36 miles from Midvale to St. Mary by car in 2.5 hours or by stagecoach in four hours. Others arrived via the Inside Trail on an overnight horseback trip, stopping at Cut Bank Chalets. After avalanches demolished two of the Many Glacier chalets and the dining hall, poor site selection prompted choosing another location for the grand Many Glacier Hotel. Finally, the luxury hotel on Swiftcurrent Lake opened its doors in 1915 with running water—both hot and cold—steam heat, telephones, and electric lights in every room.

Blackfeet Highway

In the late 1920s, the State of Montana rerouted and paved the Midvale to St. Mary road—the Blackfeet Highway, found on most maps today as Highway 49 and U.S. 89. The new route bypassed St. Mary Chalets, which fell into disuse as growing automobile traffic diverted toward Going-to-the-Sun Road and the town of St. Mary sprouted up. Saddled with the Depression and fewer people who could afford pricey hotels, the park service pressured the railroad company into building Swiftcurrent Cabins in 1933—immediately a popular place to stay at $2.25.

1936 Fire

When high winds forced the 1936 Heavens Peak fire over the Continental Divide, it made a bee-line down Swiftcurrent Valley, eating up 33 of the Swiftcurrent cabins en route to Many Glacier Hotel. Employees doused the hotel roof with water to protect the lodge. After the fire spared the hotel, employees telegrammed the railroad's vice president, apprising him of the success. His reply: "Why?" The hotels and chalets had become a financial noose around the railroad's neck. The St. Mary chalets were torn down in 1948; Many Glacier chalets succumbed to fire and avalanches. Only the historic showplace Many Glacier Hotel remains.

Exploring St. Mary and Many Glacier

Glacier's eastern ecosystem sprawls across national park lands and the Blackfeet Reservation, divided by an artificially straight border. Bears and elk know no boundaries, and sometimes neither do cattle, ranging astray inside Glacier.

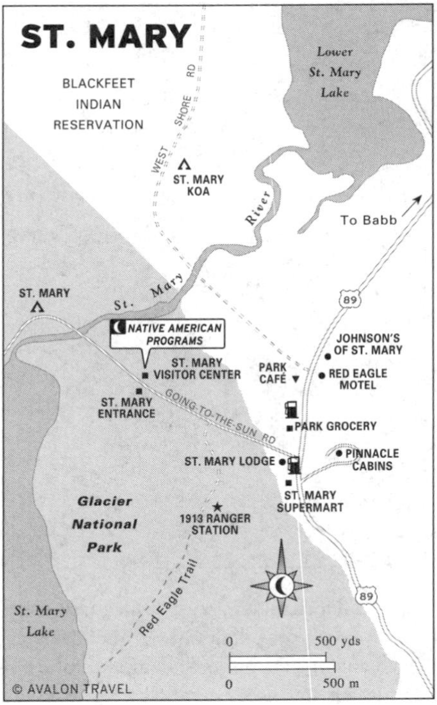

Blackfeet Reservation

Bordering the park's eastern boundary are 1.5 million acres of Blackfeet Nation lands. The boundary slices across the summits of Chief Mountain, Napi Point, and Divide Peak, crossing the lower end of Sherburne Reservoir and sliding between the two St. Mary Lakes. Permits are required for camping, fishing, hiking, and boating recreation on the reservation.

St. Mary

St. Mary is the eastern portal to Going-to-the-Sun Road. At the junction of the Sun Road and the Blackfeet Highway (U.S. 89), the town is clustered at the park boundary. Only the visitors center and St. Mary Campground are within the park; the town, restaurants, grocery stores, lodging, and commercial campgrounds are on the Blackfeet Reservation.

Many Glacier

You'll have to get used to the lingo here: Although the popular Many Glacier Hotel is in the Swiftcurrent Valley, locals refer to the whole valley area simply as Many Glacier, even though that is technically not its name; only two features actually use that name—the hotel and the campground. Many Glacier derived its name from the string of small glaciers that populated its peaks: Grinnell, Salamander, Gem, North Swiftcurrent, and South Swiftcurrent.

Babb

Between St. Mary and Many Glacier is Babb, a blink-and-you'll-miss-it village about one block long. A few houses are clustered behind a small year-round grocery store, along with two bars, two restaurants, and a tiny motel. In the middle of nowhere, it seemingly has no purpose, but its year-round post office and elementary school serve families ranching between St. Mary and the Canadian border.

Belly River

A confluence of two valleys lined with good fishing lakes, the Belly River, north of Many Glacier, is home to tales of one of the park's most notorious rangers—Joe Cosley. Guides and rangers tell stories of his exploits, which include poaching and womanizing. The Belly, as

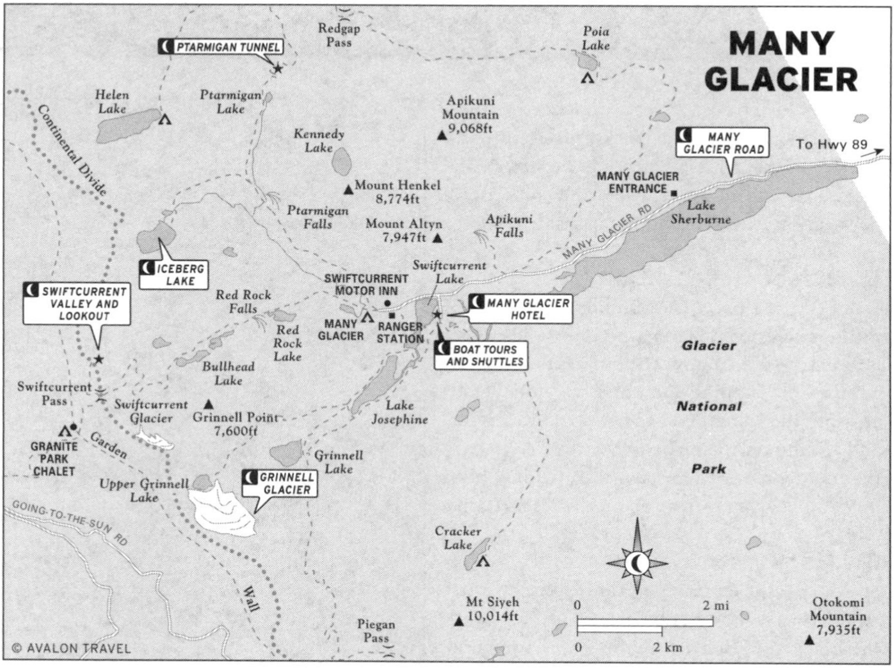

locals call it, is undeveloped backcountry; there are no hotels or restaurants. While hikers can reach a couple of the Belly's lakes in one long day, it's an area best explored by backpacking.

PARK ENTRANCE

The park staffs entrance stations at St. Mary at the eastern gateway of Going-to-the-Sun Road and in Many Glacier just inside the park boundary. Both have self-pay cash-only kiosks for when the stations are unstaffed. If you don't have an annual pass, get a seven-day pass (summer $25 per vehicle, $12 pedestrians, bicyclists, and motorcyclists).

VISITORS CENTERS

In St. Mary, **St. Mary Visitors Center** (east entrance of Going-to-the-Sun Rd., 406/888-7800, 8am-9pm daily July-Aug., shorter hours daily late May-June and Sept.) is the largest visitors center in the park. Renovated indoor facilities house a small Glacier National Park Conservancy bookstore, an enlarged theater, and displays emphasizing Native American cultural history.

Inside the center, you'll find backcountry permits, fishing regulations, Going-to-the-Sun Road updates, *Junior Ranger Activity Guides,* and information on free guided hikes and presentations with park naturalists in *Ranger-led Activities.* The indoor theater also hosts slide presentations, evening naturalist programs, and the popular Two Medicine Lake Singers and Dancers.

The visitors center is also a shuttle stop: To avoid parking hassles at Logan Pass, you can park your car here all day for free and catch the free shuttle up Going-to-the-Sun Road.

In Many Glacier, between the picnic area and Swiftcurrent parking lot adjacent to the campground, the small **Many**

Glacier Ranger Station (end of Many Glacier Rd., 406/732-7740, 7am-5pm daily late May-late Sept.) has hiking info, maps, trail conditions, bear-sighting information, guidebooks, and backcountry permits available.

TOURS AND SHUTTLES

Shuttles

St. Mary Visitors Center serves as the east-side transit hub where you can catch the **free shuttle** heading up Going-to-the-Sun Road. No tickets are needed, and no reservations are taken. Starting at 7am daily, the shuttle leaves every half hour for Logan Pass, with six stops en route at trailheads. It's a one-hour ride. At Logan Pass, you can catch the west-side shuttles into the Lake McDonald Valley. The last buses leave Logan Pass at 7pm daily to return to St. Mary.

For hikers, **Glacier Park Inc.** (406/892-2525, www.glacierparkinc.com) runs two shuttle routes on the east side of the park. For those heading to the Highline-Swiftcurrent Pass or Piegan Pass trails that end in Many Glacier, a shuttle runs from Many Glacier Hotel to St. Mary Visitor Center (July-early Sept., $10) to connect with the free National Park Service shuttle. Early June-late September, the east-side hiker vans run north-south connecting Waterton, Many Glacier, St. Mary, Cut Bank, Two Medicine, and East Glacier ($10 adults per segment one-way, children $5). Schedules are available online and at hotel activity desks, visitors centers, and ranger stations. No reservations are accepted for either shuttle; pay cash when you board.

Flathead-Glacier Transportation (406/892-3390 or 800/829-7039) runs shuttles by reservation only between Glacier International Airport and points on Glacier's east side ($200-280 one-way for the first person, $3 for each additional person). You can get to St. Mary, Many Glacier, or for the Belly River Trailhead at Chief Mountain border crossing.

Tours

Glacier Park Inc. (406/892-2525, www.glacierparkinc.com) runs daily tours leaving Many Glacier Hotel and St. Mary on the **historic red buses** (early June-mid-Sept., adults $40-75, children $20-38, not including meals or park entrance fees). Departure times vary based on location. These scenic buses are charmers; on good weather days, the jammers (tour-bus drivers) roll back the canvas tops for unlimited skyward views—no air-conditioning needed! Two tours head to Logan Pass, hitting almost every scenic stop on Going-to-the-Sun Road: the full-day Crown of the Continent tour and the half-day Eastern Alpine Tour. Both of these tours stop in St. Mary to pick up riders at St. Mary KOA and St. Mary Lodge. The International Peace Park Tour departs for an excursion to Waterton and arrives at Prince of Wales Hotel in time for afternoon tea. Passports are required. This tour, which originates in East Glacier, picks up riders in St. Mary and Many Glacier. Other tours are also available; make reservations in advance.

Departing St. Mary, **Sun Tours** (406/226-9220 or 800/786-9220, www.glaciersuntours.com, daily mid-June-mid-Sept., adults $40, children $20, not including meals and park entrance fees) drives air-conditioned 25-passenger buses with extra-large windows for big scenery, an asset on the historic Going-to-the-Sun Road. Led by local Native American guides who grew up on the reservation, the tours highlight Glacier's rich connection with the Blackfeet—Native American history in the park, plants used for traditional medicines, stories behind peak names, and life in buffalo days. A four-hour tour departs at 9am, with pickups at various St. Mary locations. Make reservations 24 hours in advance.

Boat Tours and Shuttles

In Many Glacier, jump on a pair of historic wooden boats for a tour of two lakes with

St. Mary Visitors Center sits at the east entrance of Going-to-the-Sun Road.

Glacier Park Boat Company (406/257-2426, www.glacierparkboats.com, daily mid-June-mid-Sept., adult round-trip $24, children $12). Catch the 1961-vintage *Chief Two Guns* at Swiftcurrent Lake's boat dock behind Many Glacier Hotel. In 1 hour and 15 minutes, you'll cruise across the lake, hike five minutes over a hill, hop aboard the 1945 *Morning Eagle,* and return. On this tour, you're right in the thick of moose, bear, and wolverine country. Don't forget your camera, although you may have difficulty cramming the view into the lens. Tours depart daily at 8:30am (starts mid-July), 9am, 11am, 1pm (July-Aug. only), 2pm, 3pm (July-Aug. only), and 5pm. Two of the daily launches offer a guided two-mile round-trip walk to Grinnell Lake. The guided hike tours sell out, but you can make reservations two days in advance by phone with a credit card. In person, you can purchase tickets at the dock. Once the Grinnell Glacier trail melts out, the boat company adds the 8:30am launch to the schedule, allowing hikers quicker access across the valley. The National Park Service runs a guided hike via this launch. Hikers may also catch a return boat (adults $12, children $6) at the upper Lake Josephine dock; pay cash as you board. You may have to wait for a few launches to get on, but the captain runs the boat until all hikers are shuttled.

On St. Mary Lake, boat tours on the *Little Chief* depart from Rising Sun.

SERVICES

Two gas stations are in St. Mary on U.S. 89, one on either side of the junction with Going-to-the-Sun Road. One more gas station is in Babb, across from Thronson's General Store. Many Glacier has no gas services.

In Many Glacier, public showers ($3 for 8 minutes)—which are often cold to lukewarm—and laundry facilities are available behind Swiftcurrent Campstore; purchase tokens for both in the store. In St. Mary, you'll find

© BECKY LOMAX

Boat tours run on Swiftcurrent Lake and Lake Josephine in Many Glacier.

showers at St. Mary KOA ($10) and Johnson's Campground ($4 for 6 minutes). St. Mary KOA also has a coin-op laundry. Find ATMs and pay phones at Many Glacier Hotel, Swiftcurrent Motor Inn, the Supermart in St. Mary, and St. Mary Lodge. At the junction of Many Glacier Road and U.S. 89, Babb has the nearest post office to Many Glacier; St. Mary has a seasonal post office at Johnson's Campground. The local newspaper is the *Great Falls Tribune*.

Cell Phones and Internet

Planning to use your cell phone in Many Glacier? Keep dreaming. There's no coverage. If you require cell service, stay in St. Mary. Internet access is even more evasive, with only a couple of places in St. Mary.

Shopping

St. Mary has a handful of gift shops. Expect to see merchandise heavily branded with popular moose and bear themes.

Emergencies

If you are inside the park, contact a ranger or call 406/888-7800 for emergencies. The nearest hospital is on the Blackfeet Reservation (Blackfeet Community Hospital, 760 Government Square, Browning, 406/338-6154).

Rangers like to keep apprised of all bear sightings and encounters—especially bears close to the trail. Report your sightings to the St. Mary Visitors Center or Many Glacier Ranger Station.

Find the **Many Glacier Ranger Station** (milepost 12.4, Many Glacier Rd., 406/732-7740, 8am-5pm daily late May-mid-Sept.). Contact rangers also at **St. Mary Visitors Center,** adjacent to the campground in Many Glacier. Backpackers who need assistance in The Belly can find the **Belly River Ranger Station** in the backcountry at the junction of the Cosley Lake, Elizabeth Lake, Gable Pass, and Chief Mountain border crossing trails.

DRIVING TOURS

Visitors to St. Mary have options for touring in all directions. Since St. Mary is the eastern portal for **Going-to-the-Sun Road,** most people head to Logan Pass when the road is open. Winding along St. Mary Lake and Two Dog Flats, the road reaches Logan Pass in 18 miles before dropping 32 miles to West Glacier.

Blackfeet Highway

The Blackfeet Highway, named U.S. 89 on maps, runs entirely on the Blackfeet Reservation along the east side of Glacier Park from the Canadian border at Piegan-Carway to Browning. The only gas services along the road are at Babb, St. Mary, and Browning.

Be prepared for impediments on the Blackfeet Highway. Much of the road crosses open range where you may encounter cattle or horses. Slow down and give them room. Ol' Bessie may just stand there staring at you and refuse to budge. If so, a toot on the horn can sometimes help, but avoid being obnoxious. If necessary, carefully pass in the other lane. Due to livestock, slow down at night, even though the speed limit sign says 70 mph. You'll frequently hear the screech of brakes as drivers come too quickly to a cow in the middle of the road.

Driving north from St. Mary, the highway undulates on a fairly wide road past **Lower St. Mary Lake,** where you'll see Thunderbird Island. As you round the lake's outlet, watch for waterfowl and spectacular views to the north of Chief Mountain and Old Sun Glacier on Mount Merritt. This section of the highway is one of the few roads with shoulders, making the driving significantly easier. The road runs through aspen ranchland, passing Duck Lake Road (7.3 miles north of St. Mary), Many Glacier Road and Babb (9 miles), and Chief Mountain Highway (14 miles) before reaching the Canadian border (24 miles). At the border, the highway turns into Alberta Highway 2 as it continues north in Canada.

Driving south from St. Mary, the Blackfeet Highway heads toward **Two Medicine, Browning,** and **East Glacier.** Even if you have only a couple of minutes, drive south two miles up the hill from St. Mary to get a panoramic view of the St. Mary Valley and see the results of the 2006 Red Eagle Fire. Several wide unmarked pullouts afford good places to stop for a photo. As the road climbs to St. Mary Ridge, at 6,015 feet, it crosses the Hudson Bay Divide—sending water to the Missouri or Saskatchewan River watersheds. Several lanes allow for passing, but within a few miles the road shrinks to a curvy, rolling, narrow, shoulderless trek through willow bogs and beaver ponds divided by aspen groves. Turns are blind; take them slowly in case cyclists or cows are on the road. At 20 miles from St. Mary, you can turn off onto Highway 49—a road with more curves than a snake and part of the original Blackfeet Highway—toward Two Medicine (38 miles) or East Glacier (33 miles). If you continue on U.S. 89, you'll reach Browning (32 miles).

Many Glacier Road

The 12-mile-long Many Glacier Road—also called Glacier Route 3 on some maps—is a stunning drive into **Swiftcurrent Valley.** On this road, there are two reasons to drive slowly: Motorists have a good chance of spotting wildlife, and the road is chock-full of potholes and torn-up pavement. From Babb, the road follows Swiftcurrent Creek upstream across Blackfeet Nation lands, where open range may bring you nose to nose with cows on the road. Give them room, and drive at a snail's pace around them. Watch for bears, particularly around dusk. If you spot a bear, drive by slowly to watch rather than stopping and creating a bear jam, which conditions bears to be comfortable around cars. Above all, stay in the car for safety.

After the road rises to reach Sherburne Dam (mile 4.8), it follows the reservoir's north shore, crossing into the park over the cattle grate, but

© BECKY LOMAX

A grizzly bear sow and cubs cross Many Glacier Road.

you won't reach the park entrance station for another three miles. Check the shoreline for deer, bears, and sometimes errant cows straying into the park. Aspen groves and wildflower meadows with July's pink sticky geraniums line the road. Scenic stops have views of Sherburne Reservoir and up the valley to **Grinnell, Salamander,** and **Gem Glaciers.**

At **Many Glacier Hotel** (turn south at 11.6 miles), stop to tour the historic building. After the hotel turnoff, the road passes Swiftcurrent Lake, the picnic area (mile 12.2), the ranger station, the campground, and Swiftcurrent Motor Inn, where it terminates in Swiftcurrent parking lot.

Duck Lake Road

Highway 464, known locally as the Duck Lake Road, leaves U.S. 89 at the east end of Lower St. Mary Lake (7.3 miles north of St. Mary, 1.7 miles south of Babb). Locals tend to use this road via Browning for faster access between the park's northeast sections and East Glacier. Although the mileage is longer (53 miles from St. Mary to East Glacier rather than 33 miles via U.S. 89), the straighter road affords easier driving. It's also faster: Speed limits reach 70 mph on stretches, and fences keep cattle off the road. RV drivers and those pulling trailers in particular find it easier to handle than the curvy Blackfeet Highway. The road climbs over St. Mary Ridge, passing Duck Lake at three miles. From the top of the ridge above Duck Lake—the divide between the Missouri and Saskatchewan River drainages—the highway heads southward across the Blackfeet Reservation to Browning (34 miles from U.S. 89) through bison and cattle ranchland, with Glacier's peaks dominating the western skyline across the prairie.

Chief Mountain International Highway

A seasonal road, Chief Mountain International Highway links Glacier and Waterton Parks. Its season and hours are those of the Canadian and U.S. immigration and customs stations at the border (9am-6pm daily mid-May-June and Sept., 7am-10pm daily June-Labor Day). With its start 14 miles north of Babb, the 30-mile road undulates over rolling aspen hills and beaver ponds on the Blackfeet Reservation as it curves around blocky Chief Mountain to the border and trailhead entrance to the Belly River. A few unmarked pullouts offer good photo ops. Drive this open range carefully, as cows wander the road.

As the road rounds Chief Mountain, it enters Glacier Park. There is no entrance station here, and no payment is required. The road reaches the international border and Chief Mountain border crossing at 18.6 miles. Passports are required for crossing into Canada.

SIGHTS

St. Mary River

Between St. Mary Visitors Center and St. Mary Campground, Going-to-the-Sun Road crosses St. Mary River, a waterway connecting the two St. Mary Lakes. You can park near the stone bridge to take a look—the same bridge Forrest Gump jogged across in his run across the United States. But find better parking at the visitors center and walk 0.3 miles through prairie smoke flowers to a scenic wooden bridge that connects to the campground. Watch for killdeers, among other birds. For anglers, this river offers some of the best local fishing. You can drop a line in from the wooden bridge, but not the Going-to-the-Sun Road Bridge.

St. Mary Lakes

In pockets left from 1,200-foot-deep Pleistocene ice age glaciers that gouged out St. Mary Valley, **St. Mary Lake** and **Lower St. Mary Lake** fill most of the valley floor. The lakes collect water from snowmelt and some of the largest glaciers left in the park—Blackfoot and Jackson Glaciers. Their waters then meander toward the Canadian border and into the Saskatchewan River to Hudson Bay. With the valley sucking air down from the Continental Divide, frequent winds swirl up large whitecap waves. See the lakes from Going-to-the-Sun Road and U.S. 89.

Divide Mountain

Divide Mountain rises 8,665 feet in elevation, the last in a string of peaks guarding St. Mary Valley's south. Charred remnants of the 2006 Red Eagle Fire flank its slopes. From its summit, it drops to St. Mary Ridge, running for miles onto the prairie. The ridge is a lateral moraine, deposited by the Pleistocene glacier that formed the valley. This ridge, along with Divide Mountain, separates the waters flowing into the Saskatchewan River drainage and those heading toward the Missouri River.

1913 Ranger Station

Follow the signs on a five-minute drive from Going-to-the-Sun Road (0.2 miles from the junction with U.S. 89, just south of St. Mary Visitors Center) to the 1913 Ranger Station. A small parking area leads uphill on a three-minute walk to the historic building. Adjacent to it is the Lubec Ranger Station Barn, which was moved here in 1977 for its preservation. However, with its restored weather-split logs and chinking, the barn is more photo-worthy than the original ranger station.

Grinnell Glacier

Like all glaciers in northwest Montana, Grinnell Glacier is melting. Located in Many Glacier, the ice field reached its peak size around 1850, when it filled the entire upper lake pocket under Mount Gould and connected with Salamander Glacier. Lateral moraines mark its original size. By 1930, the glacier receded—separating from Salamander and forming a lake at its snout. Today, the ice has shrunk to less than one-third of its 1850 size. By 2020 the glacier's moving ice will be gone, leaving only icebergs. You can see the glacier with binoculars from the Many Glacier Road. For a

Hikers can climb to the edge of Grinnell Glacier.

closer inspection, you can hike to the most visited glacier in the park.

Swiftcurrent Lake

Originally called McDermott Lake, Swiftcurrent Lake took its name from the Blackfeet term for swift-flowing water—a name that George Bird Grinnell promoted for the area and also used for a peak, glaciers, a creek, a waterfall, and a ridge. The lake, however, does not have fast-flowing waters. Located in Many Glacier, its bays attract loons and mergansers. Moose browse in the willows along the shoreline. A beaver lodge sits at the inlet of Swiftcurrent Creek. Enjoy the lake from Many Glacier Hotel's deck, launch a canoe from its boat ramp, ride across it on the tour boat, or walk an easy two miles around it.

Many Glacier Hotel

Built in 1915 and placed on the list of National Historic Landmarks, the five-story 211-room Many Glacier Hotel (milepost 11.5, Many Glacier Rd., 406/892-2525, www.glacierparkinc.com, mid-June-mid-Sept.) sits on Swiftcurrent Lake's shore. Listed as one of the 11 most endangered places in the country, the hotel is owned by the National Park Service and is operated by Glacier Park Inc. A $30 million restoration in the past decade straightened the leaning structure, restored the dining room to its historic look, and replaced windows, doors, the roof, siding, and decks. Warm up on a cold day around the huge fireplace in the massive lobby, or lounge on its large deck overlooking Swiftcurrent Lake and the Continental Divide. Join park naturalists for a one-hour tour of the historic hotel: Check *Ranger-led Activities* for the current schedule.

Altyn-Henkel Wildlife

Bears congregate heavily in the Swiftcurrent Valley due to abundant food sources. One of the best places to see them is feeding on the slopes of Mount Altyn and Mount Henkel on the north side of the Many Glacier Road. With binoculars, you can see bears, along with mountain goats and bighorn sheep, from the Many Glacier Hotel deck. Rangers often set up a spotting scope in the Swiftcurrent Parking Lot for wildlife watching.

Iceberg Lake

Tucked in a cirque below Mount Wilbur and Iceberg Peak in Many Glacier, Iceberg Lake is a treat for the eyes. The lake itself is in a glacial pocket, once carved by the moving ice that left a small moraine along the beach. With winter snows depositing heavy drifts in the bowl protected by Wilbur's shadow, summer icebergs float in the lake—even on the hottest August days. It's worth a quick dive in, just to say you swam with the icebergs. But the icy waters will suck the air out of your lungs.

Ptarmigan Tunnel

Built in 1931 to access the Belly River Valley from Many Glacier, Ptarmigan Tunnel is a phenomenon found on few trails. Large steel doors prevent winter snows from piling up inside; it's a good thing too, as those snows would never melt out. The doors open usually in July and close in early October. The 183-foot-long tunnel is tall enough to permit riders on horseback without scraping their heads. A walk through its dark corridor doesn't require a flashlight, but more than one hiker has encountered a bear racing through its bowels.

BELLY RIVER COUNTRY

North of Many Glacier, the Belly River is wild backcountry. No roads access the valley, meaning entry is on foot or horseback. From Many Glacier, two routes cross into the Belly—Ptarmigan Tunnel and Red Gap Pass via Poia Lake. Three other trails reach the Belly via other routes: The shortest is from Chief Mountain border crossing, and there is one from Goat Haunt over Stoney Indian Pass, and one from Lee Ridge. To locals, the area is simply known as the Belly.

The Belly is home to two headwaters of the Saskatchewan River, which flows to Hudson Bay. The **Belly River** may have been named for the Gros Ventre (French for "Big Belly") people, and the **Mokowanis River** for a Blackfeet term that refers to a buffalo's stomach. Thirty-three backcountry campsites are strung up and down the two valleys, as well as lakes: Elizabeth, Helen, Cosley, Glenns, and Mokowanis. At the confluence of the two valleys, the historic Belly River Ranger Station, which is staffed in summer, sits idyllic amid aspen groves and fields of wild sticky geraniums staring up at the three spires of Stoney Indian Peaks and Mount Cleveland, the park's highest peak.

THE LEGEND OF JOE COSLEY

The Belly is rife with legends of the park's favorite renegade ranger, **Joe Cosley.** A fur trapper long before Glacier became a national park, Cosley hunted the Belly for hides, trapped in Glacier and Waterton, and carved his name on thousands of trees.

When Glacier achieved parkhood in 1910, Cosley was hired as The Belly's first ranger. But for Cosley, ranger duties became a vehicle for poaching—even near West Glacier right under the superintendent's nose. He sold hides in Canada and furnished paying clients with big game.

Cosley's mountain man reputation grew due to his self-generated legends. He told more than one woman he named Elizabeth Lake for her, said he buried a diamond ring in a Belly poplar, and claimed to have hiked 35 miles between Polebridge and Waterton in three and a half hours for a dance.

Finally in 1914, after sending rangers to nab him poaching, the superintendent threw Joe off the payroll, despite lack of evidence. After serving with Canadian forces in World War I, Joe weaseled his way back into the Belly to trap and hunt. Meanwhile, 24-year-old **Joe Heimes,** who inherited the Belly's ranger badge, crossed a footprint leading to one of Cosley's caches. Heimes arrested Cosley, who was twice his age. After repeated attempts at escape, Cosley succumbed only when Heimes tied his feet. Heimes made Cosley carry a pack with evidence—traps and beaver pieces—for the long snowy hike over a pass, a drive, and a train ride to jail in Belton (now West Glacier).

In 1929, Glacier Park saw its most notorious trial. Cosley pled guilty but claimed Heimes framed him with the evidence. The commissioner judged him guilty with a $125 fine and 90 days in jail. Claiming a fatal disease, Cosley asked for clemency. To avoid a death in his jail, the commissioner suspended the sentence due to Joe's visibly fast-failing health. Friends paid his fine; Cosley walked free.

Two hours later, supplied with snowshoes and trail grub, the cured Cosley hiked over the Continental Divide to his cache in the Belly. Within two days after his trial, he sold 55 beaver, 21 marten, and 22 mink hides for $4,129 in Canada.

For more of Cosley's adventures, read *Belly River's Famous Joe Cosley* by Brian McClung.

Recreation

HIKING

Hiking in Many Glacier offers a wealth of trails, in contrast to St. Mary. Most **St. Mary** visitors choose to travel back up Going-to-the-Sun Road or drive 21 miles to Many Glacier, where well-marked paths access high alpine meadows, lakes, glaciers, and passes. Around St. Mary, easy trails access mosquito-ridden beaver ponds, while rough trails or scrambles lead to high peaks and bluffs. St. Mary Visitors Center has a free nontopographic map of hiking trails in St. Mary Valley, and it's also available online (www.nps.gov/glac). For hiking outside the park on Blackfeet land, pick up a $10 pp annual Tribal Conservation Permit at the St. Mary Visitors Center.

Using the hiker shuttle that runs between Many Glacier and St. Mary and the park shuttle on Going-to-the-Sun Road, visitors can do point-to-point hikes: the Highline over Swiftcurrent Pass or Piegan Pass to Many Glacier Hotel.

Hiking **Many Glacier** is a treat. Trails lead quickly up into the high country, and not much old-growth forest obliterates the views. Most trailheads are accessed from Many Glacier Hotel, Swiftcurrent parking lot, or the picnic area. Although trail junctions are extremely well signed, you'll find a map helpful to navigate the maze—especially trails crisscrossing the Grinnell Valley. Free area nontopographic hiking maps are available at St. Mary Visitors Center, Many Glacier Ranger Station, park lodge front desks, and online (www.nps.gov/glac). In Many Glacier, seasonal footbridges are usually installed in late May and removed in October. Check with the ranger station or the trail status report online for exact dates.

Because of dense bear populations and heavy hiker traffic in Many Glacier, trails are closed from time to time to let an aggressive bear cool off. Check for current trail status with the ranger station, Many Glacier Hotel's activity desk, or online.

Backcountry camping permits are available at St. Mary Visitors Center or Many Glacier Ranger Station. From St. Mary, backpackers can hike to Red Eagle Lake and Triple Divide Pass. From Many Glacier, trails lead to backcountry campsites at Cracker Lake, Poia Lake, and the Belly, but no backcountry camping is permitted at Iceberg, Ptarmigan, Red Rocks, Bullhead, and Grinnell Lakes, or at Grinnell Glacier and Piegan Pass.

The hikes below are listed in order from the south at St. Mary north to the Canadian border.

Divide Peak

- Distance: 5 miles round-trip
- Duration: 3.5 hours
- Elevation gain: 1,832 feet
- Effort: strenuous
- Trailhead: unmarked end of a dirt road
- Directions: Take U.S. 89 south of St. Mary; depart from the dirt road at milepost 25.5, on top of St. Mary Ridge.

On Blackfeet land, this hike requires a Tribal Conservation Permit ($10 pp), available at St. Mary Ranger Station. You'll have to poke around a bit to find the trail (there are several) that wanders through the 2006 Red Eagle Fire. Not only is the trail unmarked, but it's very steep—only those confident in their backcountry scrambling skills should attempt this. Several routes lead up to an old hexagonal fire lookout on Divide Peak's northeast ridge. Pick one, scouting constantly ahead for where it goes. If you don't like the steepness of what's ahead, head back down and try another trail.

At the lookout, incredible views span the St. Mary Valley up to the Continental Divide and sprawl to prairies. From the lookout, a

45-minute scramble leads to the top of the peak, where you can stand atop the divide between the Saskatchewan and Missouri drainages.

Red Eagle Lake

- Distance: 15 miles round-trip
- Duration: 7.5 hours
- Elevation gain: 269 feet
- Effort: easy but long
- Trailhead: at the 1913 Ranger Station parking lot in St. Mary

After following an old road for one mile, the trail climbs gently through the 2006 Red Eagle Fire, where wildflowers are madly growing back. The burn continues to the lake, where it started. Watch for bear diggings—places where grizzlies rototill for glacier lily bulbs or chase after ground squirrels. Red Eagle Mountain looms ahead, and grand views northwest to Going-to-the-Sun Mountain unfold. About

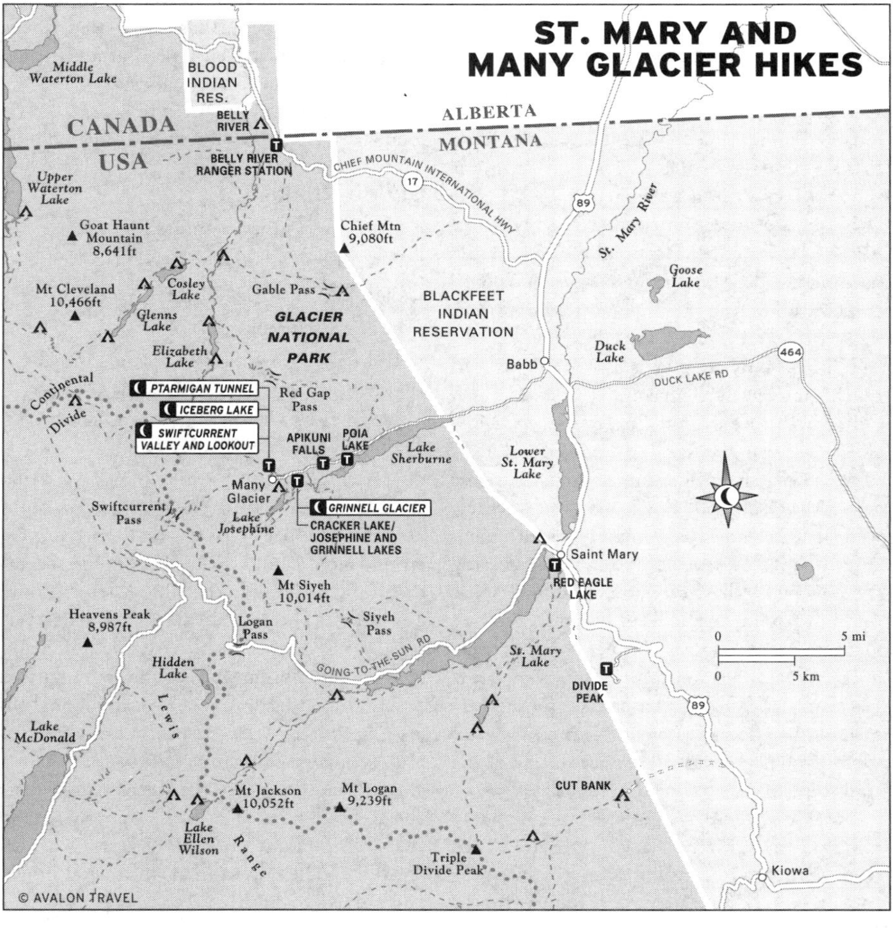

© BECKY LOMAX

Day hikers, backpackers, and anglers all enjoy Red Eagle Lake.

halfway, the trail crosses Red Eagle Creek twice on swinging bridges. Between the two bridges, the St. Mary Lake trail splits off.

In the 1920s Red Eagle Lake was home to a large tent camp, famous for its fishing. Today, die-hard anglers hike in with float tubes hitched to their packs.

Apikuni Falls

- Distance: 2 miles round-trip
- Duration: 1 hour
- Elevation gain: 550 feet
- Effort: moderate
- Trailhead: Grinnell Glacier Interpretive site, 10.4 miles west on Many Glacier Road

Apikuni Falls springs from a hanging valley, which you can see from the trailhead. The short walk starts out across a flat meadow but soon climbs uphill. In July, wildflowers bloom thickly here: geraniums, arrowleaf balsamroot, paintbrush, lupine, and stonecrop. The trail climbs to the cliffs between Altyn Peak and Apikuni Mountain, where the falls drop out of the basin above. Those with scrambling skills can climb a rough trail into the upper scenic basin.

Poia Lake

- Distance: 13 miles round-trip
- Duration: 6 hours
- Elevation gain: 1,765 feet
- Effort: moderate
- Trailhead: Grinnell Glacier Interpretive site, 10.4 miles west on Many Glacier Road

One of Many Glacier's less crowded routes, the trail to Poia Lake climbs through aspen groves and wildflower meadows blooming with pink sticky geraniums to crest the forested Swiftcurrent Ridge before dropping to the lake. Cows wandering into the Poia drainage sometimes wreak havoc on the trail before the lake. Pass through the campground and drop to the lake, where spur paths cut through the willows to the beach. The return trip requires a 400-foot climb back over the ridge. Backpackers continue on from Poia over Red Gap Pass.

Cracker Lake

- Distance: 12.2 miles round-trip
- Duration: 6 hours
- Elevation gain: 1,400 feet
- Effort: moderate
- Trailhead: south end of Many Glacier Hotel parking lot

If you can stand the muddy, horse-rutted, manure-filled first 1.5 miles, where trail rides travel multiple times a day, the rest of the hike is extremely scenic and not nearly as crowded as other Many Glacier hikes. If you meet horses, step below, not above, the trail to let them pass. At the Cracker Flats junction, leave the messy trail behind and stomp the mud and manure from your boots. Climb up switchbacks into the Cracker Valley, where avalanche paths break up the forested trail and give way to bluebell and lupine meadows in the final stretch.

Hikers go to Cracker Lake for its milky turquoise waters.

Once you reach Cracker Lake, bypass the backcountry campground and drop to the inlet for the best lunch spot on the shore. Glacial flour clouds the lake water, turning it a rich milky turquoise. The gutsy take a quick dive in the frigid water. Siyeh Peak, at 10,014 feet, rises abruptly up a gigantic cliff face, a skyscraping 4,000 feet above the lake.

Josephine and Grinnell Lakes

- Distance: 1.8-7.8 miles round-trip
- Duration: 1-4 hours
- Elevation gain: minimal
- Effort: easy
- Trailheads: on the south side of Many Glacier Hotel; at Swiftcurrent Picnic Area; or via the tour boat

With the maze of trails through Grinnell Valley, a map is helpful to navigate, even though trails are well signed. Pick up a free nontopographic map from the hotel desk or the ranger station. For a two-mile round-trip walk, catch the tour boat across Swiftcurrent and Josephine Lakes to hike to Grinnell Lake. For a longer hike, begin from Many Glacier Hotel, following the trail winding around Swiftcurrent Lake to the boat dock opposite the hotel. A third starting point begins at the picnic area, where it follows Swiftcurrent Lake to that same boat dock.

From here, head over the hill to Josephine Lake, where the trail hugs the north shore until it splits off to Grinnell Glacier. Stay on the lower trail to wrap around Josephine's west end until you reach the Grinnell Lake junction. Turn toward the lake and follow the trail over a swinging bridge. At the lakeshore, enjoy Grinnell's milky turquoise waters and the falls tumbling into the lake from the glacier basin above. Although you can return to the trailheads via the south lakeshore trail, it is not as scenic, buried in deep forest. Shorten the hike by catching the tour boat back.

Grinnell Glacier

- Distance: 11 miles round-trip
- Duration: 6 hours
- Elevation gain: 1,601 feet
- Effort: moderate-strenuous
- Trailheads: on the south side of Many Glacier Hotel; at Swiftcurrent Picnic Area; or via the tour boat

In early summer, a large steep snowdrift frequently bars the path into the upper basin; check with the ranger station for status before hiking. The most accessible glacier in the park, Grinnell Glacier still requires stamina to access, for most of its elevation gain is within two miles. For that reason, many hikers take the boat shuttle, cutting the length to 7.8 miles round-trip, or just trimming 2.5 miles off the return. To hike the entire route from the picnic area, follow Swiftcurrent Lake's west shore to the boat dock. From Many Glacier Hotel, round the southern shore to meet up with the same dock. Head over the short hill and hike around Lake Josephine's north shore.

Toward Josephine's west end, the Grinnell Glacier trail turns uphill. As the trail climbs through multicolored rock strata, Grinnell Lake's milky turquoise waters come into view below. The trail ascends on a cliff stairway where a waterfall douses hikers before passing a rest stop with outhouses. A final grunt up the moraine leads to a stunning view. Trot through the maze of paths crossing the bedrock to Upper Grinnell Lake's shore, but do not walk out on the glacier's ice, as it harbors deadly hidden crevasses.

Swiftcurrent Valley and Lookout

- Distance: 3.6-16 miles round-trip
- Duration: 2-8 hours
- Elevation gain: 100-3,496 feet
- Effort: easy-strenuous
- Trailhead: Swiftcurrent parking lot in Many Glacier

This popular trail leads to various destinations along a scenic path dotted with lakes, waterfalls, moose, glaciers, and wildflowers. The trail winds through pine trees and aspen groves as it rolls gently up to Red Rocks Lake and Falls at 1.8 miles. At the top of the falls, a knoll provides a viewpoint to scan hillsides with binoculars for bears. The trail continues level through meadows rampant with Sitka valerian in July to Bullhead Lake at 3.9 miles, a good destination with bighorn sheep wandering above on scree slopes.

From the lake, the trail is a series of uphill switchbacks. It cuts through a cliff face before reaching the pass at 6.6 miles. From here, Granite Park Chalet is 0.9 miles downhill. To reach the lookout, take the spur trail up 1.4 more miles of switchbacks—you'll lose count of them. From the lookout, you'll survey almost the entire park: glaciers, peaks, wild panoramas, and the plains. Many Glacier Hotel looks minuscule. Enjoy the one-of-a-kind view from the outhouse. For a different descent, drop to The Loop to catch a shuttle.

Iceberg Lake

- Distance: 9.8 miles round-trip
- Duration: 5 hours
- Elevation gain: 1,193 feet
- Effort: moderate
- Trailhead: behind Swiftcurrent Motor Inn cabins in Many Glacier

One of the top hikes in Glacier, the trail to Iceberg Lake begins with a short steep jaunt straight uphill, with no time to gradually warm up your muscles. Within 0.4 miles you reach a junction. Take note of the directional sign here, and watch for it when you come down. Some hikers in zombie-walk mode blaze right on past it on their return on this spur with heavy bear traffic.

© BECKY LOMAX

Icebergs float on Iceberg Lake most of the summer.

From the junction, the trail maintains an easy railroad grade to the lake. Make noise on this trail, known for frequent bear sightings. Wildflowers line the trail in July: bear grass, bog orchids, penstemon, and thimbleberry. One mile past the junction, the trail rounds a red argillite outcropping with views of the valley. As the trail swings north, it enters a pine and fir forest and crosses Ptarmigan Falls at 2.6 miles, a good break spot where aggressive ground squirrels will steal your snack. Do not feed them; feeding only trains them to be more forceful. From here, the trail traverses avalanche paths until it climbs the final bluff, where a view of stark icebergs against blue water unfolds.

Ptarmigan Tunnel

- Distance: 10.4 miles round-trip
- Duration: 5 hours
- Elevation gain: 2,301 feet
- Effort: moderate-strenuous
- Trailhead: behind Swiftcurrent Motor Inn cabins in Many Glacier

Depending on snowpack, the tunnel doors usually open in July and close in early October; check with the ranger station to confirm the status. Traversing the same trail as Iceberg Lake, the route begins with a steep uphill climb before leveling out into a gentle ascent around Mount Henkel. Just past Ptarmigan Falls, at 2.8 miles, the Ptarmigan Tunnel route leaves the Iceberg Trail. From here, it climbs aggressively uphill for nearly one mile before assuming an easier uphill grade through meadows to Ptarmigan Lake.

From the lake, the route to the tunnel leads up another 800 feet of switchbacks on a scree slope. Tiny fragile alpine plants struggle to survive on this barren slope: protect them by staying on the trail rather than cutting the switchbacks. The 183-foot tunnel, six feet wide and nine feet tall, cuts through Ptarmigan Wall. Walk through for the burst of red rock greeting you on the other side. Admire the trail engineering along the north side's cliff wall and drop down 0.25 miles to see Old Sun Glacier on Mount Merritt.

Belly River Ranger Station

- Distance: 12.6 miles round-trip
- Duration: 6 hours
- Elevation gain: 745 feet on return
- Effort: moderate
- Trailhead: Chief Mountain border crossing parking lot on Chief Mountain Highway

A trail used by backpackers to access Elizabeth, Helen, Cosley, Glenns, and Mokowanis Lakes, the Ptarmigan Tunnel, and Stoney Indian Pass, the Belly River Trail attracts day hikers more for the views en route to Chief Mountain and Pyramid Peak in the distance. Anglers also drop lines into the Belly River. The trail begins with a descent down to the valley floor. Look for scratches in the aspen bark where elk have rubbed to remove the velvet from their antlers.

As the trail undulates gently across the valley floor, it traverses aspen groves and open meadows blooming with lupine and paintbrush. At the pastoral Belly River Ranger Station, listed on the National Register of Historic Places, you can envy the backcountry rangers who spend their summers staring at Gable Mountain's colorful strata, the spires of the Stoney Indian Peaks, and Mount Cleveland, the highest peak in the park.

Guides

In Many Glacier and St. Mary, options abound for guided hikes. The National Park Service leads hikes to various scenic destinations mid-June-mid-September, including full-day hikes to Grinnell Glacier and Iceberg Lake in Many Glacier. Some trips combine with boat tours to cross Swiftcurrent and Josephine Lakes. Although park naturalist hikes are free, you'll need to pay for the boat ride. The park's guided hikes are great for solo hikers to be in the company of others in bear country and to glean tidbits of natural history, but be prepared for hiking in very large groups—some have more than 30 people in midsummer. For schedules, pick up a copy of *Ranger-led Activities* from the visitors centers, online (www.nps.gov/glac), at ranger stations, or at hotel activity desks. For full-day hikes, pack along water, snacks, lunch, and extra clothes.

Glacier Guides (406/387-5555 or 800/521-7238, www.glacierguides.com) leads day hikes and backpacking trips in the park's northeast region. While solo travelers can join the Tuesday Hikes (July-Aug., $80 pp), families and small groups can hire a guide (June-Sept., $390-470). For custom day hikes, the guide will meet you at your lodge or campground in St. Mary or Many Glacier. Many of their favorite day hikes are in Many Glacier. All hikes require reservations and include guide service, deli lunch, and transportation to the trailhead. Bring a day pack with extra clothes, a water bottle, bug spray, and sunscreen. The company also has three-, four-, and six-day backpacking trips that depart weekly (June-mid-Sept., $155 per day)—some via St. Mary and Many Glacier trailheads and frequently in The Belly.

CYCLING

Bicycling the east side of Glacier National Park is relegated to road biking, as trails do not permit mountain bikes. No bike rentals are available, so bring your own.

St. Mary and Many Glacier National Park Service campgrounds provide shared biker-hiker campsites ($5 pp) on a first-come, first-served basis. The sites have bear-resistant food storage containers and are held daily until 9pm for cyclists.

Going-to-the-Sun Road

Cyclists riding on Going-to-the-Sun Road from St. Mary to Logan Pass have no restrictions. Due to heavy traffic during July-August, riding earlier or later in the day is easier on the narrow shoulderless road.

THE EXTINCTION OF GLACIERS

"Where's the best place to go to watch the glaciers go by?" Locals chuckle when someone who slept through seventh grade earth science asks this question. Glaciers don't move like a herd of elk, but they are moving ice that scientists from the U.S. Geological Survey (USGS) estimate will melt completely between 2020-2030.

WHAT ARE GLACIERS?

Glaciers are moving ice. A glacier's upper end—the accumulation zone—piles with snow, adding to the ice's mass that presses downslope. Contrary to Alaska's giant glaciers that move several feet per day, most of the park's glaciers move less than an inch per day. A glacier needs to be 100 feet deep and have 25 acres of surface area to have the mass necessary to move. That movement separates glaciers from static snow fields. When summer heat melts the ice, water departs its snout. A glacier shrinks when the math doesn't add up—when more ice melts annually than accumulates.

Many of the park's glaciers now look similar at first glance to snow fields, but they aren't. They have crevasses, debris bands, and moraines. When ice inches over rocky humps, the rigid surface cracks into crevasses—some hundreds of feet deep. Bands of rock debris pile atop the ice, carried along in lines that reveal the glacier's movement. When the ice melts, rock rubble is left in moraines—lateral or terminal piles. Snow fields lack these features.

HOW MANY GLACIERS REMAIN?

Once glamorous diamonds, the park's glaciers are relics from a mini ice age that peaked around 1850 with more than 150 glaciers. Since then, the glaciers have thinned, shrunk, broken into pieces, or melted entirely. While early melt rates tended to be slow, by the 1920s warmer summers and less snow triggered rapid melting for two decades. Since the 1970s, melt rates skyrocketed to more than 50 percent. By 2012, only 25 glaciers remained.

WHY ARE THE GLACIERS MELTING?

Glacier Park is a laboratory for studying climate change around the globe because the park's higher elevations have warmed at three times the rate of the overall planet. Average temperatures in Glacier now run two degrees Fahrenheit hotter than they did in the mid-1900s. The park now sees 30 fewer days with below-freezing temperatures and eight more days above 90°F. Warmer summers and less snowpack are the norm. The USGS monitors the park's glaciers as climate barometers, using surface measurements, aerial photography, and repeat photography for comparisons between years.

HOW ARE THE GLACIERS MELTING?

As glaciers retreat, they fracture into patches, form lakes at their snouts, or split in two. In 1850, Sperry Glacier stretched across 960 acres, but today it covers less than one-quarter of that area. Likewise, 27 glaciers once clustered over 5,300 acres in the Mount Jackson area; now 15 of those glaciers have disappeared, and those remaining have broken into multiple pieces. Grinnell and Salamander Glaciers, once joined, split into two separate glaciers. In 1927, Grinnell Glacier's recession formed a lake, growing in size as the glacier receded. Within two decades of its onset, the lake ballooned to 20 acres and was named Upper Grinnell Lake, now larger than the shriveling glacier. Harrison Glacier, at 465 acres, is the largest, while Waterton and Two Medicine have no glaciers left.

WHAT WILL HAPPEN WHEN THE GLACIERS MELT?

Glacier National Park's ecosystem will change; the most obvious will be an increase in forest elevations. More trees aren't necessarily disastrous, but animals and birds, especially those living on the fringes of their habitat, may seek a food base elsewhere. Heat intolerant pikas, for instance, may not survive warmer temperatures. Water, now seemingly so abundant, may not shed from the mountains in the same volume or at temperatures kept cool by the ice, threatening the survival of cold-loving bull trout and affecting irrigation and salmon runs. With more forests eventually come more fires.

Follow the ongoing study of Glacier's glaciers and see comparative photography at www.nrmsc.usgs.gov. Pick up the *Climate Change* flier at visitors centers and ranger stations for more information.

Blackfeet Highway

Cycling the Blackfeet Highway (U.S. 89) from the Canadian border to St. Mary is easier than pedaling other roads in the area. The undulating road is wider, straighter, and has at least a bit of a shoulder. However, the wide-open space means only one challenge—high winds. Expect strong easterlies. If you're heading in the right direction, you will have a nice tailwind. Otherwise you'll be cursing under your breath as you push against the bluster.

Riding south from St. Mary to East Glacier on U.S. 89, however, is a different story. A wide thoroughfare with big shoulders climbs St. Mary Ridge, allowing you to breathe comfortably with the width in spite of the huffing climb. But atop the ridge, the spacious road suddenly squeezes into a narrow, curvy ribbon with blind corners and little place to go when large vehicles hog the road. From a cycling perspective, it's a fun ride with the rolling terrain, but you'll find yourself nearly steering off the road while watching for vehicles coming up behind you. Blind corners have a tendency to make riders brake for safety and then curse the loss of momentum. To avoid the heavier midsummer traffic, ride early or late in the day. Since the highway is on the open range, be prepared to encounter cow pies and brake; you may round a corner into a herd of cattle.

Many Glacier Road

Bicycling Many Glacier Road is extremely picturesque. However, keep at least one eye on the road for potholes, cattle grates, and a few short gravel sections. Also, be prepared for possible bear encounters, especially early or late in the day. While riding this road, some cyclists even whoop or holler to make noise to alert bears to their presence. With bears capable of running up to 40 mph, you won't be able to outride a bear, so muster up all your bear-country savvy when riding here.

HORSEBACK RIDING

Adjacent to the Many Glacier Hotel parking lot, **Swan Mountain Outfitters**

© BECKY LOMAX

Swan Mountain Outfitters runs daily trail rides to a variety of destinations in Many Glacier.

(406/387-4405 or 877/888-5557, corral 406/732-4203, www.swanmountainoutfitters.com/glacier, mid-June-mid-Sept., $40-165) guides one- and two-hour rides departing several times daily for Josephine Lake and Cracker Flats. Half-day rides leave twice daily for Grinnell Lake's milky blue waters or Swiftcurrent Ridge. All-day rides (lunch not included) head through aspen parklands and wildflower meadows to Poia Lake or Cracker Lake. Be aware that this is trail riding; the nose of one horse will be in the tail of another—sometimes in a long string of 15 horses. This is not the horse riding of the movies where you're galloping across Montana's prairies. However, the scenery is well worth a ride. Wear long pants and hiking boots or tennis shoes for these rides. Kids must be at least eight years old. Reservations are strongly advised.

BOATING

Powerboating is restricted in Many Glacier. The public boat dock on **Swiftcurrent Lake** is adjacent to the picnic area, but no motorized boats are allowed on the lake. Sans motors, only sailboats, kayaks, rowboats, and canoes quietly ply the waters. **St. Mary Lake** permits motorized craft with no horsepower limit as well as nonmotorized boats such as canoes, kayaks, rowboats, and rafts. The boat launch is at Rising Sun. Boating regulations in Glacier Park require all boats to pick up free permits. Boaters must show that their boats have been cleaned, drained, and dried to avoid bringing aquatic invasive species into park lakes. Permits are available at the St. Mary Visitors Center or Many Glacier Ranger Station.

On the Blackfeet Reservation, you can launch onto **Lower St. Mary Lake** via the public boat ramp at Chewing Blackbones Campground (milepost 37.3, U.S. 89). Boating is also allowed on the reservation at **Duck Lake,** at milepost 29 on Duck Lake Road (Hwy. 464). Both lakes require a $20 Blackfeet recreation label, which you can purchase at Montana's Duck Lake Lodge (3215 Duck Lake Rd., 406/338-5770) to affix to your boat. If you plan on fishing, your boat label is included in your Blackfeet fishing permit.

No motorized boat rentals are available in St. Mary, Rising Sun, or Many Glacier. However, on Swiftcurrent Lake at the boat dock behind Many Glacier Hotel, **Glacier Park Boat Company** (406/732-4480 summer, 406/257-2426, www.glacierparkboats.com, early June-mid-Sept.) rents rowboats ($18 per hour). Bring cash; no credit cards are accepted.

KAYAKING AND CANOEING

High east-side winds deter many kayakers and canoers from the larger lakes. Instead, most paddlers head to more protected waters, such as

© BECKY LOMAX

Rent boats at Many Glacier Hotel to paddle Swiftcurrent Lake.

Many Glacier's smaller lakes that are less prone to big whitecaps kicking up. A popular kayak trip crosses **Swiftcurrent Lake** and paddles the connecting slow-moving Cataract Creek upstream to Lake Josephine, where a shoreline loop makes a wonderfully scenic tour. Launch this tour from the public boat dock adjacent to Swiftcurrent Picnic Area. Pick up free boating permits at St. Mary Visitors Center or Many Glacier Ranger Station.

Rent canoes and kayaks at the boat dock behind the Many Glacier Hotel. **Glacier Park Boat Company** (406/732-4480 summer, 406/257-2426, www.glacierparkboats.com, mid-June-mid-Sept., $15-18 per hour) rents boats for use on Swiftcurrent Lake. Paddles and lifejackets are included. Bring cash; no credit cards are accepted.

FISHING

Glacier's east side is more noted more for lake fishing than for streams or rivers. Glacier's Red Eagle Lake has yielded state-record trout, and Duck Lake on the Blackfeet Reservation claims a reputation for world-class fishing.

Inside Glacier National Park, no license is required for fishing, although you must be aware of fishing regulations. Outside park boundaries, visitors on the Blackfeet Reservation need a Blackfeet fishing permit ($25 for 2 days, $75 for the season), which may be purchased at Duck Lake Lodge (3215 Duck Lake Rd., 406/338-5770, www.montanasducklakelodge.com).

St. Mary

St. Mary Lake doesn't support much in the way of good fishing with its raging winds. But it does have lake whitefish, brook trout, and rainbows. For better fishing, head instead to St. Mary River's deep channels below the lake for rainbow trout. The best local fishing requires a 7.5-mile hike to **Red Eagle Lake;** here a state-record 16-pound native westslope cutthroat was caught. Those with a serious commitment and willpower hike in float tubes.

Many Glacier

With its numerous lakes, the Many Glacier Valley offers lots of fishing holes. Grinnell, Josephine, Swiftcurrent, Red Rocks, Bullhead, Windmaker, and Ptarmigan Lakes all support varying trout populations, but don't be deceived into carrying your rod to Iceberg, Upper Grinnell, or Poia Lakes, which have no fish. Cracker and Slide Lakes are closed to fishing. Sherburne Lake—a dam-controlled reservoir partly on Blackfeet land and partly in the park—supports northern pike. Cataract Creek between Josephine and Swiftcurrent Lakes contains brookies, but other creeks in the area don't offer much.

Those willing to heft a backpack should hike through Ptarmigan Tunnel or from Chief Mountain border crossing into **The Belly.** Pools and riffles along the Belly and Mokowanis Rivers, plus Elizabeth, Cosley, Glenns, and Mokowanis Lakes, provide endless angling for arctic grayling and trout.

Duck Lake

Outside the park boundary, the Blackfeet Reservation is home to Duck Lake (milepost 29, Hwy. 464), attracting serious lake anglers year-round. One can easily spend a day on catch-and-release, pulling eight-pound rainbow trout from its waters. Some anglers commonly catch 10-12 pounders, and rainbow or brown trout can reach 15 pounds. Although you can keep the fish from this stocked and managed fishery, you may find your fishing over within an hour or so if you don't throw some back due to the catch limit. The fishing is better from a boat or a float tube: Motorized boats are allowed, with a 10 mph speed limit, and lots of float tubers launch from shore. In winter, ice fishing is permitted on the lake. The lake is surrounded by Blackfeet and private land; be conscious of private property. Pick up the current fishing regulations when you buy your license.

WATERSKIING

Waterskiing is not a big sport on Glacier's east side. But for diehards, waterskiing is permitted

ON STAGE WITH NATIVE AMERICANS

During summer months, Native Americans feature their talents around Glacier Park. Look for shows in park lodges, at campground amphitheaters, and in various Flathead Valley venues.

Renowned storytellers of the Blackfeet, Salish, and Kootenai people share stories and legends from their history in the **Native America Speaks** program, free 45-minute presentations. You can catch the Native America Speaks series at the Apgar, Many Glacier, Rising Sun, and Two Medicine campground amphitheaters and Lake McDonald Lodge. Check the *Ranger-led Activities* newspaper for the schedule.

An award-winning and Grammy-nominated singer, songwriter, and storyteller, **Jack Gladstone** combines music and narrative that weaves together Native American tradition with current cultural history. Gladstone packages a unique vision that gives insight into Blackfeet roots and Glacier's history as sacred land. Look for his performances (adults $5, under age 13 free) at Many Glacier Hotel and Lake McDonald Lodge; check the *Ranger-led Activities* newspaper for show times.

At St. Mary Visitors Center, the **Two Medicine Lake Singers and Dancers** give a glimpse into Blackfeet heritage. Dancers in full regalia perform traditional dances as well as jingle, fancy, and grass dances—each with different footwork and body movement. For the finale, visitors can join in their Round Dance. This 90-minute show sells out, so buy your tickets early (adults $5, under age 13 free). Check the *Ranger-led Activities* for current schedule.

on both Upper and Lower St. Mary Lake; however, brisk winds and cold waters inhibit the activity for most. All folks choosing to water-ski here wear wetsuits or dry suits, as the water is extremely cold. On **Lower St. Mary Lake,** the public boat launch is at Chewing Blackbones Campground (milepost 37.3, U.S. 89). For Lower St. Mary, a Blackfeet recreation permit ($10 pp per year) and boat permit ($20 per year) are required for waterskiing. Purchase the permits at Duck Lake Lodge (3215 Duck Lake Rd., 406/338-5770, www.montanasducklakelodge.com). Duck Lake does not permit waterskiing.

SAILBOARDING

Because St. Mary Lake kicks up good winds, it attracts a few skilled sailboarders, launching from Rising Sun Picnic Area. Most serious sailboarders head instead for **Duck Lake** (7 miles north of St. Mary, and then 3 miles up Duck Lake Rd./Hwy. 464), where winds blow more consistently—usually in the afternoon—and waters are warmer. Be conscientious of private property surrounding much of the shoreline. Blackfeet recreation permits ($10 pp per year plus $20 per sailboard per year) are required for sailboarding; purchase them at Duck Lake Lodge (3215 Duck Lake Rd., 406/338-5770, www.montanasducklakelodge.com).

ENTERTAINMENT

Park Naturalist Programs

Evening programs about natural history and wildlife are presented by park naturalists in Many Glacier Hotel, Many Glacier Campground Amphitheater, and St. Mary Visitors Center during summer. The free 45-minute programs run nightly at 8pm in Many Glacier Hotel and the campground amphitheater, and at 7:30pm at St. Mary Visitors Center. Indoor programs include slide shows; outdoor programs feature park naturalists.

Native American Programs

For more than two decades, Glacier's naturalist programs have included the extremely well-liked **Native America Speaks** program. Once a week, the free 45-minute evening campground amphitheater shows feature members of the Blackfeet, Salish, and Kootenai people. Speakers use storytelling, humor, and music to share their culture and heritage. You'll walk away with a new appreciation of Glacier's Native American history.

Two acclaimed Native American programs draw standing-room-only crowds. At St. Mary Visitors Center's auditorium, the **Two Medicine Lake Singers and Dancers** demonstrate Blackfeet dances in full traditional regalia once a week during summer. Tickets ($5 adults, under age 13 free) go on sale the morning of a show, and they sell out quickly. At Many Glacier Hotel, Jack Gladstone, a Blackfeet, presents his ***Buckskin PoetSongs*** (www.jackgladstone.com, $5 adults, under age 13 free), blending storytelling and music into a walk through Glacier's history from the Blackfeet perspective. For show times and days, pick up the current copy of *Ranger-led Activities* at visitors centers or check online (www.nps/gov/glac).

David Walburn Programs

Montana singer-songwriter-guitarist David Walburn (adults $8, under age 13 free) performs multimedia shows at 9pm Tuesday-Saturday in Many Glacier Hotel. He entertains with live folk music, scenic photography, and stories in a series of rotating 75-minute shows. Celebrate the West's most famous explorers and their epic trip with Walburn's outstanding narrative ***Lewis and Clark: West for America,*** or catch his re-creation of homesteading in Alaska in ***Cabin Song,*** or the colorful regional history with ***Montana: Life Under the Big Sky.*** Check the sign in the hotel lobby for a current schedule.

Accommodations

St. Mary has access to Going-to-the-Sun Road and a modern hotel; Many Glacier has a destination location. While St. Mary is convenient for exploring Logan Pass and taking day trips to Many Glacier, Waterton, and Two Medicine, Many Glacier is the best place to be smack in the heart of hiking country. You can park the car for a few days without using it. In both locations, that 7 percent Montana bed tax will still find its way onto your bill.

ST. MARY

Lodging in St. Mary is limited. The town has a large resort complex, one older motel, and cabins. Internet access is generally not available at St. Mary lodging properties. All properties are near the eastern portal of Going-to-the-Sun Road on the Blackfeet Reservation.

Resort

A large complex of hotel rooms, cabins, and motel rooms at the start of Going-to-the-Sun Road, **St. Mary Lodge** (junction of U.S. 89 and Going-to-the-Sun Rd., 406/892-2525, front desk 406/732-4431, www.glacierparkinc.com, June-Sept., $93-440) spans both sides of the highway. Glacier Park Inc., the concessionaire that runs the historic park lodges, became the owner in 2011. Although the resort surrounds itself mostly with parking lots rather than natural landscape, it has shopping, restaurants, and a bar as part of the 82-acre complex. You can walk five minutes to the park entrance and St. Mary Visitors Center.

St. Mary Lodge is comprised of several different nonsmoking options that include family to upscale accommodations. At the high end, the three-story 48-room **Great Bear Lodge** contains modern hotel comforts in chic lodge style with satellite TV (limited channels), air-conditioning, wet bars, mini fridges, and the only elevator in the immediate Glacier environs. Superior guest rooms include fireplaces and jetted tubs, and all guest rooms enjoy the sound

© BECKY LOMAX

St. Mary Lodge has a variety of lodging and dining options.

of the creek and stunning views of Singleshot Mountain from private decks. Third-floor guest rooms have larger panoramic mountain views.

Less-pricey guest rooms cluster in older lodges and small cabins. Great for small families, the **Glacier Cabins** line up along Divide Creek. The cozy, modern one-bedroom cabins include kitchenettes and porch picnic tables for enjoying the creek-side ambiance. The older **main lodge** has tiny cedar-walled guest rooms with small baths. Upgraded guest rooms in the **West Lodge** include satellite TV and air-conditioning. Older **East Motel** guest rooms do not have either, but they allow pets. Due to the proximity to the highway, some of the rooms have road noise.

Cabins

St. Mary has an abundance of cabins on various properties. In addition to the Glacier Cabins at St. Mary Resort, other cabins are available—some upscale and some rustic.

Located high on the bluff above St. Mary with spectacular views of Glacier Park, the seven upscale **Pinnacle Cabins** (106 West Shore Dr., 406/599-9285, www.glacierparkcottages.com, late May-late Sept., $250-425) offer big picture windows with the most dramatic scenery in St. Mary. The spacious two-bedroom cabins that can sleep six have large decks facing the mountains, gas barbecues, fully equipped kitchens, rock fireplaces, satellite TV, wireless Internet access, and a sleeper sofa in the living room. Check in is at the St. Mary KOA, located about 1.5 miles from the cottages. The lower rates apply early or late in the season.

Several other lodging properties in St. Mary rent out cabins. The **St. Mary KOA** (106 West Shore, 406/732-4122 or 800/562-1504, www.goglacier.com, mid-May-Sept., $90-200) has a variety of cabins. The cheapest have no baths or kitchens and require you to bring sleeping bags and towels. Showers and toilets are available in the communal building. The higher-end cabins come with baths, kitchens, and bedding. They also have glamping tents ($55-75) decked out with log beds with down duvets. Amenities at the KOA include barbecues, an outdoor pool, a hot tub, and a splash park. **Johnson's of St. Mary** (0.5 miles north of the junction of Going-to-the-Sun Rd. and U.S. 89, 406/732-5565, www.johnsonsofstmary.com, May-late Sept.) and the **Red Eagle Motel** (16 Red Eagle Trail, 406/732-4453, www.redeaglemotelrvpark.com, May-Oct.) rent a few odds and ends of cabins and modular homes.

Located 2.5 miles north of St. Mary, the **Glacier Trailhead Cabins** (milepost 34.4, U.S. 89, 406/732-4143, http://glaciertrailheadcabins.com, mid-May-mid-Oct., $130-150) are quiet, removed from the bustle of town, and set back from the highway among aspens. The 12 Spartan smoke-free knotty pine log cabins maintain quiet without TVs, Internet access, and phones (a guest phone is available in the office). Each cabin has 1-2 queen beds with a private bath, electric heat, microwaves, fridges, and a porch with a mountain view; one cabin is wheelchair accessible. Cook your own meals in the communal covered kitchen, which has an outdoor grill, sinks, a stove, picnic tables, running water, dishes, utensils, and pots.

Motel

For inexpensive motels, St. Mary has only one choice. Sitting on a bluff overlooking St. Mary, the older **Red Eagle Motel** (16 Red Eagle Trail, 406/732-4453, www.redeaglemotelrvpark.com, May-Oct., $80-95) has 23 plain nonsmoking guest rooms that have small baths with showers but no tubs. It's a place to sleep rather than lounge, but with great views of Napi Point.

BABB

Three miles southeast of Babb, **Montana's Duck Lake Lodge** (3215 Duck Lake Rd., 406/338-5770, www.montanasducklakelodge.com, year-round, $100-200) is a rustic family-owned lodge for anglers, hunters, and snowmobilers, with Duck Lake one mile away and access to local Native American hunting and fishing guides. The Spartan guest rooms have twin beds or a queen, and those on the west side look at Glacier. Some have private baths while others share a bath down the hall. The lodge great room includes a guest phone, satellite TV, a fireplace, a restaurant, and a bar.

MANY GLACIER

Two lodging options run by Glacier Park Inc. (406/892-2525, front desk 406/732-4411, www.glacierparkinc.com) are available in Many Glacier, and reservations are mandatory at both: the earlier the better for **Many Glacier Hotel** (milepost 11.5, Many Glacier Rd., mid-June-late Sept., $167-325), the most popular of the park's historic lodges due to its stunning setting. Set on Swiftcurrent Lake with access to activities from boating and trail riding to red-bus and boat tours, the nonsmoking lodge centers around its massive four-story lobby with a large fireplace. The guest rooms and suites facing the lake have views of the Continental Divide's peaks. East-side guest rooms get the sunrise, with a unique morning wake-up call as the horses jangle to the corral. A Swiss theme pervades the hotel, with bellhops dressed in lederhosen, gingerbread cutout decks, and afternoon fondue.

From being the "showplace of the Rockies," the hotel slipped into disrepair, prompting Congress to allocate $30 million to renovate the National Historic Landmark. An extensive rehabilitation straightened the structure, repaired decks, replaced windows, and renovated guest rooms by reenameling old-fashioned claw-foot tubs and adding insulation to the walls, making the guest rooms quieter. But the baths are small—many created from the original closets—with tiny sinks and skinny shower stalls in some guest rooms instead of tubs. The guest rooms have phones, but no

Historic Many Glacier Hotel offers lodging with big views.

TVs, Internet access, air-conditioning, or elevator access—even up to the fourth floor. A restaurant, a lounge, a convenience store, and a gift shop are on-site. When the hotel opened in 1915, it was considered the epitome of luxury; today, that is hardly the case, but what the hotel lacks in amenities it makes up for in historical ambience, unbelievable scenery, and convenience to trailheads. Trails to Cracker Lake, Grinnell Lake, Piegan Pass, and Grinnell Glacier depart from the hotel. Other trails depart from Swiftcurrent, one mile away.

At Many Glacier Road's terminus, **Swiftcurrent Motor Inn** (end of Many Glacier Rd., 406/892-2525, front desk 406/732-5531, early June-late Sept., $96-141 private bath, $76-86 shared bath) has austere cabins and a single-story motel. For units without baths, a central comfort station and shower house awaits. It's similar to camping, especially with the lukewarm to cold shower, but with a bed, heat, walls, and a roof for inclement weather. The nonsmoking guest rooms have no televisions, air-conditioning, Internet access, or in-room phones. Pay phones are outside the camp store; the complex also has laundry and a restaurant. Historic charm isn't the lure but rather the price and utter convenience. Trailheads for Red Rocks and Bullhead Lakes, Granite Park Chalet, Swiftcurrent Pass and Lookout, Iceberg Lake, and Ptarmigan Tunnel depart from the inn.

CAMPING

While Many Glacier has only one National Park Service campground with no hookups, St. Mary has both commercial campgrounds and a National Park Service campground. The commercial campgrounds have flush toilets, hot showers, picnic tables, and hookups for electricity, water, and sewer (and will add a 7 percent state tax to your bill), while the in-park campgrounds are limited to flush toilets, dump stations, picnic tables, fire rings with grills, and running water. Bring your own firewood for the National Park Service campgrounds; collecting it is illegal within the park. If the National Park Service campgrounds fill up, head to a commercial one in St. Mary rather than up Going-to-the-Sun Road to Rising Sun, which usually fills up first.

St. Mary is convenient for exploring Going-to-the-Sun Road, and it works as a home base for day trips to Waterton, Many Glacier, and Two Medicine. However, if you envision parking the car, setting up a tent for a couple days, and hiking straight from the campground, then Many Glacier is where you need to be.

St. Mary

Inside Glacier Park, **St. Mary Campground** (milepost 0.9, Going-to-the-Sun Rd., 406/888-7800, reservations 877/444-6777, www.recreation.gov, mid-May-mid-Sept., $23, $9 reservation fee) has 183 sites—some in open meadows, others tucked among aspens. For the best views, the C loop sites stare at Divide and Red Eagle Mountains, but in the August heat, they can be hot. Four token-operated showers with lukewarm water are available. The campground can fit RVs up to 35 feet in 25 sites. Reservations are strongly advised. A trail crosses St. Mary River on a wooden bridge to connect with the visitors center, St. Mary's restaurants, shuttles, and shops, but it has no access to St. Mary Lake. This campground is also open for primitive camping (late Apr.-May and late Sept.-Nov., $10), with pit toilets and no water.

One mile away from the hubbub of St. Mary and on Lower St. Mary Lake, **St. Mary KOA** (106 West Shore, 406/732-4122 or 800/562-1504, www.goglacier.com, mid-May-Sept., tents $37-45, RV hookups $56-65) is on the St. Mary River and Lower St. Mary Lake in a huge meadow where elk often browse. With views of surrounding peaks from an outdoor pool and hot tub, the campground has little shade and can be quite windy. You can rent canoes, kayaks, and mountain bikes. In addition to the usual commercial campground amenities, it has a grocery store, espresso, a putting green, laundry, a gift shop, free Wi-Fi, a playground, pet sitting, and the A-OK Grille (June-Aug.), which serves sourdough pancake breakfasts and barbecue dinners. Prime campsites flank the river.

Sitting atop a bluff with premium RV sites that have a panoramic view of Glacier, the older **Johnson's Campground** (0.5 miles north of the junction of Going-to-the-Sun Rd. and U.S. 89, 406/732-4207, www.johnsonsofstmary.com, May-late Sept.), just above St. Mary, sprawls in a grassy setting broken up by chattering aspens. With 75 tent sites ($25) plus 82 RV sites with hookups ($36-45)—some with fire rings—the campground can usually accommodate latecomers when National Park Service campgrounds are full. The baths are old. Amenities include a camp store, laundry, and a dump station. Restaurants and shops in St. Mary are a five-minute walk down the hill.

Many Glacier

At the end of Many Glacier Road in the park, **Many Glacier Campground** (406/888-7800, late May-mid-Sept., $20) packs 110 shaded sites into a treed setting at the base of Grinnell Point. Because of the popularity of its location, it fills up by noon in midsummer. Plan to arrive by 11am or earlier to claim a site, as they are all first come, first served; 13 sites can accommodate RVs up to 35 feet. Nearby trails depart for Red Rocks, Bullhead, and Iceberg Lakes as well as Ptarmigan Tunnel and Swiftcurrent Pass. From the picnic area, a five-minute walk down the road, trails depart to Josephine and Grinnell Lakes, Grinnell Glacier, and Piegan Pass. Across the parking lot at Swiftcurrent Motor Inn, you have access to a restaurant, laundry, hot showers, and a camp store. If bears frequent the campground, tent camping may be restricted, with only hard-sided vehicles allowed. Check www.nps.gov/glac or 406/888-7800 for status. Seasonal primitive camping (mid-Sept.-Oct., $10) involves pit toilets and no water.

Backcountry Camping

From St. Mary, you can find a series of backcountry campsites on the Continental Divide Trail to Cut Bank and Two Medicine. The most popular campsites are at both ends of **Red Eagle Lake,** a fishing mecca. Hikers then continue southward over Triple Divide Pass to **Atlantic Creek** or farther on to **Morningstar Lake.** The first campground is buggy in thick dog-hair timber, but the lake is tucked under sunrise-catching cliffs that are home to mountain goats and a golden eagle nest.

Most of Many Glacier's spur valleys are reserved for day hiking only; however, **Cracker Lake** campground is on a bluff above a turquoise lake at the base of Mount Siyeh's monstrous face. North of Many Glacier via Ptarmigan Tunnel, the Belly houses seven gorgeous lakeshore backcountry campgrounds.

Elizabeth, Helen, and **Cosley** are the most popular, but all offer outstanding scenery and good fishing. Accessing the same lakes, the trail from Chief Mountain border crossing leads first to **Gable Campground,** hidden in aspens and surrounded by wildflower meadows near the Belly River Ranger Station.

Pick up permits (adults $5 pp per night, ages 8-15 $2.50, under age 8 free) at Many Glacier Ranger Station, St. Mary Visitors Center, or the Apgar Permit Office (406/888-7900). Permits must be picked up in person 24 hours in advance. A limited number can be reserved in advance ($30) online (www.nps.gov/glac).

Food

Because Many Glacier has minimal choices, locals staying here for several days will drive to Babb (12 miles away) or St. Mary (21 miles away) to hit their favorite eateries. Nothing beats driving back in to Many Glacier at sunset, with ample opportunities for wildlife watching. Be aware that restaurants and grocery stores in Babb and St. Mary do not serve alcohol during Indian Days, a reservation-wide four-day celebration beginning the second Thursday in July. Alcohol sales are also prohibited on other selected days, such as graduation in June. Because of their location in the park rather than on the reservation, the restaurants in Many Glacier can still serve alcohol on those days.

For hikers and those driving Going-to-the-Sun Road, the restaurants run by Glacier Park Inc. at St. Mary Lodge, Many Glacier Hotel, and Swiftcurrent sell sack lunches to go ($9); order these one day in advance.

RESTAURANTS

St. Mary

Located in St. Mary Lodge (junction of Going-to-the-Sun Road and U.S. 89, 406/892-2525, front desk 406/732-4431, www.glacierparkinc.com, daily June-Sept.), the **Snowgoose Grille** looks up at Singleshot Mountain. The dining room serves up breakfast (6:30am-10am daily, $8-16) with omelets and berry crepes. Lunch (11:30am-3pm daily, $10-15) includes salads, wraps, sandwiches, and burgers, while dinner (5pm-9:30pm daily, $16-27) fill plates with pasta, beef, pork, fish, and chicken. You can also get vegetarian dishes. Reservations are not available, which can sometimes mean waiting in line. For an alternative, you can order sandwiches and appetizers in the adjacent **Mountain Bar** (11:30am-10pm daily, $8-15), or on warm days sit on the deck overlooking Divide Creek to watch the sunset with a Montana microbrew.

Also in the resort, **Curly Bear Café** (10am-8:30pm daily, $6-10) is the closest thing to fast food with subs and ice cream.

The **Park Café** (3147 U.S. 89, 406/732-4482, http://parkcafe.us, 7:30am-10pm daily July-Aug., shorter hours daily late May-June and Sept.) bakes top-notch homemade fruit pies ($4.50 per slice); try the triple berry or peach. If your heart is set on a particular pie, order it when you order dinner, in case they run out. The restaurant serves breakfast, lunch, and dinner with an eclectic menu all its own: creative veggie meals, burgers, greens, wraps, and Southwestern-style items (most $6-18). Be ready for long waiting lines in midsummer, as they don't take reservations, and it's a favorite haunt of locals. No alcohol is served in the restaurant, but you can get a Moose Moss shake made with chocolate chunk mint ice cream.

For a throwback experience, **Johnson's World Famous Historic Restaurant** (0.5 miles north of the junction of U.S. 89 and Going-to-the-Sun Rd., 406/732-5565, www.johnsonsofstmary.com, 7am-9pm daily late May-late Sept., $7-23) serves up most of its

© BECKY LOMAX

The Park Café is known for its fresh baked fruit pies.

daily large-portion specials family style with home-baked bread. Located at Johnson's Resort of St. Mary, the small old-fashioned restaurant with red-checked tablecloths serves its eggs, bacon, and hash browns all on one big platter for the entire table. Lunch soup shows up in a large tureen; ladle it yourself. Dinner features country foods, with fried chicken on Sunday. On Sunday, lunch is replaced by the dinner menu starting at 11:30am. No alcohol is served.

Babb

Four miles north of St. Mary, in a bright purple building with the walls inside covered with license plates and bumper stickers, **Two Sisters Café** (3600 U.S. 89 N., 406/732-5535, www.twosistersofmontana.com, 11am-10pm daily June-Sept., $9-25) serves up homemade fare, with big portions for lunch and dinner. Cajun grilled chicken dinners are accompanied by corn on the cob and freshly baked bread. The Red burger is topped with bacon, cheese, grilled mushrooms and onions, and Creole sauce. Montana microbrews, wine, and margaritas are available, and there are monstrous ice cream sandwiches for dessert.

Not for vegetarians, the **Cattle Baron Supper Club** (junction of U.S. 89 and Many Glacier Rd., 406/732-4033, 5pm-10pm daily mid-June-Sept., $30-50) is a beef palace. Up the log spiral staircase above the Babb Bar, once known as the roughest bar in Montana, the restaurant serves dinners where the baked potato isn't the biggest thing on the plate. Be ready to gorge, for steak cuts are humongous at 16-20 ounces. The rib eyes are even larger. Salads, grilled veggies, baked bread yanked from the oven, and a potato accompany most entrées. The log lodge pays tribute to Blackfeet history with painted wall stories and a sculpture of a buffalo jump. During midsummer, make reservations.

Many Glacier

Many Glacier has three restaurants, all operated

© BECKY LOMAX

The Ptarmigan Dining Room has been revamped to return to its 1920s look.

by the same concessionaire (Glacier Park Inc., 406/892-2525, front desk 406/732-4411, www.glacierparkinc.com) and open daily mid-June-mid-September. No reservations are accepted for any of them, so you may have to wait for a table in midsummer. Hiker sack lunches are available ($9); order them one day in advance.

In Many Glacier Hotel, the **Ptarmigan Dining Room** (milepost 11.6 on Many Glacier Rd.) underwent a renovation in 2012 that removed the drop ceiling and unmasked the original railroad beams. New furnishings have elevated the ambiance with massive windows looking out on Swiftcurrent Lake, Grinnell Point, and Mount Wilbur. For the best views to watch the bears, ask to sit near the north windows facing Altyn Mountain. Breakfast (6:30am-10am daily, $8-15) is a multiple-table buffet spread of fruits, pastries, eggs, french toast, bacon, sausage, biscuits and gravy, and pancakes. While the buffet has selection and quantity to feed hikers carb-loading for a long day, entrées are sometimes lukewarm, but you can get a waffle hot off the iron. The menu also has á la carte breakfasts. The dining hall is also open for lunch (11:30am-2pm daily, $9-14) with deli and grilled sandwiches, burgers, and salads. For dinner (5pm-9:30pm daily, $16-25) the menu includes steaks, fish, pasta, and vegetarian entrées.

Grab lighter meals—appetizers, sandwiches, and burgers—in the adjacent **Interlaken Lounge** overlooking Swiftcurrent Lake or the cozy **Swiss Room** bar (11:30am-11pm daily, $8-15). Their traditional Swiss fondue for two ($15) of four cheeses or chocolate is served 2pm-5pm daily or in the dining room as an appetizer or dessert.

At the Swiftcurrent complex, the **Swiftcurrent Restaurant** (milepost 12.5, Many Glacier Rd., 406/892-2525, front desk 406/732-5531) appeals to families with a broad menu and kid favorites. It serves standard café fare for breakfast (6:30am-10am daily, $7-13). Lunch and dinner (11:30am-9:30pm daily, $9-18) menus include burgers, sandwiches, soups, pizza, and pasta, while full dinners are added after 5pm. A gluten-free pizza crust is available, as are Montana microbrews and wine. The restaurant crowds with families due to its convenient location near the campground.

CAFFEINE

For a jolt to get you going, find espresso in St. Mary at two locations: **Glacier Perk** (inside St. Mary Lodge, daily June-Sept., 406/892-2525) and at the **Park Grocery and Gift Shop** (3147 U.S. 89, 406/732-4482, http://parkcafe.us). In Many Glacier, get espresso drinks at **Heidi's Snack Shop** (Many Glacier Hotel basement, daily mid-June-late Sept.).

GROCERIES

In Many Glacier, you'll find only two small options for groceries—both open daily mid-June-mid-September. In the basement of

Many Glacier Hotel, **Heidi's Snack Shop** (406/892-2525, 6:30am-9pm daily) sells hot dogs, coffee, espresso, soda pop, snacks, newspapers, beer, wine, and other convenience-store items. Located across the parking lot from Many Glacier Campground in the Swiftcurrent Motor Inn, the **Swiftcurrent Campstore** (milepost 12.5, Many Glacier Rd., 406/892-2525, 7am-10pm daily) carries groceries, camping and hiking supplies, T-shirts, gift items, newspapers, beer, wine, firewood, and ice. Hikers can put together lunches from either store.

In St. Mary, you can stock up on supplies at two grocery stores on U.S. 89. The largest grocery store, the **St. Mary Supermart** (St. Mary Lodge Resort, 406/892-2525, www.glacierparkinc.com, 8am-8pm daily June-Sept.) is more like an oversize convenience store rather than a full market. It carries a bit of fresh produce, meats, beer, and wine along with minimal camping, fishing, and automotive supplies. It is fully stocked in midsummer but skimpy on fresh fare in the shoulder seasons. The **Park Grocery and Gift Shop** (3147 U.S. 89, 406/732-4482, http://parkcafe.us, 7:30am-10pm daily July-Aug., shorter hours daily late May-June and Sept.) carries a great selection of Montana microbrews, along with convenience-store items, groceries, fishing tackle, and backpacking supplies. St. Mary stores do not sell alcohol during Blackfeet celebration days, including North American Indian Days (2nd Thurs.-Sun. in July). For big grocery stores, head to Browning.

Located in Babb, **Thronson's General Store** (4013 U.S. 89, 8am-7pm daily summer, 8am-7pm Mon.-Fri. fall-spring) stocks convenience-store items but no beer or wine.

PICNICKING

Many Glacier's small picnic area (milepost 12.2, Many Glacier Rd.) is a great place to sit with binoculars and scan for bears on Altyn Peak—even if you aren't picnicking. It's a popular picnic site and can be crowded in midsummer at lunchtime. If you want to roast marshmallows in one of the fire pits, bring your own firewood, because gathering wood is prohibited. The picnic area is also one of the trailheads for hiking to Lake Josephine, Grinnell Lake, Piegan Pass, and Grinnell Glacier.

TWO MEDICINE AND EAST GLACIER

Quiet and removed, Glacier's southeast corner harbors a less-traveled wonderland. It's away from the harried corridor of Going-to-the-Sun Road with its endless line of cars. With no hotel in Two Medicine, you'll find trails far less clogged on day hikes than at Many Glacier. Just because it sees fewer people, however, does not make it less dramatic. For many locals, it's their favorite park locale.

A string of three lakes curves through the Two Medicine Valley below Rising Wolf—a red hulking monolith. Its sheer mass is larger than any other peak in the park. Even though glaciers vacated this area within the past 150 years, their footprints are left in swooping valleys, cirques with blue-lakes, and toothy spires. Two Medicine Lake—the park's highest road-accessible lake, a mile high in elevation—shimmers in a valley strewn with hiking trails.

Around the corner, the tiny East Glacier burg on the Blackfeet Reservation buzzes in summer. The Great Northern Railway's historic headliner hotel, Glacier Park Lodge, dominates the town with its immense Douglas fir lobby. Train travelers taste the history as they step from the depot across a garden walkway to the hotel, framed by the mountains of Dancing Lady and Henry. Hiking, golf, Native American and red-bus tours, horseback riding, and swimming delight guests. At night, quiet stretches across the sky, broken only by the rumble of trains rolling by.

HIGHLIGHTS

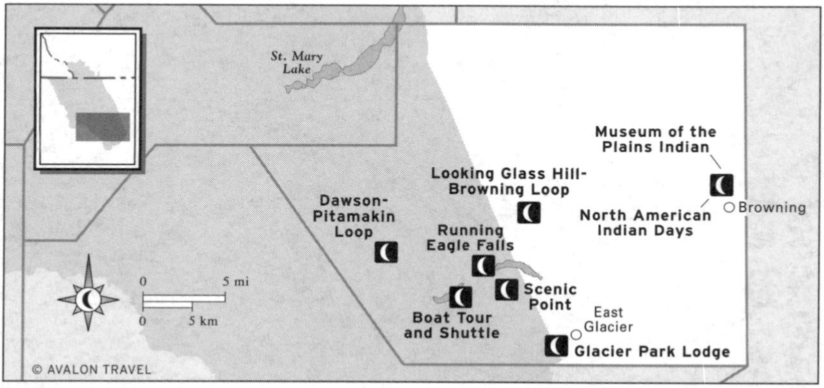

LOOK FOR ☾ TO FIND RECOMMENDED SIGHTS, ACTIVITIES, DINING, AND LODGING.

☾ **Boat Tour and Shuttle:** Hop on the historic *Sinopah* for the best way to see Two Medicine Lake. The wooden tour boat has plied these waters since 1927 (page 157).

☾ **Looking Glass Hill-Browning Loop:** Drive up the dramatic and sometimes scary Highway 49. The narrow, bumpy, curvy road lends stupendous views of Two Medicine Valley (page 160).

☾ **Running Eagle Falls:** Catch sight of water cascading from an underground chute. Named for Pitamakin, a Blackfeet woman warrior, the falls also have another name–Trick Falls (page 161).

☾ **Glacier Park Lodge:** Walk the gardens leading up to the front door of the headliner hotel for the historic chain of Great Northern hostelries. Lounge in its massive lobby held up by three-story Douglas firs (page 162).

☾ **Museum of the Plains Indian:** Sample Blackfeet history and culture in Browning at this museum, crammed with intricate beadwork. Local artisanal crafts also fill the gift shop (page 162).

☾ **Scenic Point:** Hike high above Two Medicine Lake to a top-of-the-world view. Stare across the plains, and maybe if it's clear enough, you'll see Minneapolis (page 163).

☾ **Dawson-Pitamakin Loop:** Skitter on a narrow trail along the Continental Divide thousands of feet above blue lakes and green forested valleys. Bighorn sheep summer on the three high passes (page 166).

☾ **North American Indian Days:** Join the Blackfeet celebration for four days. The colorful early July festival in Browning features regalia, horse racing, and rodeos (page 169).

HISTORY

Two Medicine acquired its name from Blackfeet legends. According to one story, two Piegan tribes planned to meet for a medicine ceremony in the valley. Failing to find each other, they both celebrated independently. In another version, two lodges for the sun dance sat on either side of Two Medicine Creek. Either way, the name stuck.

The 1896 land sale between the Blackfeet and the federal government included the Two Medicine area. Starving and nearly decimated as a nation, the Blackfeet swapped part of their reservation land from the Continental Divide

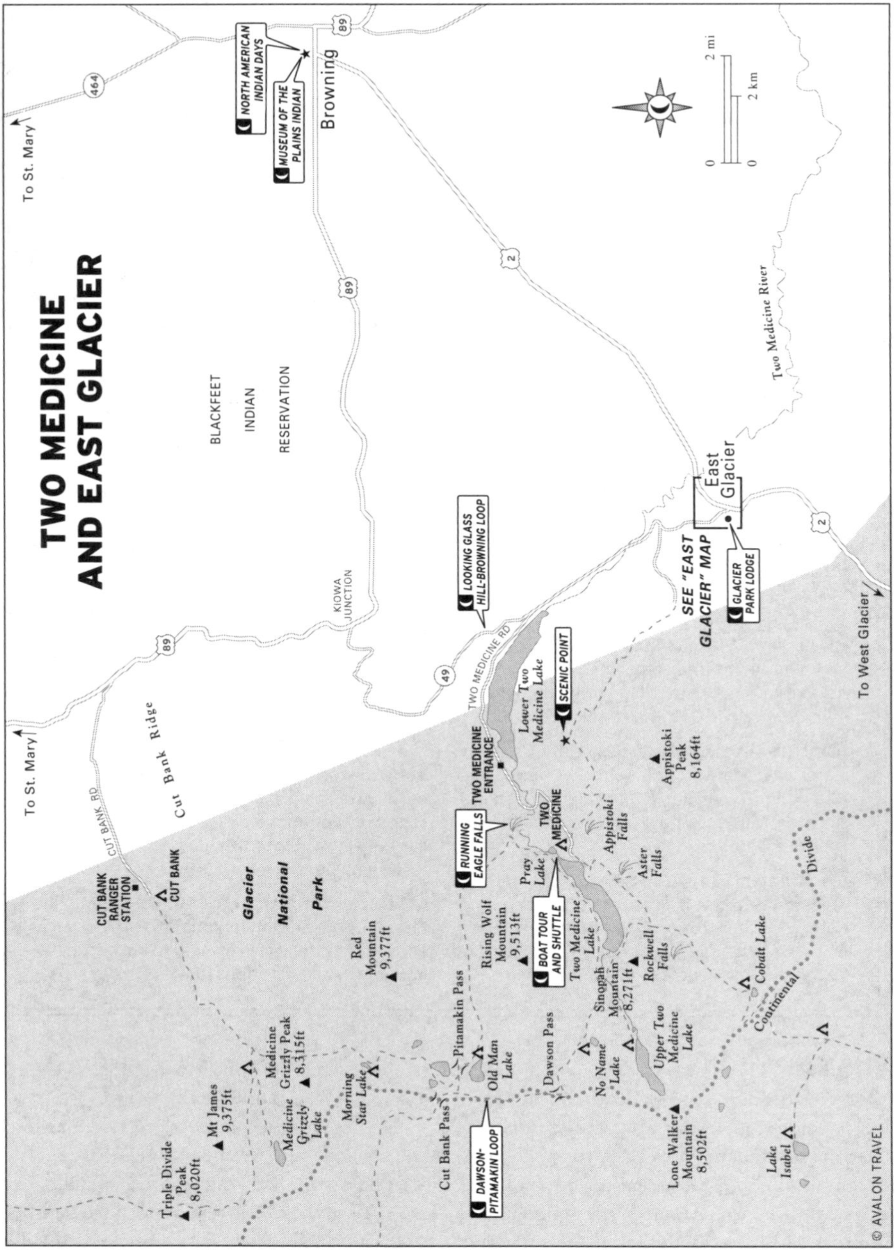
TWO MEDICINE AND EAST GLACIER
BLACKFEET INDIAN RESERVATION
To St. Mary
464
89
NORTH AMERICAN INDIAN DAYS
MUSEUM OF THE PLAINS INDIAN
Browning
2
Two Medicine River
East Glacier
SEE "EAST GLACIER" MAP
GLACIER PARK LODGE
To West Glacier
KIOWA JUNCTION
LOOKING GLASS HILL-BROWNING LOOP
49
TWO MEDICINE RD
Lower Two Medicine Lake
SCENIC POINT
Appistoki Peak 8,164ft
TWO MEDICINE ENTRANCE
Cut Bank Ridge
CUT BANK RD
To St. Mary
CUT BANK RANGER STATION
CUT BANK
Glacier National Park
RUNNING EAGLE FALLS
TWO MEDICINE
Appistoki Falls
Pray Lake
Aster Falls
BOAT TOUR AND SHUTTLE
Two Medicine Lake
Rockwell Falls
Red Mountain 9,377ft
Rising Wolf Mountain 9,513ft
Sinopah Mountain 8,271ft
Pitamakin Pass
Dawson Pass
Upper Two Medicine Lake
Cobalt Lake
Continental Divide
Medicine Grizzly Peak 8,315ft
Old Man Lake
No Name Lake
Mt James 9,375ft
Morning Star Lake
Medicine Grizzly Lake
Cut Bank Pass
DAWSON-PITAMAKIN LOOP
Lone Walker Mountain 8,502ft
Lake Isabel
Triple Divide Peak 8,020ft
0 2 mi
0 2 km
© AVALON TRAVEL

to the current reservation boundary for $1.5 million—a mere pittance considering what the parklands are worth.

In April 1891 the Great Northern Railway began laying tracks from Cut Bank to Midvale (East Glacier) and over Marias Pass toward West Glacier. As railroad developer James J. Hill sought means to increase ridership on his new line, he spawned a grand plan: a lodge to greet Eastern guests first arriving at Glacier and several chalets sprinkled in the park's most scenic spots for places to tour. For early visitors getting off the train in Midvale in 1911, Two Medicine Lake was the first stop in Glacier's backcountry after a bumpy wagon ride. Originally a tepee enclave with canvas walls and wooden floors, the hugely successful camp prompted the railroad to add two log chalets—a dormitory and a dining hall. By 1915, guests arrived on horseback via trail, the first leg on the Inside Trail connecting to Cut Bank and St. Mary Chalets, on Park Saddle Horse Company tours—a three-day trip costing $13.25.

In 1913, Great Northern's headliner hotel—the Glacier Park Lodge—finally welcomed arriving train guests, awed at the first glimpse of Glacier. Built on reservation land purchased from the Blackfeet, the posh lodge with a plunge pool in the basement erected its elegantly large lobby with 500- to 800-year-old Douglas firs sent from western Washington and Oregon. Rooms touted such high-class amenities as electric lights and steam heat. The nine-hole golf course followed 14 years later—on which employees were not allowed to play for fear of upsetting high-class tourists.

In 1929, Great Northern introduced the *Empire Builder,* named after J. J. Hill, as its modern train for the 2,200-mile Chicago-Seattle trip that packaged Glacier Park travel for its passengers. This is still the name for the Amtrak line here. It's the only U.S. train outside Alaska that stops regularly at a major national park.

In the wake of the Depression, World War II closures, and increasing auto traffic, the Two Medicine chalets met their demise and were torn down building by building until only the dining hall remained. It's now the Two Medicine store.

Today, East Glacier is home to less than 400 year-round residents. Brutal winters keep it small. High winds accompanied by frigid temperatures pound the town so strong that they've blown trains off the tracks.

Exploring Two Medicine and East Glacier

ENTRANCE STATION

East Glacier sits outside park boundaries, but Two Medicine is within the park, with an entrance station location approximately four miles up Two Medicine Road. It is staffed during daylight hours seven days a week in the summer. During shoulder seasons, staffing is reduced to weekends only or not at all, but you can use the self-pay cash-only kiosk. If you don't have an annual pass, get a seven-day pass ($25 per vehicle, $12 pedestrians, cyclists, and motorcyclists). Maps and the biannual *Waterton-Glacier Guide* are available.

Even though the Cut Bank Road enters the park, it lacks both an entrance station and a self-pay kiosk.

RANGER STATIONS

The **Two Medicine Ranger Station** (406/888-7800, 8am-4:30pm daily summer), at the terminus of Two Medicine Road at the campground junction, has current trail information and issues backcountry campsite permits. You can also pick up copies of *Ranger-led Activities* for park naturalist programs, fishing information, and free nontopographic maps of trails in the area. The ranger station plots bear sightings

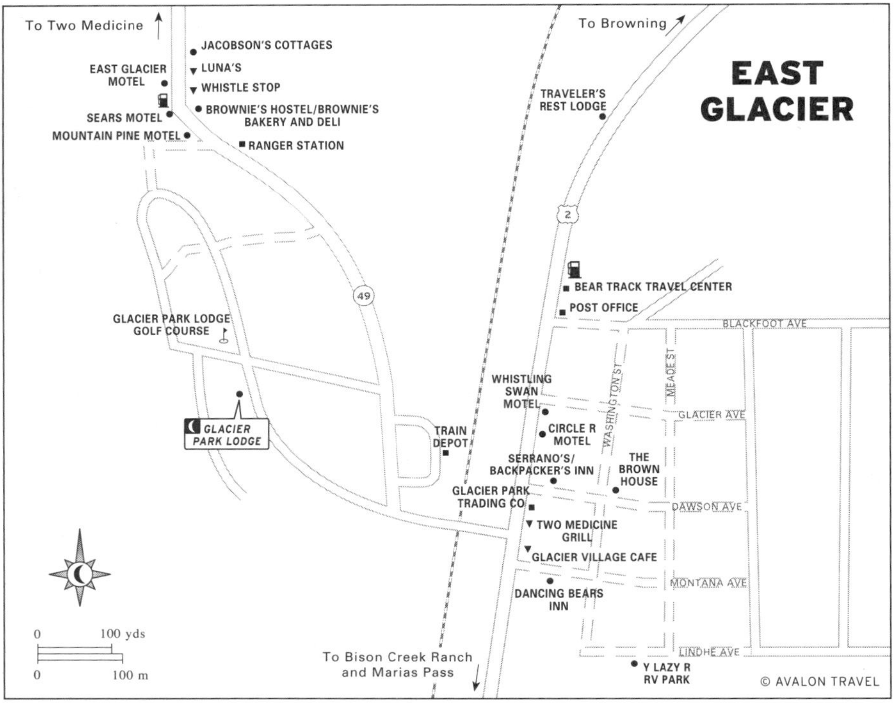

on a large wall map, which is worth a look just for bear trivia. The ranger station sells Blackfeet conservation permits ($10 pp per year) for those hiking over Scenic Point to East Glacier. The **East Glacier Ranger Station** (824 Hwy. 49, 406/888-7800) has a small staff year-round, but it doesn't maintain public hours.

SHUTTLES AND TOURS

Shuttles

The hiker shuttle operated by **Glacier Park Inc.** (406/892-2525, www.glacierparkinc.com, adults $10-50, children $5-25 one-way) aids getting to trailheads. The east-side shuttle runs daily early June-late September and connects East Glacier, Two Medicine, Cut Bank Road Junction, St. Mary, Many Glacier, and Waterton. Pay cash when you board. Shuttles heading to Two Medicine connect with tour boat departure times. Ask for schedules at the hotel front desk. At St. Mary Visitors Center, riders can connect to the free Going-to-the-Sun Road shuttles (July-Labor Day). No shuttle runs directly from East Glacier to West Glacier via U.S. 2. For trailheads at Marias Pass, for instance, you must drive or hitchhike, which is legal in Montana.

While in theory the shuttle is a great way to access trailheads, consider where you are and how long it will take you to get to Logan Pass—three hours. For the most efficient use of your time while staying in East Glacier, you're better off hiking in Two Medicine; then, move north to St. Mary or Many Glacier to hike trails in the park's core.

Flathead-Glacier Transportation (406/892-3390 or 800/829-7039) runs shuttles between Glacier International Airport and East

Glacier or Two Medicine (by reservation only, $140-180 one-way for the first person, $3 each additional person).

Bus Tours

Historic **Red Buses** (406/892-2525, www.glacierparkinc.com, adults $45-80, children $23-40) depart from Glacier Park Lodge in East Glacier. Driven by storytelling jammer drivers who roll the canvas tops back when the weather permits, the vintage tour buses are not just a treat for their historic ambience but also for the whole-sky views. The eight-hour **Big Sky Circle Tour** (daily mid-June-mid-Sept.) packs in the best of the park for those who have limited time to explore all its corners. The tour travels over Marias Pass to Lake McDonald Lodge, then crosses Logan Pass on Going-to-the-Sun Road to St. Mary and back to the lodge. The three-hour **Two Medicine Tour** (twice daily late May-late Sept.) includes a boat tour on Two Medicine Lake. For an excursion to Many Glacier and Waterton, the 8.5-hour **International Peace Park Tour** (daily early June-mid-Sept.) for Waterton Lakes National Park. Prices do not include meals or park entrance fees. Reservations are required and can be made by phone or at the hotel front desk.

© BECKY LOMAX

The *Sinopah* provides boat tours and shuttles hikers across Two Medicine Lake.

Departing East Glacier, **Sun Tours** (29 Glacier Ave., 406/226-9220 or 800/786-9220, www.glaciersuntours.com, 8am daily mid-June-mid-Sept., adults $75, children $25, meals and park entrance fees not included) runs 25-passenger air-conditioned buses with extra-large windows to catch the big views on Going-to-the-Sun Road. Tours go through St. Mary to Logan Pass and back. Led by local guides who live on the reservation, the 8.5-hour tour highlights Glacier's connection with the Blackfeet. You'll learn the background of peak names as well as the cultural history of the park. The guides, most of whom are excellent storytellers, also know about plants, wildlife, and geology. Those staying in Browning can hop on the bus at 8:30am. While last-minute spots are sometimes available, it's best to make reservations at least 24 hours in advance.

Boat Tour and Shuttle

The ***Sinopah*** (Glacier Park Boat Company, 406/257-2426, www.glacierparkboats.com, mid-June-early Sept., adults $12 round-trip, children $6) started service on Two Medicine Lake in 1927 and has never left its waters. The 45-foot, 49-passenger wooden boat cruises up-lake four times daily for 45-minute tours (10:30am, 1pm, 3pm, and 5pm) while the captain narrates history, trivia, and natural phenomena. Two trips daily also incorporate a short guided hike to Twin Falls (0.9 miles one-way). For July-August, the boat company adds a 9am hiker express. Purchase tickets at the boat dock, or make reservations by phone with a credit card. To shorten the 10-mile round-trip Upper Two Medicine Lake hike to four miles, catch the boat both directions. For a three-mile jaunt, hike one-way along the northern lakeshore through avalanche gullies under Rising Wolf's flanks and hop the boat back. You can pay half price cash for one-way return rides on boarding. If too many people are waiting, the boat runs extra trips to retrieve all hikers waiting at the upper dock.

Blackfeet Reservation Tours

Darrell Norman, a Blackfeet member who runs the Lodgepole Tipi Village and Art Gallery in Browning, leads private **Blackfeet Cultural Historical Tours** (406/338-2787, www.blackfeetculturecamp.com, May-Sept.) to buffalo jumps and old tepee ring sites on the Blackfeet Reservation. He accompanies up to four people in your car for half-day or full-day tours ($120-180, additional participants $30-50 each).

SERVICES

Two Medicine has no gas station, but East Glacier has two: an Exxon at the Bear Track Travel Center at the east end of town on U.S. 2 and Grizzly Gas on Highway 49 at the Sears Motel. Browning has several gas stations. ATMs are at Glacier Park Trading Company and Glacier Park Lodge. There is a post office (15 Blackfoot Ave., East Glacier, 8:30am-noon and 1:30pm-5pm Mon.-Fri.). The area's daily newspaper is the *Great Falls Tribune.*

In East Glacier, a launderette is at Y Lazy R RV Park (Lindhe Ave. and Meade St.), and it offers coin-op showers available to drop-ins. Showers ($5) are also available at Aspenwood Resort.

May-September you can rent cars in East Glacier through Dollar Rent-A-Car at **Sears Motel** (1023 Hwy. 49, 406/226-4432 or 800/457-5335, www.searsmotel.com, www.dollar.com) or Avis at **Glacier Park Trading Company** (316 U.S. 2, 406/226-9227, or 800/230-4898, www.seeglacier.com, www.avis.com).

Cell Phones and Internet

Some cell phones have reception in East Glacier and Browning. No reception is available at Two Medicine. Internet access is available at Brownie's, Bear Track Travel Center, and a few motels.

Shopping

East Glacier has a few gift shops to browse, and it is home to the unique **Spiral Spoon** (1012 Hwy. 49, www.thespiralspoon.com, 406/226-4558) that creates artfully hand-carved spoons made with different woods. For the largest collection of Native American art, stop in Browning at the **Blackfeet Heritage Center and Art Gallery** (333 Central Ave., 406/338-5661, www.blackfeetnationstore.com, 9am-6pm daily). It houses the beadwork, jewelry, paintings, and sculptures of more than 500 artists and craftspeople. You can also find rawhide, buffalo hides, and bison skulls.

Water

In 2012, a new $22 million treatment system improved water quality for East Glacier and Browning. The old system required frequent "boil orders" to make the water clean enough to drink, but that's no longer the case. The State of Montana gave its stamp of approval to the local water system, and you can now fill up water bottles at taps.

Emergencies

In Glacier Park, contact a park ranger for emergencies (406/888-7800). You can also walk into the **Two Medicine Ranger Station** (8am-4:30pm daily summer), on Two Medicine Road at the campground junction. The nearest hospital is on the Blackfeet Reservation (Blackfeet Community Hospital, 760 Government Square, Browning, 406/338-6154).

DRIVING TOURS

Two Medicine Road

Four miles north of East Glacier, Two Medicine Road diverges off Highway 49 for a 7.5-mile scenic venture up Two Medicine Valley. Beginning on the Blackfeet Reservation, it winds through

BLACKFEET NATION

Bordering Glacier National Park on the east side, Blackfeet land extends from the Canadian border to south of East Glacier, covering 1.5 million acres. About half of the nation's 15,000 members live on the reservation.

Originally from north of the Great Lakes, the Blackfeet are related by language to the Algonquin peoples. As Europeans landed in North America in the 1600s, the Blackfeet were one of the first nations to move westward, adopting a nomadic lifestyle hunting buffalo in what is now Saskatchewan, Alberta, and Montana. Small bands, each led by a chief, met for summer medicine-lodge or sun-dance rituals and separated for winter.

The loose Blackfeet Confederacy contained three nations: The **North Blackfeet** and **Bloods** gravitated into Alberta, and the **Piegan** to Montana. All three hunted using buffalo jumps, lighting fires to stampede bison over a cliff. (*Siksika,* or "black feet," may have referred to moccasins ash-darkened from these prairie fires.) When the Blackfeet acquired horses in the 1700s from the Kootenai, Flathead, and Nez Percé and guns from French fur traders, their hunting methods altered.

The 1800s brought devastating misery to the Blackfeet. A smallpox epidemic in 1837 killed 6,000 people, two-thirds of the population. Buffalo herds declined, leading to Starvation Winter in 1884, claiming the lives of 600 Blackfeet. By the middle of the 19th century, the first treaty with the U.S. government defined Blackfeet territory as two-thirds of eastern Montana, starting at the Continental Divide. White settlers arrived, rankling the Blackfeet, who raided settlements. To squelch hostilities, in 1870 the U.S. Army sent Colonel E. M. Baker to kill the raid leader, Mountain Chief. But Baker mistakenly attacked Heavy Runner's peaceful band, slaughtering 200 and capturing 140 women and children.

Blackfeet leaders, desperate to help their destitute people, negotiated with the U.S. government for their survival. They sold off portions of the reservation in trade for tools, equipment, and cattle. Glacier Park, from the Continental Divide to the eastern boundary, was one of these trades, purchased by the U.S. government for a mere $1.5 million in 1896.

Today, the Blackfeet economy is based on some cattle ranching, but 90 percent of their income depends on oil and gas extraction. Browning, the center of Blackfeet culture, houses the small but outstanding **Museum of the Plains Indian,** which chronicles their history and displays amazing beadwork. In July, the nation celebrates **North American Indian Days** (406/338-7521, www.blackfeetnation.com), hosting regional indigenous people for the four-day powwow that includes rodeos, games, dancing, traditional regalia, singing, and drumming.

BEST WAYS TO EXPLORE NATIVE AMERICAN ROOTS

The Blackfeet once used Glacier for hunting and sacred ceremonies. You can learn about Blackfeet history and culture by visiting Browning to tour the **Museum of the Plains Indian,** to sleep in a tepee at the **Lodgepole Gallery and Tipi Village,** or to attend **North American Indian Days. Sun Tours** runs Going-to-the-Sun Road trips, narrated by Native American guides. Performances by **Jack Gladstone** at several hotels and the **Two Medicine Singers and Dancers** at St. Mary Visitors Center also give insight into Blackfeet culture, and many evening interpretive programs at campgrounds and park hotels include Native American speakers.

quaking aspen above Lower Two Medicine Lake. In September, the aspens turn bright yellow, almost emitting a light of their own. **Scenic Point** rises across the lake, and the red flanks of Rising Wolf fill the upper valley. About three miles up, you'll enter the park, crossing over a cattle guard, but you won't reach the entrance station until 4 miles. A few minutes past the entrance station (5.2 miles), stop for the short nature walk to **Running Eagle Falls.** As the road climbs into the Two Medicine Basin, look for blue camas, fleabane, paintbrush, and lupine.

RISING WOLF

The most prominent feature in Two Medicine Valley is the hulking 9,513-foot **Rising Wolf Mountain.** It is named for the first person of European descent to meet the Blackfeet. Born Hugh Monroe in Quebec, Canada, in 1798, the 16-year-old traveled west as an apprentice for the Hudson's Bay Company.

With an intense interest in the Indians, he was sent to live with the Small Robes band of Piegans, a tribe of the Blackfeet nation, to learn their language and to find beaver-trapping territory. The band's chief, **Lone Walker,** took a liking to the congenial Monroe. After several seasons with the Piegans, Monroe married **Sinopah,** Lone Walker's daughter, and lived permanently with them.

When officially admitted to the band, Monroe was given the name Rising Wolf. Despite the lack of written records, it is presumed that Monroe was the first person of European descent to set eyes on St. Mary Lake and much of Glacier's eastern lands. He served as a guide and interpreter for territorial survey teams and early reconnaissance of Glacier National Park. He later left the Hudson's Bay Company for the American Fur Company, which established trading posts on the Marias River in Blackfeet country. Rising Wolf died in 1892, the same year the Great Northern Railway laid tracks over Marias Pass.

While there is some discrepancy as to Monroe's birth date, it is apparent he lived to a ripe old age, even after losing sight in one eye in a fight with a Sioux. Many of Monroe's descendants still live on the Blackfeet Reservation. Lone Walker peak sits at the head of Upper Two Medicine Lake; Sinopah rises straight out of Two Medicine Lake opposite Rising Wolf.

Once you cross the apex, the peaks of Two Medicine pop out: Sinopah, Lone Walker, and Rising Wolf. After passing the campground and picnic area entrance (7.1 miles), the road terminates in the parking lot at **Two Medicine Lake,** where you can catch a boat tour on the lake or stop in the historic chalet, now a camp store selling ice cream.

Looking Glass Hill-Browning Loop

From East Glacier, a 49-mile scenic drive twists up Highway 49 and loops through Browning. Because the section from Two Medicine Road to Kiowa Junction is closed November-April, this tour is a summer drive only. State law restricts the size of trailer combinations and RVs to 21 feet on shoulderless Highway 49, which has more curves than a snake, but you'll see many anyway. Wet downpours cause landslides, which frequently cause road closures and chew up the pavement. As the road climbs to a high vantage point on Looking Glass Hill above **Lower Two Medicine Lake,** three miles past the Two Medicine junction, find unmarked pullouts overlooking the valley for great photo ops before descending to Kiowa Junction.

Drive slowly; "open range" means no fences. Cattle wander willy-nilly where they please. You'll round a corner into cows standing smack in the middle of the road and may have to wait for them to move. They are not speedy creatures, but they can dent your car with a good kick, so give them room. Because the road is narrow and curvy, take it slow. You'll have less chance of putting a cow imprint across your grille.

At Kiowa, turn on U.S. 89 toward Browning to make the loop through the Blackfeet Reservation. Stop at the Museum of the Plains Indian, and turn back to East Glacier on U.S. 2 past the Blackfeet National Bison Reserve. From Kiowa, an alternate tour continues north on U.S. 89 to St. Mary along the Rocky Mountain Front—a scenic but narrow curvy drive.

Blackfeet Trail

Looping south and east of Browning, a 70-mile

Blackfeet Trail Tour winds on mostly paved roads through the Blackfeet Reservation following 15 historical markers. The sites paint a picture of the West as seen through Blackfeet eyes. Download a map online (www.blackfeetcountry.com).

SIGHTS

Two Medicine Lake

The largest of three lakes, Two Medicine Lake is the highest road-accessible lake in Glacier, sitting almost one mile high in elevation and flanked by peaks rich in Blackfeet history. Its waters collect snowmelt from peaks over 8,000 feet high but devoid of glaciers. The lakes are all that remain of the monster 1,000-foot-thick ice field that covered nearly 500,000 acres, flowing out onto the prairie past Browning. To explore Two Medicine Lake, jump on the historic *Sinopah* tour boat, or if the waters are calm, rent a canoe to paddle its shoreline, swim in its chilly clear waters, or fish for brook trout.

Two Medicine Chalets

Little remains of Two Medicine Chalets, but the dining hall, now operating as the Two Medicine Campstore, is designated a National Historic Landmark. Built in 1912-1913, the chalets replaced the original tepee camp for visitors. The log two-story chalet was once the hub of the small colony, the first stop on the Inside Trail horse trip with the Park Saddle Company in the 1920s. The dining hall's most famous guest—Franklin Delano Roosevelt—addressed the nation from here in an unofficial fireside chat in 1934.

Running Eagle Falls

A short nature trail (0.6 miles round-trip) leads to Running Eagle Falls, also known as Trick Falls. In high runoff, water gushes over the top of the falls, spraying those standing nearby. But in lower flows, you can see the trick. Part of the falls runs underground and spits out through a cavern halfway down the cliff face. Running

Mile-high Two Medicine Lake lures waders on hot days.

Eagle, the Blackfeet name for the falls, honors a female warrior named Pitamakin who had her vision quest here. She gained renown for stealing horses from the Kootenai but was eventually killed during a raid.

Glacier Park Lodge

In East Glacier, Glacier Park Lodge stands as the headliner hotel for the historic chain of Great Northern hostelries built throughout Glacier. Set within the Blackfeet Reservation, the 155-room hotel, built in 1915, started its life providing train visitors with a first taste of Glacier. Since the advent of Going-to-the-Sun Road, additional avenues into the park stole some of the lodge's thunder. Today, the hotel is listed on the National Register of Historic Places. Even if you are not staying here, walk the gardens leading up to the front door, lounge in its massive lobby held up by three-story Douglas firs, and catch the historic photo display chronicling the hotel's glory days.

Blackfeet Sentries

Blackfeet artist Jay Laber gives new life to garbage in what he calls "reborn Rez Wrecks." Using farm tools, jewelry, hubcaps, and barbwire, he sculpted a not-to-be-missed sculpture series—*Blackfeet Reservation Sentries*—posted on the reservation's four boundaries. Each pair of life-size sentries rides atop horses. Posted in East Glacier, one pair guards the reservation's western entrance (U.S. 2, 0.2 miles west of town).

Blackfeet Nation Bison Reserve

While driving between East Glacier and Browning, you may catch sight of the buffalo herd managed by the Blackfeet. Bison provided food, shelter, and clothing for the nomadic Blackfeet until the buffalo were exterminated in the 1800s.

Museum of the Plains Indian

Located 12 miles from East Glacier, the Museum of the Plains Indian (junction of U.S. 2 and U.S. 89, Browning, 406/338-2230, www.blackfeetcountry.com, 9am-4:30pm daily June-Sept., 10am-4:30pm Mon.-Fri. Oct.-May, adults $4, seniors $3, children $1, under age 6 free, all ages free winter) is a small but very informative center for Blackfeet culture and history. A five-screen multimedia show narrated by Vincent Price tells the story of the Blackfeet people, well worth the 20 minutes it takes to watch it. Displays cluster phenomenal beadwork, leather, tools, and clothing to tell the story of the Northern Plains Indians. Seeing the life-size beaded ceremonial regalia is worth the price of admission.

Recreation

HIKING

Hiking at Two Medicine is in a class by itself. Except for a few short hikes from the lake's upper boat dock, hikers here find solitude even on the most crowded hot summer days. For hikes on reservation land (those leaving directly from East Glacier or the latter half of the Scenic Point trail), a Blackfeet recreation permit ($10) is required, available at the Two Medicine Ranger Station or Bear Track Travel Center (Exxon gas station) in East Glacier.

With a maze of trail junctions breaking off the north-shore and south-shore Two Medicine Lake trails, you'll find one of the park's nontopographic trail maps helpful. These are available at the ranger station and the Glacier Park Lodge activity desk. For longer hikes, such as the Dawson-Pitamakin Loop, take a good topographic map; you can buy one in the Two Medicine Campstore.

In Two Medicine, hikers use the tour boat as a shuttle up-lake to prune miles off hikes and get

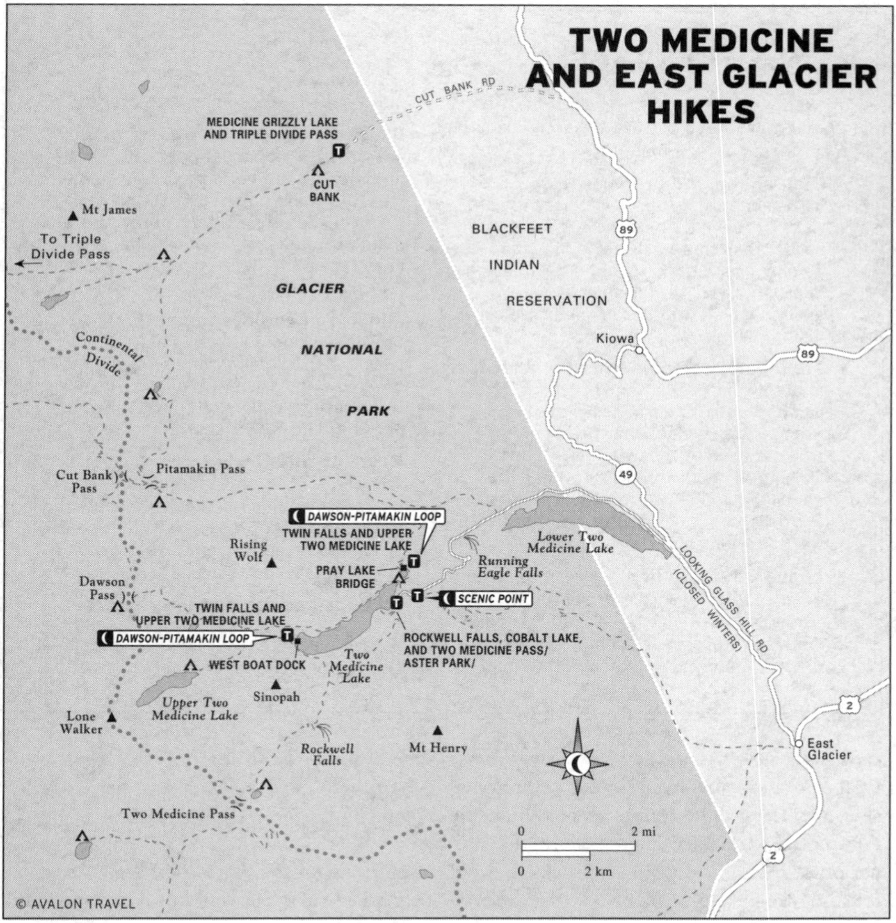

farther into the backcountry faster. Glacier Park Inc. also runs a shuttle from Glacier Park Lodge to Two Medicine for hiking; the shuttles arrive in time to catch the boat across Two Medicine Lake.

Scenic Point

- Distance: 6.2 miles round-trip
- Duration: 3-4 hours
- Elevation gain: 2,124 feet
- Effort: moderate-strenuous
- Trailhead: milepost 6.9 up Two Medicine Road

Scenic Point is one short climb with big scenery. The trail launches up through a thick subalpine fir forest. A short side jaunt en route allows a peek at Appistoki Falls. As switchbacks line up like dominoes, stunted firs give way to silvery dead and twisted limber pines. Broaching the ridge, the trail enters seemingly barren alpine tundra. Only alpine bluebells and pink mats of several-hundred-year-old moss campion cower in crags.

The trail traverses a talus slope, to be avoided

LEAVE NO TRACE

To keep Glacier pristine, visitors to this unique park need to take an active role in maintaining its well-being.

- **Plan ahead and prepare.** Hiking in Glacier's backcountry is inherently risky. Three miles here may be much harder than three miles through your neighborhood park back home. Choose appropriate routes for mileage and elevation gain with this in mind, and carry hiking essentials.
- **Travel and camp on durable surfaces.** In both front-country and backcountry campgrounds, camp in designated sites. Protect fragile plants by staying on the trail, refusing to cut switchbacks, and walking single file on trails—even in the mud. If you must walk off the trail, step on rocks, snow, or dry grasses rather than wet soil and delicate plants.
- **Leave what you find.** Flowers, rocks, and goat-fur tufts on shrubs are protected park resources, as are historical cultural items. For lunch stops and camping, sit on rocks or logs where you find them rather than moving them to accommodate your camp.
- **Properly dispose of waste.** Whatever you bring in, you must pack out. Pack out all garbage. If toilets are not available, pack out toilet paper. Urinate on rocks, logs, gravel, or snow to protect soils and plants from salt-starved wildlife, and bury feces 6-8 inches deep at least 200 feet from water.
- **Minimize campfire impacts.** Make fires in designated fire pits only, not on beaches. Use small wrist-size dead and downed wood, not live branches. Be aware that fires and collecting firewood are not permitted in many places in the park.
- **Respect wildlife.** Bring along binoculars, spotting scopes, and telephoto lenses to aid in watching wildlife. Keep your distance. Do not feed any wildlife, even ground squirrels. Once fed, they become more aggressive.
- **Be considerate of other visitors.**

For more Leave No Trace information, visit www.LNT.org.

early in the season as it is covered in steep snows (you can climb a worn path that circumvents the snow field). The trail descends to Scenic Point. To reach the actual point above the trail, cut off at the sign, stepping on rocks to avoid crushing fragile alpine plants. At the top, you have a view several thousand feet straight down to Lower Two Medicine Lake. Return the way you came, or drop seven miles to East Glacier, passing outside the park boundary, where cow pies buzz with flies. Blackfeet recreation permits are required for this option, available at the ranger station.

Aster Park

- Distance: 3.8 miles round-trip
- Duration: 2 hours
- Elevation gain: 610 feet
- Effort: easy
- Trailhead: adjacent to Two Medicine boat dock

Beginning on the south shore trail, Aster Park is reached via a spur trail just past Aster Creek. About 1.2 miles southwest of the boat dock, turn left at the signed junction and follow the trail past Aster Falls as it switchbacks up to a flower-covered knoll. This overlook provides grand views of Two Medicine Lake and Rising Wolf.

Rockwell Falls, Cobalt Lake, and Two Medicine Pass

- Distance: 6.8-15.8 miles round-trip
- Duration: 4-8 hours
- Elevation gain: minimal-2,518 feet

© BECKY LOMAX

Hikers get treated to views of Lone Walker on the Upper Two Medicine Lake trail.

- Effort: easy-strenuous
- Trailhead: adjacent to the Two Medicine boat dock

Follow the gentle south shore trail along Two Medicine Lake past beaver ponds and bear-scratched trees to Paradise Creek, where a swinging bridge makes you think of Indiana Jones movies, but it's not as scary. At 2.3 miles, turn left at the signed junction. The trail wanders through avalanche paths with up-rooted trees shredded like toothpicks. At 3.4 miles, you reach Rockwell Falls. Spur trails explore the falls.

Continuing on to Cobalt Lake, the trail climbs up several switchbacks into an upper basin, crossing the creek. Then it ascends at a moderate pitch for the last two miles. Tucked in the uppermost corner of the basin, Cobalt Lake sits below mountain-goat cliffs.

Another 2.2 miles climbs above the tree line through alpine tundra along the wind-blown Two Medicine Pass. From the highpoint atop Chief Lodgepole Mountain, you'll stare straight down a dizzying drop to Cobalt Lake with Two Medicine Lake in the distance.

Twin Falls and Upper Two Medicine Lake

- Distance: 1.8-10 miles round-trip
- Duration: 1-5 hours
- Elevation gain: 0-231 feet
- Effort: easy
- Trailhead: Two Medicine Lake west boat dock, or Pray Lake Bridge in Two Medicine Campground

Set in a subalpine bowl, Upper Two Medicine Lake is reached by a trail passing Twin Falls—a double flume of cascades. Taking the boat both ways on Two Medicine Lake shortens the hike: Twin Falls, 1.8 miles round-trip; the upper lake, 4.4 miles. Taking the boat one-way and hiking the remaining distance shortens the hike to 7.2 miles. For the longest route, you can hike both up and back on the north shore trail or loop around Two Medicine Lake.

The trail climbs gently, passing the short spur trail to Twin Falls. After crossing avalanche gullies thick with huckleberries, you'll crest a prominent rock ledge to the lake. If you are eating lunch at the lake, help maintain the safety of those sleeping in the backcountry campground here by not eating in the sleeping sites. Sit in the cooking area to eat, or in late season, hike up the north shoreline. Early season high water floods the beach.

Dawson-Pitamakin Loop

- Distance: 16.9 or 18.8 miles
- Duration: 7-9 hours
- Elevation gain: 2,909 feet
- Effort: strenuous
- Trailhead: Two Medicine Lake west boat dock, or Pray Lake Bridge in Two Medicine Campground

Although this loop can be done from either direction, both with the same elevation gain up to 8,000 feet, the approach to Dawson Pass is much steeper than to Pitamakin Pass. It crams all of its elevation gain within three miles, while Pitamakin Pass is less steep as the elevation gain is spread out over eight miles. So pick your route based on your preference or aversion to uphill grunts and knee-pounding descents. If you catch the Two Medicine boat one direction or the other, you'll chop off 1.9 miles.

In its loop around Rising Wolf, the route actually crosses three passes: Pitamakin, Cut Bank, and Dawson. The latter two passes have frequent winds that are sometimes strong enough to knock you off balance. Starting toward Pitamakin, the trail crosses Dry Fork and follows it up to Old Man Lake (6.8 miles), a good fishing lake, before climbing to the pass (8.8 miles), where you'll often see bighorn sheep. The narrow trail is exposed high on a several-mile goat traverse between Cut Bank and Dawson (12.1 miles) passes, and those with a fear of heights will be uncomfortable. For most, it's the best part of the trail, walking a tightrope between vertigo and soaring.

Medicine Grizzly Lake and Triple Divide Pass

- Distance: 12 or 14.4 miles round-trip
- Duration: 6-7.5 hours
- Elevation gain: 540 or 2,223 feet
- Effort: easy-strenuous
- Trailhead: terminus of Cut Bank Road
- Directions: Locate the signed Cut Bank Road six miles north of Kiowa Junction on U.S. 89. Follow the narrow dirt road over cattle grates into the park and past the ranger station. The trailhead is about four miles up just before the campground.

Due to its location up the rough Cut Bank Road, many hikers are deterred. But it's a popular trail for anglers as Medicine Grizzly Lake harbors 12-inch rainbows. Check with the ranger station before leaving, as bear activity frequently closes the lake and its spur trail. The trail follows Atlantic Creek up a forested drainage to a signed junction at four miles. Turn right, climbing 0.6 miles past the Atlantic Creek campground to the junction for the pass or lake. For Medicine Grizzly Lake, continue straight for 1.4 miles.

For Triple Divide Pass, climb north at the junction. The trail bursts out of the trees, traversing a rocky face below Mount James as it looks down on the lake. After winding into a large bowl, look for bighorn sheep frequently browsing. Tucked at the base of Triple Divide Peak, the pass actually stands on the split between the Saskatchewan and Missouri River drainages, beginning here as Hudson Bay Creek and Atlantic Creek.

Guides

The National Park Service guides free hikes mid-June-mid-September to a variety of destinations in Two Medicine: Upper Two Medicine Lake, Scenic Point, Dawson Pass, Rockwell Falls, and Cobalt Lake, as well as a daily boat ride and hike to Twin Falls. The hike is free, but you still need to pay for the boat ride. Grab a copy of *Ranger-led Activities* from the ranger station for the current schedule.

Glacier Guides (406/387-5555 or 800/521-7238, www.glacierguides.com) will pick you up at your lodge, transport you to the trailhead, and bring along a deli lunch and snacks. You just need to bring your pack, sunscreen, insect repellent, water, and extra clothes. You can hire a guide (June-Sept., $390-470). Solo travelers can also hook up with the Tuesday Hikes (July-Aug., $80 pp), which depart from the company's West Glacier office, an hour from East Glacier. The guide service also has 3-6-day backpacking trips (June-mid-Sept., $155 per day)—that depart weekly, some on routes out of Two Medicine. Reservations are mandatory.

CYCLING

Bicycling around the park's southeast corner is usually restricted to narrow, curvy, shoulderless roadways. Although most drivers are fairly courteous toward bicyclists, be prepared to have large RVs nearly shove you off the road, simply due to their size in comparison to the skimpy pavement. It's an area where you may encounter bears on the roadway, especially on Two Medicine Road; on Highway 49, with open range, you can round a corner into a small herd of cows. For some reason, no matter which direction you're riding, a strong headwind always blasts. Since mountain biking is not permitted on trails within Glacier, riding is restricted to roadways and, for kids, the campground loops. Bicyclists do day tours from East Glacier to Two Medicine Lake and back. Bike rentals are not available.

For bicyclists, Two Medicine Campground has shared hiker-biker campsites ($5 pp). These are reserved until 9pm for cyclists and have bear-resistant food storage containers on-site.

TRAIL RIDING

Across the street from Glacier Park Lodge on Highway 49, **Glacier Gateway Trailrides** (406/226-4408 or 406/338-5560, June-early Sept.) leads trail rides and cowboy-style horseback rides—ones that tour cross-country rather than riding single file. Led by Native American guides, the tours roam outside Glacier Park on adjacent Blackfeet Reservation land. Rides wander along Two Medicine River Gorge through aspens and blooms of early-season shooting stars and late-summer lupine—all at the foot of the park's front range. Rides lasting 1-3 hours depart several times daily ($30 pp per hour). Those dreaming of riding the open range rather than riding head-to-tail can take a full-day ride (minimum 6 people, $185 pp) to two buffalo jumps. Wear long pants and sturdy shoes, such as hiking boots or tennis shoes. Kids must be at least seven years old and have some experience riding. Reservations are recommended, especially in midsummer.

BOATING, CANOEING, AND KAYAKING

Two Medicine is the highest lake you can drive to in the park; it's also one of the windiest. Boaters need to keep an eye on waves; if whitecaps pop up, paddlers should consider getting off the lake. Two Medicine Road terminates at the public boat ramp, so it's easy to find. Hand-powered craft and up to 10-hp motorized boats are allowed, but Jet Skis are not allowed, so the lake maintains pleasant quiet. On calm days, kayakers and canoers tour the lake's shore. On Lower Two Medicine Lake, you won't see many boats. The lack of a boat ramp and no access trails preclude most visitors.

Boating regulations in Glacier Park require free permits for all boats, motorized and non-motorized. Boats must be cleaned, drained, and dried to avoid bringing aquatic invasive species into park lakes. Free permits are available at the Two Medicine Ranger Station.

Located at the Two Medicine boat dock, **Glacier Park Boat Company** (406/226-4467 summer, 406/257-2426, www.glacierparkboats.

© BECKY LOMAX

Paddlers tour Pray Lake to avoid winds on Two Medicine Lake.

com) rents canoes, kayaks, and small motorboats ($15-20 per hour, cash only).

FISHING

Two Medicine River links together the three lakes by the same name, with brook trout populating much of the water. For fishing **Upper Two Medicine Lake,** hike two miles after taking the boat shuttle across Two Medicine Lake. It's an attractive lake to fish, but its shoreline is brushy, and the outlet is clogged with downed timbers. Anglers in **Two Medicine Lake** may have more success tossing in a line from a boat rather than fishing from the heavily timbered and brushy shore. On the valley's south side, Paradise Creek harbors some trout, but Aster and Appistoki Creeks are empty. On the dam-controlled **Lower Two Medicine Lake,** half of which is in the park with the other half on the Blackfeet Reservation, only a few anglers go after the 10-12-inch rainbows and brookies due to difficult access with no public trails or boat ramp. Other area lakes—**No Name** and **Old Man**—support trout, but Cobalt is barren. In the Cut Bank Valley, **Medicine Grizzly Lake** lures anglers, but reality doesn't live up to legend, and the lake is frequently closed due to bear activity.

Licenses and Regulations

No fishing license is required inside Glacier Park, but pick up park fishing regulations at the ranger station in Two Medicine. On Lower Two Medicine Lake or Two Medicine River, you will need a Blackfeet fishing permit ($25 for 2 days, $75 for the season). Purchase Blackfeet fishing permits at **Bear Track Travel Center** (Exxon station, 20958 U.S. 2, East Glacier, 406/226-5504, daily 7am-10pm spring-fall, shorter hours winter).

GOLF

Built in 1927, the **Glacier Park Lodge Golf Course** (406/892-2525, tee times 406/226-5342, www.glacierparkinc.com, late May-Sept., 9 holes $20, 18 holes $30) is the oldest grass greens in Montana. The nine-hole course winds through aspen groves with views of Dancing Lady, Henry, Calf Robe, and Summit peaks. Don't be surprised if bears (or more commonly stray dogs) roam across the course. Because the course is on Blackfeet land, each hole is named after a former Blackfeet Nation chief—Rising Wolf, Bad Marriage, Long Time Sleeps, and Stabs-by-Mistake. You can rent clubs ($14-21) and power carts ($20-30).

A public nine-hole pitch-and-putt miniature golf course covers half of the front lawn of Glacier Park Lodge. Pick up clubs and a souvenir ball ($10 pp) at the front desk. Ground squirrel holes add challenge to the course.

CROSS-COUNTRY SKIING

Late December-April, **Two Medicine Road** (15 miles round-trip) makes a delightfully moderate but long ski, with frozen Two Medicine Lake as

© BECKY LOMAX

Anglers fish in Pray Lake near Two Medicine Campground.

the destination. Snow piles up enough to bury the restrooms. While the going is not tough and the gentle terrain undulates, except for one long hill, winds can scour the road free of snow in places, requiring skiers to take their skis off and walk. Headwinds also frequently blow in both directions. Nevertheless, it's a stunning trip, with relatively little avalanche danger.

When snow permits, skiing **Looking Glass Hill** on Highway 49 is also popular. An eight-mile round-trip tour leads from the junction with Two Medicine Road to spectacular overlooks of Two Medicine Valley and Lake Creek drainage to Divide Mountain by St. Mary. Sometimes winds blow the pavement bare, so be prepared to take your skis off and put them on again.

No equipment rentals are available in East Glacier; the nearest rentals are at the Izaak Walton Inn (milepost 179.7, U.S. 2, Essex). Be prepared for winter travel: Do not venture out without a complete pack full of emergency gear, ready for self-rescue.

ENTERTAINMENT

On summer evenings National Park Service naturalists present free 45-minute talks (usually 8pm daily) on natural history and wildlife in the Two Medicine Amphitheater. Once a week, the presentations feature **Native America Speaks**—storytellers who bring to life the history of local indigenous people and their involvement in Glacier. For a current schedule, pick up a copy of *Ranger-led Activities* at visitors centers and ranger stations.

Glacier Park Lodge sponsors entertainment from time to time—Native American speakers and entertainers as well as musicians such as the Trapp Family Singers. Check the sign in the lobby near the front desk for the current schedule.

North American Indian Days

Over four days beginning the second Thursday in July, North American Indian Days (406/338-7406, www.blackfeetcountry.com) celebrates

© BECKY LOMAX

The Blackfeet celebrate their culture at the annual North American Indian Days.

native culture in vibrant, stunning color. In Browning, behind the Museum of the Plains Indian, the powwow grounds (4th Ave. NW and Boundary St.) become home to tepees, dancing, drumming, singing, games, rodeos, horse racing, sporting events, food, and crafts. Hosted by the Blackfeet, this family event, which bans alcohol on the reservation for the duration, draws regional indigenous people from the United States and Canada. Traditional regalia show off exceptional craftsmanship with feathered headdresses and beadwork. Nonnative people are welcome to attend, and it's free to watch the performances and events.

Casino

Gaming and slot machines on the Blackfeet Reservation are at **Glacier Peaks Casino** (junction of U.S. 2 and U.S. 89, Browning, 406/338-2274 or 877/238-9946, http://glacierpeakscasino.com, 10am-2am daily). The 33,000-square-foot casino contains 300 slot machines, live poker, and a restaurant.

Accommodations

Two Medicine has no lodging, just a campground. But there are accommodations in East Glacier, located on the Blackfeet Reservation. You'll find motels, cabins, lodges, hostels; at **VRBO** (www.vrbo.com) there are vacation rentals that range from small cabins to large homes. Bring earplugs; some motel rooms catch the rumble and clatter of passing trains and trucks on the highway. On one side of the railroad tracks, historic Glacier Park Lodge is on Highway 49 along with a compact strip of motels—think very rustic, not a highway megastrip. On the south side of the tracks along U.S. 2, East Glacier has several motels within a few blocks of restaurants. All of these fill completely in midsummer, so reservations are strongly advised.

Lodges

Historic **Glacier Park Lodge** (1 Midvale Rd., 406/892-2525, front desk 406/226-5600, www.glacierparkinc.com, late May-late Sept., $140-471) is outside the park boundary on the Blackfeet Reservation right across from the train depot. It's the only historic park lodge with an outdoor swimming pool (heated, but still chilly), a golf course, and a pitch-and-putt. In the gigantic lobby, huge western red cedars hold aloft a several-story ceiling. The main lodge connects to guest rooms in the west wing via a scenic enclosed walkway. Get a room facing the mountains to enjoy the sunrises and sunsets casting orange glows. Lodge rooms, suites, and family rooms are available, along with a chalet. All guest rooms are

© BECKY LOMAX

Glacier Park Lodge was built by Great Northern Railway some 100 years ago.

nonsmoking. West wing guest rooms tend to be larger. Expect rustic—tiny baths converted from original closets, thin walls, slanted floors, cantankerous hot water, and no TV, Internet access, air-conditioning, or elevators; revel in the historical ambience instead. Reservations are strongly advised for June and September, and are an absolute must for July-August.

A restaurant, lounge, snack shop, and gift shop are near the lobby, and Remedies Day Spa offers massages for trail-weary muscles. Red-bus tours depart from the hotel, and trail riding is across the street. Trails to Scenic Point and Firebrand Pass depart nearby. In the evening, Native American speakers often give fireside talks.

Cabins

On the east edge of town, **Traveler's Rest Lodge** (20987 U.S. 2 E., 406/226-9143 summer, 406/378-2414 winter, http://travelersrest-lodge.net, May-Sept., $130-160 d) has clean, roomy, nonsmoking mortise-and-tenon log cabins with gas fireplaces and fully equipped kitchenettes amid aspen trees. Each is positioned so that its covered deck has privacy and views of the Bob Marshall Wilderness. The nicely decorated cabins sleep 2-4 in log-hewn beds; there are TVs and CD players but no phones (a phone is available in the office). In one of the cabins, owners Diane and Bob Scalese have their engraving workshop. They are well-known artisans who design, craft, and engrave spurs, bits, belt buckles, and saddle silver.

Located 1.5 miles from East Glacier, **Bison Creek Ranch B&B** (milepost 207.4, 20722 U.S. 2, 406/226-4482 or 888/226-4482, www.bison-creekranch.com, mid-May-Sept., $70-110 for 2 people, $12 for each additional person) combines rustic cabin stays with a continental breakfast. Remodeled one-bedroom Gandy Dancer cabins (built as bunkhouses for railroad repair workers) and two-bedroom A-frame chalets are spread among the firs and meadows. It appeals to those who want real quiet without phones, Internet access, or TVs but with electricity and private baths. Be ready for slow-arriving hot water. A small fishing stream runs nearby, and an on-site restaurant serves Western dinners.

Motels

East Glacier has seven basic older family-run motels, some with cabins and all within walking distance to restaurants, stores, and the train station. Advance reservations in midsummer are wise. Some motels offer pickups at the train depot.

Four summer-only motels line Highway 49's strip north of Glacier Park Lodge. The area hops in midsummer, but highway traffic virtually disappears at night. Train noise still filters through the trees to some of the motels. The **Mountain Pine Motel** (909 Hwy. 49, 406/226-4403, www.mtnpine.com, May-Sept., $75-175) offers 25 tidy guest rooms—some adjoining for families—lined up surrounding a lawn tucked under tall shady trees. The nonsmoking guest rooms have queen beds, wireless Internet access, and TVs. Spring and fall rates drop substantially. **East Glacier Motel and Cabins** (1107 Hwy. 49, 406/226-5593, www.eastglacier.com, June-Aug., $76-140) has six large motel rooms and 11 small cabins with private baths, and some with kitchenettes. Early in the season, the rates are lower.

In "downtown" East Glacier, south of the tracks, are three year-round motels. Rates are highest in summer and lowest in winter. The **Whistling Swan Motel** (512 U.S. 2, 406/226-4412 or 406/226-9227, www.whistlingswanmotel.com, from $68) is run by the same family that owns the Two Medicine Grill and the Trading Post. Their 10 pine-walled guest rooms offer various bed configurations, and you can get loads of advice from the owners on how to see Glacier. The **Dancing Bears Inn** (40 Montana Ave., 406/226-4402, http://dancingbearsinn.com, $90-190) received a facelift to the exterior in 2012. Its 16 guest rooms come with continental breakfast and wireless Internet access. Some guest rooms have kitchenettes.

Guesthouses

Art aficionados can rent a room from a professional potter and sculptor at **The Brown House** (402 Washington St., 406/226-9385, June-Sept., $75 d), which has three remodeled nonsmoking guest rooms, each furnished with antiques and with a private entrance and bath. The upstairs guest room has a view of the park's peaks. Originally a 1920s store, the building still has some of the fixtures from that era. The gift shop also sells the works of local artisans.

Hostels

For budget travelers, East Glacier has two hostels open May-September. Located one block from the train depot, **Backpacker's Inn** (29 Dawson Ave., 406/226-9392, www.serranosmexican.com) has three dorms ($12 pp), plus two cabins ($30) located in the backyard of Serrano's Mexican Restaurant—a little outdoor oasis in the middle of town that serves as a common area. The buildings are renovated original 1920 prefab cedar Sears and Roebuck homes. Bring your own sleeping bag for the beds in the dorm rooms; the cabins have one queen bed. **Brownie's Hostel** (1020 Hwy. 49, 406/226-4426, www.brownieshostel.com) is in a renovated old two-story 1908 building that used to house railroad workers. An easy six-block walk from the train station and adjacent to restaurants, the hostel has a fully equipped communal kitchen and three dorms ($20 pp). Private bedrooms ($22-40) are also available. Cinnamon rolls scent the air in the morning from the downstairs bakery. It also has a deli and a convenience store with Internet access.

CAMPING

RVers requiring hookups will need to stay in East Glacier or Browning, as Glacier Park campgrounds have no hookups. If the campgrounds are full, check the Marias Pass and Essex districts.

Glacier Park Campgrounds

Two National Park Service campgrounds are

© BECKY LOMAX

Brownie's offers a store and deli downstairs and hostel upstairs.

in Glacier's southeast corner—one with easy paved access and the other via a dirt road. Both offer campsites outfitted with picnic tables and fire rings with grills. Bring your own firewood; gathering wood in the park is prohibited. All campsites are first come, first served.

Two Medicine Campground (406/888-7800, late May-late Sept., $20) yields views of bears foraging on Rising Wolf Mountain, especially from the A and C loops. In early summer, ruby-crowned kinglets call out "teacher, teacher" from the trees. The campground is set back from Two Medicine Lake, surrounding the calmer waters of small Pray Lake, a good place for paddling and chilly swimming or fishing. With 99 sites, the campground fills up in midsummer, but often not as early in the day as those on Going-to-the-Sun Road; try to claim a campsite by early afternoon. Tenters should choose sheltered sites due to abrupt high winds that can flatten tents. Flush toilets, water, and a dump station are provided. The north shore trail departs right from the campground, leading in both directions around Rising Wolf Mountain. A seven-minute walk or a several-minute drive puts you at the boat tour and rental dock, and the Two Medicine Campstore can cover what you've forgotten. Only 13 sites can handle RVs up to 32 feet. In late September-October, the campground allows primitive camping ($10) with pit toilets and no water.

Located 19 miles north of East Glacier on U.S. 89, **Cut Bank Campground** (406/888-7800, early June-early Sept., $10) is at the end of a five-mile potholed dirt road. The campsites can only accommodate very small RVs, and trailers are not recommended. To locate the road, look for the campground sign six miles north of Kiowa Junction. The ultra-quiet campground is rustic, with only pit toilets and no running water. Atlantic Creek runs nearby, but you'll need to filter the water or boil it for five minutes. With only 14 sites set in deep shade under large firs, it's a great place to escape the crowds. The campground has fishing in Atlantic Creek as well as the nearby trailhead to Medicine Grizzly Lake and Triple Divide Pass.

Glacier Park Backcountry Camping

Two Medicine has plenty of backcountry campsites that work as good destinations for kids as well as connections on the Continental Divide Trail. For kids, reduce the mileage by using the boat and head to **Upper Two Medicine** or **Cobalt Lake.** Those backpacking the Dawson-Pitamakin Loop will need permits for camping at **No Name** and **Old Man Lake.** Those backpacking the Continental Divide Trail to St. Mary will want to continue on to **Morningstar,** with its lake tucked against a cliff wall with a golden eagle nest and mountain goats, before hitting **Atlantic Creek** and **Red Eagle Lake.** Pick up permits ($5 pp per night, ages 8-15 $2.50, under age 8 free) in person 24 hours in advance at Two Medicine Ranger Station or the Apgar Permit Office (406/888-7900). Advance reservations ($30) are available online (www.nps.gov/glac).

East Glacier

A small campground on three acres on the Blackfeet Reservation, **Y Lazy R RV Park** (junction of Lindhe Ave. and Meade St., 406/226-5505, mid-May-Sept., tents $20, hookups $25) is two blocks off U.S. 2. With only a few aspen trees, its open rough grass and dirt setting overlooks Midvale Creek and affords big views of surrounding mountains. Amenities include flush toilets, picnic tables, coin-op showers, a dump station, a large laundry, and hookups for electricity, water, and sewer. The campground is an easy few blocks' walk from restaurants.

Browning

On a prairie wildflower knoll west of Browning in view of Glacier's peaks, the **Lodgepole Gallery and Tipi Village** (U.S. 89, 2.5 miles west of Browning, 406/338-2787, www.blackfeetculturecamp.com, May-Sept., $60 for the first person, $15 each additional person, under age 12 $10) is different—and not just because a small herd of nearly extinct Spanish mustangs, the original Indian horse, runs free on the property (they're not for riding, just for watching). Ten traditional double-walled canvas tepees with a fire pit inside each serve as tents. Supplied wood heats the tepees on cooler nights. Bring your sleeping bag, air mattress, and flashlight, or rent them ($10). A central bathhouse with flush toilets and showers serves all the tepees. Meals—breakfast or a traditional southern Blackfeet dinner—are available by reservation. A Blackfeet art gallery and art classes are available on-site. The owners can arrange Blackfeet-guided tours, fishing trips, and horseback riding.

West of Browning, with views of Glacier's eastern front range, **Aspenwood Resort** (U.S. 89, 9.5 miles west of Browning or 2.3 miles east of Kiowa Junction, 406/338-3009, www.aspenwoodresort.com, mid-May-mid-Oct., $18-35) is on the Blackfeet Reservation with two beaver ponds that offer fishing, paddleboating, wildlife-watching, and walking. The campground includes flush toilets, hookups for electricity and water, tent and RV campsites, showers, a disposal station, and a restaurant. The resort also arranges for Native American-guided fishing trips, tours, and horseback riding. Reservations are required for powwow weekends. Pets and horses are welcome.

Food

Because Two Medicine has no restaurants, campers must hit East Glacier to dine out. During special days on the Blackfeet Reservation, such as graduation and North American Indian Days, none of the restaurants, groceries, or bars serves alcohol, including East Glacier. The four-day celebration is usually scheduled beginning the second Thursday in July.

EAST GLACIER

The town is small, so you can walk to restaurants from your accommodations.

Lodges

In the historic Glacier Park Lodge, the **Great Northern Steak and Rib House** (1 Midvale Rd., 406/892-2525, front desk 406/226-5600, late May-late Sept.) has the best views of any restaurant in town. Ask to be seated near the west windows facing Dancing Lady Mountain: The sunrise smears it with pink, and the sunset casts orange alpenglow across its face. The nonsmoking restaurant serves up three meals per day with a menu similar to all the park lodges. It has kids' menus too. Breakfast (6:30am-10am daily, $7-15) has two options—a huge buffet or á la carte. The buffet has stacks of fruit, pastries, eggs, sausage, bacon, french toast, and pancakes. You won't walk away hungry, but the mass-produced entrées are sometimes only lukewarm. Dinner (5pm-9:30pm daily, $15-27) specializes in prime rib, steak, chicken, fish, and pasta. Vegetarian dishes are available. The restaurant doesn't take reservations, so high season can mean waiting lines. Order hiker sack lunches ($9) one day in advance. Adjacent to the restaurant, the **Sunset Lounge** (11:30am-midnight daily, $8-15), also known as the Empire Bar, serves up Montana microbrews, wine, and cocktails. Lunch is served in the lounge rather than the dining room; the windows yield a terrific view of Dancing Lady and Mount Henry. You can get salads, sandwiches, burgers, and appetizers, including healthier options, for lunch or dinner.

Located 1.5 miles west of East Glacier, **Bison Creek Ranch** (20722 U.S. 2, 406/226-4482 or 888/226-4482, 5pm-9pm daily May-Sept., $7-25) has served up the Schauf family's Western home cooking since the 1950s. The house favorite is fried chicken, but you can also get burgers, steaks, and fish. Come hungry because dinners are large, complete with a salad bar, soups, homemade bread, veggies, and ice cream.

Mexican

Waiting lines on the front porch of **Serrano's Mexican Restaurant** (29 Dawson Ave., 406/226-9392, www.serranosmexican.com, 5pm-10pm daily May-Sept., $8-18) attest to its tasty food. The made-from-scratch Veggie Delight and Enchilada Especial top the choices of house specialties. Nachos as appetizers and huge plate-loads of food pacify hungry hikers. The smoke-free building is the oldest house in East Glacier; you can eat inside its cozy dining room with wooden booths or sit on the deck out back while watching the sunset. Either way, the margaritas go down easy.

Cafés

Open year-round, **Two Medicine Grill** (314 U.S. 2, 406/226-9227, www.whistlingswanmotel.com, 6:30am-9pm daily spring-fall, closes earlier daily winter, $7-18) is a local hangout for diner-type breakfast, gooey homemade cinnamon rolls, bison burgers, and wild huckleberry shakes. You can sit on one of the eight stools at the bar to grill owner Mark Howser about hiking trails, or eat in the tiny dining room. The funky diner was built in Choteau in 1935 but was moved to East Glacier.

© BECKY LOMAX

Serrano's Mexican Restaurant sometimes runs a special of bison tacos.

The **Glacier Village Cafe** (304 U.S. 2 E., 406/226-4464, www.glaciervillagecafe.com, 7am-9pm daily June-Sept., $7-20) is one place you can get vegetarian and low-fat meals. The café—run by the owners of Izaak Walton Inn—serves breakfast, lunch, and dinner daily, with specialties such as buffalo brats, wraps, entrée-size salads, and buffalo meatloaf. You can also get beer, wine, and picnic lunches.

The **Whistle Stop Restaurant** (1024 Hwy. 49, 406/226-9292, 7am-9pm daily June-Sept., $6-24) is in a funky and rickety-looking old building with outside seating in good weather. The breakfast specialty is french toast stuffed with huckleberries or hazelnut-vanilla filling. For kids, the Grizzly Paw French toast is served with chocolate sauce. The house dinner features barbecue ribs and chicken in different styles and portions. Beer and wine are available, and the huckleberry pie is a must.

Luna's Restaurant (1112 Hwy. 49, 406/226-4433, 6:30am-9pm daily mid-May-Sept., $6-18) serves up café fare with popular biscuits and gravy. Unique offerings such as zucchini fries, Indian tacos, wasabi coleslaw, and bison brats add to menu favorites, as well as home-fried red potato chips. Luna's huckleberry pie is made with a graham cracker crust and a cream cheese layer. Food is not precooked, so expect a wait. The restaurant does not have an alcohol license, but you can bring in your own beer and wine for dinner.

CAFFEINE

Espresso is ubiquitous in East Glacier, with caffeine jolts available in multiple locations. The two places that can make espresso drinks beyond the basic latte order are the **Two Medicine Grill** (314 U.S. 2, 406/226-9227, www.whistlingswanmotel.com, 6:30am-9pm daily spring-fall, closes earlier daily winter) and **Brownie's** (1020 Hwy. 49, 406/226-4426, www.brownieshostel.com, 7am-9pm daily June-Sept.).

GROCERIES

A small grocery and two convenience stores in East Glacier can provide supplies for your trip, but for full-size grocery stores, you'll need to head 12 miles east to Browning: In 2012 the Blackfeet opened the new **Glacier Family Foods** (601 SE Boundary St., Browning, 406/338-7283). On the Blackfeet Reservation, alcohol sales are banned during graduation and North American Indian Days.

Two East Glacier stores sell groceries daily year-round. **Glacier Park Trading Company** (316 U.S. 2 E., 406/226-9227, www.seeglacier.com, 8am-9pm daily summer, 9am-8pm daily winter) sells fresh veggies, dairy products, wine, meat, and staples. It also carries a broad selection of Montana microbrews. The deli makes sandwiches good for hiker lunches as well as pizzas to go. The **Bear Track Travel Center** (Exxon station, 20958 U.S. 2, 406/226-5504, 7am-8pm daily winter, 7am-10pm daily summer) sells convenience-store foods, ice, firewood, camping and fishing supplies, beer and wine, propane, and fishing licenses. In summer, **Brownie's Bakery and Deli** (1020 Hwy. 49, 406/226-4426, www.brownieshostel.com, 7am-9pm daily June-Sept.) is an everything place—a bakery, a deli, a convenience store, an ice cream shop, an espresso stand, and an Internet café. It's a great place to pick up a deli sandwich for hiking or grab a light breakfast of muffins or bagels. The bakery churns out cookies and brownies.

On the shore of Two Medicine Lake, **Two Medicine General Store** (end of Two Medicine Rd., 406/892-2525, 7am-9pm daily mid-June-mid-Sept.) now operates in what used to be the historic dining hall for Two Medicine Chalets. It sells a few groceries, camping and hiking supplies, newspapers, maps, gifts, books, beer, wine, ice, and ice cream. Hikers can build a trail lunch from convenience items.

PICNIC AREA

Two Medicine has the only picnic area, adjacent to the campground. With running water and flush toilets, it is in a scenic spot right on the shore of Two Medicine Lake amid cottonwoods. Most of the sites have some trees, which provide a good windbreak on days when the wind howls and scant shade on hot days. Sites include a picnic table and a fire ring with a grill, but bring your own firewood; it's illegal to gather wood here.

MARIAS PASS AND ESSEX

The Theodore Roosevelt Highway (U.S. 2) runs 2,119 miles from Minnesota to Washington; 57 of its miles border Glacier National Park. Tiny, rustic mountain enclaves dot the route. Both Marias Pass and Essex gained their notoriety through the railroad: Marias Pass as the route chosen for the railroad to cross the Continental Divide, Essex as a train community to work the tracks. The history of this Rocky Mountain corridor, as much as its scenery, adds to its appeal.

Running through John F. Stevens Canyon, the year-round highway accesses wild country. With 1.5 million acres of the Bob Marshall Wilderness Complex to the south and Glacier's one million acres to the north, the road bisects the largest grizzly bear habitat in the Lower 48. The Middle Fork of the Flathead River, designated a Wild and Scenic River, races through the canyon, creating a playground for rafters, kayakers, and anglers. The canyon also draws mountain goats in search of minerals and bighorn sheep and elk for wintering. From this passageway, most of Glacier is only accessible on foot. Hikers soak up solitude on remote trails, while horseback riders, anglers, and hunters dive into the Bob Marshall Wilderness.

Backwoodsy and removed from the accoutrements of civilization, the southern route around Glacier is devoid of stores and fast-food restaurants. Services are few and far between. Most visitors just drive through, but for hikers, anglers, and river floaters, it's an area rich with recreation.

© BECKY LOMAX

HIGHLIGHTS

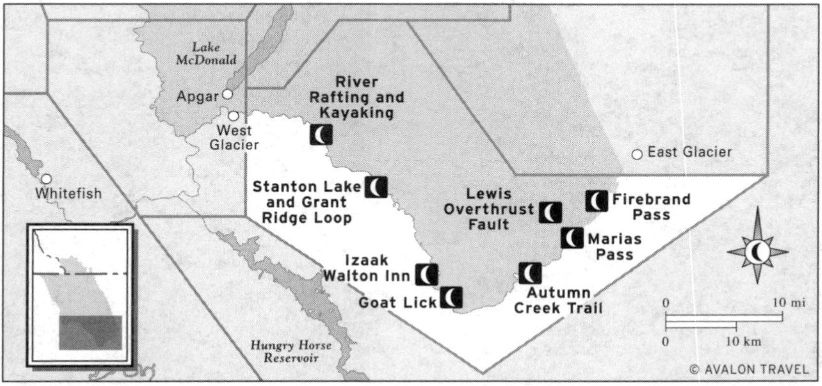

LOOK FOR TO FIND RECOMMENDED SIGHTS, ACTIVITIES, DINING, AND LODGING.

Marias Pass: Drive over the Continental Divide on one of the lowest passes through the Rockies. From the pass, peaks sweep up above 8,000 feet, revealing remarkable geology (page 183).

Lewis Overthrust Fault: Catapult back in time 65 million years to when the Lewis Overthrust pushed older rock on top of younger sediments. See this stone story in the cliff face along Summit and Little Dog Mountains (page 184).

Goat Lick: Mountain goats congregate for minerals May-early July at the Goat Lick. Bring your binoculars to see the shaggy white beasts strutting across death-defying cliffs (page 184).

Izaak Walton Inn: Stop for lunch at the historic inn that used to house Great Northern Railway workers. The hotel now attracts train aficionados, cross-country skiers, and those looking for a taste of history (page 185).

Firebrand Pass: Climb uphill through wildflowers. Fields below the pass may make you want to break out in songs from *The Sound of Music* (page 187).

Stanton Lake and Grant Ridge Loop: Hike in the Great Bear Wilderness to one of the best panoramic views of the park's southern monoliths. You'll spot Stimson, Jackson, and St. Nicholas (page 190).

River Rafting and Kayaking: Float the Middle Fork of the Flathead River below the Goat Lick. You'll stare up at the nimble creatures cavorting along the cliffs (page 191).

Autumn Creek Trail: Cross-country ski or snowshoe beneath the ramparts of Marias Pass. Elk Mountain and Little Dog make a dramatic backdrop for the trail, which winds through lodgepole pine forest (page 194).

HISTORY

Marias Pass

When Lewis and Clark passed through Montana in 1805, they failed to find Marias Pass. They came within 25 miles but swung south on the Missouri River to cross the Continental Divide on a much higher and more difficult pass. Lewis named the Marias River, calling it "Maria's River" after his cousin. The apostrophe got lost through history, much like the pass with the same name.

Reports of a "lost" pass filtered through

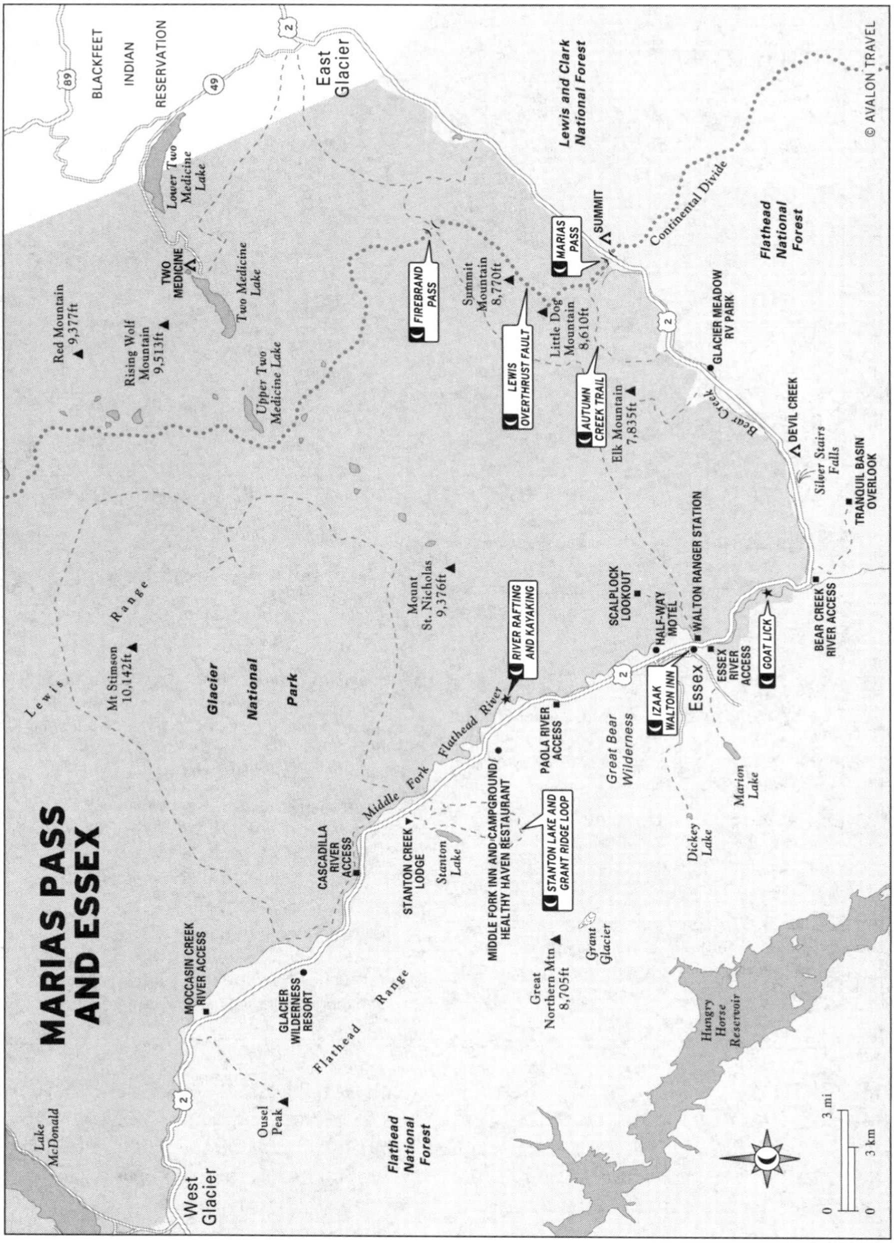
MARIAS PASS AND ESSEX
BLACKFEET INDIAN RESERVATION
East Glacier
West Glacier
Lower Two Medicine Lake
TWO MEDICINE
Two Medicine Lake
Upper Two Medicine Lake
Red Mountain 9,377ft
Rising Wolf Mountain 9,513ft
FIREBRAND PASS
Summit Mountain 8,770ft
LEWIS OVERTHRUST FAULT
Little Dog Mountain 8,610ft
MARIAS PASS
SUMMIT
Continental Divide
Lewis and Clark National Forest
AUTUMN CREEK TRAIL
Elk Mountain 7,835ft
GLACIER MEADOW RV PARK
Bear Creek
DEVIL CREEK
Silver Stairs Falls
TRANQUIL BASIN OVERLOOK
Flathead National Forest
Lewis Range
Mt Stimson 10,142ft
Glacier National Park
Mount St. Nicholas 9,376ft
RIVER RAFTING AND KAYAKING
SCALPLOCK LOOKOUT
HALF-WAY MOTEL
WALTON RANGER STATION
BEAR CREEK RIVER ACCESS
GOAT LICK
ESSEX RIVER ACCESS
Essex
IZAAK WALTON INN
Middle Fork Flathead River
PAOLA RIVER ACCESS
Great Bear Wilderness
Marion Lake
Dickey Lake
MIDDLE FORK INN AND CAMPGROUND/ HEALTHY HAVEN RESTAURANT
STANTON LAKE AND GRANT RIDGE LOOP
CASCADILLA RIVER ACCESS
STANTON CREEK LODGE
Stanton Lake
Great Northern Mtn 8,705ft
Grant Glacier
MOCCASIN CREEK RIVER ACCESS
GLACIER WILDERNESS RESORT
Flathead Range
Ousel Peak
Lake McDonald
Hungry Horse Reservoir
Flathead National Forest
0 3 mi
0 3 km
© AVALON TRAVEL
2
49
89

the ranks of fur traders and mountain men. Government-funded expeditions went looking, but to no avail, while mountain men and Native Americans wandered through the real Marias Pass—yet "undiscovered." Rumors of the pass reached Great Northern Railroad developer J. J. Hill, prompting him to dispatch railroad engineer John F. Stevens and his Flathead guide Coonsa to see if the fable was true. While temperatures plummeted to -40° in December 1889, the pair traveled on rawhide snowshoes through deep snow. Unable to slog on, Coonsa stayed behind with a fire as Stevens ventured on solo. He found the lost pass, deeming it appropriate for the railroad crossing. Within two years, Hill had a rail line built across the Continental Divide at Marias Pass in his push to complete his transcontinental railroad.

Building a Highway

As auto travel enchanted Americans, the demand for a road through John F. Stevens Canyon rose to a clamor. To transport an auto over the Continental Divide, you had to cough up $12.50 to put your car on a Great Northern Railway flatbed. While building Going-to-the-Sun Road dragged on for 20 years, the road over Marias Pass went through in a jiffy. Finished in 1930, the road over Marias Pass was much easier to build than chipping a route through the cliffs over Logan Pass.

Lodges

In 1906 the Great Northern Railway built Summit Station at Marias Pass as one of its early depots. When Glacier Park Lodge and its depot in East Glacier attracted more visitors, Summit's use died.

In 1939, Great Northern Railway constructed Izaak Walton Inn to house railroad workers who cleared the tracks of snow in winter. The railroad planned to convert it to guest lodging when the park service built a southern road entrance into Glacier. When the Depression and World War II sent park visitation plummeting, the park scrapped the south entrance. Today, Glacier's southern valleys remain remote bastions of wilderness, accessible only by trail, some only after fording the Middle Fork. The building eventually became an inn, but not under the Great Northern Railway's umbrella.

Exploring Marias Pass and Essex

With 2.5 million acres of public lands surrounding U.S. 2—Glacier National Park, Lewis and Clark National Forest, Flathead National Forest, and the Bob Marshall Wilderness Complex—only small strips of private land line the valley floor. The result is a necklace of tiny mountain communities, none barely large enough to warrant the title of "village." Truly, if you blink, you will miss them.

SEASONAL CONCERNS

U.S. 2 is considerably easier to maintain than Going-to-the-Sun Road. It is wider, more gradual, and for the most part, follows a fairly long, gentle 2,000-foot ascent from West Glacier to Marias Pass. However, even though Marias Pass is 1,500 feet lower than Logan Pass, winter still poses difficulties. While plows clear and sand the road frequently to keep it passable for winter travel, cornices thousands of feet above break loose, sending avalanches careening down across its path. In some winters the highway is closed for several days while road crews clear a path through ice, rock, and tree debris.

SHUTTLES AND TOURS

No hiker shuttles regularly run along U.S. 2. You either have to drive yourself to trailheads or use your thumb, which is legal in Montana. By reservation, you can arrange for a shuttle with **Flathead-Glacier Transportation** (406/892-3390 or 800/829-7039). They take backpackers hiking point-to-point trails, dropping you off at one trailhead and picking you up at another several days later ($40-140 one-way for one person, $3 for each additional person). The company also runs shuttles to Izaak Walton Inn ($90).

The historic **red buses** run by Glacier Park Inc. (406/892-2525 www.glacierparkinc.com, mid-June-mid-Sept., adults $85-90, children $43-45) drive a loop around Going-To-The-Sun Road, Logan Pass, and Marias Pass on their eight-hour tour. Buses originating in East Glacier can pick up riders at Glacier Meadows RV Park or Izaak Walton Inn.

SERVICES

This 60-mile corridor through wild untamed wilderness is a road where the usually expected conveniences of civilization are not available. You won't find gas stations between East Glacier and West Glacier; fill up in either of those towns before you leave.

While you can find some newspapers sold in the inns and restaurants along the highway, you'll need to head to East Glacier or West Glacier for ATMs, laundry, and anything resembling espresso. **The Half Way Restaurant** (14840 U.S. 2 E., Essex, 406/888-5650, www.thehalfwaymotel.com) runs the Essex post office. For hot showers ($5), you can pop in to Glacier Meadow RV Park or Glacier Haven Campground.

Even though U.S. 2 lacks many services, public restrooms are plentiful. Most are vault toilets with no running water and are open spring-fall. Find these at all river access points, Walton Picnic Area, the Goat Lick, and Marias Pass.

For maps, guidebooks, and information on outdoor activities in the Great Bear Wilderness and the Bob Marshall, contact the **Hungry Horse Ranger Station** (10 Hungry Horse Dr., Hungry Horse, 406/387-3800, www.fs.fed.us/r1/flathead), nine miles west of West Glacier. It is the place for information on river rafting, fishing, hiking, hunting, and horse packing in the national forest. For Lewis and Clark National Forest information, call the Rocky Mountain Ranger Station (1102 Main Ave. NW, Choteau, 406/466-5341, www.fs.fed.us/r1/lewisclark).

Cell Phones and Internet

Because of John F. Stevens Canyon and surrounding steep mountains, you'll find cell reception intermittent to nonexistent on U.S. 2, but you can stop to use old-fashioned public pay telephones at Stanton Creek Lodge, Izaak Walton Inn, and Snow Slip Inn. The nearest Internet services are in East Glacier and West Glacier, as well as Glacier Meadow RV Park, Snow Slip Inn, and Izaak Walton Inn.

Emergencies

For highway or river emergencies, call 911. A seasonal **Urgent Care Clinic** (100 Rea Rd., West Glacier, 406/888-9224, 9am-4pm daily Memorial Day-Labor Day) operates in West Glacier. Regional hospitals in Flathead Valley include **Kalispell Regional Medical Center** (310 Sunny View Lane, Kalispell, 406/752-5111) and **North Valley Hospital** (1600 Hospital Way, Whitefish, 406/863-3500). The east side is served by the **Blackfeet Community Hospital** (760 Government Square, Browning, 406/338-6154).

The **Walton Ranger Station** (milepost 180.5, U.S. 2, 406/888-7800), at Walton Picnic Area on the southernmost tip of Glacier National Park, is staffed only in summer, and not full time, as the rangers patrol miles of backcountry trails. If you need assistance, use the pay phone at Izaak Walton Inn (0.8 miles west of the Walton Ranger Station) to call Glacier Park Headquarters (406/888-7800).

PUBLIC LANDS: WHAT'S THE DIFFERENCE?

Many people find it confusing to differentiate the various types of public land. In the greater Glacier ecosystem, national park lands border national forests and wilderness areas. National parks, national forests, and wilderness areas are each managed with different purposes:

- **National parks** fall under the U.S. Department of the Interior. Parks are set aside for their historical, geological, cultural, or biological significance and are geared toward public recreation. Hunting is not permitted, nor is picking mushrooms or berries for commercial use. Mining and logging are also taboo. Leases for developing recreation like ski resorts are not available. Generally, dogs are not allowed on trails; neither are mountain bikes. Permits are needed for backcountry camping.
- **National forests** come under the U.S. Department of Agriculture. Hunting, timber harvesting, and commercial berry picking are generally allowed by permit. National forest land is leased for recreational development, such as ski areas. Your pooch can go with you on hikes; you can mountain bike as long as no special designation says otherwise. Permits are not needed for backcountry camping.
- **Wilderness areas** are administered usually by the national forest that contains the wilderness boundaries. Two concepts set wilderness apart: no mechanical transportation and no permanent human inhabitants. Wilderness areas do not have roads inside them. While hunting is permitted and Fido can go along on the trail, mountain biking is not allowed. Permits are not needed for backcountry camping.

DRIVING TOUR

U.S. 2

After driving the dramatic Going-to-the-Sun Road, most visitors are less impressed with this southern highway. But this two-lane road still has gorgeous scenery. The drive from East Glacier to West Glacier takes 70 minutes or so. Locals use the road as a faster route across the Continental Divide when too many cars clog Going-to-the-Sun Road in midsummer. Large RVs and trailers must use it, as they are banned from driving Going-to-the-Sun Road. You can start from East Glacier or West Glacier.

You'll see several white crosses along this highway. One cross equals one traffic fatality. Begun in 1953, the American Legion-sponsored program works with the Montana Department of Transportation to use the crosses as safety reminders. An estimated 2,000 sobering crosses line the state's highways.

SIGHTS

U.S. 2 sights are listed here from East Glacier to West Glacier.

Lewis and Clark National Forest

From south of East Glacier to Marias Pass, U.S. 2 passes through the Lewis and Clark National Forest. Its 1.7 million acres serve as the headwaters for the mighty Missouri River. High prairies at 4,500 feet in elevation climb up to Rocky Mountain Peak, at 9,362 feet, along the Rocky Mountain Front in an extremely diverse ecosystem that is home to species like lynx and grizzly bears. Around milepost 198, you'll get good views south of 46,000 burned acres from the 2007 Skyland Fire.

Marias Pass

At 5,220 feet, Marias Pass (milepost 197.9) is the lowest Continental Divide saddle north of New Mexico. Two monuments mark the pass: A statue of John F. Stevens commemorates his discovery of the route for the railroad, and a tall obelisk stands in memory of Theodore Roosevelt, for whom the highway is named. Legend has it that he visited Many Glacier in 1910, but no official records indicate that. At

© BECKY LOMAX

The Marias Pass obelisk commemorates Theodore Roosevelt.

the pass, the 3,100-mile Continental Divide Trail crosses into Glacier National Park, where hikers and skiers launch onto Autumn Creek Trail. With the area's broad flat forest, you'd be hard-pressed to realize you were crossing the Continental Divide.

Lewis Overthrust Fault

Opposite Marias Pass, the Lewis Overthrust Fault shoved older 1.6-billion-year-old rocks on top of 80-million-year-old stones. This fault exposed some of the oldest sediments in North America—ancient Precambrian rocks that formed as Belt Sea sediments solidified. On the face of Summit and Little Dog Peaks, look for an obvious upward line where the younger Cretaceous rock from the dinosaur age shows up as black or brown. This is the site where in the 1890s geologists discovered the Lewis Overthrust Fault, which extends into Canada and sets Glacier apart as a World Heritage Site.

Silver Stairs Falls

Tumbling thousands of feet, an unmarked and unsigned pullout on the highway's south side stares up Silver Stairs Falls (milepost 188.2). The waterfall cascades down stair steps created from eroding sedimentary layers. In June-July, water rages down in torrents, but by late August it slows to a trickle. You can catch a glimpse with a drive-by, but with trees surrounding the falls, you'll get a better view by stopping.

Goat Lick

Much of Glacier National Park's wildlife tends to be mineral deficient. Because their bodies crave minerals from their winter-deprived condition, during spring and early summer mountain goats congregate at the Goat Lick (milepost 182.6). The lick is actually a huge mass of gray rock cliffs, an exposed fault containing salts like calcium, magnesium, and potassium. Goats hop surefooted along the steep cliff faces as if they

© BECKY LOMAX

Mountain goats craving minerals congregate at the Goat Lick.

were on flat land to slurp the minerals. The well-marked overlook has a couple of viewing areas with interpretive signs. Bring your binoculars for better viewing. You can also catch sight of the goats on the slopes above the Goat Lick bridge on the highway.

Bob Marshall Wilderness Complex

While Glacier rises to the north of the highway, to the south the Bob Marshall Wilderness Complex spans nearly 1.5 million acres. It actually comprises three wilderness areas: the Bob (as locals call it), the Great Bear, and the Scapegoat. The Great Bear is the section bordering U.S. 2. The Bob Marshall was one of the country's first wilderness areas, dedicated in 1964 concurrent with the Wilderness Act. Scapegoat was added in 1972, and Great Bear six years later. While roads do not enter the wilderness areas and mechanized vehicles are prohibited (no mountain bikes or snowmobiles), a plethora of trails lead off U.S. 2. Short day hikes access the Great Bear, while longer overnight treks reach the Bob, a world-class area for horse packing, fishing, and big-game hunting.

Izaak Walton Inn

Listed on the National Register of Historic Places, Izaak Walton Inn (milepost 179.7) is opposite the southernmost point of Glacier National Park at Essex. The hotel stands adjacent to the train tracks, luring train aficionados, cross-country skiers, and those looking for something a bit different, like sleeping in a renovated caboose. Loaded with historical photos and memorabilia, the inn makes you feel almost like you've been transported back to a different era. In the downstairs bar, check out photos of avalanches burying the railroad tracks. Eat lunch on Great Northern Railway plates in the small dining room, and cozy up to the warm lobby fire.

BOB MARSHALL WILDERNESS COMPLEX

The largest wilderness area in Montana, the Bob Marshall Wilderness Complex straddles 1.5 million acres along 110 miles of the Continental Divide. It is home to a huge ungulate population of deer, elk, moose, mountain goats, and bighorn sheep. They feed predators like lynx, grizzlies, black bears, mountain lions, and wolves. Over 1,000 miles of trails crisscross its ranges, with peaks reaching 9,000 feet high. The 1,000-foot-high Chinese Wall escarpment runs for 22 miles along the Continental Divide.

The complex is named for Bob Marshall, a young forester who became a local legend in 1925 with marathon 30-mile mountain treks around the Missoula area. Later, he penned *The Problem of Wilderness*, a treatise defining principles that would shape the movement to preserve the country's wildlands. In a one-man crusade as the U.S. Forest Service's Lands Division chief, he placed 5.4 million acres of vulnerable land under wilderness protection. Along with Aldo Leopold and others, he launched the Wilderness Society in 1935, but he died four years later at age 38.

In 1941, the South Fork, Pentagon, and Sun River areas south of Glacier were set aside as primitive zones, and finally, after 66 drafts, the 1964 Wilderness Act protected them from development. As part of the act, the three primitive-zone areas were combined to create the one-million-acre **Bob Marshall Wilderness.**

Unprecedented lobbying by a citizens group from the town of Lincoln led by a hardware store owner resulted in the adjacent **Scapegoat Wilderness,** adding 239,936 acres to the south end of the area in 1972. Scapegoat is home to 50 miles of the 3,100-mile-long Continental Divide Trail. Six years later, a third wilderness area was added to the complex—the **Great Bear Wilderness,** adding 286,700 acres of land to the northwest. Tucked between Hungry Horse Reservoir and Glacier National Park, the Great Bear has 300 miles of trail and the elevation tops out at 8,700 feet on Great Northern, the sweeping peak seen from Flathead Valley.

Together these three wilderness areas, along with Glacier National Park, provide 2.5 million acres of habitat for species such as grizzly bears, lynx, and wolves. The wilderness complex is managed jointly by Flathead, Lewis and Clark, Lolo, and Helena National Forests.

Mount St. Nicholas

The toothy 9,376-foot spire of St. Nicholas is easy to pick out on the skyline—especially when rimmed with winter snow. Look for a notched spire with precipitous cliffs on its southern face. Get good views of this forbidding-looking peak driving eastward on U.S. 2. For more in-your-face views, hike Grant Ridge Loop counterclockwise or climb to Scalplock Lookout.

John F. Stevens Canyon

Named for the Great Northern Railway engineer who verified the feasibility of Marias Pass as a railroad route, John F. Stevens Canyon begins just west of the pass and follows Bear Creek and the Middle Fork of the Flathead until its terminus near West Glacier. U.S. 2 and the railroad traverse the canyon's entire 40-mile distance. In places the canyon broadens into wide valleys; in others it tightens up into narrow channels, frothing with wild waters. Although its more dramatic sections are best seen from a raft or kayak on the river, several highway pullouts offer good photo ops.

Flathead National Forest

From the Continental Divide west past Flathead Valley and extending 120 miles south of the Canadian border, Flathead National Forest is broken up by state and private land but still tallies up a healthy 2.3 million acres. Within its glaciated mountains, it has 2,600 miles of trails. Over 46 percent of the forest is designated wilderness area.

Spruce, Douglas fir, lodgepole, larch, and pine cover its slopes—home to wolverines, grizzly bears, and wolves.

Middle Fork of the Flathead River

Draining Glacier National Park and the Bob Marshall Wilderness Complex, the Middle Fork of the Flathead River is no small tributary. Designated a Wild and Scenic River, its 95-mile length is known for some of the best white-water rafting and kayaking in Montana. Dropping at 35 feet per mile, the Great Bear section teems with Class III-IV rapids; the lower waters break up long scenic floats with Class II-III rapids with such names as Jaws and Bonecrusher. Hook up with one of the four West Glacier rafting companies to splash in its waves or float it yourself.

Wintering Range

Belton Mountain, to the road's north (milepost 155-157), is quite a different ecosystem from the heavily forested south slopes. Fires, winds, and a dry exposure have minimized forest growth. Winds create a lower snowpack, and south-facing slopes melt off early—both keys to making the area a prime wintering range for ungulates such as deer, elk, and bighorn sheep. Grizzly and black bears also forage on its slopes. Even in summer, it's worth a stop at one of the several pullouts to scan the slopes with binoculars.

Recreation

HIKING

U.S. 2 is one road where hiker shuttles are not available; you must get to the trailheads on your own. Most of Glacier's trails on the south end are long valley hikes accessing little-used areas. Additional short hikes, mostly in the Great Bear Wilderness, round out the options—especially for hikers with Fido. While trails within Glacier do not allow dogs, canine friends can tag along on a leash in the wilderness area. However, hiking in bear country with a dog will not guarantee protection from bears.

While trails within Glacier National Park are well signed and frequently maintained, trails in the wilderness areas are not; signs, if any, may be just a wooden trail number or name nailed to a tree—no mileages. Take a good topographic map, which you can purchase from the **Hungry Horse Ranger Station** (10 Hungry Horse Dr., Hungry Horse, 406/387-3800), and know how to read it. Be prepared to encounter deadfall, downed trees, and heavy brush. Trail crews in the national forests do not have the staff numbers of the national park trail crews; it takes them longer to get to damaged or buried trails. Unlike in Glacier, bear-warning signage does not exist, except in extreme cases. Make noise and take precautions in bear country.

Hikes are listed here from east to west along U.S. 2.

Firebrand Pass

- Distance: 9.6 miles round-trip
- Duration: 4.5 hours
- Elevation gain: 2,210 feet
- Effort: moderate
- Trailhead: at milepost 203 on the north side of U.S. 2

From the trailhead, the path crosses into Glacier Park, wanders by beaver ponds, passes the old Lubec ranger station site, and follows Coonsa Creek northward. At 1.4 miles, turn right at the Autumn Creek Trail junction and ascend through aspens and meadows thick in July with valerian, lupine, paintbrush, and penstemon to another junction about one mile later. Take a left, gaining elevation as the trail

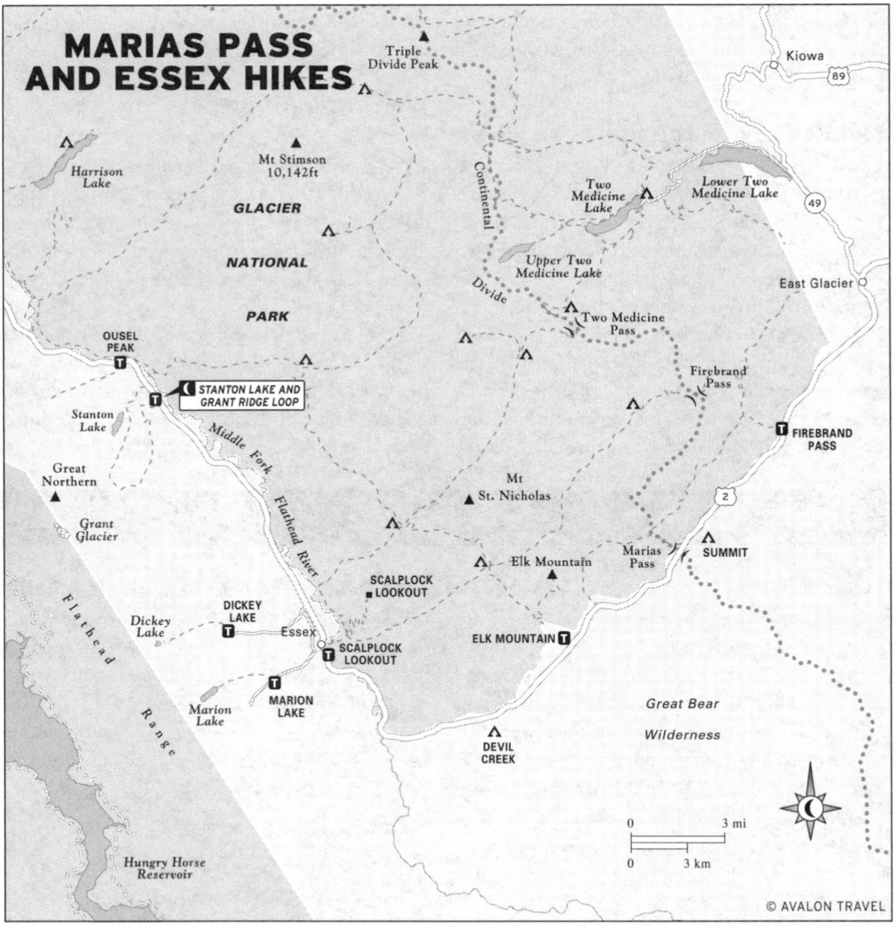

circumvents Calf Robe's lower slopes. Make noise, for this is prime bear country.

As the trail breaks out of the trees, you'll have views of Dancing Lady and East Glacier. The trail rounds Calf Robe into a hanging basin and then ascends to the pass, where you can look down Ole Creek and into Glacier's remote southern peaks. Scrambles up Calf Robe or Red Crow lend even better views, but don't go off trail unless you're ready to deal with steep scree hillsides.

Elk Mountain

- Distance: 7 miles round-trip
- Duration: 6 hours
- Elevation gain: 3,332 feet
- Effort: strenuous
- Trailhead: turn north off U.S. 2 at Fielding (milepost 192), and follow the dirt Forest Road 1066 about 0.5 miles to the trailhead.

Hike up through private logged land to the railroad tracks and cross into Glacier Park.

The trail to Firebrand Pass climbs through a high open basin.

The trail starts off deceptively easy enough, but shortly after turning right at the junction near a ranger cabin, the trail climbs and climbs. *Steep* does not come close to describing the pitch as it ascends to an open saddle. No wonder you have so much solitude here. From here, you can see the remainder of the trail, climbing sharply again across a talus slope to the summit.

From the top, among debris from what was once the lookout, the views make the grunt worthwhile. Panoramas both north and south line up peak tops for miles into Glacier's remote southern sector and the Bob Marshall Wilderness Complex. A knife ridge leads east toward the Continental Divide, and the view down Autumn Creek is dizzying.

Scalplock Lookout

- Distance: 9.4 miles round-trip
- Duration: 5 hours
- Elevation gain: 3,079 feet
- Effort: strenuous
- Trailhead: Walton Picnic Area (milepost 180.5)

This can be a gorgeous hike in early July, with bluebells in the high meadows, but be prepared for snow on top in June. Beginning in the Walton Picnic Area, the trail wanders along the Middle Fork of the Flathead in the first mile, crossing Ole Creek on a swinging bridge over a small gorge and ascending to the Ole Creek trail. Turn west on this trail for 0.4 miles to a second junction where the climb begins. In the remaining three miles, the trail grunts up switchbacks at nearly 1,000 feet per mile as the sounds of the highway and train reverberate from below.

Peek-a-boo views of the Middle Fork of the Flathead River are the only respite from the relentless ascent. Near the top, the trail breaks out of the trees to climb up a ridge flanked with wildflower meadows. At the top, Scalplock Lookout has a commanding view of the entire Middle Fork drainage, with Mount St. Nicholas's spire in your face.

Marion Lake

- Distance: 3.4 miles round-trip
- Duration: 2 hours
- Elevation gain: 1,739 feet
- Effort: short but strenuous
- Trailhead: turn south on the Dickey Lake Road (milepost 178.7 on Forest Rd. 1640) at Essex, and follow the left fork 2.3 miles to the Flathead National Forest-signed trailhead

The trail is popular and sees quite of bit of summer traffic, making it well-worn and quite obvious to follow until you encounter heavy foliage. From the start, it taxes your lungs on its steep climb up Marion Creek Valley. You will encounter thick heavy brush in the trail's midsection. Cow parsnip, nettle, elderberry, and false huckleberry nearly suffocate the trail. Make noise here to avoid surprising a bear.

© BECKY LOMAX

Grant Ridge Loop affords panoramic views of Glacier's southern peaks.

You know you're nearing the lake when the trail assumes a more moderate pitch. Marion Lake sits in a photo-worthy glacial cirque surrounded by cliffs and the outlet congested with logs. Anglers should bring rods, as the lake harbors westslope cutthroat trout up to 12 inches long.

Dickey Lake

- Distance: 4.8 miles round-trip
- Duration: 2.5 hours
- Elevation gain: 1,446 feet
- Effort: moderate
- Trailhead: turn south on Dickey Lake Road (milepost 178.7 on Forest Rd. 1640) at Essex, and follow the right fork three miles to an unmarked spur where the Flathead National Forest trail begins

This short trail in the Great Bear Wilderness gives rather decent rewards for its efforts, and anglers will want to tote a fishing rod. After wading Dickey Creek, the forested trail climbs up a large bowl riddled with avalanche paths, which means deadfall, limbs, and uprooted and downed trees. In places, thick brush chokes the path, but you can still follow it to the headwall near the basin's end. From here, a rock cairn, which may be buried in snow that hangs late in the season, marks the trail, ascending steeply through false huckleberry bushes dangling with pale apricot blossoms and into a hanging valley.

Upon reaching the upper basin, the trail pops out on the edge of Dickey Lake. The shallow tarn, flanked by meadows and steep talus slopes, is a scenic lunch spot. You'll most likely find solitude here. Anglers will enjoy fishing for cutthroats in the small lake.

Stanton Lake and Grant Ridge Loop

- Distance: 2 miles round-trip or 10.2-mile loop
- Duration: 1 or 5 hours
- Elevation gain: 600 or 3,605 feet
- Effort: easy or strenuous
- Trailhead: Stanton Lake Trailhead on U.S.

2 at mile marker 169.9 in the Flathead National Forest

An easy short hike takes hikers and anglers to the shores of Stanton Lake, or a longer strenuous loop explores the very scenic Grant Ridge, both in the Great Bear Wilderness. From the trailhead, a steep grunt heads straight uphill. But it soon levels out into a nice forested walk that leads into the basin cradling Stanton Lake. For a short hike to a well-traveled destination, stop here. Anglers should bring rods to fish for westslope cutthroat, rainbows, and mountain whitefish. Some maps show the trail continuing above Stanton Lake; however, that trail peters out promptly in willow bogs.

For the Grant Ridge Loop, take the left fork before the lake and ford the outlet creek. The trail climbs a forested hillside with peek-a-boo views of Great Northern, the highest peak in the Great Bear Wilderness. At the ridge top, follow a faint intermittent trail 0.25 miles south to a rocky outcrop to lunch overlooking the waterfall springing from the Grant Glacier's snout. With views of Glacier's southern monoliths, the trail wanders north below the ridgeline before descending switchbacks to the highway 0.5 miles from the starting point. Many hikers prefer to do this loop clockwise, staring at Grant and Great Northern during the ridgeline walk.

Ousel Peak

- Distance: 5.2 miles round-trip
- Duration: 3.5 hours
- Elevation gain: 3,818 feet
- Effort: very strenuous
- Trailhead: mile marker 159.6 on U.S. 2 in the Flathead National Forest

Do the math: This trail gains well over 1,000 feet per mile, and from the first minute it makes no bones about heading straight uphill. If the uphill doesn't tax your lungs, the downhill will pound your knees. Nevertheless, the view from the top is outstanding and well worth the effort or pain. Sitting on the northern edge of the Great Bear Wilderness, the trail climbs through a forest canopy littered with various microclimates, from wet seeps to dry, arid slopes. The path finally breaks out of the forest with glimpses of Glacier's peaks. At the top, remnants of the old lookout scatter across the hillside amid tiny yellow stonecrop. Look into Glacier to see Mounts Jackson and Stimson along with Harrison Glacier.

CYCLING

Cross-country cyclists use U.S. 2 to cross the Continental Divide when Going-to-the-Sun Road is not open. Many use it also to make a big loop through and around Glacier (Going-to-the-Sun Rd., U.S. 89, Hwy. 49, and U.S. 2). Compared to the rest of Glacier's roads, U.S. 2 is definitely an easier ride, because it has shoulders in some sections and is a bit wider and less curvy. However, due to heavy traffic in summer, it can be downright dangerous, with large rigs that nearly blow cyclists off the road. Tackle it only if you can handle riding with semis and RVs whipping by your elbows at 60 mph.

Be prepared for winds, especially at Marias Pass. They are usually blowing eastward, so those riding toward West Glacier encounter substantial headwinds. Also, be extra cautious in the five curvy miles east of West Glacier, as severe turns reduce the visibility of drivers on the road. Even though no law requires wearing a helmet, think twice about leaving your brain bucket off. Most drivers here are gawking at scenery or trying to spot wildlife rather than keeping their attention totally on the road.

Mountain bikes are not permitted on trails in the wilderness areas nor in Glacier Park.

RIVER RAFTING AND KAYAKING

Designated as a Wild and Scenic River, the **Middle Fork of the Flathead River** is the local hot spot for rafting and kayaking. The river

Rafters splash in whitewater on the Middle Fork of the Flathead River.

has two sections—the wilderness above Bear Creek and the lower section below Bear Creek.

With headwaters starting in the Great Bear Wilderness, you'll need to fly in to Schaeffer Meadows or pack in on a horse to float the upper 26 miles. Contact the Flathead National Forest Ranger Station (406/387-3800) in Hungry Horse for details on rafting and floating this upper wild section. The normal float season (Class III-IV) runs mid-May-mid-July. During peak runoff in May, the trip can often be more challenging, with several rapids becoming Class V and spring snows chilling the air.

From Bear Creek to the confluence with the North Fork of the Flathead, the river runs 46 miles, with easy river access from locations on U.S. 2: Bear Creek (milepost 185), Essex (milepost 180), Paola (milepost 175.2), Cascadilla (milepost 166), Moccasin Creek (milepost 160.5), and West Glacier (follow signs to the golf course). With the float season running mid-May-early September, the river accesses make for easy half-day or full-day float trips. Between Bear Creek and Cascadilla, rapids rate Class III-IV. Waters flatten to a float trip from Cascadilla to Moccasin Creek, but be wary of deadly log jams. From Moccasin to West Glacier, rapids range Class II-III, with some Class IV stretches during late-May high water. The average float time in July from Bear Creek to Cascadilla is usually 6.5 hours, and from Moccasin Creek to West Glacier 2.5 hours.

Flathead National Forest manages the river, even though it borders Glacier National Park. Consult the Flathead National Forest Ranger Station (10 Hungry Horse Dr., Hungry Horse, 406/387-5243), located nine miles west of West Glacier, for assistance in planning a self-guided overnight trip. Toilet systems are required for overnights, and fire pans are required in the wilderness. Rafters and kayakers should purchase the *Three Forks of the Flathead Floater's Guide* ($13) available through Glacier National Park Conservancy (406/888-5756, www.

glaciernationalparkconservancy.org) for location of rapids and public land for camping. No permits are needed for overnights, but no camping is allowed on the Glacier Park side. In the Great Bear Wilderness, sites are not restricted, but in the section below Bear Creek, private land abuts national forest land, much of it unmarked.

Guides

Four local river companies operate out of West Glacier, guiding half-day, full-day, and overnight trips on the Middle Fork of the Flathead. **Glacier Raft Company** (406/888-5454 or 800/235-6781, www.glacierraftco.com) is the only one that guides trips in the wilderness section above Bear Creek. Glacier Raft Company, **Montana Raft Company** (406/387-5555 or 800/521-7238, www.glacierguides.com), **Great Northern Whitewater** (406/387-5340 or 800/735-7897, www.gnwhitewater.com), and **Wild River Adventures** (406/387-9453 or 800/700-7056, www.riverwild.com) guide trips between Bear Creek and West Glacier.

Rentals and Shuttles

Two West Glacier raft companies rent rafts, kayaks, camping gear, toilet systems, and fire pans: **Montana Raft Company** (406/387-5555 or 800/521-7238, www.glacierguides.com) and **Glacier Raft Company** (406/888-5454 or 800/235-6781, www.glacierraftco.com). Glacier also provides shuttle services on the Middle Fork in your vehicle or theirs ($30-315).

FISHING

Rivers and Streams

In Glacier Park, Ole, Park, Muir, Coal, and Nyack Creeks are closed to fishing. However, anglers can drop lines in Summit, Railroad, and Badger Creeks, which flow from Marias Pass east through Lewis and Clark National Forest and onto the Blackfeet Reservation. **Badger Creek,** in particular, has a good reputation for rainbow trout. **Bear Creek,** good for westslope cutthroat, mountain whitefish, and some rainbow trout, drops west from Marias to its confluence with the Middle Fork of the Flathead River. The **Middle Fork** has plenty of river accesses for fishing: Bear Creek, Essex, Paola, Cascadilla, and Moccasin.

Lakes

Inside the park, good cutthroat trout fishing lakes such as Ole, Harrison, and Isabel usually require backpacking or fording the Middle Fork of the Flathead. It's actually easier to get to lakes in the Great Bear Wilderness on the south side of the highway. **Stanton Lake** is a quick destination with westslope cutthroat trout, mountain whitefish, and rainbow trout, but it's somewhat overfished because of its ease of access. Dickey and Marion Lakes also harbor cutthroat.

Guides

For guided fishing on Blackfeet Nation lands, contact **Blackfeet Fish and Wildlife** (406/338-7207, www.blackfeetfishandwildlife.com) for a list of licensed outfitters. From West Glacier, four fishing companies guide fly-fishing trips on the Middle Fork of the Flathead River.

Licenses and Regulations

Fishing regulations along U.S. 2 vary depending on land ownership. Check carefully where you are before dropping a line into the water. The road passes through Blackfeet land, Glacier National Park, and national forests. No licenses are required inside Glacier Park. You'll need to plan ahead to get the appropriate fishing licenses, as none are available along the highway. Purchase Blackfeet fishing permits ($25 for two days, $75 for the season) at **Bear Track Travel Center** (Exxon station in East Glacier, 20958 U.S. 2, 406/226-5504). For Montana State licenses, go to **Glacier Outdoor Center** (11957 U.S. 2 E., West Glacier, 406/888-5454 or 800/235-6781, www.glacierraftco.com). Montana residents can buy two-day ($13) or season ($26) licenses. Nonresidents can get two-day

($25), 10-day ($54), or season ($70) licenses. Children under age 12 fish free. Ages 12-14 and Montana seniors can buy licenses for $8. You can also order one online (www.fwp.mt.gov).

HUNTING

Hunting is illegal in Glacier National Park, but south of U.S. 2, the famed Bob Marshall Wilderness boasts world-renowned big-game hunting for bighorn sheep, elk, and black bears. East-side grasslands are also famous for bird hunting. For hunting in the Bob Marshall Wilderness or in national forests, get regulations and license info from **Montana Fish, Wildlife, and Parks** (406/444-2535, www.fwp.mt.gov). The **Blackfeet Reservation** (406/338-7207, www.blackfeetfishandwildlife.com) has separate regulations and licenses for its land. Check also with each entity for the names of licensed outfitters.

© BECKY LOMAX

Kids can cross-country ski, too!

CROSS-COUNTRY SKIING AND SNOWSHOEING

In winter, ski and snowshoe routes off U.S. 2 are popular for their ease of access. You'll find everything from groomed skate and classic skiing trails to snowmobile-packed tracks and off-piste break-your-own-trail treks.

Izaak Walton Inn

With 20 miles of track groomed daily for skate and classic skiing late November-mid-April, Izaak Walton Inn (290 Izaak Walton Inn Rd., 406/888-5700, www.izaakwaltoninn.com) becomes a great cross-country skiing destination in winter. At the inn, trails range from easy meanders to steep grunts. One short section of trail is lit for night skiing. Trail passes for day skiers and inn guests cost $12 per day. Although the area never feels crowded, the most popular time is late December-late February. Lessons are available from the lodge as well as ski or snowshoe rentals, and the rentals can be taken elsewhere to use. The inn also guides half-day snowshoe tours and full-day ski tours in Glacier.

Autumn Creek Trail

One of the most popular ski trails in Glacier is Autumn Creek Trail at Marias Pass, which can be skied point-to-point if you set up a car shuttle or hitchhike, which is legal in Montana. Park for the west trailhead at milepost 193.8 on U.S. 2, and ski up the railroad access road and across the tracks. Park for the other trailhead at Marias Pass and locate the trailhead north of U.S. 2 and the railroad tracks. Orange markers on trees denote the six-mile trail. Beginners will find the Marias Pass section easier than the steep Autumn Creek section. To avoid the narrow, steep 660-foot downhill plummet, begin on the west end and finish at the pass.

SNOWMOBILING

Snowmobilers gravitate to groomed and ungroomed roads in Lewis and Clark National

Forest (406/791-7700) and Flathead National Forest (406/758-5204). The most popular snowmobiling is in the Marias Pass and Skyland-Challenge complex, both straddling the Continental Divide south of U.S. 2. The Cut Bank Snowgoers and Flathead Snowmobile Association groom about 40 miles of trail, which are open for snowmobiling December-mid-May. Contact them via the Montana Snowmobile Association (406/788-2399, www.m-s-a.org). Snow depths in both of these snowmobiling areas vary 150-250 inches. Some restrictions apply to the designated connecting trails, so get a good snowmobile map from the Forest Service. The nearest rentals are in Flathead Valley.

ENTERTAINMENT

The U.S. 2 corridor is backwoods Montana, but small homespun music festivals have started at the **Snow Slip Inn** (15644 U.S. 2 E., Essex, 406/226-4400, www.snowslipinn.com). Look for the **Shields Mountain Music Festival** in early July and the **Highline Music Festival** in early September.

Accommodations

Along U.S. 2, lodging includes historic inns, rustic cabins, and tiny motels. Regardless of the type, that 7 percent Montana state bed tax will find your bill. Many lodging properties boast of being near Glacier, but from U.S. 2, the only access is on foot, horseback, or by raft, with exception of Walton Picnic Area and the Goat Lick.

Lodges

With some of the most unique lodging around Glacier, **Izaak Walton Inn** (290 Izaak Walton Inn Rd., Essex, 406/888-5700, www.izaakwaltoninn.com, year-round, $100-300) celebrates its railroad heritage with accommodations in historic lodge rooms, cabooses, and a luxury locomotive. The resort also has log cabins. From the lobby fireplace to the Dining Car Restaurant or the swinging seat on the porch, the nonsmoking National Historic Landmark is a place to unwind and relax. The inn maintains its historic ambience with no TVs, in-room phones, air-conditioning, or elevators; a pay phone is off the lobby. Lodge guest rooms vary in size, although most baths are fairly small. A short walk over a footbridge above the railroad tracks leads to four heated cabooses set in the trees that sleep four each, with kitchenettes and full baths. In the same glen, six log cabins with kitchens were added in 2008. They sleep up to six in bedrooms and lofts. The luxury locomotive, which sleeps four, looks out of the picture window on the train tracks. Two nights minimum are required for the cabooses and the locomotive.

Amenities include a sauna, coin-op laundry, wireless Internet access in the Flagstop Bar, restaurant, cross-country ski trails in winter, walking trails, and railroad ambience. You can arrive and depart by train, as it's an Amtrak stop. Bring earplugs, as trains rumble by each night. You can rent skis or snowshoes in winter. In summer, red-bus tours pick up riders here for an all-day loop around Going-to-the-Sun Road. To get good deals, check the inn's packages, which include skiing, rafting, park sightseeing, and special weekends for railroad fans.

Motels

Several small no-frills family-run motels with restaurants dot U.S. 2, all within close earshot of the highway and train noise. Bring earplugs to survive the night. The **Snow Slip Inn** (milepost 180, 15644 U.S. 2 E., Essex, 406/226-4400, www.snowslipinn.com, year-round, $95 summer, $65 off-season) has six motel rooms and wireless Internet access. Sitting half way

© BECKY LOMAX

Izaak Walton Inn houses a restaurant and bar, in addition to lodging.

between East Glacier and West Glacier at milepost 178, **The Half Way Motel** (14840 U.S. 2 E., Essex, 406/888-5650, year-round, $90 summer, $65 winter) has four remodeled motel rooms with TVs. At milepost 173.8, **Glacier Haven Inn** (14305 U.S. 2, 406/888-5720, www.glacierhaveninn.com, year-round, $150 summer, discounted off-season) has small guest rooms with two double beds and satellite TV. The full house ($299-349) with a kitchen, a barbecue, and laundry can sleep up to eight people.

Cabins

Flathead National Forest (406/387-3809, www.fs.fed.us/r1/flathead) rents two quiet rustic cabins (reservations 877/444-6777, www.recreation.gov, $9 service fee per reservation) with three-night maximum stays. Both are accessible from U.S. 2 and must be reserved. Decked out with propane, mattresses, and kitchen utensils, the cabins are reasonably well equipped and warm with either propane heat or woodstoves (wood is supplied). A seven-mile ski or snowmobile ride up Skyland Road (milepost 195.8 on U.S. 2), tiny one-room **Challenge Cabin** (Dec.-Mar., $30) sleeps six people stacked like sardines. A much larger two-bedroom cabin that sleeps eight, **Zip's Place** (June-Mar., $50) is off U.S. 2; turn at milepost 191.9 and drive two miles, following the signs. In winter, it requires a ski or snowshoe trip to reach the front door. Bring your own food and sleeping bags. Both cabins are nonsmoking, and neither allow pets.

The closest lodging to West Glacier, **Glacier Wilderness Resort** (milepost 163 on U.S. 2, 406/888-5664, www.glacierwildernessresort.com, year-round, $215-295) is in a woodsy setting abutting the Great Bear Wilderness. With an indoor heated pool, its 11 time-share 1-2-bedroom log cabins sleep 4-6 people and come with fireplaces, satellite TV, DVD players or VCRs, fully equipped kitchens, and private hot tubs. Summertime usually requires a five-night minimum stay; other seasons require a two-night minimum. In summer, you can use an outdoor picnic pavilion and walking trails. In winter, cross-country skiing and snowshoeing trails allow you to tour the property.

Bed and Breakfast

You'll feel the hunting heritage at **Bear Creek Guest Ranch** (milepost 192, U.S. 2, 406/226-4489, www.bearcreekguestranch.com, May-Oct., $70-150 d) with elk, moose, bears, and fish mounted on the walls at this ranch that has been operating since 1933. Lodging is in rustic log cabins with private baths or small guest rooms in the main lodge. Rates are at the lower end during spring and fall. You can add on horseback riding lessons or an all-day trail ride. The ranch offers cattle drives on the Blackfeet Reservation in June and other special Western days throughout the summer.

CAMPING

U.S. 2 has no drive-in national park campgrounds; to camp in Glacier requires backpacking. U.S. Forest Service and private campgrounds line the highway, where noise from trains and trucks permeates the night.

U.S. Forest Service Campgrounds

Two fairly small summer-only Forest Service campgrounds are adjacent to U.S. 2, tucked in dog-hair timbers for shade and monitored by campground hosts. Expect to find picnic tables (some wheelchair accessible), fire rings with grills, vault toilets, drinking water, but no hookups. You must also pack your own garbage away with you. Sites are first come, first served, so get there by early afternoon in high season, especially if you want to nab one of the campsites farthest from the highway. Firewood is not available; you can collect it in the woods here. At Marias Pass, the **Summit Campground** (Lewis and Clark National Forest, 406/791-7700, $10) has 17 sites. You can hop onto the Autumn Creek Trail across the highway and railroad tracks. At milepost 190, **Devil Creek Campground** (Flathead National Forest, 406/387-3800, $10) has 14 sites, a few of which can handle up to 40-foot RVs. From the campground, a trail leads 5.9 miles up to Elk Lake or 8.2 miles to Moose Lake.

Private Campgrounds

Two private campgrounds are available along U.S. 2. If these fill up, a couple of restaurant-bar-cabin businesses also offer a few campsites. The 7 percent Montana bed tax is added to the rates, which usually cover two people; each additional person is $5. Bring earplugs, because all are near the highway and train tracks.

Located 16 miles west of East Glacier between milepost 191 and 192, **Glacier Meadow RV Park** (406/226-4479, www.glaciermeadowrvpark.com, mid-May-mid-Sept., hookups $36, tents $20) has 41 sites on a 58-acre meadow and forest setting with a dump station, laundry, a playground, full hookups, flush toilets, showers, and wireless Internet access. The campground is in full view of the highway, and all the sites are open, providing good satellite dish reception, but there isn't much privacy from your neighbors. In the evening and early morning, elk sometimes browse in the meadow. Red-bus tours heading over Logan Pass pick up passengers here.

Between milepost 173 and 174 west of Essex, **Glacier Haven Campground** (14297 U.S. 2 E., 406/888-5720, www.glacierhaveninn.com, May-Oct.) is part of the Glacier Haven Inn. The treed campground is tucked between the highway and the railroad tracks, with 19 RV hookup campsites ($40), including three that can accommodate large RVs, and room for five tents ($28) in a large camping zone. Facilities include flush toilets, showers, full hookups, a

COAL-NYACK LOOP

"Remote" doesn't come close to describing the Coal-Nyack Loop, an ancient Kootenai trail. A rough 38-mile trail encircles Mount Stimson, at 10,142 feet one of the six highest peaks in Glacier Park. While other trails require camping in designated sites, the Coal-Nyack Loop is wild, with wilderness camping at large–which means you can camp wherever you can find a flat place to sleep, and you must abide by Leave No Trace principles. Bear-resistant canisters are the way to carry food.

The loop is not a place for the faint of heart. Creeks require fording because there are no bridges, and snowmelt creates plenty of them in spring. Frequent avalanches splinter trees across trails, and thick brush cloaks routes. The only access to the loop is by trail or fording the Middle Fork of the Flathead River. Only those with experienced backcountry savvy should tackle its primitive isolation on foot or on horseback. For those who do, wilderness solitude awaits.

Permits are required for backcountry camping in the Coal-Nyack Loop. Call 406/888-7800 or check for details at www.nps.gov/glac.

launderette, a camping cabin with linens ($75), and a restaurant. Rates are for two people, and each extra person is $5. Kids under age 10 under stay free, and rates are reduced in spring and fall.

Backcountry Camping

On U.S. 2's north side, trails lead up Glacier's remote rugged valleys. With multiple creek fords and primitive or undesignated campsites, the **Coal-Nyack Loop** keeps the undedicated out. Its best campground—**Beaver Woman Lake**—is in Martha's Basin in goat-watching terrain. Pick up permits (adults $5 pp per night, ages 8-15 $2.50, under age 8 free) in person at ranger stations, visitors centers, or the Apgar Permit Office (406/888-7900) 24 hours prior to your trip. Advance reservations ($30) can be made online (www.nps.gov/glac).

Backcountry camping on Forest Service land south of U.S. 2 requires no special permit. Any destination works as long as you follow Leave No Trace ethics. Campsites are not maintained or designated. Overused campsites attest to the popularity of **Marion** and **Stanton Lakes**—short-hike destinations good for anglers and families with young kids. **Tranquil Basin** ranks as one of the most scenic places for 1-2 nights. Call Hungry Horse Ranger Station (406/387-3800) for information.

Food

Restaurants along U.S. 2 vary from old dives to family cafés—no fine dining. Off-season, don't be surprised if one is closed when its hours say otherwise—if the fish are biting, the owners may lock up.

RESTAURANTS

Located three miles west of East Glacier, **Ramsey's Food and Ale** (20629 U.S. 2, East Glacier, 406/226-9374, 4pm-10pm daily year-round, $10-25), also known as Firebrand Food and Ale, has a mixed menu of burgers, sandwiches, pasta, fish, and steaks along with more than 50 types of beer. The food rates much better than the building would imply, and it fills with local characters. It's convenient for dining after hiking to Firebrand Pass or cross-country skiing the Autumn Creek Trail.

At Izaak Walton Inn, the **Dining Car Restaurant** (290 Izaak Walton Inn Rd., Essex, 406/888-5700, www.izaakwaltoninn.com, 7am-9pm daily year-round) serves up scrumptious meals on replicas of the Great Northern Railway's historic dinnerware. (The gift shop sells the dishes, too.) The cozy restaurant is a great place to grab a breakfast ($8-11) of huckleberry pancakes or french toast with homemade bourbon maple sauce before hiking, or lunch favorites ($10-13) like a buffalo burger or gourmet burger of the day and a Montana microbrew. Enjoy a leisurely dinner ($16-25) of osso buco, filet mignon with port glaze, or grilled rainbow trout accompanied by a glass of wine as trains rumble past your window. Leave room for the huckleberry cobbler dessert. You'll also find vegetarian dishes and a kids' menu. Be sure to head downstairs to the Flagstop Bar for a nightcap or at least to look at the historic photos of local railroad disasters.

CAFÉS

Inexpensive family-run cafés, favorites for locals and good for after-hike burgers, are the mainstay of U.S. 2. Lighter meals at these establishments run $7-10; full dinners run up to about $20. Located six miles west of Marias Pass, the **Snow Slip Inn** (15644 U.S. 2 E., Essex, 406/226-4400, www.snowslipinn.com, 7am-10pm daily year-round) has upgraded its menu to home-style cooking, with a mean jalapeno bacon burger, but still has its circa 1945 historic bar. Half way between East and West Glacier, **The Half Way Restaurant** (14840 U.S. 2 E., Essex, 406/888-5650, 8am-9pm Mon.-Sat. summer, shorter hours off-season) features good portions of simple, tasty "slow-cooked" fare that hasn't been premade. Also midway, the **Healthy Haven Cafe** (14305 U.S. 2 E., Essex, 406/888-5720, www.glacierhaveninn.com, 8am-10am and 6pm-8pm Tues.-Sat., 8am-10am Sun. Memorial Day-Labor Day) serves a breakfast buffet of home-baked breads, seasonal fresh fruit, design-your-own omelets, waffles, and mostly organic ingredients. Homemade dinners with fresh ingredients include salmon, steaks, and buffalo burgers. Leave room to finish dinner with huckleberry pie, made with 100 percent hucks rather than fillers. Closest to West Glacier, the small **Stanton Creek Lodge** (13951 U.S. 2 E., Essex, 406/888-5040, www.stantoncreeklodge.com, 11am-7pm daily mid-May-Oct., bar open later Fri.-Sat.) serves lunch and dinner—convenient for refueling after hiking the Grant Ridge Loop. This is one of Montana's funky old full-service bars, where patrons used to ride horses through the building and shoot at the floor. If you see the buck sing, you've stayed too long.

GROCERIES

U.S. 2 lacks grocery stores, but at milepost 178, the Half Way Restaurant (14840 U.S. 2 E., Essex, 406/888-5650) carries convenience-store items: chips, soda pop, and a few staple groceries. To stock up for camping, you'll find seasonal grocery stores in East Glacier and West Glacier. Larger food markets are in Browning on the east side and Hungry Horse and Columbia Falls on the west side.

PICNIC AREAS

There is only one designated picnic area on U.S. 2, and that is **Walton** (milepost 180.5). Behind the Walton Ranger Station, the small picnic area is under thick trees adjacent to the Middle Fork River. Picnic tables, pit toilets, and fire rings with grills are available, but you'll need to bring your own firewood; gathering wood is prohibited. Trails to Ole Creek, the Middle Fork, and Scalplock Lookout depart from the picnic area.

With several river accesses along the Middle Fork of the Flathead, there are plenty of additional places sans tables for picnicking at a scenic spot and soaking your feet in cold water. Cascadilla and Paola offer the best beaches.

WATERTON

For such a small park, Waterton Lakes National Park packs a punch. It houses rare plants found nowhere else and a plethora of wildlife that rivals its large northern sisters of Banff and Jasper. It is at a nexus of major bird migration routes and weather systems. On the Continental Divide's east side, mountains meet the prairie; with no transitional foothills, eastern peaks plummet directly to grasslands, a phenomenon caused by geological overthrusts that exposed the oldest sedimentary rock in the Canadian Rockies. Although active glaciers vacated Waterton's borders years ago, the results of ice gnawing on its landscape left lake pockets strewn through the park. A long glacier-gouged trough forms Upper Waterton Lake, the deepest lake in the Canadian Rockies and one that straddles the U.S.-Canada border. The lake frequently kicks up with winds, proving the park's ranking as the second-windiest place in Alberta.

Dominated by the Prince of Wales Hotel and Waterton Lake, the park serves as a destination itself as well as an entrance to Glacier's remote north country. On any summer day, the Waterton Townsite bustles with shoppers, bicyclists, backpackers, boaters, and campers. It's a quintessential Canadian mountain town that embodies what Banff used to be before booming commercialism. The MV *International* shuttles hikers and sightseers across Waterton Lake and the international boundary to Goat Haunt, USA. Only two roads pierce the park's

© BECKY LOMAX

HIGHLIGHTS

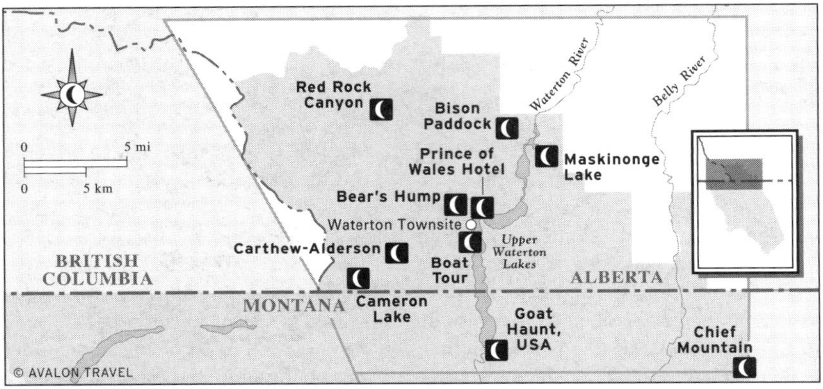

LOOK FOR ☾ TO FIND RECOMMENDED SIGHTS, ACTIVITIES, DINING, AND LODGING.

☾ **Boat Tour:** Hop aboard the historic MV *International* for a ride on the deepest lake in the Canadian Rockies. You'll float across the international boundary to Goat Haunt, USA (page 208).

☾ **Chief Mountain:** Spot this 9,080-foot mountain, sacred to the Blackfeet, from Chief Mountain Highway. In Glacier National Park rather than Waterton, the mountain stands adjacent to Ninaki ("the mother"), and Papoose peeks up behind it (page 212).

☾ **Prince of Wales Hotel:** Drop in to the historic 1927 hotel sitting regally atop a knoll. Part of the chain of Swiss-style hostelries built by the Great Northern Railway, the hotel maintains British ambience with kilt-wearing bellhops and afternoon high tea (page 213).

☾ **Goat Haunt, USA:** Walk to the International Peace Park Pavilion. Accessible only by boat or on foot, Goat Haunt is at Waterton Lake's southern end in Glacier Park—a launch pad to Glacier's remote northern trails (page 214).

☾ **Cameron Lake:** Rent a boat to paddle the lake, or walk the pathway to Grizzly Gardens. The lake at Akamina Parkway's terminus receives snowmelt from the remnants of Herbst Glacier across the international boundary (page 214).

☾ **Red Rock Canyon:** Tread around a colorful mosaic of sediments. Argillites in striking reds and greens are layered atop one another—evidence of its origins as an ancient inland sea (page 215).

☾ **Maskinonge Lake:** Focus your binoculars on unusual bird sightings. Located on the axis of two migratory flyways, Waterton is home to trumpeter swans, yellow-headed blackbirds, and Vaux's swifts (page 215).

☾ **Bison Paddock:** Drive through a paddock harboring majestic bison. In a tribute to the great wild herds that once roamed the prairies in vast numbers, Parks Canada maintains a small herd of these large mammals (page 215).

☾ **Bear's Hump:** Climb up the short grunt for a grand panoramic view. The trail gives you an eagle-eye shot of Waterton Townsite and Waterton Lake (page 218).

☾ **Carthew-Alderson:** Cross over a high windswept alpine pass on a scenic trail between Cameron Lake and the Waterton Townsite. You'll be wowed by the peaks as you walk past icy blue jewels (page 219).

KOOTENAI BROWN

John George "Kootenai" Brown was influential in the formation of Waterton Lakes National Park, but he also became the stuff of legend. Born in Ireland in 1839, he served with the British Army in India before coming to North America in 1861. With no money, he followed the Cariboo Gold Rush to Barkerville, British Columbia. He spent the money he made from gold, departing several years later broke.

At age 26, he crossed the Continental Divide at South Kootenay Pass in what would become Waterton Lakes National Park. He fell in love with the area, called Kootenay Lakes at the time, and inherited his name through his close ties to the Kootenai people.

Local legend is full of Brown's escapades. When Blackfeet shot him in the back with an arrow, he reputedly pulled the arrow out himself and cleaned the wound with turpentine. He spent 12 years in Montana as a trader, a pony express rider, a scout for Custer, and a buffalo hunter. When buffalo became scarce, he hunted wolves. While he rode for the U.S. Army pony express, Chief Sitting Bull and the Sioux captured him, stripping him and tying him to a stake while they debated his fate. He escaped in the middle of the night.

In 1869, he married and started a family with a métis woman, Olivia Lyonnais. After being hauled into a Fort Benton court on murder charges and acquitted, he and his family packed up and went to Alberta. He built a cabin by Upper Waterton Lake, working as a guide, commercial fisherman, hunter, rancher, trader, and scout for the Rocky Mountain Rangers during the 1885 North-West Rebellion, the same year Olivia died. He later married Isabella, a Cree.

When Canada established the Kootenay Lake Forest Reserve in 1885, Brown became its first game warden and fisheries officer. In 1910, he was promoted to Forest Ranger in Charge. A year later, when Kootenay Lakes officially became Waterton Lakes, he stepped in as its first superintendent.

Kootenai Brown died in 1916 and is buried with his two wives along the entrance road to Waterton.

remarkable interior, both gateways to lakes, waterfalls, canyons, peaks, and wildlife.

HISTORY

In 1858, Lieutenant Thomas Blakiston, a European explorer, scoured southern Alberta for a railroad route through the Canadian Rockies. Arriving at Waterton Lakes, he named them for the British naturalist Charles Waterton, who never visited the area.

When the area became Kootenay Lakes Forest Park in 1895—Canada's fourth national park and the brainchild of Pincher Creek rancher F. W. Godsal—the legendary Kootenai Brown took the reins as the first game guardian and fisheries inspector. In 1911 he became Waterton's first superintendent, and the park's name officially changed to Waterton Lakes National Park.

Waterton produced Western Canada's first oil well in 1902, but within four years the site closed down as the yield trickled to nothing. Meanwhile, an oil well near Cameron Falls produced one barrel a day and prompted building the Waterton Townsite. When oil riches dissipated in 1910, tourism arrived, fueled in part by Great Northern Railway's Glacier development. The Townsite sprouted cottages, a hotel, a golf course, packhorse outfitters, and boating.

In 1913 the Great Northern Railway scouted Waterton for an appropriate hotel site, but World War I and a proposed dam in Waterton delayed its construction. Ironically, Prohibition in the United States prompted it to be built. Alcohol, after all, was still legal in Canada, attracting scads of Montanans for thirst quenching. In 1927 the Prince of Wales Hotel finally opened on the wind-battered knoll above the town, and the 72-foot MV *International* took its first sightseers up Waterton Lake. Within five years the park gained status in conjunction with Glacier as the world's first International Peace Park.

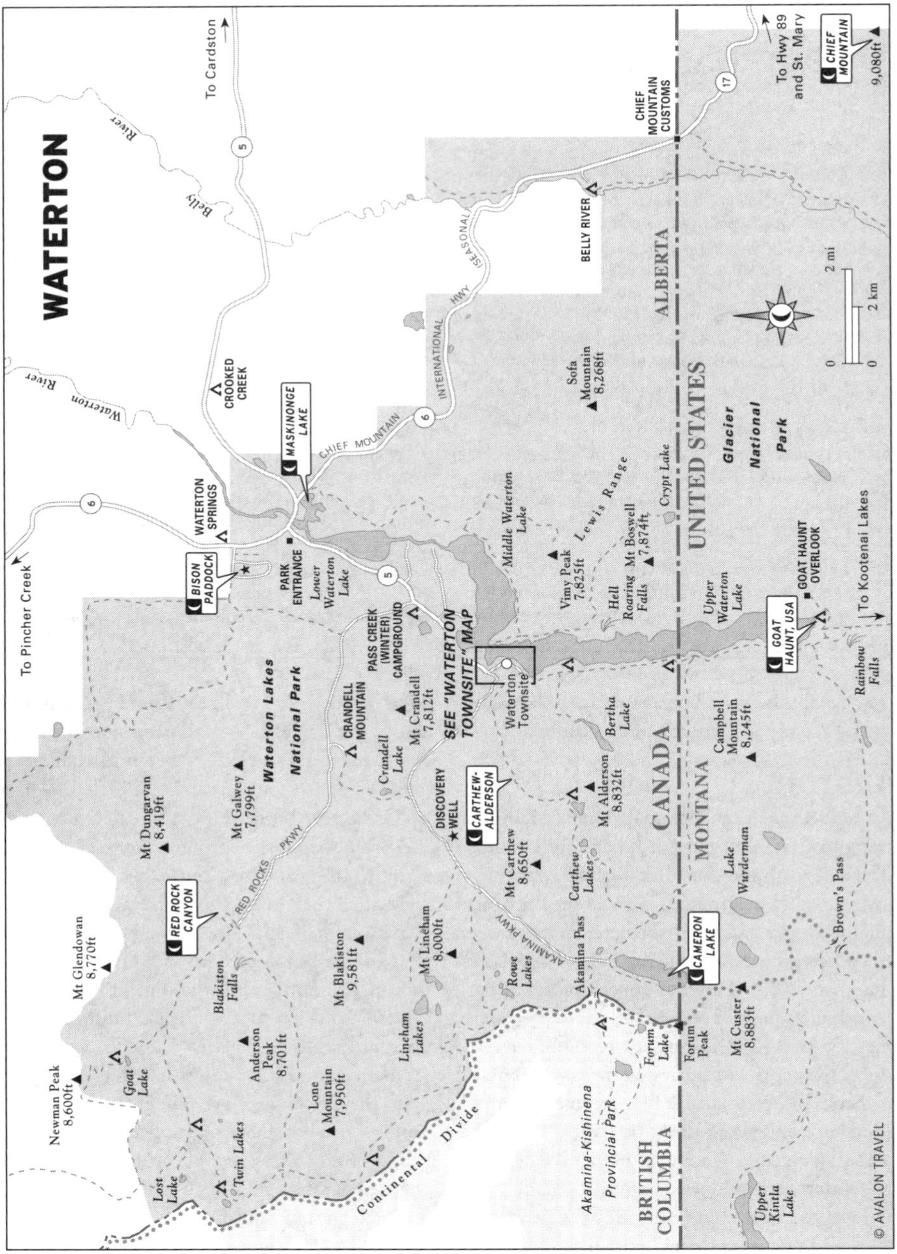
WATERTON
To Cardston
To Pincher Creek
Belly River
Waterton River
CROOKED CREEK
MASKINONGE LAKE
WATERTON SPRINGS
BISON PADDOCK
PARK ENTRANCE
Lower Waterton Lake
CHIEF MOUNTAIN INTERNATIONAL HWY SEASONAL
CHIEF MOUNTAIN CUSTOMS
BELLY RIVER
To Hwy 89 and St. Mary
CHIEF MOUNTAIN
9,080ft
ALBERTA
UNITED STATES
Glacier National Park
Sofa Mountain 8,268ft
Middle Waterton Lake
Lewis Range
Crypt Lake
Vimy Peak 7,825ft
Mt Boswell 7,874ft
Hell Roaring Falls
Upper Waterton Lake
GOAT HAUNT OVERLOOK
GOAT HAUNT, USA
To Kootenai Lakes
Rainbow Falls
PASS CREEK (WINTER) CAMPGROUND
SEE "WATERTON TOWNSITE" MAP
Waterton Townsite
Waterton Lakes National Park
CRANDELL MOUNTAIN
Mt Crandell 7,812ft
Crandell Lake
Bertha Lake
CANADA
Campbell Mountain 8,245ft
Mt Dungarvan 8,419ft
Mt Galwey 7,799ft
DISCOVERY WELL
CARTHEW-ALDERSON
Mt Alderson 8,832ft
MONTANA
RED ROCKS PKWY
RED ROCK CANYON
Mt Carthew 8,650ft
Carthew Lakes
Lake Wurdeman
Mt Glendowan 8,770ft
Blakiston Falls
Mt Blakiston 9,581ft
Mt Lineham 8,000ft
AKAMINA PKWY
Akamina Pass
CAMERON LAKE
Brown's Pass
Rowe Lakes
Mt Custer 8,883ft
Newman Peak 8,600ft
Goat Lake
Anderson Peak 8,701ft
Lineham Lakes
Forum Lake
Forum Peak
Lone Mountain 7,950ft
Twin Lakes
Lost Lake
Continental Divide
Akamina-Kishinena Provincial Park
BRITISH COLUMBIA
Upper Kintla Lake
2 mi
2 km
0
© AVALON TRAVEL

WATERTON

ECOLOGICAL SIGNIFICANCE

Despite its tiny size, Waterton is a nexus. The park is on a narrow north-south wildlife corridor and is at the axis of two major migratory bird flyways. Over 250 bird species nest or use the park's rich habitat for migration stopovers. It is one of the last places in North America where grizzly bears roam into the fringes of their original grassland habitat. Over 45 different habitats shelter 10 species of amphibians and reptiles, 24 species of fish, and 60 species of mammals. Rare trumpeter swans nest here, as do Vaux's swifts.

Because arctic and Pacific weather systems collide at Waterton, a breadth of vegetation abounds. With more than 1,370 plants, mosses, and lichens, Waterton is home to more than half of Alberta's plant species, 179 of which are considered rare and 22 of which are found nowhere else in the province. Moonwort, a small fern, grows in eight varieties; one is found only in Waterton. The park's diminutive acreage has more plant diversity than the much larger Banff, Jasper, Kootenay, and Yoho parks combined. Because of its extremes and such rarities, the United Nations Educational, Scientific, and Cultural Organization (UNESCO) has named Waterton a **Biosphere Reserve** and a **World Heritage Site.**

Exploring Waterton

Waterton's 52 square miles are tiny compared to Glacier. The Townsite is at 4,200 feet in elevation, but surrounding peaks climb to 9,000 feet. While the Townsite is home to about 100 people in winter, in summer it balloons to nearly 2,000 residents. The park has less than 400,000 annual visitors—about 20 percent of Glacier's crowds.

Waterton and Glacier meet at the 49th parallel, which is the international border, yet the parks are connected because they form one ecosystem, recognized by UNESCO as a **World Heritage Site** and a **Biosphere Reserve.** Humans can cross between the two via Waterton Lake, and grizzly bears roam back and forth. The two parks, which include part of the longest undefended border in the world at 5,525 miles, form **Waterton-Glacier International Peace Park.**

PARK ENTRANCE

U.S. park passes are not valid in this Canadian park, although many Americans expect them to be. Even though Waterton-Glacier is an International Peace Park, no combined park pass is sold. To enter Waterton, you must purchase a separate Parks Canada day pass (adults C$8, seniors C$7, ages 6-16 C$4, under age 6 free, family or single-vehicle group C$20), valid until 4pm the following day. You can also get an annual Waterton pass (adults C$40, seniors C$35, ages 6-16 C$20, family C$99) or a one-year pass good for 27 Canadian National Parks (adults C$68, seniors C$58, ages 6-16 C$34, family or vehicle C$137). While the entrance gate is open 24-7 year-round, it is only staffed early May-early October. Admission to the park is free on Canada Day (July 1).

VISITORS CENTER

The **Waterton Lakes Visitor Information Centre** (7.6 km/4.6 miles south of the park entrance station on the park entrance road, 403/859-5133, 8am-7pm daily July-Aug., 9am-5pm daily early May-June and Sept.-early Oct.) is across from the entrance road to Prince of Wales Hotel. It provides information, wilderness-use permits, road conditions, fishing licenses, maps, and the Bear's Hump trailhead.

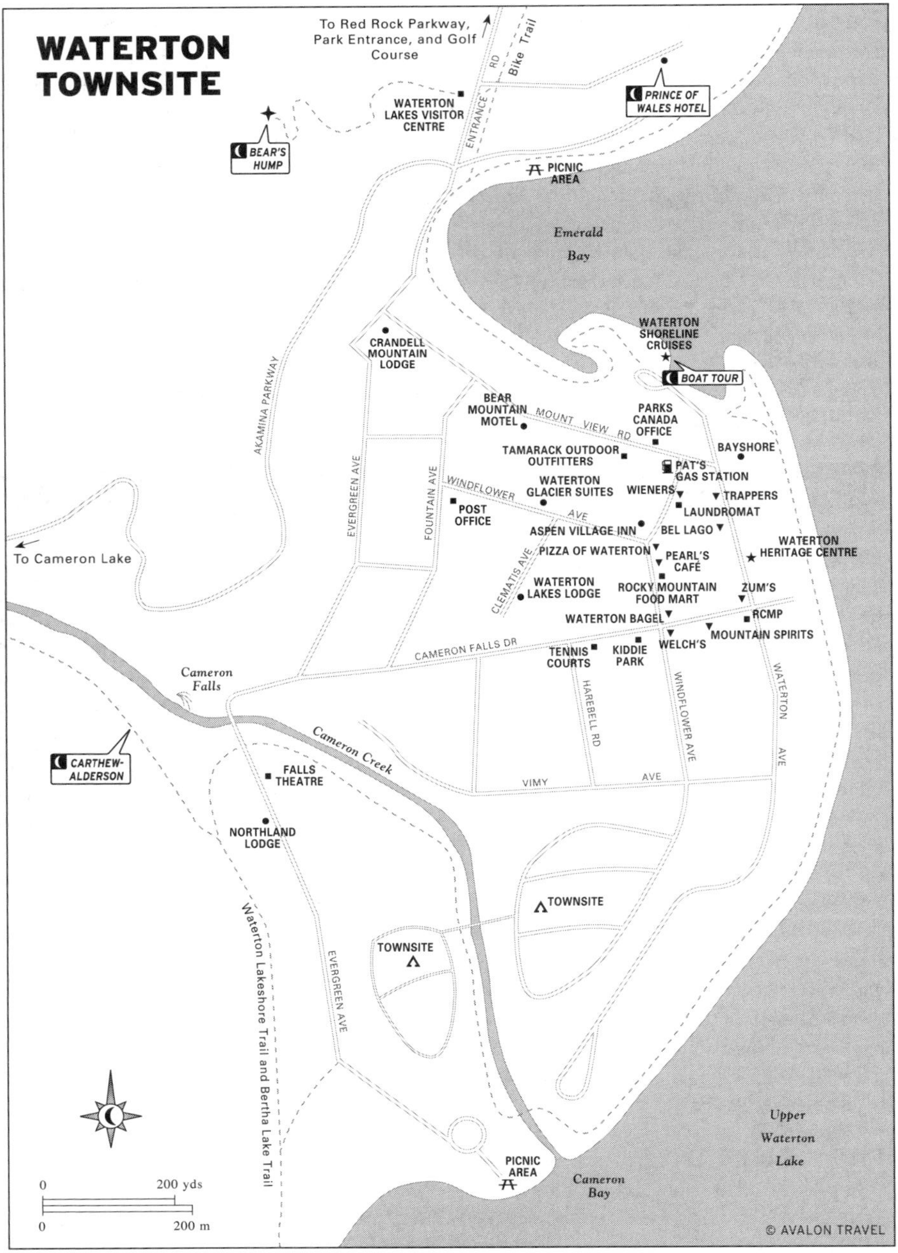
WATERTON TOWNSITE
To Red Rock Parkway, Park Entrance, and Golf Course
Bike Trail
ENTRANCE RD
WATERTON LAKES VISITOR CENTRE
BEAR'S HUMP
PRINCE OF WALES HOTEL
PICNIC AREA
Emerald Bay
AKAMINA PARKWAY
CRANDELL MOUNTAIN LODGE
WATERTON SHORELINE CRUISES
BOAT TOUR
BEAR MOUNTAIN MOTEL
MOUNT VIEW RD
PARKS CANADA OFFICE
TAMARACK OUTDOOR OUTFITTERS
BAYSHORE
PAT'S GAS STATION
WATERTON GLACIER SUITES
WIENERS
TRAPPERS
LAUNDROMAT
EVERGREEN AVE
FOUNTAIN AVE
WINDFLOWER AVE
POST OFFICE
ASPEN VILLAGE INN
BEL LAGO
To Cameron Lake
PIZZA OF WATERTON
PEARL'S CAFÉ
WATERTON HERITAGE CENTRE
CLEMATIS AVE
WATERTON LAKES LODGE
ROCKY MOUNTAIN FOOD MART
ZUM'S
WATERTON BAGEL
RCMP
MOUNTAIN SPIRITS
WELCH'S
KIDDIE PARK
TENNIS COURTS
CAMERON FALLS DR
Cameron Falls
HAREBELL RD
WINDFLOWER AVE
WATERTON AVE
Cameron Creek
CARTHEW-ALDERSON
FALLS THEATRE
VIMY AVE
NORTHLAND LODGE
TOWNSITE
TOWNSITE
Waterton Lakeshore Trail and Bertha Lake Trail
EVERGREEN AVE
Upper Waterton Lake
PICNIC AREA
Cameron Bay
0 200 yds
0 200 m
© AVALON TRAVEL

In winter, you can get the same information, licenses, and permits from the Parks Canada office (215 Mount View Rd., 403/859-2224, 8am-4pm Mon.-Fri. year-round).

GOAT HAUNT RANGER STATION

Located at the southern tip of Waterton Lake, **Goat Haunt Ranger Station** is in Glacier National Park in the United States. It is only accessible by boat or on foot. Visitors may debark the tour boat to walk to the International Peace Park Pavilion at Goat Haunt and back without going through immigration control; however, hikers must go through immigration at the ranger station 11am-5pm to access Glacier's trails and backcountry campsites. All hikers must have appropriate passports or passport cards. Those entering Waterton from Glacier via Goat Haunt-area trails are required to call the Canada Border Services Agency (403/653-3535 or 403/653-3009) from the Waterton Townsite.

SHUTTLES AND TOURS

Shuttles

Getting between Glacier and Waterton by shuttle is complicated by the international border. From Glacier's east side, you can get to Waterton on the **Glacier Park Inc.** shuttle (GPI, 406/892-2525, www.glacierparkinc.com, early June-mid-Sept., depending on distance $10-50 adults, children $5-25). Originating at Glacier Park Lodge in East Glacier, the shuttle stops Two Medicine, Cut Bank Creek, St. Mary Visitor Center, Many Glacier Hotel, and Chief Mountain border crossing before reaching the Prince of Wales Hotel. It runs once daily in each direction, with departure times varying depending on the starting point. For the return connection between Waterton and Glacier, riders may not originate in Canada with GPI. Instead, you must use the **Chief Mountain Shuttle** (Tamarack Outdoor Outfitters, 214 Mount View Rd., 403/859-2378, www.hikewaterton.com, June-Sept.). The shuttle runs on demand by reservation from Waterton to Chief Mountain border crossing for those who need to set up a car shuttle for backpacking from the U.S. border station through the Belly River to Goat Haunt or vice versa. A shuttle ($20 pp) also departs Tamarack Village Square at 2:30pm daily for Chief Mountain border crossing, where you walk through the border control station to catch the 3:45pm GPI shuttle running down Glacier's east side.

Hikers can access Waterton trailheads via shuttles on land or water. The **Crypt Lake Water Shuttle Service** (Waterton Shoreline Cruises, 403/859-2362, www.watertoncruise.com, daily late May-early Oct., adults C$20 round-trip, children C$10) departs from the marina at 9am daily (June-Aug. only) and 10am daily for a 15-minute ride across Upper Waterton Lake to Crypt Landing, where the 17.2-kilometer (10-mile) round-trip trail begins. The return boats depart Crypt Landing at 4pm daily (June-Aug. only) or 5:30pm. No reservations are taken for this shuttle; arrive at least 20 minutes before departure. The tour boat to **Goat Haunt** functions also as a hiker shuttle (daily late May-late Sept., adults C$25 one-way, C$40 round-trip, children C$9-12 one-way, $12-18 round-trip). It accesses trailheads in northern Glacier and provides transportation back to Waterton after hiking the shoreline trail to Goat Haunt. Buy your return ticket that morning before hiking down the lake. You can also pay in cash (exact change in U.S. or Canadian dollars) when you board in Goat Haunt. Day hikers should catch the 10am boat from Waterton Townsite to Goat Haunt. Notify the ticket agent of which boat you plan to catch to return. Be aware of the border regulations for hiking and using this shuttle.

Departing from Tamarack Village Square, the **Cameron Express** (Tamarack Outdoor Outfitters, 214 Mount View Rd., 403/859-2378, www.hikewaterton.com, 8am

The MV *International* lands at Goat Haunt, USA.

Mon.-Fri., 8am and 9:30am Sat.-Sun. June-Sept., C$13) shuttles hikers to the popular Carthew-Alderson trailhead for a point-to-point 18-kilometer (11-mile) hike back to the Townsite. Mountain bikers can take the shuttle to ride the Akamina trails and then ride back to town. Reservations are a good idea in midsummer and are required for cyclists; you can make them with a credit card by phone. The morning **Tamarack Trail Shuttles** ($60 for 2 people, reservations required) help backpackers set up car shuttles between Red Rocks Trailhead and Rowe Lakes Trailhead. The company also provides custom shuttles to other trailheads for a minimum of $80 for two people.

Boat Tour

Waterton Shoreline Cruises (at the marina at the junction of Mount View Rd. and Waterton Ave., 403/859-2362, www.watertoncruise.com, 10am, 1pm, 4pm, and 7pm daily July-Aug., 10am and 1pm daily May-June and Sept.-early Oct., adults C$40 round-trip, kids C$12-18, under age 4 free) operates the historic MV *International* on Upper Waterton Lake. During the two-hour tour on the wooden 200-passenger boat, which has been cruising here since 1927, knowledgeable guides punctuate their patter with humor. For the best views, go for a sunny seat on the boat's top deck. If the weather is brisk, just bundle up. June-mid-September, the boat docks for 30 minutes at Goat Haunt—time enough to walk to Goat Haunt's tiny International Peace Park Pavilion. Because advance reservations are only taken for large groups, get to the dock early in midsummer.

Interpretive Tours

Waterton Outdoor Adventures (214 Mount View Rd., 403/859-2378, summer) offers interpretive tours (2.5 hours, C$20 pp, 4 people minimum) of Cameron Valley and Red Rock

Parkway. You can learn about Canadian aboriginal heritage, early explorers, and wildlife from local guides who have intimate knowledge of the park. The tours are offered on demand by reservation.

SERVICES

Gas up before you head north across the border—gas in Canada is usually $0.50-0.80 per gallon more expensive than in the United States. Also, be aware that gas is sold by the liter in Canada, so the price on the pump will look pretty darn good. To convert the price, remember 3.8 liters equals one U.S. gallon.

While several private websites provide Waterton travel information, two sources have the most accurate and complete details. **Parks Canada** (215 Mount View Rd., 403/859-2224, www.pc.gc.ca/waterton, 8am-4pm Mon.-Fri. year-round) provides the official national park information on camping, boating, hiking, trail conditions, fishing, and other activities. For information on motels, restaurants, and shops, consult the **Waterton Chamber of Commerce** (403/859-2224, www.mywaterton.ca).

Pat's Gas Station (224 Mount View Rd., 403/859-2266) is much more than a place to gas up or buy propane for the RV. While Pat can magically perform minor car repairs, the shop's claim to fame is its rental line: surrey bikes (C$25 per hour), mountain bikes (C$40 per day, C$10 per hour), and mopeds (C$150 per day, C$35 per hour), baby backpacks or strollers (C$15), binoculars (C$15), and tennis rackets (C$3 per hour). Pat's also sells food and convenience items as well as Cuban cigars, fishing tackle, park permits, and newspapers.

There is a coin-op **launderette** (302 Windflower Ave., 7am-9pm daily May-Oct.). Showers (C$6) are available at the **Waterton Health Club and Recreation Centre** at the Waterton Lakes Lodge (101 Clematis Ave., 403/859-2150). The new **Serenity Spa** (111 Waterton Ave., 403/859-2404, daily 11am-7pm summer) offers a full line of massages, manicures, pedicures, and facials (C$30-160).

The Townsite has a **post office** (102 Windflower Ave., 8am-4:30pm Mon.-Fri. year-round). Remember to use Canadian postage stamps rather than U.S. stamps to send mail from Canada. To get Canadian currency, ATMs are located at Pat's Gas Station, Tamarack Village Square, Rocky Mountain Food Mart, Mountain Spirits Liquor Store, the Bayshore Inn, and the Prince of Wales Hotel. *The Calgary Herald* carries regional, national, and international news.

Cell Phones and Internet

Many cell phones can get service in the Townsite, but not in the rest of the park. Pearl's Café (305 Windflower Ave., 403/859-2498) has wireless Internet access, as do several of the lodges, but Internet service is unreliable; don't plan on streaming or downloading music and big files.

Shopping

Shopping in Waterton features souvenirs that are decidedly Canadian, with moose and red maple-leaf T-shirts. Most shops are open daily May-September but close in winter. During shoulder seasons, hours are shorter, often 10am-5pm daily, but in midsummer shops stay open until 7pm-8pm. Many stores and restaurants sell specialty Cuban cigars, unavailable in the United States, but these cannot be taken back over the U.S. border.

If you need outdoor gear, **Tamarack Outdoor Outfitters** (214 Mount View Rd., 403/859-2378, www.hikewaterton.com, mid-May-Sept.) can outfit you from head to toe with hiking, backpacking, camping, and fishing gear. The shop carries good reputable brands at reasonable prices as well as topographic maps for hiking. Chocoholics gravitate toward a sister shop to one in Banff—**Welch's Chocolate Shop** (401 Windflower Ave., 403/859-2363)—that stocks international chocolates and makes its

© BECKY LOMAX

The new Serenity Spa offers a full line of massages, facials, and pedicures.

own fudge and candy. Get wine, beer, and liquor at **Mountain Spirits** (504 Cameron Falls Dr., 403/859-2015).

Currency Exchange

In Waterton, most businesses, including restaurants, shops, and lodges, will accept U.S. currency; however, return change will be given in Canadian currency. For conversions, most businesses use the bank exchange rate, but some have their own policies. For the best exchange rates, use a credit card as much as possible. Waterton has no banks; the nearest banking services are in Cardston and Pincher Creek, but **Tamarack Village Square** (214 Mount View Rd., 7:30am-7:30pm daily July-Aug., shorter hours mid-May-June and Sept.) offers currency exchange for U.S. and Canadian dollars only.

Emergencies

For emergencies, dial 911 or contact the **Royal Canadian Mounted Police** (RCMP, 202 Waterton Ave., 403/859-2244 or 403/627-2113) during summer months or **Parks Canada Wardens** (215 Mount View Rd., 403/859-2224) year-round. The nearest hospitals are 50 kilometers (30 miles) away: **Pincher Creek Hospital** (1222 Bev McLachin Dr., Pincher Creek, 403/627-1234) and **Cardston Health Centre** (144 2nd St. W., Cardston, 403/653-5234). To contact the park's one emergency ambulance, call 403/859-2636.

DRIVING TOURS

Chief Mountain Highway

The Chief Mountain International Highway provides a summer-only connection between Glacier and Waterton Parks. Its hours are linked to the Canadian and U.S. immigration and customs stations at the border (7am-10pm daily June-Labor Day, 9am-6pm May and Sept.). You may want to top off on gas in the United States since gas is generally more expensive in Canada. The nearest gas is in Babb, Montana,

© BECKY LOMAX

Waterton overlook along Chief Mountain Highway

or in Waterton Townsite. The 30-mile road undulates over rolling aspen hills and past beaver ponds as it curves around Chief Mountain, imposing and alone on Glacier's northwest corner. A few unmarked pullouts offer good photo ops. Drive this open range carefully, for cows wander the road. Your car also may need a good cleaning if wet cow pies litter the road.

From the United States, as the road rounds Chief Mountain, it enters Glacier Park. There is no entrance station here, and no payment is required. The road reaches the international border and Chief Mountain border crossing at 18.6 miles. After crossing the border, the road enters Alberta and Waterton Lakes National Park, but you won't reach a park entrance station until nearly at the Townsite. After the road crosses the Belly River, it briefly exits the park, crossing the Blood Indian Reserve (the Blood are part of the Blackfoot family) before reentering the park. Regrowth from the 1998 Sofa Mountain Fire lines both sides of the road. As you crest a big rise, stop at the overlook (45 kilometers, 28 miles) to gaze at the Waterton Valley. For the descent, shift into second gear to avoid burning your brakes.

Park Entrance Road

From Highway 6, the eight-kilometer (5-mile) road connecting the park entrance station with Waterton Townsite is worth a drive with a pair of binoculars. Linnet, Maskinonge, and Lower Waterton Lakes attract scads of birds as well as moose, bear, elk, and smaller wildlife. Stop at a picnic area along the route for wildlife-watching: Knight's Lake (1 km/0.6 miles), Hay Barn (4 km/2.5 miles), or Marquis (6.5 km/4 miles). The Waterton Lakes Visitor Information Center is 7.7 kilometers (4.8 miles) from the entrance station.

Akamina Parkway

A 16-kilometer (10-mile) paved drive climbs above Waterton Townsite along the base of

AKAMINA-KISHINENA PROVINCIAL PARK

Where Waterton Lakes National Park meets the Continental Divide, Akamina-Kishinena Provincial Park begins. It flanks the international boundary of Montana's Glacier National Park and runs westward to the North Fork of the Flathead River. This remote 27,000-acre park is accessible only on foot from Akamina Parkway in Waterton Lakes or on trails from the end of a 109-kilometer (68-mile) dirt road that starts 16 kilometers (10 miles) south of Fernie, British Columbia.

The small park is part of the same slice of the Rockies that provides corridors for grizzly bears and wolves. Geologic wonders display themselves in Forum Peak's 1.3-billion-year-old sedimentary rocks, and rare plants like the pygmy poppy grow here.

From Waterton, hikers and mountain bikers can access the park via a circa-1920 trail that connects the Cameron Valley to the North Fork of the Flathead Valley. At Akamina Pass, the boundary between Waterton National Park and the provincial park, you can mountain-bike to Wall Lake or hike to Forum Lake.

On both sides of the international border, a growing movement is lobbying to make Akamina-Kishinena a national park. The addition would complete the protection of the "Crown of the Continent" ecosystem, matching the entire distance of Glacier's international boundary with lands protected under the Canadian national park system.

Contact British Columbia Parks (205/489-8540, www.gov.bc.ca/bcparks) for information on visiting the park. For information on lobbying efforts, see www.flathead.ca.

Crandell Mountain on Akamina Parkway. The paved road is open year-round, although in winter the plow only goes as far as Little Prairie. Just west of the Waterton Visitor Information Center, the signed Akamina Parkway turns off and begins climbing steeply from Waterton Townsite as it curves up above the Cameron Creek Gorge. It passes the **Oil City Historic Site** as well as trailheads to Crandell Lake, Lineham Falls, Rowe Lakes, Akamina Pass, and Forum Lake. For those looking to picnic along Cameron Creek, picnic tables, pit toilets, and shelters are at McNeally's (6.4 km/4 miles) and Little Prairie (13 km/8 miles). The road ends at **Cameron Lake.** On the return trip, shift into second gear for the steep descent back to the Townsite; you can always smell the hot brakes of those who forget.

Red Rocks Parkway

Red Rocks Parkway (May-Oct.) is self-descriptive, as the paved road ends at Red Rock Canyon. Locate the signed turnoff on the park entrance road (3.5 km/2.2 miles from the Townsite; 4 km/2.8 miles from park entrance station). The 15-kilometer (9.3-mile) narrow road climbs through grasslands, squeezes through a canyon, and opens up into meadows along Blakiston Creek. Through the canyon, the road is quite narrow but passable for trailers and RVs. Bring your binoculars for watching bears and bighorn sheep. Crandell Mountain Campground (7.5 km/4.6 miles) is accessed via this road. The parkway ends at an improved parking area, which has restrooms. A self-guided trail leads around **Red Rock Canyon.** To picnic along Red Rocks Parkway, you'll find tables, pit toilets, and shelters at three spots: Coppermine Creek (8 km/5 miles), Dungarvan (13 km/8 miles), and Red Rocks (15 km/9.3 miles).

SIGHTS

Chief Mountain

Located along Chief Mountain Highway, Chief Mountain abruptly rises 9,080 feet from aspen parklands and prairie. It is the northeasternmost peak in Glacier National Park. Legend

Prince of Wales Hotel sits on a bluff overlooking Waterton Lake.

tells of a young Flathead brave who carried a bison skull to its summit and remained there for four nights wrestling the Spirit of the Mountain. When he finally prevailed, the spirit gave him a protection totem to keep him safe in battle and hunting.

Prince of Wales Hotel

Designated a Canadian National Historic Site, the 122-foot-tall, four-story, 90-room Prince of Wales Hotel took more than a year to build. Constructed by the Great Northern Railway as a link in its Glacier chain, the hotel opened its doors in 1927. Even if you are not staying here, drop in to see its massive lobby with floor-to-ceiling windows looking down Waterton Lake. Kilt-wearing bellhops haul luggage, and the lobby serves high tea in the afternoon. Walk out on the bluff for the best photographic views of Waterton Lake. Beware the howling winds that can rips off hats.

Waterton Lake

Set in a north-south trough gouged by Pleistocene ice age glaciers, Waterton Lake is the deepest lake in the Canadian Rockies. (It's actually Upper Waterton Lake, which feeds Middle and Lower Waterton Lakes, but no one calls it that.) Its 487-foot depths hold 50-pound lake trout and tiny relics of the ice age—the opossum shrimp. Spanning the international boundary, the 0.5-mile-wide and nearly seven-mile-long lake conveys visitors over its waters in the 1927 wooden MV *International.*

The U.S.-Canada Border

For Waterton visitors, the border inside the park is an attraction. The long, straight swath is cleared every 20 years by the International Boundary Commission. The boat tour down Waterton Lake crosses this unnatural forest line en route to Goat Haunt, where visitors can walk to the Peace Park Pavilion without going

© BECKY LOMAX

The border crossing at Chief Mountain celebrates the world's first peace park at adjoining Waterton and Glacier Parks.

through immigration control. Hikers can also walk over the border swath on the Waterton Lake Trail.

Goat Haunt, USA

A tiny seasonal enclave housing rangers, Goat Haunt, USA, is at Waterton Lake's southern end in Glacier National Park. Accessed only by boat or on foot, Goat Haunt sees hundreds of visitors per day in midsummer. Most arrive via the MV *International.* Walk the paved pathway to Goat Haunt's International Peace Park Pavilion, where displays tell the story of the peace park. Trailheads depart to Goat Haunt Overlook, Kootenai Lakes, Rainbow Falls, and beyond.

Cameron Lake

Tucked in a glacial cirque at the terminus of Akamina Parkway, Cameron Lake reflects the steep slopes of Mount Custer. Look across the glacially fed lake to Herbst Glacier: You're looking across the international boundary into Montana. Avalanches preen the slopes into good bear habitat. Rent a rowboat or canoe to paddle around the lake's shoreline, or saunter the pathway along the west shore, watching for moose, shorebirds, and bears. From here, hikers climb the Carthew-Alderson trail to trek to the Townsite.

Waterton Heritage Centre

Operated by the Waterton Natural History Association, Waterton Heritage Centre (117 Waterton Ave., 403/859-2267, daily mid-May-Sept., free) is a small museum housed in the old fire hall with displays on Waterton's natural and cultural history, including local favorite renegade Joe Cosley. Books—from hiking guides to coffee table picture books—are also sold here.

Cameron Falls

Picturesque Cameron Falls is on the edge of Waterton Townsite on Evergreen Avenue. In June, water roars through its slots, but the flow drops substantially by August. Cameron Creek has eroded a massive fold of the Waterton Formation, a 600-million-year-old rock layer. Sit on a bench at the base, or climb the short steep trails on both sides of the creek to reach overlooks. Opt for the north-side switchback trail for better views.

Waterton Townsite

A quaint little tourism town frequented by bighorn sheep and deer, Waterton Townsite is in a dramatic location at the foot of Waterton Lake. Paved walking trails lead through the town, connecting the few-blocks-long shopping district with the campground and picnic areas. Find Waterton's International Peace Park Pavilion adjacent to the marina. Waterton Townsite hums in summer with visitors riding surrey bikes but is quiet in winter under the snow.

Cameron Falls spews from a gorge with such force that mist sprays onto the bridge.

Red Rock Canyon

Red Rocks Parkway begins at Blakiston Creek and terminates at Red Rock Canyon, a colorful narrow gorge. Walk the 0.7-kilometer (0.4-mile) pathway up one side and down the other to take in all its flaming red hues. Iron-rich argillite sediments are layered on top of each other, some turning red from oxidization, others remaining green. Evidence of the ancient Belt Sea, these sediments are some of the region's oldest exposed sedimentary rock, created 1.5 billion years ago. Look for sea evidence of mud cracks and ripple marks.

Maskinonge Lake

Birders and wildlife-watchers migrate to Maskinonge Lake for its rich diversity. Located east of the park entrance, the aspen-rimmed lake attracts waterfowl, ospreys, trumpeter swans, yellow-headed blackbirds, and kingfishers. Because Waterton is on the axis of two migratory flyways, it sees over 250 species of birds. The lake also attracts huge Shiras moose, weighing 1,500 pounds, plus muskrats, mink, and tiny vagrant shrews. When rare trumpeter swans nest here in midsummer, some of the area closes to protect their offspring. Bring binoculars and spotting scopes for wildlife watching.

Bison Paddock

Once roaming the plains in vast numbers 150 years ago, wild bison, also called buffalo, have all but vanished from North America. Two kilometers (1.2 miles) west of the park entrance road on Highway 6, the Bison Paddock contains a small herd. Bison weigh close to 2,000 pounds and look like shaggy cows. But don't be lured into thinking they are docile: They may look big, lunky, and dumb, but they are extremely unpredictable and aggressive. You can see the bison from a viewing area or via a narrow, roughly paved four-kilometer (2.5-mile) loop through the grassland paddock.

Discovery Well and Oil City

Located on the Akamina Parkway, two stops mark the site of Western Canada's first oil well and its accompanying town site. Find the 1902 Discovery Well site eight kilometers (4.8 miles) up the road. Continue on a bit to the original town site for Oil City, where a five-minute walk leads to the foundation of the hotel—all that remains of the 20-block city that became a ghost town within four years.

Recreation

HIKING

Waterton has more than 200 kilometers (124 miles) of trails. Among them, three kilometers (2 miles) of walking trails—both paved and dirt—connect sights, restaurants, lodging facilities, the campground, and picnic areas in Waterton Townsite. From the marina to Cameron Bay, the trail follows the shoreline. Trails also connect to the Falls Theater, Cameron Falls, Bertha Lake and Waterton Lake trailheads, Emerald Bay, and the Prince of Wales Hotel. Contrary to Glacier's backcountry rules, Waterton's trails permit dogs on a leash, but keep your pet under control and away from wildlife.

For updated trail conditions, look at current reports on the Parks Canada website (www.pc.gc.ca) under Public Safety. The visitors center also has trail conditions information, but if you want to talk to the experts about trails, head to **Tamarack Outdoor Outfitters** (214 Mount View Rd., 403/859-2378) to check their hike board and get advice.

For hiking, you'll find the best Waterton topographic map at the visitors center and Tamarack Outdoor Outfitters. The Gem Trek map (877/921-6277, www.gemtrek.com, C$10), also available online, includes roads, trails, bike routes, and trail descriptions for easy, moderate, and strenuous hikes, plus trails in Akamina-Kishinena Provincial Park and at Goat Haunt.

For those planning to camp in the backcountry, wilderness permits are necessary (adults C$10 pp per night, under age 17 free) for all of the nine designated backcountry campsites. Reservations (C$12 per trip) are available 90 days in advance beginning April 1 each year. You can get permits and reservations at the Waterton Visitor Information Center (403/859-5133) or Waterton's Parks Canada office (403/859-5140).

Shuttles by water and land make for easy trailhead access. Waterton Shoreline Cruises (403/859-2362, www.watertoncruise.com) operates the Crypt Lake and Goat Haunt boats. Waterton Outdoor Adventures (Tamarack Outdoor Outfitters, 214 Mount View Rd., 403/859-2378, www.hikewaterton.com) operates the land shuttles.

Hikers heading on trails in Glacier beyond the Goat Haunt Ranger Station must have valid passports or approved passport cards. International visitors from countries other than Canada or the United States must also have an I-94 form or I-94W status, available at Class A Ports of Entry but not at Goat Haunt. The immigration station at Goat Haunt is open 10am-5:30pm daily June-September.

Bertha Lake

- Distance: 11.4 km (7 miles) round-trip
- Duration: 3-4 hours
- Elevation gain: 1,480 feet
- Effort: mostly strenuous
- Trailhead: southwest corner of Waterton Townsite off Evergreen Avenue

The trail starts as a signed interpretive path to Lower Bertha Falls. The path climbs gradually along the western shore of Waterton Lake to an overlook with views of Mount Cleveland, the

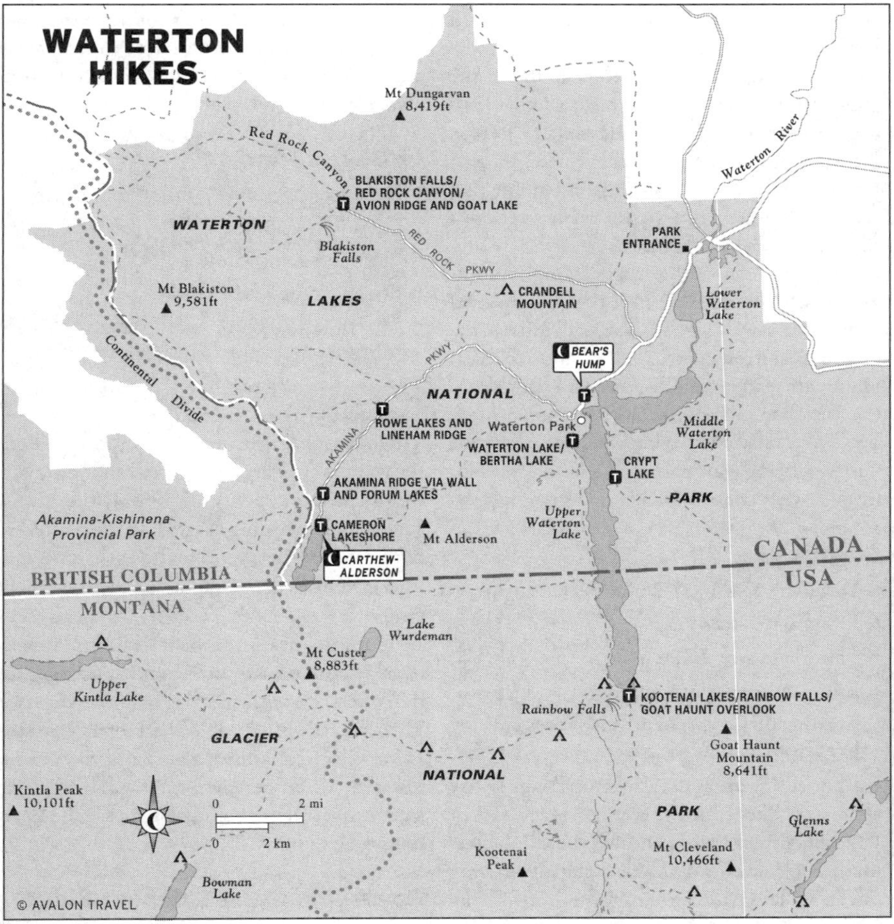

highest peak in Glacier. At the junction, take the right fork and head across the dry open hillside to Lower Bertha Falls, where pounding waters crash through bedrock. For a destination, the falls is 6.4 kilometers (4 miles) round-trip.

To continue to Bertha Lake, cross the bridge below the falls and climb incessant switchbacks up through a forested hillside beside Upper Bertha Falls, a larger sister of the lower falls. Soon the trail crests a timbered knoll high above narrow Bertha Lake for the best view of the lake. To reach the shore, descend 160 meters (500 feet) to the campground near its outlet.

Waterton Lake Trail

- Distance: 13 km (8.7 miles) one-way
- Duration: 4-5 hours
- Elevation gain: minimal
- Effort: easy by elevation gain, moderate by length
- Trailhead: southwest corner of Waterton Townsite off Evergreen Avenue

Bordering the west lakeshore of Waterton Lake, the trail begins at the Bertha Lake Trailhead. After 1.5 kilometers (1 mile), the trails diverge, with the Waterton Lake Trail dropping in a quick steep descent to Bertha Bay Campground on the lakeshore. The trail wanders through cottonwoods, subalpine firs, lodgepole pines, and aspen, with overlooks that offer views of the lake.

The trail crosses the international boundary at 6.1 kilometers (3.8 miles) before connecting to a well-signed maze of trails at the end of Waterton Lake. Follow signs to Goat Haunt and catch the MV *International* back to the Townsite. Before you leave in the morning, book your return trip with Waterton Shoreline Cruises. Bring your passport; you'll need it for immigration control in Goat Haunt.

Crypt Lake

- Distance: 17 km (11.2 miles) round-trip
- Duration: 5-6 hours
- Elevation gain: 2,300 feet
- Effort: moderate-strenuous
- Trailhead: Crypt Landing, accessible by boat from Waterton

Catch the water taxi operated daily by Waterton Shoreline Cruises to reach Crypt Landing. From Crypt Landing, the climb bolts up through a wooded hillside along Hellroaring Creek Valley. An alternate route leads to the edge of Hellroaring Creek and its waterfalls; you can take one route up and one down this short section. Soon the trail passes Twin Falls, and lodgepole pines give way to open meadows and boulder fields.

The trail appears to dead-end in a headwall, but an iron ladder climbs up to a four-foot-high tunnel with an awkward walk or crawl. The tunnel emerges on a cliff with a steel cable for assistance in crossing. The trail breaks into a tight cirque housing Crypt Lake, which drains from an underwater channel. The international boundary crosses the lake's southern end. In a mad dash, hikers suddenly check their watches, and all jump up to speed down the trail en masse to catch the return boat.

Bear's Hump

- Distance: 2.8 km (1.7 miles) round-trip
- Duration: 1.25 hours
- Elevation gain: 550 feet
- Effort: strenuous but short
- Trailhead: Waterton Lakes Visitor Information Centre parking lot

The trail heads promptly uphill, piling on switchback after switchback in a vertical ThighMaster. At least it offers benches along the way to rest. Partially forested and thick with thimbleberry and virgin's bower, the hike is cool in early morning or late afternoon after the hump shades the east slope from the sun. Pick up a free interpretive guide for the trail at the visitors center.

Topping out on the Bear's Hump, a rocky outcropping on Mount Crandell's ridge, the trail offers one of the best views of the Waterton Townsite, the Prince of Wales Hotel, Waterton Lake, Glacier National Park, and the prairie. On top, three benches offer good spots to gaze at the scenery before you tackle the knee-pounding descent.

Rowe Lakes and Lineham Ridge

- Distance: 8.4 km (5 miles) round-trip to Lower Rowe Lake; 12.8 km (7.7 miles) round-trip to Upper Rowe Lakes; 17.2 km (10.6 miles) round-trip to Lineham Ridge
- Duration: 2.5-6 hours
- Elevation gain: 3,116 feet
- Effort: moderate-strenuous
- Trailhead: Rowe Tamarack Trailhead, 10.9 km (6.7 miles) up Akamina Parkway

In July this trail bursts with wildflowers: yellow arnica, paintbrush, and purple lupine.

© BECKY LOMAX

A short, steep trail leads to Bear's Hump, with one of the best views of Waterton Lake.

The climb starts through thin forest broken by avalanche paths, following Rowe Creek. At 3.9 kilometers (2.4 miles), a 10-minute spur trail splits off to Lower Rowe Lake, a destination for those wanting the shortest trek. Continuing on from the junction, the trail ascends into a broad meadow at the base of a giant cirque. After you cross the creek at 5.2 kilometers (3.1 miles), the left fork climbs steep switchbacks to Upper Rowe Lakes, a pair of scenic shallow lakes fringed with alpine larch.

For Lineham Ridge, the right fork after the creek crossing swings around the cirque to climb from subalpine wildflower meadows into alpine tundra. Red argillite colors the mountainside. From the ridge, Lineham Lakes appear below. At the saddle below Mount Lineham, you can opt to climb off-trail east to the peak or continue on the rugged trail west up Lineham Ridge to look down Blakiston Creek.

Cameron Lakeshore

- Distance: 3.2 km (1.9 miles) round-trip
- Duration: 1 hour
- Elevation gain: none
- Effort: easy
- Trailhead: end of Akamina Parkway

This short trail follows the lake's western shoreline to a wooden platform and small interpretive display called Grizzly Gardens, where trees are starting to cut the view. Although the trail is flat, watch your footing on tree roots. Several points reach the shoreline for photos of Mount Custer and Herbst Glacier. At the trail's terminus, scan the avalanche slopes for grizzly bears feeding on glacier lilies. Do not continue farther; bears depend on quiet here for denning, feeding, and rearing cubs.

Carthew-Alderson

- Distance: 18 km (11.8 miles) one-way

- Duration: 6 hours
- Elevation gain: 1,440 feet
- Effort: moderate-strenuous
- Trailhead: end of Akamina Parkway

Catch the Cameron Express hiker shuttle to Cameron Lake. One of the most popular hikes in Waterton, the trail climbs 4.5 miles to Carthew Summit, where alpine tundra stretches along a windswept ridge. Be prepared for strong winds here, even on a sunny summer day. Some winds may even force you to crawl over the pass. Views span deep into Glacier's interior.

The descent is a knee pounder, dropping over 3,000 feet in elevation. From the summit, the trail passes by several high tarns, sometimes flanked with snow fields into July. The path drops along a cliff wall before reaching Alderson Lake. Once you depart the lake, only peek-a-boo views of avalanche chutes break out from the thick timber en route to Cameron Falls at Waterton Townsite.

© BECKY LOMAX

Akamina Ridge offers stunning views into Glacier's remote northwest corner.

Akamina Ridge via Wall and Forum Lakes

- Distance: Akamina Ridge Loop, 18.3 km (11.4 miles); 8.8 km (5.4 miles) round-trip to Forum Lake; 10.4 km (6.4 miles) round-trip to Wall Lake
- Duration: 6-7 hours
- Elevation gain: 3,199 feet
- Effort: strenuous
- Trailhead: Akamina Pass Trailhead, 14.8 km (9.2 miles) up Akamina Parkway

This hike begins in Waterton Park, but within one mile reaches low, forested Akamina Pass, where it crosses over the Continental Divide and into Akamina-Kishinena Provincial Park. Hikers looking for shorter adventures can choose either lake as a destination, but the longer loop hike gets the views. Continue 700 meters (0.4 miles) to the Forum Lake junction, turning left; Wall Lake is to the right, and it's the way you will return. The trail climbs to the snowmelt-fed Forum Lake, surrounded by steep talus and larch slopes. From the lake, follow the rough unmaintained trail that ascends the western ridge up through a 16-foot rock band where you'll need to use your hands for climbing. Once above the band, the ridge walk begins.

The five-kilometer (3-mile) Akamina Ridge walk is truly spectacular. Rolling over peaks and knolls, the alpine tundra is devoid of trees but rampant with miniature plants like pink moss campion struggling to survive. To the south, Glacier's remote Kintla Peak stands with Agassiz Glacier while a sea of peaks stretches in all directions. At the end of the ridge, the trail drops steeply back into forest to Wall Lake, a dramatic cirque tucked against abrupt limestone walls. From Wall Lake, hike three kilometers (1.8 miles) back to the Forum Lake junction and return to the trailhead over Akamina Pass.

Blakiston Falls

- Distance: 2 km (1.2 miles) round-trip
- Duration: 45 minutes
- Elevation gain: 100 feet
- Effort: easy
- Trailhead: end of Red Rocks Parkway

Turn left just after you cross Red Rocks Creek. After crossing Bauerman Creek, turn right and ascend through a coniferous forest. At Blakiston Falls, two wooden decks overlook the roaring falls of Blakiston Creek. Mount Blakiston is visible above the falls.

© BECKY LOMAX

Wooden viewing platforms overlook Blakiston Falls.

Red Rock Canyon

- Distance: 1 km (0.6 miles) loop
- Duration: 30 minutes
- Elevation gain: 130 feet
- Effort: easy
- Trailhead: end of Red Rocks Parkway

From the bridge over Red Rocks Canyon, walk down and up either side of the loop. Water chiseled the canyon, exposing the lustrous red mudstone. At the top of the loop, you'll stare down a dizzying drop more than 23 meters (75 feet) to the creek, a distance that took up to 10,000 years to carve.

Avion Ridge and Goat Lake

- Distance: Avion Ridge Loop, 22.5 km (14 miles); 12.6 km (7.8 miles) round-trip to Goat Lake
- Duration: 4 hours
- Elevation gain: 1,750 feet
- Effort: moderate-strenuous
- Trailhead: at end of Red Rocks Parkway

The Avion Ridge Loop begins and ends on the Snowshoe Trail, an old overgrown roadway that permits bicycles. It's easiest done clockwise, but some hikers prefer the vertical ascent via Goat Lake in favor of a less-steep descent. At 4 kilometers (2.4 miles) up the Snowshoe Trail, you'll reach the Goat Lake junction. Those heading to Goat Lake abruptly climb a relentless uphill into the hanging valley above to Goat Lake, known for its rainbow trout.

For Avion Ridge Loop, continue up the Snowshoe Trail from the Goat Lake junction. At 8.2 kilometers (5.1 miles), you'll reach the Snowshoe Warden Cabin and campsites. Take the trail heading north toward Lost Lake and climb to Avion Ridge. An eight-kilometer (5-mile) unmaintained trail ascends the ridgeline through larch before popping out of the trees on a barren windswept ridge. The trail circles above a cirque right on the boundary of Waterton National Park (you'll see signs). Endless peaks parade in all directions. As the trail swings north, it descends to a saddle, traverses a steep side hill, and reaches a pass above Goat Lake. A knee-pounding descent through wildflower meadows plummets to the lake and then to the Snowshoe Trail junction. Turn left to return to the trailhead.

Rainbow Falls

- Distance: 2.3 km (1.4 miles) round-trip
- Duration: 1 hour
- Elevation gain: minimal
- Effort: easy
- Trailhead: behind the ranger station at Goat Haunt in Glacier National Park

Rainbow Falls is one option for a short hike from the boat tour on Waterton Lake. Check with Waterton Shoreline Cruises for a schedule, and book a return boat that allows enough time to complete your hike. Take your passport to pass through immigration control in Goat Haunt.

Follow the paved trail to the first junction, taking the right fork onto dirt. The trail wanders through thick forests, filled with mosquitoes in early summer. Just before reaching Waterton River, take a left turn at the signed junction, heading up the east bank toward Rainbow Falls. The falls is actually a series of cascades cutting troughs in the bedrock, but it's a great place to sit.

Goat Haunt Overlook

- Distance: 3.2 km (2 miles) round-trip
- Duration: 2 hours
- Elevation gain: 844 feet
- Effort: very strenuous
- Trailhead: behind the ranger station at Goat Haunt in Glacier National Park

Goat Haunt Overlook is another option for a short hike from the boat tour on Waterton Lake. Check with Waterton Shoreline Cruises for a schedule, and book a return boat that allows enough time to complete your hike. Take your passport to pass through immigration control in Goat Haunt.

Follow the paved trail past the first right-hand turn to a dirt trail and hike 160 meters (500 feet) on the Continental Divide Trail, heading south toward Fifty Mountain. At the signed junction, turn left. The trail climbs gently for a few hundred feet before it turns straight up a steep uphill. It's a grunt, but the view is well worth the climb. At the overlook, you can flop on a conveniently placed log to eat lunch and gander down-lake to the Waterton Townsite and the Prince of Wales Hotel.

Kootenai Lakes

- Distance: 9 km (5.6 miles) round-trip
- Duration: 3-3.5 hours
- Elevation gain: minimal
- Effort: easy
- Trailhead: behind the ranger station at Goat Haunt in Glacier National Park

Kootenai Lakes attracts hikers for its often-seen moose and sometimes-seen nesting trumpeter swans. Access is via the tour boat. Check with Waterton Shoreline Cruises for a schedule, and book a return boat that allows enough time to complete your hike. Take your passport to pass through immigration control in Goat Haunt.

At Goat Haunt, follow the paved trail past the first right-hand turn and hike on the Continental Divide Trail, heading south toward Fifty Mountain. The trail wanders through old-growth forest. At four kilometers (2.5 miles), take the right junction toward the campground. If you eat lunch here, do so on the beach or in the cooking area and protect the cleanliness of the tenting sites for those sleeping in bear country.

International Peace Park Guided Hike

Interpretive rangers from Waterton and Glacier jointly lead the International Peace Park Hike (10am Wed. and Sat. July-Aug.). The 14-kilometer (8.7-mile) hike leaves from the Bertha Lake Trailhead. Bring a sack lunch, water, and extra clothes, and wear sturdy walking shoes. You'll stop at the international boundary for a hands-across-the-border ceremony and photos before hiking to Goat Haunt and returning by boat to the Townsite by 6pm. Group size is limited to 35, so you'll need to preregister at the Waterton Lakes Visitor Information Center (403/859-5133) or Glacier's St. Mary Visitor Center (406/732-7750). It's free, but you'll need to pay for the boat ride and make reservations through Waterton Shoreline Tours. Passports are required.

Guides

Parks Canada naturalists guide free hikes to several destinations, usually Wednesday-Monday in summer. Destinations include Rowe Lake and Summit Lake, suitable hikes for families with children. Check at the visitors center for the current schedule or look online (www.pc.gc.ca/waterton).

The Baker family has been hiking in Waterton for more than 90 years, and the youngest generation now operates the commercial guide service **Waterton Outdoor Adventures** (Tamarack Outdoor Outfitters, 214 Mount View Rd., 403/859-2379, www.hikewaterton.com, June-Sept.). Lead guide Carey Tetzlaff provides interpretive services, trail knowledge, and ground transportation to the trailhead. Reservations are required. In general, a full-day hike starts at C$160 for 1-2 people. Half-day hikes and paddle-hike combos are available too. Bring your own trail snacks, lunches, and water.

CYCLING

All roadways in Waterton offer good cycling, but be ready to ride with cars at your elbows with minimal shoulders and narrow corners on Akamina and Red Rocks Parkways. You can also encounter bears on both roads. In 2010, the new seven-kilometer (3.5-mile) paved Kootenay Brown Trail opened, connecting the park entrance with Waterton Townsite, offering the best family-friendly bicycling option. For campers traveling by bicycle, both the Townsite and Crandell Mountain Campgrounds have bear-resistant food storage facilities.

Parks Canada levies heavy fines of up to C$2,000 for riding on sidewalks, grass, or trails designated for hiking only. Alberta law requires children under age 18 to wear a helmet while bicycling. Given the narrow roads and the fact that most drivers are gaping at the scenery or looking for bears, and that winds can be strong enough to knock you off your bike, it's a wise idea for riders of all ages to wear helmets.

Mountain Bike Trails

Four unpaved trails in Waterton permit bikes. For these, mountain bikes are best at handling the trail rubble, roots, and terrain. For current trail conditions, check with the visitors center.

Near the end of Akamina Parkway, **Akamina Pass Trail** climbs a stiff, steep 1.3 kilometers (0.8 miles) on a forested trail to the Continental Divide—the boundary of Waterton National Park, Akamina-Kishinena Provincial Park, Alberta, and British Columbia—before rambling to Wall Lake (10.4 km/6.4 miles round-trip).

At the end of Red Rocks Parkway, the **Snowshoe Trail** is 16.4 kilometers (9.8 miles) round-trip along Bauerman Creek to the Snowshoe Warden Cabin. An abandoned fire road with a fairly wide berth, the trail has some steep sections and creek fords for spice. Savvy hikers do biking-hiking trips—bicycling to the Snowshoe Cabin, then hiking to Lost or Twin Lake.

Leaving Chief Mountain Highway less than one kilometer (0.5 miles) from the Highway 5 junction, the 21-kilometer (12.6-mile) round-trip **Wishbone Trail** rolls on an old wagon road through aspen parklands before narrowing in brush to traverse above Lower Waterton Lake.

The 21-kilometer (12.6-mile) **Crandell Mountain Loop** offers the most challenging ride, with rough terrain and washouts, to circle the massive mountain. You can start at three different trailheads: Crandell Lake Trailhead six kilometers (3.6 miles) up Akamina Parkway, six kilometers (3.6 miles) up Red Rocks Parkway on the Crandell Campground turnoff, or at Waterton Townsite.

Rentals

Pat's Gas Station (224 Mount View Rd., 403/859-2266) rents mountain bikes by the hour (C$10) or full day (C$40). The shop carries full-suspension mountain bikes, and helmets come free with rentals. You'll see Pat's famous two-person four-wheel surrey bikes tootling around the Townsite (C$25 per hour); they're fun for a spin on the flat Townsite roads, but hills are difficult.

HORSEBACK RIDING

Alpine Stables (4 km/2.4 miles from the park entrance on the park entrance road, 403/859-2462, www.alpinestables.com) offers guided rides (9am-5pm daily May-Sept., C$35) that leave on the hour touring on open grasslands with big views of surrounding peaks. During shoulder seasons, the first ride starts at 10am. With small saddles, the stables can take kids as young as four years old. You can either reserve a spot or simply show up about 20 minutes ahead. Wear long pants and tennis shoes or boots. Other rides range 1.5-8 hours (C$48-145). Two-hour rides that depart at 10am, 1pm, and 5pm daily cruise through wildlife habitat where you can often see elk. The 3-4-hour rides depart at 1:30pm daily for the Bison Paddock. Those traveling with their own equines can board horses. Backcountry camping with horses is allowed only at Lone Lake and Snowshoe Cabin (permit required).

BOATING

Motorized boats are permitted on two lakes: **Upper** and **Middle Waterton Lakes.** Jet Skis are not allowed. You can launch boats on ramps at Linnet Lake Picnic Area (1.1 km/0.7 miles north of the Townsite) on Middle Waterton Lake or the marina on Upper Waterton Lake. The marina sells gas and also has overnight mooring services operated by Waterton Shoreline Cruises (403/859-2362). Free permits, available at the entrance station and visitors center, are required for launching.

Boaters are not allowed to camp in their watercraft, but three Upper Waterton Lake campsites are accessible by boat—Bertha Bay and Boundary Creek in Waterton, and Goat Haunt in Glacier. Permits are required; you can get permits and reservations at the Waterton Visitor Information Center (403/859- 5133) or Waterton's Parks Canada office (403/859-5140) for Bertha Bay and Boundary Creek (adults C$10 pp per night, under age 17 free) and Goat Haunt (adults $5 pp per night, ages 8-15 $2.50, under age 8 free, credit card only).

KAYAKING AND CANOEING

Canoeing, kayaking, and rowing are perfect activities for many of Waterton's road-accessible lakes. However, be aware that whitecaps are common, with an average wind speed of 20 mph on Waterton Lake. A free permit is required for boats; you can pick one up at the visitors center.

Waterton Lakes

A few paddlers tackle Upper Waterton Lake, hugging shorelines because of the wind. More kayakers and canoers opt for Middle Waterton Lake, the Dardanelles (the waterway connecting the two lakes), and Lower Waterton Lake for exceptional wildlife-watching, birding, and less-hefty gales. Hay Barn and Marquis Picnic Areas offer good put-ins for paddling these sections.

Cameron Lake

Cameron Lake is an ideal spot for kayaking, canoeing, and rowing. Winds are often less cantankerous than at Waterton Lakes, and the views are equally as tantalizing. Avoid beaching to hike on the slopes surrounding the southern half of the lake; this is prime grizzly bear habitat. Canoes, kayaks, paddleboats, and rowboat rentals (Cameron Lake Boat Rentals, 403/859-2396, www.cameronlakeboatrentals.com, 8am-6:30pm daily mid-June-mid-Sept., shorter hours in shoulder seasons, C$25-35 per

© BECKY LOMAX

the marina in Waterton Townsite

hour) are available at the lakeshore. Life jackets and paddles are included in the rates.

FISHING

As in Glacier, fish are no longer stocked in Waterton Lakes National Park; however, introduced species still populate the waterways: arctic grayling, British Columbia and Yellowstone cutthroat, and rainbow, eastern brook, and brown trout. Conscientious anglers practice catch-and-release, especially to protect 17 species of native fish, including bull trout, ling, lake chub, deepwater sculpin, northern pike, pygmy whitefish, and spottail shiner.

In **Waterton Lake,** home to rainbow trout, whitefish, and pike, fish feed on the tiny opossum shrimp, a crustacean that is a relic of pre-ice age days. The record lake trout caught in Waterton Lake was 51 pounds. Some hiking destinations, like **Goat Lake,** offer decent rainbow trout fishing.

Season

The general fishing season runs July-October, but anglers may fish Upper and Middle Waterton Lakes, Crandell Lake, Cameron Lake and Creek, and Akamina Lake mid-May-early September. Waters closed year-round include Maskinonge Lake and inlet, plus several creeks—Blakiston, Bauerman, Sofa, Dungarvan, and the North Fork of the Belly River.

Regulations

Waterton Park requires a fishing permit (daily C$10, annual C$35) to fish within park boundaries. Purchase one at the visitors center, Parks Canada office, campground kiosks, Cameron Lake boat rentals, or Pat's Gas Station. The license is valid in all Canadian mountain parks. Kids under age 16 can either purchase their own permit to catch a full limit or share limits with an adult. Check for species limits when you purchase fishing licenses. Anglers planning to fish Wall and Forum Lakes in Akamina-Kishinena Provincial Park need British Columbia provincial fishing licenses.

© BECKY LOMAX

Rent kayaks, canoes, paddleboats, and rowboats at Cameron Lake.

Regulations on catch-and-release of native fish and limits of nonnative fish may be changed due to concerns with the aquatic ecosystems. Check for current limits at the visitors center. Barbless hooks are required. Lead weights less than 50 grams (1.8 ounces) are not permitted due to contamination of waterfowl. As in Glacier, bull trout are a protected species in Waterton. Follow the adage "No black, put it back."

WATERSKIING

Waterskiing is permitted only on Upper and Middle Waterton Lakes; however, most water-skiers gravitate to the middle lake. It's more sheltered and less windy than its upper sister. You'll find boat ramps at Linnet Lake Picnic Area (1.1 km/0.7 miles north of the Townsite) on Middle Waterton Lake or the marina on Upper Waterton Lake. Because the water is extremely cold, water-skiers wear dry suits or full wetsuits. Floating debris—logs, sticks, and branches—is common; keep your eyes open for these hazards. Waterton has no water-ski boat or ski rental service. Boats must pick up a free permit at the visitors center before launching.

SAILBOARDING

It's a rare day when Waterton doesn't see wind. Winds don't just blow, they rage. That's why traveling sailboarders with their own gear (no rental gear is available in Waterton) gravitate to Upper Waterton Lake. The glacier-fed lake, however, is freezing cold. Wear a dry suit or wetsuit to prevent hypothermia. To sailboard here, you should know how to water-start and self-rescue; it's not a place for beginners. For the best launching on the upper lake, head to **Windsurfer Beach** on Waterton Avenue, one block west of Vimy Avenue. For safety, check the current weather report at the Waterton Visitor Information Center before launching into a big wind.

SCUBA DIVING

Scuba divers go after a spot in Emerald Bay where a sunken circa 1900 paddle steamer, *The Gertrude,* provides exploration at a depth of 20 meters (65 feet). For the clearest waters, early spring and fall are best for diving. Just remember that historic artifacts, which include anything on the wreck, are protected by the park; leave everything where you find it. Bring your own gear, as the nearest scuba shop for rentals and repairs is 130 kilometers (78 miles) east in Lethbridge.

SWIMMING

Beaches at Waterton Lake attract swimmers, but the water is chilly, and winds can howl. For a heated indoor pool, head to the **Waterton Health Club and Recreation Centre** (7am-10pm daily year-round, C$6) in the Waterton Lakes Lodge (101 Clematis Ave., 888/985-6343). The facility includes a hot tub and fitness center. For kids, there is a fun outdoor water-spray playground (Cameron Falls Dr. and Windflower Ave.).

GOLF

Focusing on your putting can be difficult with huge scenery. Not only are sand traps a hazard, but sometimes grizzly bears are too. Located three kilometers (1.7 miles) north of the Townsite, the 18-hole **Waterton Golf Course** (403/859-2114, www.golfwaterton.com, dawn-dusk May-Oct., C$49) is an original Stanley Thompson design like the Banff Springs and Jasper courses—rolling fairways bordered with aspens. The pro shop rents golf carts (C$35) and clubs (C$7-20), and a licensed clubhouse keeps guests fed and watered on its patio, which has outstanding views. Many of Waterton's hotels offer golf packages in May and after mid-September.

TENNIS

There are four hard-surface outdoor public tennis courts (Cameron Falls Dr. and Harebell Dr.). **Pat's Gas Station** (224 Mount View Rd., 403/859-2266) rents tennis rackets (C$3 per hour). The free unlit courts, which are snow-covered in winter, are available on a first-come, first-served basis.

CROSS-COUNTRY SKIING AND SNOWSHOEING

In winter, when heavy snows render many of the roads impassable by vehicle, the parkways become ideal cross-country ski trails. Skiers can also glide down Waterton Lake after it freezes. Cross-country ski and snowshoe gear is available to rent through Waterton Lakes Lodge ($15 per day). With no snowmobiles allowed, a quiet backcountry experience is guaranteed on the park's ski trails.

Waterton is a land of winter extremes. It records the highest precipitation levels in Alberta, much of it as snowfall. It also records winter winds over 60 mph, which can plummet wind chills. With winter chinooks, the park is also one of Alberta's warmest areas, with an average of 28 days above freezing in winter. With this diversity, you can expect all types of snow—from dry light powder to heavy wet glop—and conditions that change within an hour. Most cross-country skiers sacrifice speed for reliable glide by using waxless skis.

Two designated ski trails are marked: **Cameron** and **Dipper Ski Trails,** both off Akamina Parkway, which is plowed to the trailheads at Little Prairie. Other trails such as Crandell Lake, Rowe Trail, and Akamina Pass offer more options, but be prepared with avalanche gear. Popular snowshoe trails lead to Bertha Falls and Crandell Lake. Contact the Waterton Parks Canada office (403/859-2224) for details and avalanche conditions.

ENTERTAINMENT

Parks Canada offers evening slide shows and indoor programs (8pm daily summer) at the Falls Theater (across Evergreen Ave. from Cameron Falls) and Crandell Mountain Campground. Varying programs cover wildlife, ecology, and geology. Call 403/859-2445 for a current schedule, which is also posted in the visitors center and campgrounds.

New owners of the **Waterton Opera House** (309 Windflower Ave., 403/859-2466, www.watertonlakesoperahouse.ca, summer) took out the 100-year-old theater seats to revamp the building for live music and dining. Music offerings are broad but don't include opera.

Waterton celebrates festivals. For 10 days in late June, the **Waterton Wildflower Festival** (800/215-2395, www.watertonwildflowers.com) pulls together hikes, art shows, photography courses, watercolor painting workshops, drawing classes, slide shows, and free evening lectures in a tribute to the park's rare and diverse wildflowers. Some events are single-day programs lasting two hours; others are multiday. All are taught by regional experts. Course fees range C$10-299, but several are free. You can register online. The **Blackfoot Arts and Heritage Festival** stages exhibition pow-wows for several days in early August. In late September, when the elk bugle and animals congregate on Blakiston, the town celebrates the **Waterton Wildlife Festival** (800/215-2395, www.watertonwildlife.com), which includes the International Wildlife Film Festival and special wildlife-watching and photography excursions.

Accommodations

In Waterton, everything is within walking distance, with the compact town less than a mile across. No matter where you stay, you can walk to restaurants, shopping, boat tours, or hiking. Several hotels have wireless Internet access, but the service is erratic; you won't be able to stream movies or download big files. All of the hotel rooms in Waterton are smoke-free, and reservations are absolutely mandatory for midsummer.

While the town bustles in summer, minimal services remain open in winter. All accommodations have the 5 percent Goods and Services Tax and the 4 percent tourism tax added to the rates; together they add up, so don't be surprised that your final room bill tallies higher than you might have expected. Many of the hotels offer golf, seasonal activity packages, and specials; ask or check their websites for current deals. You'll get better deals in Waterton in the off-season (May-early June, late Sept.-Oct., and winter), when most lodging properties drop their rates substantially, making travel cheaper at a crowd-free time. Waterton lodging is at a premium in midsummer during the big visitor season. If you don't want to pay the high rates, you can drive 35 minutes north to Pincher Creek for less-expensive chain motels.

Plans for rebuilding the Kilmorey Lodge (117 Mount View Rd., 403/859-2150, www.thekilmoreylodge.com), which burned to the ground in 2009, are still afloat; the owner is working on approval from Parks Canada.

Lodges and Inns

Located on a bluff above Waterton Lake, historic **Prince of Wales Hotel** (across from the visitors center, 7.6 km/4.6 miles south of the park entrance station, 406/892-2525, 403/236-3400, front desk 403/859-2231, www.glacierparkinc.com, mid-June-mid-Sept., C$200-300, suites C$600-800) is a four-story wonder named for the prince who later became King Edward VIII. Kilted bellhops greet visitors, and high tea is served in the afternoon. Its lobby, with floor-to-ceiling windows, swings with a huge rustic chandelier. Lake-view guest rooms allow you to shower while looking into Glacier Park, and mountain-view guest rooms let you spy on bighorn sheep. But despite its grand facade, the building is old, creaky, and thin-walled, and the upper stories seem to sway in high winds. Be prepared for tiny sinks and small baths, many installed in what were once closets. The guest rooms have phones but no other amenities. A cantankerous elevator accesses upper floors but requires a bellhop to run, rendering it unavailable at all hours. Top-floor lodgers often get a workout climbing the stairs. A restaurant, a gift shop selling English bone china and Waterford crystal, and a lounge surround the lobby. You can reach town via a 5-minute drive or a 15-minute walk down a trail.

With mountain views from many of the guest rooms, the **Waterton Lakes Lodge Resort** (101 Clematis Ave., 403/859-2150 or 888/985-6343, www.watertonlakeslodge.com, year-round, C$195-450 mid-June-mid-Sept., $120-225 mid-Sept.-mid-June) has 80 modern air-conditioned guest rooms, plus kitchenettes, suites, guest rooms with fireplaces and jetted tubs, and pet-friendly options. The pleasant accommodations are in 11 two-story chalets

© BECKY LOMAX

historic Prince of Wales Hotel

that have an intimate feel. All guest rooms have TVs, coffeemakers, wireless Internet access, and phones. Guests get free use of the on-site Waterton Spa and Recreation Center pool, hot tub, and workout room.

The 17-room **Crandell Mountain Lodge** (102 Mount View Rd., 403/859-2288 or 866/859-2288, www.crandellmountainlodge.com, year-round, C$145-240 mid-June-mid-Sept., C$100-190 mid-Sept.-mid-June) is tucked beneath its namesake peak. The two-story circa-1940 inn has a variety of country-themed guest rooms—from standard rooms up to three-room suites with full kitchens and fireplaces. In a private garden area, a huge deck with a barbecue and lounge chairs begs for afternoon relaxation.

Motels

The Bayshore (Mount View Rd. and Waterton Ave., summer 403/859-2211 or 888/527-9555, www.bayshoreinn.com, May-early Oct., C$122-282) offers lakefront guest rooms with prime views from private balconies. Family rooms, deluxe suites, and pet-friendly rooms are available, along with less pricey guest rooms with mountain views. New bedding and curtains recently upgraded the guest rooms. The complex has restaurants, a lounge, a saloon, a hot tub, a gift shop, satellite Internet access, an ice cream shop, and spa services. It is adjacent to the marina, shopping, and additional restaurants. The Townsite Loop trail system passes between the inn and the lake.

With mountain views and the most spacious guest rooms in town, the **Waterton Glacier Suites** (107 Windflower Ave., 403/859-2004 or 866/621-3330, www.watertonsuites.com, year-round, C$232-292 mid-June-mid-Sept., C$99-159 mid-Sept.-mid-June) has 26 units with private balconies for enjoying the scenery. Guest room amenities include fridges, microwaves, satellite TV, air-conditioning, wireless Internet access, and whirlpool tubs. Some guest rooms have fireplaces.

WHAT IS GST?

Everywhere in Canada, a 5 percent **Goods and Services Tax** (GST) is applied to some purchases and services. In most cases, it is added onto your bill, not already included.

In general, groceries, prescription drugs, health care, and medical devices are not taxed. But you will pay GST on motels, campground fees, restaurant bills, souvenirs, clothing, gas, recreation rentals, and tours.

Nonresident visitors on tours and foreign conventioneers can get a rebate on a portion of the tax on the tour, provided the tour company does not offer the rebate. Not all tours qualify–only those with short-term accommodations of less than one month (camping, motels, hotels, lodges) plus guide services, interpreter services, or transportation. In general, lodging, meals, admission fees, car rentals and gas, RV rentals, golf greens fees, recreational equipment, and park entrance fees do not qualify.

Nonresidents on tours that qualify need to save their original receipts and detailed itineraries to be eligible for a refund on the GST. Refund forms are available online (www.cra-arc.gc.ca).

Sporting unique red metal roofs (you won't get lost), the **Aspen Village Inn** (111 Windflower Ave., 403/859-2255 or 888/859-8669, www.aspenvillageinn.com, mid-May-early Oct., C$99-259) has standard hotel rooms, pet-friendly rooms, and cottages with kitchens in its aging two-story buildings. The guest rooms have been upgraded and include TVs and wireless Internet access. Cottages accommodating 2-8 people work well for families. The units surround mowed lawns, a playground, and an outdoor barbecue picnic area.

For the most affordable rooms in town, your answer is the **Bear Mountain Motel** (208 Mount View Rd., 403/859-2366, www.bearmountainmotel.com, mid-May-early Oct., C$75-199). The 1960s wood-and-masonry motel revamped its 36 small 1-3-bedroom units, several of which have tiny kitchenettes. You can expect clean basic guest rooms but no in-room phones or extras. Pay phones are available near the office.

Bed-and-Breakfast

For park-history buffs, the **Northland Lodge** (408 Evergreen Ave., 403/859-2353, www.northlandlodgecanada.com, mid-May-mid-Oct., C$135-215) has a certain attraction. Louis Hill, builder of the Prince of Wales Hotel and many of Glacier Park's historic hotels, constructed the Swiss-style lodge as his private residence circa 1948, although he never lived here. Two of the lodge's nine guest rooms share a bath, and the rest have private baths; guest rooms are split among three levels. Wireless Internet access is available. A large balcony is great for soaking up the views with coffee and homemade muffins with saskatoon-berry jam in the morning. A 10-minute walk puts you in the heart of shopping and restaurants via the scenic Townsite Loop trail, just across the street.

CAMPING

Inside the Park

Waterton Park campgrounds have flush toilets, drinking water, kitchen shelters, and bear-resistant food-storage lockers. Some sites have fire rings, and firewood is supplied, but you pay $9 per site for a burning permit in addition to your campground fee. Trailheads are adjacent to all campgrounds.

Smack in the heart of town, the **Waterton Townsite Campground** (403/859-2224, www.pc.gc.ca, May-mid-Oct., unserviced sites C$23-28, full hookups C$38) is citified with a mowed lawn, but it sits on prime real estate with gorgeous views. The 238-site campground borders the Townsite Loop trail and the beach. A few trees shade some sites, but most are open, offering little privacy. Go for the most scenic unserviced spots in the G loop—sites 26-46—but be prepared for strong winds. For more sheltered scenery, go for the Cameron Creek E loop sites (even numbers 2-16). Fires are only permitted in the kitchen shelters, but the campground includes hot showers and a dump station. In midsummer, the campground fills early; plan on arriving by noon to claim a site, or make reservations (C$11) starting in early April through the National Parks Canada Campground Reservation Service (877/737-3783, www.pccamping.ca). Early or late in the season, you'll have your pick of sites without a reservation; off-season, the campground is virtually empty.

On the opposite side of Crandell Mountain from the Townsite and six kilometers (3.8 miles) up the Red Rocks Parkway, **Crandell Mountain Campground** (403/859-2224, www.pc.gc.ca, mid-May-early Sept., C$22) is nestled in the woods along Blakiston Creek. With many sites deep in the trees, the campground has a remote feel, with greenery providing privacy between sites. Sometimes you can see bears and moose around Blakiston Creek. The 129 sites offer no hookups, but a dump station is available. The campground takes no reservations, so plan on claiming your site by midday in July-August. A, B, C, and D loops are in thicker trees; E, F, G, and H loops are more open, with views of surrounding peaks. Five tepees (reservations 403/859-5133 or at the visitors center, $55, reservation fee $11) are available for rent.

On Chief Mountain Highway and 26 kilometers (17 miles) from Waterton Townsite, the **Belly River Campground** (403/859-2224, www.pc.gc.ca, mid-May-mid-Sept., C$16) has 24 pleasant sites for small RVs and tents in aspen groves with hand-pumped well water and some pit toilets in addition to the flush toilets. Some sites are shaded, and some are in

© BECKY LOMAX

Waterton Townsite Campground sits on Upper Waterton Lake.

meadows. It is a good location for watching wildlife and birding, and it is the closest campground to Chief Mountain border crossing for those who want to travel across the boundary first thing in the morning.

In winter, when all other campsites have closed, free sites are available at **Pass Creek Winter Campground** (403/859-2224, www.pc.gc.ca, mid-Oct.-mid-Apr.). Located on the entrance road five kilometers (3.1 miles) from the Townsite, the eight sites offer primitive camping with only a pit toilet and a woodstove in the kitchen shelter. Water from the creek may be boiled or purified for use.

Backcountry Camping

Waterton has nine backcountry campgrounds, called "wilderness campsites." Some backpackers break up the Avion Ridge traverse with stays at **Snowshoe** and **Goat Lake,** but **Twin Lakes** and **Lost Lake** put you farther away from day hikers. Required permits (adults C$10 pp per night, free under age 17) are available at the visitors center (403/859-5133) or Waterton's Parks Canada office (403/859-5140) in person 24 hours in advance or by reservation (C$12) up to 90 days in advance.

Outside the Park

Just outside the park boundary, two private campgrounds can handle the overload when the park campgrounds are full. GST will be added to your camping fees. On Highway 6 to Pincher Creek, **Waterton Springs Campground** (2.5 km/1.5 miles north of the park entrance road, 403/859-2247, www.watertonspringscamping.com, May-Sept.) has 70 full-hookup sites (C$30) in an open dusty parking lot-type setting that fit big rigs, along with 75 partial-hookup sites (C$24-30) and tent sites (C$18) around small ponds and a creek in a rough aspen parkland. Amenities include token-operated showers and a launderette, flush toilets, picnic tables, a camp store, a playground, and fire rings.

Operated by Waterton Natural History Association, **Crooked Creek Campground** (6 km/3.8 miles east of the park entrance road, 403/653-1100, www.wnha.ca, May-Sept., hookups C$25-30, tents C$18) has 33 sites adjacent to the highway. Amenities include flush toilets, showers, a kitchen shelter, a dump station, firewood, a launderette, and hookups for power, water, and sewer.

Food

In this remote resort oasis in a national park, food prices can be exorbitant, but a few good, less expensive options have recently opened. If you're camping or backpacking, consider bringing supplies with you. You'll also find your final bill increased by the 5 percent GST.

RESTAURANTS

With the exception of the Prince of Wales Hotel, restaurants in the Townsite are clustered in one block along Waterton and Windflower Avenues. The two streets have a European feel with patio and sidewalk dining. For the kids and on hot days, ice cream shops abound. For adults, the revamped **Thirsty Bear Saloon** (111 Waterton Ave., 403/859-2211) usually rolls out C$10 beer jugs on Monday, and several locations serve espresso. Many restaurants offer hiker lunches (C$10-15) for the trail. In the off-seasons (June and Sept.), restaurants may shorten their hours or days. Only one restaurant stays open through the winter.

Casual Fine Dining

At Waterton Lakes Lodge, **Vimy's Lounge and Grill** (101 Clematis Ave., 403/859-2150 or

888/985-6343, www.vimys.com, 7:30am-10pm daily, shorter hours Mon.-Fri. winter) is the only restaurant open year-round. It offers two dining rooms: a lounge downstairs, and upstairs dining with a view of Mount Cleveland. Outside dining is also available on a patio and upper deck. Breakfast (C$7-13) includes multiple variations on eggs Benedict, while lunch (C$11-15) has burgers plus the locally sourced Yak-beef Dip. You can also test the Canadian classic *poutine:* homemade french fries drowning in cheese curds and gravy. Dinner entrées (C$24-30) rotate seasonally with bison tenderloin, trout, and vegetarian options, which can be accompanied by international and Canadian wines.

Located in the Prince of Wales Hotel (406/892-2525, 403/236-3400, front desk 403/859-2231, www.glacierparkinc.com, early June-mid-Sept.), the **Royal Stewart Dining Room** looks out massive floor-to-ceiling windows down Waterton Lake, which garners the restaurant its fame more than its culinary uniqueness. Breakfast (6:30am-9:30am daily, C$7-17) specializes in eggs Benedict and omelets, while lunch (11:30am-2pm daily, C$11-16) serves up salads, burgers, sandwiches, and wraps. The dinner menu (5pm-9:30pm daily, C$23-30) includes a few entrées with a Scottish-Canadian twist: Ballymaloe Irish Stew or Buffalo Bangers and Mash. Reservations are recommended in midsummer. Lighter meals are served in the **Windsor Lounge** (2pm-10pm daily, C$8-16), a cozy place to sit that has a big view.

The British atmosphere of the Prince of Wales Hotel goes into full swing with **Afternoon Tea** (1pm-5pm daily, adults C$30, children C$16) in the hotel lobby overlooking Waterton Lake. It's a full meal of finger sandwiches, scones, and a sugar-fest of desserts: pastries, fruits, and berries. Pour your tea from signature porcelain servers. It's a unique experience, but it is more about the atmosphere than

© BECKY LOMAX

Vimy's Lounge and Grill is the one restaurant open year-round in Waterton.

© BECKY LOMAX

Pearl's Café is a hiker's haunt with fresh baked goodies.

anything else. Reservations and prepayment are recommended. If you partake in high tea, you can forgo a big evening dinner.

Located in the Bayshore, the **Bayshore Lakeside Chophouse** (111 Waterton Ave., 403/859-2211 or 888/527-9555, www.bayshoreinn.com, 7am-10pm daily May-mid-Oct.) has the view going for it, as the restaurant is right on Waterton Lake with outdoor dining on a patio. Breakfast and lunch (C$9-15) have an array of choices on the menu. This is the place to go for dining on Alberta steaks and game (C$19-38).

Italian

Dine indoors or alfresco at **Bel Lago Ristorante** (110 Waterton Ave., 403/859-2213, www.bellagoristorante.com, 11am-10pm daily May-Sept.). Homemade pastas with Alberta ingredients—natural beef and organic veggies-catapult the flavors up a notch. Lunch (C$8-17) features salads, pasta, and paninis. Dinner entrées (C$15-32) run from pastas to tenderloin and can be paired with a bottle of Italian wine. Reservations are required for dinner in midsummer.

With indoor and patio seating, the tiny **Pizza of Waterton** (303 Windflower Ave., 403/859-2660, 5pm-10pm Mon.-Thurs., noon-10pm Fri.-Sun. May-Oct., C$14-28) is known for creative handcrafted pizzas, huge calzones, big salads, and a local vibe. Order a pizza to go for campsite dinners.

Cafés

Known as the hiker's haunt, **Pearl's Café** (305 Windflower Ave., 403/859-2498, www.pearlscafe.ca, 7am-9pm daily May-Sept., C$7-14) serves breakfast, lunch, and dinner. Find homemade energy bars, baked goods, espresso, French toast, wraps, chili, salads, wine, beer, wireless Internet access, and a dinner pasta bar.

Wieners of Waterton (301 Windflower Ave., 403/339-1079, www.wienersofwaterton.com, 7am-9pm daily mid-May-Sept., $4-9) is Waterton's newest eatery, started by brothers Jon and Max Low in 2010. It's a hot dog shop, but one that piles the dogs with creative toppings. The dogs hail from local butchers as well as New York, and the Anti-Dog (falafel with hummus and *tzatziki*) appeases vegetarians. The sweet-potato fries come with a variety of tasty homemade dipping sauces, and the breakfast sausage dog works for a grab-and-go start to the day.

The **Glacier Bistro** (111 Waterton Ave., 403/859-2211, 7am-11pm daily) serves lighter meals for breakfast, lunch, and dinner (C$6-12): croissants, pizza, and burgers, plus a selection of dessert goodies.

Family Dining

Two family eateries (8am-9pm daily May-Sept.) provide large diverse menus to appease any palate. Located at opposite ends of the same block, you can browse their outdoor menus and assess the crowds at **Zums Eatery** (116 Waterton Ave., 403/859-2388) and the new **Trappers Mountain Grill** (106 Waterton Ave., 403/859-2445). Both restaurants offer indoor or shaded outdoors sidewalk dining. Breakfasts and lunches range $7-16; dinner (C$13-23) at Zums features ribs barbecued in Guinness or fried chicken. The wildberry pie (C$5)—a combination of raspberries, blueberries, blackberries, rhubarb, and apple—is a must. Trappers dinner ($16-35) specializes in hickory smoked ribs, wings, and pulled pork.

Caffeine

Over the past few years, espresso has boomed in Waterton. You can linger over your favorite cappuccino or latte or get it to go at five different locations-all a few steps from each other on Waterton and Windflower Avenues. Pearl's Café is the locals' fave.

GROCERIES

While several outlets in town carry convenience foods, only one grocery store—**Rocky Mountain Food Mart** (307 Windflower Ave., 8am-8pm daily May-Sept.)—stocks fresh produce, meats, dairy, deli, and baked goods. It's tiny, so expect limited selection, and prices can be high. It also carries ice, firewood, and camping supplies. Off-season, find the closest grocery stores in Pincher Creek.

FLATHEAD VALLEY

The Flathead Valley is an outdoor recreation paradise. Surrounded by mountain ranges and abundant lakes, back doors open on fishing, skiing, hiking, hunting, biking, and boating. With 2.5 million acres of wilderness and national parklands, there's no shortage of space to get away from it all and play outdoors. One of the country's largest national forests fringes the valley floor, which is dotted with lakes, including the largest freshwater lake west of the Mississippi. Summer brings flat-water kayaking and river floating. Anglers drop lines from drift boats, golfers hit the links, and hikers climb to wildflower-strewn heights with huge views of the vast valley.

Strip-mall culture has made some inroads into the valley, paving once pastoral farmlands. Housing developments sprout between towns, blending the borders of one with another. People who want to create another Aspen have thrown up multimillion-dollar mansions on the hillsides. But an underlying culture remains—one where ripped Carhartts and a duct-taped jacket rank as fashion. Rather than hit the nine-to-five office hours, lots of folks here work seasonally—in Glacier or Flathead National Forest in summer and at ski areas in winter.

When snow falls, logging roads and golf courses become ski and snowshoe trails, while two alpine ski areas rack up the vertical for skiers and snowboarders. Many in the valley

© BECKY LOMAX

HIGHLIGHTS

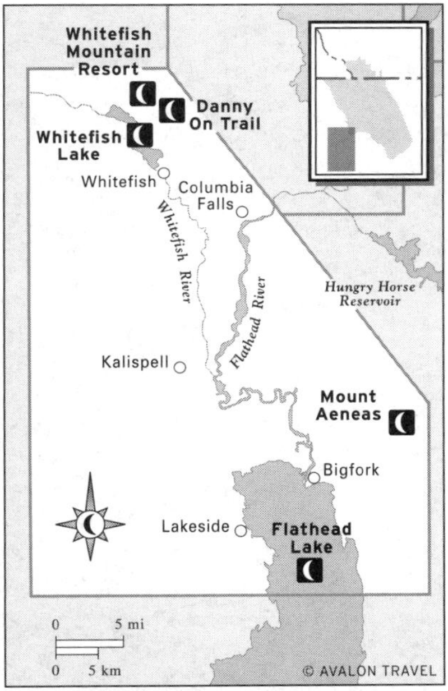

LOOK FOR ☾ TO FIND RECOMMENDED SIGHTS, ACTIVITIES, DINING, AND LODGING.

☾ **Flathead Lake:** Sail its blue waters or drive around its perimeter. The largest freshwater lake west of the Mississippi draws waters from Glacier and Canada (page 239).

☾ **Whitefish Lake:** Cool off on hot summer days in a lake hopping with water-skiers and anglers. Three parks and a marina provide different access options (page 240).

☾ **Mount Aeneas:** Hike the short trail up the highest peak in Jewel Basin. From the summit are views into the Great Bear Wilderness, down on Flathead Lake, and north to Glacier (page 242).

☾ **Danny On Trail:** Ride a chairlift to the top of Big Mountain to hike down the most popular trail in the Flathead. It's a romp through mounds of wildflowers with panoramic views of Glacier Park (page 243).

☾ **Whitefish Mountain Resort:** Ski or snowboard this winter wonderland, or go for summer adventures: mountain biking, zip-line tours, an aerial park, an alpine slide, or scenic chairlift rides (page 249).

adhere to the six-inch rule: If six inches or more of snow falls, call in late for work.

HISTORY

Originally the home of the Flathead, Salish, and Kootenai people, the Flathead Valley saw its first person of European descent—famed explorer David Thompson—in 1809. Within 40 years, trappers, homesteaders, and ranchers edged their way into the valley. By the end of the 19th century, the Great Northern Railway had laid tracks through the Flathead, prompting Kalispell to be plotted for township in 1890, in theory to become the next St. Paul.

Growing with ranchers, farmers, and timber harvesters, the Flathead soon sprouted other towns clustered around its lakes and rivers. In 1901 the Great Northern Railway rerouted its tracks through Whitefish to access Canadian coal, transforming the tiny lakefront community of Whitefish into a railroad town. The mid-1900s saw tremendous change in the Flathead, with the construction of the Hungry Horse dam spawning an aluminum plant, the Plum Creek Timber Company, and the Whitefish Mountain Ski Resort. Today, while valley ranching, farming, and timber still support many families, part of the Flathead economy for its 90,000 residents comes from technology industries and tourism.

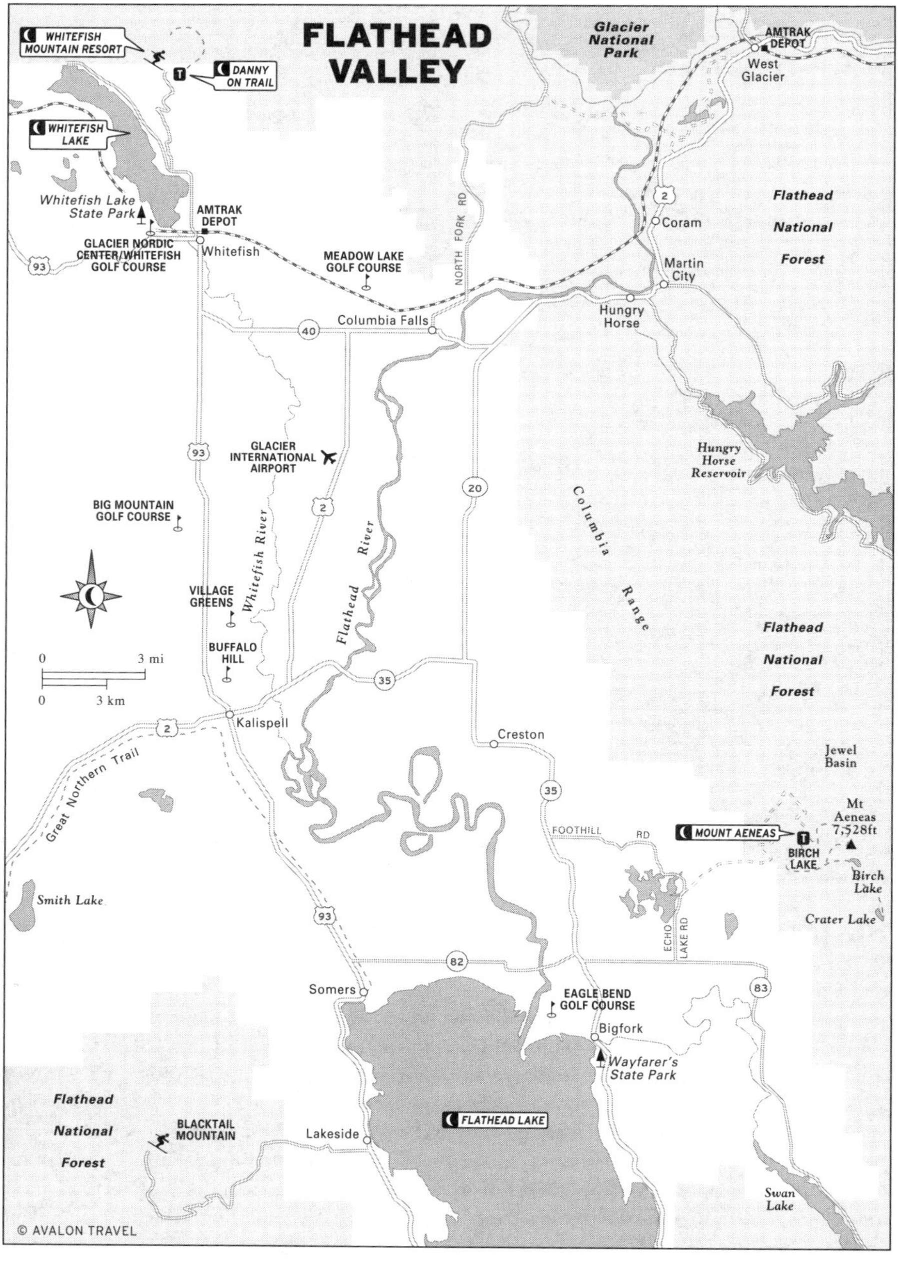

FLATHEAD VALLEY

Exploring Flathead Valley

Flathead Valley centers around four main towns: Kalispell, Whitefish, Columbia Falls, and Bigfork. Each has its own draw in the form of seasonal recreation in each area. Flathead Valley is a casual place. Don't bother with a suit and tie or fancy dinner dress, even in the priciest restaurants. Recreational clothing is suitable everywhere.

Outside the four main towns, small burgs dot Flathead Lake's shoreline. Lakeside buzzes with summer water fun and serves as the launching point to reach Blacktail Mountain Ski Area in winter. Somers is a blink-and-miss-it town but is popular for its marina.

Kalispell

The nucleus of Flathead Valley, with three golf courses, restaurants, and shopping, the area's largest town has moved beyond its cow-town past. In historic downtown Kalispell, you can tour the pre-1900s Conrad Mansion and unique art spots. In August, catch the Northwest Montana Fair and Rodeo, and in October, join in the Glacier Jazz Stampede.

Whitefish

The recreation capital of Flathead Valley, Whitefish is busy in summer with boating in Whitefish Lake and golf at the valley's only 36-hole course. In winter, skiing becomes the passion at Whitefish Mountain Resort. Surrounded by rampant new housing developments, downtown Whitefish fits compactly into several square blocks with boutiques, restaurants, art galleries, and theaters.

Columbia Falls

The gateway to Glacier, Columbia Falls never had a waterfall of its own until the town built one. Those in search of old-time bargains head to its antiques stores. Recently, the town has boomed with restaurants in its downtown area, upgrading the quality of its dining. Beside its rebuilt public outdoor swimming pool, Columbia Falls is home to Big Sky Waterslides.

Bigfork

A summer resort town, Bigfork combines easy access to the Swan Mountains with boating on Flathead Lake. Bigfork Summer Playhouse dominates the town, packing restaurants before nightly shows. Quaint gift shops and multiple art galleries fill its several-block-long village, and its one-lane steel bridge crosses the Swan River. In early June, the town hops with the Bigfork Whitewater Festival, when kayakers shoot the Swan's Wild Mile.

VISITORS CENTERS

One of the easiest ways to get additional information on the Flathead is to contact the visitors centers. Flathead Valley has six: **Flathead Valley Convention and Visitors Bureau** (406/756-9091 or 800/543-3105, www.fcvb.org), **Kalispell Chamber of Commerce** (15 Depot Park, Kalispell, 406/758-2800, www.kalispellchamber.com), **Whitefish Chamber of Commerce** (520 E. 2nd St., Whitefish, 406/862-3501, www.whitefishchamber.com), **Whitefish Convention and Visitors Bureau** (www.explorewhitefish.com), **Columbia Falls Chamber of Commerce** (233 13th St. E., Columbia Falls, 406/892-2072, www.columbiafallschamber.com), **Bigfork Chamber of Commerce** (Olde Town Center, Bigfork, 406/837-5888, www.bigfork.org), and **Lakeside Chamber of Commerce** (406/844-3715, www.lakesidechamber.com).

SIGHTS

Flathead Lake

Stretching 28 miles long and 15 miles wide,

© BECKY LOMAX

Downtown Bigfork houses restaurants, shops, and the Bigfork Summer Playhouse.

Flathead Lake is the largest freshwater lake west of the Mississippi. Its 188 square miles, six state parks, islands, deep fishing waters, and wildlife refuges make it a summer play land. Highways encircle the lake, providing public access at 13 different points. The southern half of the lake is in the Flathead Indian Reservation, home to the Salish and Kootenai people. Kayakers and boaters can explore **Wild Horse Island,** home to wild horses, bighorn sheep, and big views of Flathead Lake.

Two boat tours offer different modes of travel. From Bigfork, **Questa Sailing Charters** (150 Flathead Lake Lodge, 406/837-4391) launch from Flathead Lake Lodge's dock. Two 51-foot 1928-1929 Q-class sloops each carry 12 passengers. On the beautifully restored boats, there are regular tours (1:30pm daily mid-June-Aug., adults $39, seniors and under age 13 discounted) and the adults-only sunset cruise (7pm daily, $44), which includes wine. From Lakeside, **Far West Boat Tours** (7135 U.S. 93 S., 406/844-BOAT—406/844-2628, www.flatheadlakeboattour.com, 1pm Tues.-Sun., 7pm Tues.-Wed. and Sun. late June-early Sept., adults $19, ages 6-12 $10) launches a 23-foot cabin cruiser. Sit upstairs in the sun for bigger views.

Whitefish Lake

The 3,315-acre lake in Whitefish buzzes in summer. Anglers hit the lake in early morning and evening, while midday is a frenzy of water-skiers, Jet Skiers, party barges, kayakers, and canoers. Swimmers cool off at Whitefish State Park, City Beach, and Les Mason Park. In winter, when ice covers the lake, hockey players make their own rinks, and anglers ice fish.

Flathead River

In Hungry Horse, the South, Middle, and North Forks of the Flathead River converge. The Flathead River then snakes 55 miles across the valley to Flathead Lake. Seven river access

© BECKY LOMAX

Lifeguards watch swimmers at City Beach on Whitefish Lake.

points allow anglers, canoers, and floaters to get onto its meandering pace. Toward Flathead Lake, the river takes several sharp S-turns in sloughs and estuaries, bird habitat for ospreys and waterfowl.

Whitefish Mountain Resort

Skiers and snowboarders flock to Whitefish Mountain Resort's 3,000 acres in winter. Twelve lifts access an average 300 inches of snow per year. Snow ghosts—ice-encrusted bent firs—compete with the view of Glacier National Park from the mountain's 6,817-foot summit. During summer the resort runs its lift for sightseeing, hiking, and mountain biking. Other summer activities include zip-lines, an aerial park, an alpine slide, and treetop tours.

Museums

In Kalispell, the historic Victorian **Conrad Mansion** (Woodland Ave. between 3rd St. and 4th St., 406/755-2166, www.conradmansion.com, 10am-5pm Tues.-Sun. mid-May-mid-Oct., adults $8, seniors $7, children $3) preserves 26 rooms with their original 1895 furniture. Vintage clothing and toys recall the days of rummaging through Grandma's attic.

Also in Kalispell, the **Hockaday Museum of Art** (302 2nd Ave. E., 406/755-5268, www.hockadayartmuseum.org, 10am-5pm Tues.-Sat. year-round, adults $5, seniors $4, under age 13 free) features Montana pottery, jewelry, and paintings—particularly by Native American and Glacier Park artists.

Atop Big Mountain at Whitefish Mountain Resort, the **USFS Summit Nature Center** (406/862-2900, www.skiwhitefish.com, 10am-5pm daily late June-Labor Day, free) requires a hike or a lift ride ($8-12 round-trip) to reach its hands-on exhibits. Free guided flower walks are offered in July-August, and there's a Junior Ranger program for kids.

Recreation

The Flathead Valley is a four-season recreation mecca. Lakes draw summertime paddlers and swimmers, fall lures hunters, ski resorts cater to powder hounds, and spring explodes with hikers and mountain bikers.

HIKING

Since Flathead National Forest surrounds Flathead Valley, hikers have no shortage of trails within spitting distance of the back porch. Most trails are multiuse, permitting mountain bikes and motorcycles, but a few—such as the Jewel Basin trails or the Danny On Memorial Trail on Big Mountain—are limited to hikers.

In the Swan Mountains, **Jewel Basin** has 50 miles of hiking paths. Open for hiking June-October, depending on snow, the 15,349-acre hiker-only area is called the Jewel for the 27 alpine fishing lakes that sparkle in its basins. Paths tromp across huckleberry meadows and high ridges with top-of-the-world views. Fido can go if he's on a leash. It's extremely popular: Fourth of July weekend sees 200 people per day. Trail signage is scanty, so find maps in local sports shops or contact **Flathead National Forest** (406/758-5208, www.fs.fed.us/r1/flathead) or **Swan Lake Ranger Station** (200 Ranger Station Rd., Bigfork, 406/837-7500).

A narrow, curvy seven-mile Forest Service dirt road climbs up to 5,717 feet above the valley floor to the Jewel. Leave low-clearance vehicles and trailers behind, as it's riddled with washboards, rollers, and limited turnouts. To reach the Camp Misery Trailhead, with its less-than-inspiring name, catch the Swan Highway (Hwy. 83) two miles north of Bigfork. Follow it to Echo Lake Road, and head north approximately three miles to Jewel Basin Road (Forest Rd. 5392).

Mount Aeneas

- Distance: 5.9-mile loop
- Duration: 3 hours
- Elevation gain: 1,779 feet
- Effort: moderate-strenuous
- Trailhead: Camp Misery Trailhead in Jewel Basin

Mount Aeneas, at 7,528 feet, is the highest peak in the Jewel and offers big views for little work, but don't expect solitude at the summit. From the top, you'll see Flathead Lake, Glacier National Park, the Bob Marshall Wilderness Complex, and the Swan Mountains—a lot of scenery for a short hike. Combined with Picnic Lakes, the trail loops on a ridge and through a lake basin.

Begin hiking up trail 717, a wide roadbed. In 1.5 miles, the trail reaches a four-way junction—stay on 717, heading uphill. After a few switchbacks, you'll pass an ugly microwave tower before waltzing with the mountain goats along an arête to the summit. From the summit, drop down through the Picnic Lakes Basin. At the lakes, take trail 392, then right onto trail 68, and left onto trail 8. At 1.7 miles from Camp Misery, Picnic Lakes makes a good little-kid destination—just reverse the route.

Birch Lake

- Distance: 6 miles round-trip
- Duration: 3 hours
- Elevation gain: 800 feet
- Effort: moderate
- Trailhead: Camp Misery Trailhead in Jewel Basin

A short hop over a ridge along with a skip down a trail puts hikers on the shore of Birch Lake—a great destination for kids. Swim in the lake's west end, but don't expect balmy waters. This clear snowmelt pond retains its chill even in August. For those with more gumption, another 2.5 miles puts you on the boulder shoreline of Crater Lake.

HUCKLEBERRY MANIA

The huckleberry—a small dark-purple berry about the size of the tip of your little finger—resembles a blueberry but is much sweeter and more flavorful. It grows only in the wild on low deciduous bushes with leaves that turn red in fall. Growing mostly at elevations above 4,000 feet, the berries ripen late July-September.

The berry has yet to be successfully cultivated. In Flathead Valley, you'll find berry stands selling hucks that have been picked by commercial permit in national forests or on private lands. Expect to pay near $50 per gallon for the precious purple gems (now you know why huckleberry pie is so expensive). Be cautious when purchasing berries in early summer, as you may be buying frozen berries from last year rather than freshly picked ones. The frozen berries are still yummy but are a little softer when they thaw. Fresh ones start hitting the stands in late July.

You can pick your own huckleberries to eat—no permit needed. You'll find them on many trails in Glacier and Flathead National Forest. While locals don't usually divulge their prized secret stashes, you can usually find good huckleberry picking on Big Mountain at Whitefish Mountain Resort. Glacier Park rules permit plucking a few berries to eat, but not commercial harvesting.

Two mammals crave the berries: bears and humans. High in vitamin C, the berries are healthy and low in fat. They enliven any pastry, pie, sauce, or fruit concoction. They're tasty in smoothies and delightful on pancakes.

You'll find huckleberries in everything from ice cream to beer; syrup, jam, and jelly top everyone's favorites. Hucks also flavor and scent chocolate, honey, cocoa, barbecue sauce, tea, salad dressing, ice cream toppings, a daiquiri mix, lotion, lip balm, bubble bath, shampoo, soap, and more.

One word of advice: Avoid using huckleberry shampoo before hiking in bear country.

Begin hiking up the broad roadway of trail 717 to the four-way junction. Take the right fork on trail 7. The trail curves around the lower flanks of Mount Aeneas as it descends to Birch Lake; you'll have to hike up this on the way out. A trail circles the lake, but the best place to stop is on its clearly visible peninsula.

Danny On Trail

- Distance: 4 miles one-way
- Duration: 2 hours
- Elevation gain: 2,400 feet
- Effort: moderate
- Trailhead: next to the Chalet at Whitefish Mountain Resort
- Directions: drive seven miles north of Whitefish, following signs

The Danny On Trail hosts over 14,000 hikers annually. At Big Mountain's summit, the USFS Summit Nature Center provides interpretive resources for the trail. Catch the chairlift up to hike down or hike up and then ride down ($6 pp one-way). While you can hike with your pooch on a leash, dogs may not ride up or down the chairlift.

After beginning in Whitefish Mountain Resort Village, the trail switchbacks up through a forested slope and crosses ski runs as it sweeps around the mountain. Valerian and penstemon bloom in July; huckleberries scent the air in August. Junctions to Flower Point are well marked: Stay left at both to go directly to the top. You can also loop through Flower Point for a 5.6-mile hike. At the East Rim junction, turn left for a gentle, scenic loop before the final steep ascent. Panoramas at the top span Glacier Park to Flathead Lake.

CYCLING

Oodles of two-lane highways and paved country lanes make long loops around Flathead Lake or short farmland tours for roadies, and there are many single-track and dirt-road choices for mountain bikers. For the best list of itineraries

© BECKY LOMAX

The Danny On Trail climbs to the top of Big Mountain.

to suit your interests and abilities, check Glacier Cyclery's website (www.glaciercyclery.com) for popular area routes. The shop also maintains a ride board with recent trail updates.

In Kalispell, the **Great Northern Historical Trail** (www.railstotrailsofnwmt.com) runs 12 miles of paved bike trail from Meridian Street to Smith Lake in Kila. You can stop partway for lunch at Kila's Cottage Inn (4220 U.S. 2 W., 406/755-8711). Another 12-mile segment links Meridian with Somers, where you can lunch at the Somers Bay Café (47 Somers Rd., 406/857-2660) and enjoy Flathead Lake. Find trailhead parking for both at Meridian Road and Derns Road.

In Whitefish, the expanding **Whitefish Trail,** at more than 20 miles, provides a curvy multiuse dirt single-track trail with fun terrain for mountain bikers. Current maps to trailheads can be found at www.whitefishlegacy.org. For single-track lift-served mountain biking, **Whitefish Mountain Resort** (end of Big Mountain Rd., Whitefish, 406/862-2900, www.skiwhitefish.com, late June-Labor Day) hauls bikes and riders up its chairlift ($14-28), depending on your age and duration. Several routes descend from the summit—the easiest is via switchback traverses, while the others drop on steep hair-raising downhill descents. Natural obstacles put both trails into the "have some experience first" category. Whitefish Mountain Resort has bicycles available to rent ($30-65).

Rentals and Repairs

Glacier Cyclery (326 E. 2nd St., Whitefish, 406/862-6446, www.glaciercyclery.com) rents touring bikes, roadies, hybrids, and mountain bikes ($35-55 per day). They can also equip you with car racks ($20 per day), utility trailers ($30 per day), and Burleys ($20 per week). **Mountain Mike's** (417 Bridge St., Bigfork, 406/837-2453, 10am-4pm daily May-Sept.) rents kid and adult mountain bikes ($20-35, depending on duration), convenient for touring Swan Valley. You can also hire a guide ($35-45 pp, reservations required) for half-day dirt-road or single-track tours. Both shops include helmets with rentals, offer weekly rates, and do repairs. There are several other bike shops in Flathead Valley.

BOATING

Popular boating lakes dot Flathead Valley; the two largest are Flathead and Whitefish Lakes. Both have several launch sites, and rentals are available. Expect to pay hourly rates for Jet Skis ($60-75), water-ski boats ($85-125), and pontoon fishing boats and party barges ($85-120). In addition to your rental fee, you'll need to pay for the gas you use. Hand-propelled craft like canoes, kayaks, and rowboats ($15-20 per hour) are also available.

Flathead Lake

On Flathead Lake's north end, three communities—Bigfork, Somers, and Lakeside—serve boaters with marinas (usually May-Oct.).

The new Whitefish Trail offers more than 20 miles of single-track mountain biking.

The lake also has 13 public access points, six of which are state parks ($5 per day) maintained by Montana Fish, Wildlife, and Parks (406/752-5501, www.fwp.state.mt.us). Boat rentals are available at **Wild Wave Watercraft** (7220 U.S. 93 S., Lakeside, and 180 Vista Lane, Bigfork, 406/253-5800 or 406/257-2627, www.wildwaverentals.com).

Whitefish Lake

For launching boats, you'll find public ramps at Whitefish Lake State Park ($5 per day) and City Beach ($5 launch fee). For rentals, mooring, and fuel service, **Whitefish Lake Lodge Marina** (1390 Wisconsin Ave., 406/863-4020, mid-May-Sept.) is the only option.

WATERSKIING

Most vacationers don't come to the Flathead solely for waterskiing since glacial-fed lakes are downright cold. Wetsuits are advised for those used to warm water. Water-skiers hit Whitefish Lake and Flathead Lake as well as smaller valley lakes. The marinas rent waterskiing boats and gear ($85-95 per hour plus gas).

KAYAKING AND CANOEING

Sea kayakers and canoers paddle anywhere they can in the Flathead. Lakes such as **Flathead** and **Whitefish** provide flat water, although Flathead can kick up with big winds. The most popular Flathead Lake paddling destination is **Wild Horse Island,** launching from the public beach in Dayton. Ambling portions of the **Flathead, Whitefish,** and **Swan Rivers** also flow slowly enough for flat-water paddling.

White-water kayakers wearing dry suits in freezing cold water gravitate to the Swan River outside Bigfork. For Class IV-V rapids, the **Swan River Wild Mile,** a short 1.25-mile stretch that drops 100 feet below Bigfork Dam, sees its best water May-July, and specifically Wednesday nights during summer when the dam releases flows.

© BECKY LOMAX

Swan River's Wild Mile attracts whitewater kaykers, especially during the annual Bigfork Whitewater Festival.

Rentals and Guides

You can rent kayaks to take into Glacier or onto lakes in the Flathead. **The Sportsman** (145 Hutton Ranch Rd., Kalispell, 406/755-6484, and Mountain Mall, Whitefish, 406/862-3111) rents canoes and tandem kayaks ($40 for 24 hours). Life jackets and paddles are included in the rates.

Valley Wide Sea Kayaking Adventures (8537 Hwy. 35, Bigfork, 406/212-5647 or 406/871-5045) is a new company run by Sam Stone that offers smaller recreational sea kayaks, tandems, sit-on-tops, canoes, and standup inflatable and fiberglass paddleboard rentals ($40-130). Life jackets, dry bags, and paddles are included in the rates. Introductory 20-minute sessions ($20) for beginner paddlers are available. Stone runs guided adventures ($75-225) on most rivers and lakes in Flathead Valley as well as shuttle services for floating the Swan River or other area rivers. Although the company is located on the highway in Bigfork, with another outlet in downtown Bigfork, he delivers gear anywhere in Flathead for an extra fee.

FISHING

Lakes, estuaries, and rivers abound for fishing. Flathead Valley is home to the **Flathead River,** a giant highway for migrating fish. Because of dam control and the cold glacial water, do not expect blue-ribbon trout fishing. But the river doesn't see lots of fishing pressure. It carries many nonnative species—especially northern pike lurking in larger southern sloughs. Seven river access points offer places to fish and to launch boats downstream: Blankenship Bridge, the U.S. 2 bridge at Hungry Horse, a spur road at Bad Rock Canyon's west end, Kokanee Bend, Pressentine Bar, the old Steel Bridge, and the Stillwater mouth. Most anglers hit the stretch between Columbia Falls and the Old Steel Bridge in Kalispell.

Flathead Lake teems with cutthroat, giant trophy lake trout, mountain and lake whitefish, largemouth bass, bull trout, and yellow perch. It's good for all types of fishing: bait, lure, fly-fishing, and trolling. Anglers need a Montana fishing license, good only on the north half of the lake and available at sporting goods stores.

Whitefish Lake draws anglers for its lake trout and whitefish. During winter, some anglers ice fish. Northern pike, lake trout, and kokanee are common, and it is regularly stocked with westslope cutthroat trout.

Licenses

Montana fishing licenses are required. Montana residents can buy two-day ($13) or season ($26) licenses. Nonresidents can get two-day ($25), 10-day ($54), or season ($70) licenses. Children under age 12 fish free. Ages 12-14 and Montana seniors can buy licenses for $8. Licenses are available in sporting goods stores and fly shops. You can also order one online (www.fwp.mt.gov).

Fly Shops and Guides

Hit up fly-fishing shops in the Flathead for locally made hand-tied flies and tackle as well as advice on where the fish are biting. Most of the following shops also offer guide services ($450-490 for 2 people per day). Rates usually do not include Montana fishing licenses.

Lakestream Flyshop (334 Central Ave., Whitefish, 406/862-1298, www.lakestream.com) guides fly-fishing trips on the main Flathead River plus all three tributaries. **Stumptown Anglers** (5790 U.S. 93 S., Whitefish, 406/862-4554, www.stumptownangler.com) guides trips on several northwest Montana rivers, including the Flathead. For guided fishing on the Swan or Flathead River, head to **Bigfork Anglers** (405 Bridge St., Bigfork, 406/837-3675, www.bigforkanglers.com).

Montana has no shortage of independent fly-fishing guide services operating unattached to shops; you can find them in business listings and on the Internet. Be sure the guide service is licensed with the state before hiring one.

Charter Fishing

Charter fishing services on Flathead Lake (half-day $350, full-day $700 for 2 people) operate May-September. From two locations on Flathead Lake, **A Able Fishing and Tours** (688 Lakeside Blvd., Lakeside, and Marina Cay, Bigfork, 406/257-5214, www.aablefishing.com) operates three boats. Other charter services also run fishing charters on Flathead Lake.

SWIMMING

Swimming beaches are available at state parks on Flathead Lake and Whitefish Lake (406/752-5501, www.fwp.mt.gov, $5 per vehicle). Kids can build sandcastles only at City Beach on Whitefish Lake (406/863-2475) due to sand imported decades ago.

Two seasonal outdoor pools attract kids. The renovated **Pinewood Family Aquatic Center** (925 4th Ave. W., Columbia Falls, 406/892-3500, Mon.-Sat. June-Aug., $2-5 pp) has a bromine 25-meter pool and kids' play pool. In Kalispell, the outdoor pool at **Woodland Park** (Woodland Park Dr. and Shady Glen Dr., 406/758-7812, daily June-Aug., $2-5 pp) has slides, a current stream, and diving pools.

Big Sky Waterslides (7211 U.S. 2 E., Columbia Falls, 406/892-5025, www.bigskywp.com, 11am-7pm daily Memorial Day-Labor Day, $15-30) is a great place to take the kids to unwind after a hot day and a long drive. The park has 10 slides—both big and little—along with mini golf and bumper cars. After 4pm, rates drop slightly.

Flathead Valley has two large physical-fitness complexes that include weights, cardio machines, indoor swimming pools, and hot tubs. To drop in for a day (adults $12, children $5-10), call for current hours. **The Summit** (205 Sunnyview Lane, Kalispell, 406/751-4100) also has a climbing wall. **The Wave** (1250 Baker Ave., Whitefish, 406/862-2444) has a fun kids' pool with a slide and a water fountain.

HUNTING

With Flathead Valley surrounded by Flathead National Forest, it is popular for hunting big game and birds. Get hunting regulations, seasons, and license info from Montana Fish, Wildlife, and Parks (406/752-5501, www.fwp.mt.gov).

GOLF

Golf Digest rated Flathead Valley as one of the world's 50 greatest golf destinations—not just because the scenery is good and the prices are reasonable but because of the nine championship courses. With daylight lasting 16 hours in June, courses are open dawn-dusk, adjusting tee times as daylight hours change. Depending on snowmelt, most courses are open April-October. All of the Flathead courses have rentals, pro shops, restaurants, and lounges.

Flathead Valley summer greens fees run

Whitefish Lake Golf Course is the busiest course in Montana.

$50-100, depending on the course, but you can get cheaper greens fees in spring, fall, and daily after 3pm. Club rentals range $10-30 and carts $16-35.

You can find one-stop Flathead golf information at www.golfmontana.net, with stats for most of the local courses. A central number (800/392-9795) provides guaranteed advance reservations and golf packages.

Courses

With the highest greens fees, **Eagle Bend Golf Course** (279 Eagle Bend Dr., Bigfork, 406/837-7310 or 800/255-5641, www.eaglebendgolfclub.com) is ranked among the top 50 public courses in the country. The challenging 27-hole course is a Jack Nicklaus design with big variety in its hole layouts. From different tees, you can see Flathead Lake, Swan Mountains, and Glacier Park; ospreys fly overhead.

Four courses offer summer greens fees in the $60-70 range. The city-owned **Whitefish Lake Golf Course** (1200 U.S. 93 N., Whitefish, 406/862-4000, www.golfwhitefish.com) is Montana's only 36-hole course. The north course tours through large cedars and firs; the south course runs past Lost Loon Lake. Both have mountain views. **Meadow Lake Golf Course** (490 St. Andrews Dr., Columbia Falls, 406/892-2111, www.meadowlakegolf.com) has 18 holes among woods, with some tight fairways and lots of adjacent houses. A couple of ponds and a creek separate the fairways, and some trees shade the course. **Big Mountain Golf Course** (3230 U.S. 93 N., Kalispell, 406/751-1950 or 800/255-5641, www.golfmt.com) is a Scottish links-style course. Since its 18 holes sit mid-valley, with few trees, views open up to Big Mountain and Glacier Park. The Stillwater River runs adjacent to the back nine. **Buffalo Hill** (1176 N. Main St., Kalispell, 406/756-4530 or 888/342-6319, www.golfbuffalohill.com) combines an older course with a newer course for 27 holes. The older Cameron Nine abuts the highway; the newer 18-hole course is moderately difficult with a lot of terrain variety.

With the least expensive greens fees, **Village Greens** (500 Palmer Dr., Kalispell, 406/752-4666, www.montanagolf.com) surrounds its bent-grass greens with a few trees, ponds, and houses. The 18 holes afford a pleasant place to play on one of the easier courses.

OUTDOOR ADVENTURES

Whitefish Mountain Resort (end of Big Mountain Rd., 406/862-2900, www.skiwhitefish.com, daily mid-June-Labor Day, Sat.-Sun. Sept.) beefed up their summer adventure programs. **Zipline Tours** ($50-85, lowest rates in June and Sept.) let you sail through the air 20-300 feet above the ground. The longest—the AdrenaLine—stretches 1,900 feet. **Walk in the Treetops** ($51) is a boardwalk tour through the tree canopy at 70 feet in the air. You're clipped in with a safety harness. Multiple tours go out each day for both guided tours. Reservations are a must as both tours fill completely.

You can also tackle individual adventures at your own speed with no reservations needed: Scenic lift rides ($8-12) whisk riders via gondolas or open chairs to the summit of Big Mountain for views of Flathead Valley and Glacier Park. The **Alpine Slide** ($8 per ride) offers speed thrills sledding down a track. Even little kids can ride with adults. For a physical challenge, tackle the new **Aerial Adventure Park** ($24-39). You'll traverse bridges, cables, zip-lines, and more suspended 10-50 feet above the ground in courses of varied difficulty—all with the safety of being clipped in with a harness.

SKIING

Whitefish Mountain Resort

Located seven miles north of Whitefish, Whitefish Mountain Resort (end of Big Mountain Rd., 406/862-2900, www.

© BECKY LOMAX

Whitefish Mountain Resort is known for the ice-crusted snow ghosts on the summit.

skiwhitefish.com, early Dec.-early Apr., adults under $70) lives up to its former name of Big Mountain with 3,000 acres of skiing terrain, 2,400 feet of vertical drop, 12 lifts, and 91 named runs. Big bowls, glades, and long cruisers head off the summit in every direction. You can even find good tree skiing in the mountain's famous fog. The resort's village contains restaurants, shops, rental gear, ski school, day care, and lodging from economy to upscale condos.

Blacktail Mountain

Sitting above Flathead Lake, Blacktail Mountain (end of Blacktail Mountain Rd., Lakeside, 406/844-0999, Wed.-Sun. and holidays mid-Dec.-early Apr., adults under $40) attracts families for its smaller 1,000 acres, four lifts, and family-friendly pricing.

CROSS-COUNTRY SKIING

Several small cross-country ski areas dot Flathead Valley, with trails groomed for classic and skate skiing mid-December-March. You need to bring your own skis for Blacktail Mountain, central Flathead Valley, Foothills, and Round Meadows, or rent from **Sportsman** (145 Hutton Ranch Rd., Kalispell, 406/755-6484, and Mountain Mall, Whitefish, 406/862-3111). **Glacier Nordic Center** ($8) grooms 7.5 miles on Whitefish Golf Course, with the **Glacier Nordic Shop** (406/862-9498) renting skate and classic gear ($15-25) and teaching lessons ($35-77) in both disciplines. The shop also rents cross-country skis for touring in Glacier Park. Grooming 16 miles of trails, **Stillwater Nordic** (750 Beaver Lake Rd., 406/862-7004, $10-15) provides undulating, more technical routes.

SNOWMOBILING

The Flathead Valley is surrounded by 200 miles of groomed snowmobile trails December-mid-April, but some trails close April 1. Flathead Valley Snowmobile Association (www.flatheadsnowmobiler.com) maintains the grooming on nine popular trails near Whitefish, Columbia Falls, and Bigfork. For those striking out on their own, check conditions with Flathead Avalanche Center (406/257-8402, www.flatheadavalanche.org).

Rentals are available at **Extreme Motorsports** (6191 U.S. 93 S., Whitefish, 406/862-8594, www.wfmextrememotorsports.com) and **J & L Rentals** (830 1st Ave. W., Columbia Falls, 406/892-7666, www.jandlsnowmobile.com). Expect to pay $150-200 per day for renting a snowmobile, helmets included; snowmobile suits, boots, and gloves are extra. Guided tours are available, too.

ENTERTAINMENT AND EVENTS

Theaters

In Bigfork, the **Bigfork Summer Playhouse** (526 Electric Ave., 406/837-4886, www.bigforksummerplayhouse.com, mid-May-late Aug.) presents five shows in repertory during each summer, from Broadway musical favorites to comedies. In Whitefish, **Whitefish Theater Company** (1 Central Ave., 406/862-5371, www.whitefishtheaterco.org) sponsors plays, concerts, speakers, and art films in the O'Shaughnessey Center. Broadway veterans formed the acclaimed **Alpine Theatre Project** (Whitefish, 406/862-7469, www.alpinetheatreproject.org), which produces plays during the summer at Whitefish Performing Arts Center. Beloved musicals, classic comedies, and first-run plays highlight its summer schedule, along with big names like John Lithgow, Olympia Dukakis, and Henry Winkler for single-evening shows.

You can catch a just-released blockbuster movie in the Flathead—but don't expect a hotbed of foreign, independent, or avant-garde films. Whitefish has one movie theater, **Mountain Cinema** (Mountain Mall, U.S. 93, 406/862-3130). In Kalispell, you'll find 14 movies showing at **Stadium 14** (185 Hutton Ranch Rd., 406/752-7804, www.signaturetheatres.com).

Vikings, penguins, yetis, and onlookers crowd the streets during Whitefish's Winter Carnival Parade.

Rodeos and Fairs

Located mid-valley between Whitefish and Kalispell, **Majestic Valley Arena** (3630 U.S. 93 N., 406/755-5366, www.majesticvalleyarena.com) is the hub for big events: concerts, rodeos, equestrian competitions, and trade shows. Special attractions include calf roping, pro rodeos, and horse jumping. For cowpoke wannabes, the annual **Northwest Montana Fair and Rodeo** opens in mid-August at the Flathead County Fairgrounds (265 N. Meridian, Kalispell, 406/758-5810). The five-day, six-night event features Professional Rodeo Cowboys Association (PRCA) rodeo events, fireworks, animal and produce exhibits, team penning, musical concerts, and livestock sales.

Events

The annual **Glacier Jazz Stampede** (406/755-6088, www.glacierjazzstampede.com) is for those who love traditional jazz, swing, ragtime, Dixieland, and big-band sounds. The October event crams four days with 12-14 bands from across the United States and Canada, pounding out nearly nonstop music in four different Kalispell venues. Bands, schedules, and ticket prices vary yearly for each event, but you can order a ticket for all events.

Attracting hundreds of spectators even in soggy weather, the **Bigfork Whitewater Festival** (www.bigfork.org) runs kayakers down the Class IV Wild Mile of the Swan River at the peak of spring runoff. Traditionally held for two days over Memorial Day Weekend, competitions run the gamut from slalom to boater-cross. Local pubs and restaurants party with nightly entertainment.

In the doldrums of winter, Whitefish celebrates its wacky **Winter Carnival** (406/862-3501, www.whitefishchamber.org), a three-day spree of ski races, ice hockey, the penguin plunge, figure skating, a torchlight parade, fireworks, the rail jam, and skijoring, held the first weekend in February. Hundreds of people line the few blocks of downtown Whitefish for an old-fashioned "drive the old tractor down main street" parade disrupted by raucous yetis and Viking women.

Art events abound in the Flathead. Whitefish hosts their **Gallery Nights** on the first Thursday of each month May-October, and their three-day **Huckleberry Days** art festival in mid-August in Credit Union Park. Kalispell celebrates their three-day **Arts in the Park** in late July in Depot Park and a late-November **Art Walk** through downtown galleries. The **Bigfork Festival of the Arts** takes place in early August on the town's main street.

Casinos

While gambling is legal in Montana, casinos haven't rocketed to Las Vegas style—or even to the level of those found on some Native American reservations. Most Flathead bars have a few slot machines squirreled away in a corner; some even run a card table or two. In a twist to the usual gas station-convenience mart, some gas chains add small, dark, and smoky casinos featuring gaming machines and poker tables.

Shopping, Services, and Information

SHOPPING

While Flathead Valley thankfully has no Mall of America clone or factory outlet mall, it does have its share of strip malls and chain stores—most located on U.S. 93 north of Kalispell. However, if you can, head to the few strikingly different shops worth browsing: art galleries, jewelry stores, and eclectic gift shops. Most of the one-of-a-kind locally owned stores cluster in the few blocks of downtown Whitefish, Bigfork, and Kalispell. Columbia Falls features several antiques stores within a few blocks.

For classy high-quality toys—inventive, classic, and educational—stop in **Imagination Station** (221 Central Ave., Whitefish, 406/862-5668, and 132 Main St., Kalispell, 406/755-5668). They'll even ship your toys home for you so you don't have to haul everything on the airplane. In Kalispell, visit **Sassafras** (120 Main St., 406/752-2433), an artist and antiques co-op, featuring the works of 30-40 local northwest Montana artists. Pieces range from watercolors and cards to pottery, jewelry, clothing, furniture, and sculptures. In Whitefish, be sure to pick up exquisite handmade chocolates at **Copperleaf Chocolate Company** (242 Central Ave., 406/862-9659) and handmade soaps at **Sage and Cedar** (214 Central Ave., 406/862-9411).

Outdoor Gear

For outdoor gear—camping, backpacking, skiing, snowboarding, and fishing clothing and equipment—several shops carry good brand-name selections and know how to fit equipment to individual people. **Rocky Mountain Outfitter** (135 Main St., Kalispell, 406/752-2446, www.rockymountainoutfitter.com) specializes in hiking, backpacking, climbing, and skiing. Don Scharfe, the owner, is well known for first ascents on several of Glacier's peaks.

The folks at **The White Room** (130 Lupfer Ave., Whitefish, 406/862-7666, www.whiteroomshop.com) are the local telemark and backcountry ski experts, but in summer, the shop outfits hikers, backpackers, and climbers with gear and clothing. With two stores, **Sportsman** (145 Hutton Ranch Rd., Kalispell, 406/755-6484, and 6475 U.S. 93, Whitefish, 406/862-3111) carries gear and clothing for skiers, snowboarders, hikers, backpackers, anglers, hunters, campers, tennis players, cyclists, and ice skaters. In two locations, **Stumptown Snowboards** (128 Central Ave., Whitefish, 406/862-0955, and Whitefish Mountain Resort, Whitefish, 406/862-5828) are the local experts in snowboarding and skateboarding, with full equipment and clothing lines.

Maps and Books

To stock up on good topographic maps of Glacier and Flathead National Forest, you'll find the widest selection at **Rocky Mountain Outfitter** (135 Main St., Kalispell, 406/752-2446, www.rockymountainoutfitter.com) or **Sportsman** (145 Hutton Ranch Rd., Kalispell, 406/755-6484, and 6475 U.S. 93, Whitefish, 406/862-3111). Likewise, both shops carry guidebooks for hiking, fishing, and cross-country skiing in the area along with a few field guides. You can also find guidebooks and books on natural history, Lewis and Clark, Montana history, and field guides for flowers, birds, and animals at **Bookworks** (244 Spokane Ave., Whitefish, 406/862-4980, and 38 1st

MADE IN MONTANA

Want local souvenirs to take home? Look for the blue "Made in Montana" logo. Only arts, crafts, food, and other products made by Montana residents and grown or produced within the state can use the label. More than 2,600 businesses—some producing only one item—use the distinctive marker.

Find the "Made in Montana" logo on foods like coffee, jams and jellies, preserves, teas, pasta, salad dressings, barbecue sauces, herbs, cheese, jerky, and cookies. There are also personal health-care products ranging from soaps and shampoos to lotions and oils. Toys, games, pet goodies, furniture, and clothing also may sport the logo, as can arts and crafts like photography, music, lithographs, paintings, candles, and more.

One Made in Montana company, **Montana Coffee Traders,** has been roasting beans in Flathead Valley since 1981. Their coffees celebrate Montana with the light- and medium-roasted Montana Blend as well as the Glacier Blend, light-roasted with a bit of vanilla and almond. The Grizzly Blend promotes the protection of crucial grizzly-bear habitat, and the Wild Rockies Blend promotes protection and restoration of wildlands habitat. Look for these products in local grocery stores and at Montana Coffee Traders cafés and outlets (5810 Hwy. 93 S. and 110 Central Ave., Whitefish; 30 9th St. W., Columbia Falls; 328 W. Center St., Kalispell) or order by phone (406/862-7633 or 800/345-5282) or online (www.coffeetraders.com).

For a Made in Montana product fix after you get home, check www.madeinmontanausa.com for companies that sell Made in Montana products online.

Ave. E., Kalispell, 406/755-4980). **Glacier National Park Conservancy** (402 9th St. W., Columbia Falls, 406/892-3250) also has an outlet on U.S. 2 in Columbia Falls.

SERVICES

Spas

Whitefish is home to two unique day spas. **Remedies Day Spa** (119 Central Ave., 406/863-9493, www.remediesdayspa.com, 10am-5pm Mon.-Sat., by appointment Sun.) makes all their products for massages, soaks, and wraps from natural food ingredients found in the kitchen. The spa offers its signature kitchen "fassage" (massage for the face), whipped cream wrap, honey and cream hot-rock foot rub, scrubs, soaks, and traditional massages ($40-150 per treatment). In an upscale quiet lakeside setting, **The Spa at Whitefish Lake** (1380 Wisconsin Ave., 406/863-4050, www.lodgeatwhitefishlake.com, 9am-7pm daily, $50-195 per treatment) offers traditional spa facials, waxing, massage, scrubs, wraps, manicures, and pedicures. Their 90-minute Stone Silence uses hot Flathead Valley river stones and aromatherapy oils, like coconilla, in a deep muscle massage.

Post Offices

Each major town in Flathead Valley has one post office; Kalispell has two. Locations are in Bigfork (265 Holt Dr., 406/837-4479, 8:30am-5:30pm Mon.-Fri., 10am-2pm Sat.), Columbia Falls (65 1st Ave. E., 406/892-7621, 8:30am-4:30pm Mon.-Fri., 10am-2pm Sat.), Kalispell (350 N. Meridian Rd., 406/755-6450; 248 1st Ave. W., 406/755-0187, 8:30am-5:30pm Mon.-Fri., 10am-1pm Sat.), Whitefish (424 Baker Ave., 406/862-2151, 8:30am-5:30pm Mon.-Fri., 10am-2pm Sat.), Somers (150 Somers Rd., 406/857-3330, 8am-4:45pm Mon.-Fri.) and Lakeside (7196 U.S. 93 S., 406/844-3224, 7:30am-11am and noon-4pm Mon.-Fri.).

Banks

Banks and ATMs are common in Flathead Valley, but several banks have branches in more than one town. Find **Glacier Bank** (www.glacierbank.com) in Kalispell (202 Main St.,

406/756-4200), Bigfork (Old Town Center, 406/837-5980), Columbia Falls (822 Nucleus Ave., 406/892-7100), and Whitefish (319 E. 2nd St., 406/863-6300). **First Interstate Bank** (www.firstinterstate.com) is located in Kalispell (2 Main St., 406/756-5200, and 100 Hutton Ranch Rd., 406/756-5222), Bigfork (8111 Hwy. 35, 406/837-7200), and Whitefish (306 Spokane Ave., 406/863-8888).

Cell Phones and Internet

Contrary to Glacier's sketchy cell and Internet service, Flathead Valley has ubiquitous coverage. Most motels have added wireless and DSL Internet services. You can also get online in the local county public libraries on their computers for a limited amount of time in Kalispell (247 1st Ave. E., 406/758-5820), Columbia Falls (130 6th St. W., 406/892-5919), Bigfork (525 Electric Ave., 406/837-6976), and Whitefish (9 Spokane Ave., 406/862-6657). Each library has its own access policies; call for hours (mostly Mon.-Sat.).

A few cafés have wireless Internet access available for patrons: **Montana Coffee Traders Cafes** (110 Central Ave., Whitefish, 406/862-7667; 1st Ave. W. and U.S. 2, Columbia Falls, 406/892-7633; and 328 W. Center St., Kalispell, 406/756-2326, www.coffeetraders.com) as well as **Colter Coffee** (424 Main St., Kalispell, 406/755-1319, www.coltercoffee.com).

GROCERIES

The Flathead Valley has no shortage of supermarket chains and local grocers. But for seasonal locally grown produce, try one of the summer **farmers markets,** held in Whitefish (north end of Central Ave., Tues. May-Sept.), Bigfork (Bigfork High School, Wed. and Sat. May-Sept.), Columbia Falls (Discovery Square, Thurs. May-Sept.), and Kalispell (Kalispell Center Mall, Sat. May-Sept.). You can also get organic food at several local shops, including **Third Street Market** (3rd St. and Spokane Ave., Whitefish, 406/862-5054) or **Withey's Health Foods** (1231 S. Main St., Kalispell, 406/755-5260).

INFORMATION

Newspapers and Magazines

The local valley daily news comes in the *Daily Interlake* and the weekly news in the free *Flathead Beacon,* with the daily updated online version at www.flatheadbeacon.com. You'll also find other northwestern Montana newspapers around, such as *Great Falls Tribune* and *The Missoulian.* Community weeklies, which cover everything from local events to politics, include Columbia Falls's *Hungry Horse News,* the *Whitefish Pilot,* and the *Bigfork Eagle.*

Emergencies

For medical, fire, or police emergencies in Flathead Valley, call 911. For medical emergencies in Whitefish and Columbia Falls, the new **North Valley Hospital** (1600 Hospital Way, Whitefish, 406/863-3500) is closest. For emergencies in Kalispell, Bigfork, and Lakeside, the upgraded **Kalispell Regional Medical Center** (310 Sunny View Lane, Kalispell, 406/752-5111) is closest.

City police stations have jurisdictions inside city limits only; much of Flathead Valley is covered by the county sheriff's department. In an emergency, when you dial 911, you don't have to think about whether you are inside city boundaries or not; your emergency will be relayed to the appropriate jurisdiction. But just in case, here are the police and sheriff contacts you may need: **Flathead County Sheriff** (920 S. Main St., Kalispell, 406/758-5585), **Columbia Falls Police** (130 6th St. W., 406/892-3234), **Kalispell Police** (312 1st Ave. E., 406/758-7780), and **Whitefish Police** (2nd St. and U.S. 93, 406/863-2420).

Ranger Stations

The Flathead National Forest surrounds the Flathead Valley, so you can pick up maps, current trail and camping information, forest and ski conditions, and regulations in several national forest offices and ranger stations, including **Flathead National Forest and Talley Lake Ranger Station** (650 Wolfpack Way, Kalispell, 406/758-5200) and **Swan Lake Ranger Station** (200 Ranger Station Rd., Bigfork, 406/837-7500).

Bigfork Lodging, Camping, and Food

Bigfork's location on Flathead Lake attracts scads of visitors to the summer resort town. Lake and river activities are big, along with hiking, golf, and the playhouse. In the off-season, you may have the town nearly to yourself. Of the four major towns in Flathead Valley, Bigfork is the farthest south from Glacier (65 minutes) and Glacier Park International Airport on U.S. 2 (35 minutes).

BIGFORK ACCOMMODATIONS

You can find a full list of Bigfork lodging options at www.bigfork.org and locate lake, river, or golf vacation homes to rent through **Eagle Bend Flathead Vacation Rentals** (406/837-4942 or 800/239-9933, www.mtvacationrentals.com). Lodging rates are lowest fall-spring. Properties will add on the 7 percent state bed tax.

Motels and Cottages

The town's most reasonably priced lodging is **Timbers Motel** (8540 Hwy. 35 S., 406/837-6200 or 800/821-4546, www.timbersmotel.com, Apr.-Oct., $100-125 d), which puts you within a five-minute drive of Eagle Bend Golf Course and just a couple of minutes from the

© BECKY LOMAX

Bridge Street Cottages offer riverside lodging in Bigfork.

FLATHEAD VALLEY

A GUIDE TO LOCAL BREWS

Montanans relish their local microbreweries. To help you navigate the mystery of the brews, here's a guide to the local beers.

- **Bayern Brewing** (Missoula): Bayern Amber is the backbone of this brewpub, but Dancing Trout, a filtered German wheat ale, is favored by anglers.
- **Big Sky Brewing** (Missoula): One of the most well-known brown ales in northwest Montana, Moose Drool may have gained its notoriety through merchandising its name, but it tastes darn good too. Two other popular brews are Scape Goat Pale Ale, a lighter English-style ale, and Trout Slayer, a filtered wheat ale.
- **Blackfoot River Brewing** (Helena): Look for the seasonal Woollybugger Wheat, a German *hefeweisen*, and Missouri River Steamboat Lager, a light, hoppy amber.
- **Flathead Lake Brewing** (Bigfork): The brewery with an accompanying restaurant named its headliner light-bodied hoppy ale after Flathead Lake's waves: Whitecap Pale Ale. Also, try the Wild Mile Wheat, an unfiltered summer wheat beer named after the town's famous white water.
- **Glacier Brewing** (Polson): This brewery's award-winning beers are the Golden Grizzly Ale, a light-bodied German Külsch-style brew, and the Slurry Bomber Stout, with a creamy roasted chocolate flavor.
- **Great Northern Brewing** (Whitefish): The brewery's popular lighter beers include a *hefeweisen* called Wheatfish and the medium-bodied Hellroaring Amber. If you haven't overdosed on huckleberries, try the Wild Huckleberry Wheat Lager. In winter, look for Snow Ghost, named for the snow-laden trees on top of Whitefish Mountain Resort.
- **Tamarack Brewing** (Lakeside): Northwest Montana's newest brewery and restaurant puts out a light golden Bear Bottom Blonde and robust amber Yard Sale Ale—named after ski lingo used to describe a skier who crashes hard, littering the hill with skis and poles.

Bigfork Summer Playhouse. It is on a small knoll above the highway and has a heated pool, a hot tub, a sauna, and continental breakfast.

In downtown Bigfork, **Bridge Street Cottages** (309 Bridge St., 406/837-2785 or 888/264-4974, www.bridgestreetcottages.com, $95-300) offers higher-end lodging. Four of the units are right on the Swan River. Surrounded by small perennial gardens, these well-furnished, well-kept one-bedroom cottages come with Internet access, cable TV, air-conditioning, and fully equipped kitchens. Suites are smaller, with just a fridge and a microwave.

Bed-and-Breakfast

A short 3.5 miles south of Bigfork puts you at **Candlewycke Inn Bed & Breakfast** (311 Aero Lane, 406/837-6406 or 888/617-8805, www.candlewyckeinn.com, $100-170). On 10 acres, the nonsmoking cedar-and-log inn, serving a full breakfast in the morning, has five folk-art-themed guest rooms with pillow-top beds and private baths, some with jetted tubs. Walk on trails around the property, cross-country ski in winter, or lounge on the massive decks or in the outdoor hot tub.

Flathead Lake Resorts

Averill's Flathead Lake Lodge (Flathead Lake Lodge Rd., Bigfork, 406/837-4391, www.flatheadlakelodge.com, mid-June-Aug.) is a family-owned working dude ranch on 2,000 acres. Lodging, meals, and activities are all included in one big price for 7 or 14 days: rates run around $3,500 per week for adults, with rates for children less depending on their age. With horseback riding, fishing, swimming, waterskiing, tennis, and sailing, the ranch centers around the classy log lodge and cabins. You can park the car and dive into vacation mode for several days, as the ranch coordinates all the activities.

At the mouth of the Swan River at Flathead Lake, **Marina Cay Resort** (180 Vista Lane, Bigfork, 406/837-5861 or 800/433-6516, www.marinacay.com, $150-400) has courtyard and waterfront suites and 2-3-bedroom condos along with restaurants, a seasonal outdoor pool and hot tub, and a marina with boat rentals. Although it's a little dated, the new owners may be remodeling.

Bigfork Camping

Located on Flathead Lake, **Wayfarer's State Park** (0.5 miles south of Bigfork on Hwy. 35, 406/837-4196, www.fwp.state.mt.us, May-Sept., $15-23) is great for boating and fishing. The park is one of the lake's largest campgrounds, with 30 sites on 68 acres, a boat ramp, a swimming area, and 1.5 miles of hiking trails. Pets are allowed on a leash. Campground amenities include firewood, a fire grill, flush and vault toilets, showers, picnic tables, and drinking water. Four other state parks also rim the lake.

BIGFORK DINING

For a tiny town, Bigfork packs in the tasty restaurants, most of which sit downtown within two blocks' walking distance of the theater. On performance nights at the theater, you won't get into a restaurant for dinner unless you make reservations. Stop in for espresso and oversize chocolate-chip cookies baked fresh daily at **Brookies Cookies** (191 Mill St., 406/837-2447). You can even mail cookies home. For grab-and-go breakfast bagels and hiking lunches, stop by **MontanaBearFood** (475 Electric Ave., 406/837-0811).

Breakfast

Located on the way to hike in Jewel Basin, **Echo Lake Café** (1195 Hwy. 83, 406/837-4252, www.echolakecafe.com, 6:30am-2:30pm daily, $6-12) is a local haunt that frequently has waiting

© BECKY LOMAX

Showthyme serves up eclectic dinners in Bigfork.

lines. Breakfast is served all day, with blueberry waffles, artichoke omelets, and eggs Benedict. Lunch features sandwiches, wraps, and salads.

Burgers

For burgers and beer, drop in at the **Garden Bar and Grill** (451 Electric Ave., 406/837-9914, 11am-2am daily, $7-10). You can eat inside or out back in the funky garden, where live music is played on summer weekend evenings. The bar, which serves as local headquarters for the annual whitewater festival, features 20 microbrews on tap.

Eclectic Cuisine

Known for exceptional food at modest prices, **Showthyme!** (548 Electric Ave., 406/837-0707, www.showthyme.com, 5pm Tues.-Sat., $18-26) dishes up a broad repertoire: fresh fish, pasta, wild game, and steaks. One friend swears by the before-dinner wicked gin and tonic. Start dinner with the warm brie cheese salad or just dive straight into an entrée of Angel's chicken-stuffed green chilies smothered with red sauce. The wine list features Australian and New Zealand imports as well as West Coast vintners. For dessert, try the house specialty: a huckleberry ice cream crepe. The cozy old two-story brick bank building adjacent to the theater has outside seating in summer.

In 2012 owner-chef Marc Guizol revamped his French restaurant into **Mosaic** (408 Bridge St., 406/837-2923, lunch 11am-2:30pm Tues.-Sat., dinner 5pm-10pm Tues.-Sat., $7-23) with indoor or outdoor seating and a large new bar. Flavors now reflect worldwide influences but with local and regional ingredients. The lunch menu includes deli-style quiche, baguette sandwiches, paninis, and organic greens. Cuban, Asian Fusion, French, Italian, and Moroccan flavors enliven meats, fish, and pasta.

Sushi

Located upstairs in Twin Burch Square, **SakeTome Sushi** (459 Electric Ave., 406/837-1128, www.saketomesushi.com, 5pm-9pm Tues.-Sat.) garners a loyal following, making reservations a must. The restaurant includes a bar, indoor seating, and deck seating. Specialty rolls ($10-17) feature fun twists, with spicy crab or ahi. *Nigiri* and *maki* rolls ($4-9) come raw or cooked.

Columbia Falls Lodging, Camping, and Food

Columbia Falls is the closest town to Glacier and Glacier Park International Airport (on U.S. 2), but in opposite directions, about 18 minutes from West Glacier and 12 minutes from the airport. It has fewer lodging, dining, and shopping options compared to other Flathead towns. Rather than a tourist town, it's a working-class lumber-mill town.

COLUMBIA FALLS ACCOMMODATIONS

Surrounding Columbia Falls, cabins and vacation homes are scattered in the woods and on the Flathead River. Locate vacation homes and cabins rented by their owners via **VRBO** (www.vrbo.com). Summer rates are highest, but you can find lower rates and deals during the rest of the year. A 7 percent bed tax is added to lodging rates.

Motels

Good for those on a budget, the town has a Super 8 chain motel plus two small independent motels, all located on U.S. 2 near the waterslide and Flathead River. **Glacier Inn Motel** (1401 2nd Ave. E., 406/892-4341, www.glacierinnmotel.com, $50-100) is a small mom-and-pop motel with air-conditioning, clean guest rooms, and friendly owners.

Bed-and-Breakfast

On 10 quiet acres 10 minutes from town, **Bad Rock Bed and Breakfast** (480 Bad Rock Dr., 406/892-2829 or 888/892-2829, www.badrock.com, $125-225) is four log cabins surrounding a river-rock and log-frame house. Cabin guest rooms have handcrafted log furniture, while the three house guest rooms are decorated in different styles. All have private baths. Breakfast is a large Montana-style affair, sometimes featuring Belgian waffles heaped with strawberries.

Golf Resort

Outside Columbia Falls, among big trees and quiet, **Meadow Lake Resort** (100 St. Andrews Dr., 406/892-8700 or 800/321-4653, www.meadowlake.com) is on an 18-hole golf course, with a restaurant, indoor and outdoor swimming pools, a spa, and tennis courts. For lodging ($125-620), the resort has 24 hotel rooms, condos with 1-3 bedrooms, and vacation homes. In winter the resort provides a ski shuttle to Whitefish Mountain Resort.

COLUMBIA FALLS CAMPING

Two private campgrounds are on U.S. 2 and Highway 40, with Glacier Park about 20 minutes away. Be prepared for road noise with the highway locations. Both have sites for tents ($20-28) and sites for RVs ($25-40) with hookups; other amenities include flush toilets, hot showers, dump stations, wireless Internet access, and laundries.

With 55 full-hookup sites in a renovated grassy setting surrounded by trees right in town, **Columbia Falls RV Park** (103 U.S. 2 E., 406/892-1122 or 888/401-7268, www.columbiafallsrvpark.com, Apr.-Oct.) is the closest to Glacier and one mile from the waterslides, an outdoor community swimming pool, and grocery stores. A few blocks' walk puts you at the restaurants in town. **Glacier Peaks RV Park** (3185 Hwy. 40, 406/892-2133 or 800/268-4849, www.glacierpeaksrvpark.com, year-round) is easy to spot, with its flower-painted VW bug and trailer as a sign. Sixty grassy full-hookup sites sprawl under partial shade. With its location at the junction of Highway 40 and U.S. 2, driving access is quick to Columbia Falls, Whitefish, and Kalispell.

COLUMBIA FALLS DINING

Columbia Falls has never been known as a dining mecca—until recently. New restaurateurs ushered in new tastes, catapulting the cuisine beyond the fast-food enterprises along the highway.

Cafés

Coffee Traders Columbia Falls Café (1st Ave. W. and U.S. 2, 406/892-7633, 7am-2pm daily, $6-10) is a place to grab an espresso, breakfast, or lunch of huge breakfast omelets, salads, wraps, and deli sandwiches, including the decadent Lobster Artichoke Melt. Given the location en route to Glacier, many folks grab an espresso with muffins, scones, or cookies for the drive and a sandwich to go for the trail.

Dining

When **Three Forks Grille** (729 Nucleus Ave., 406/892-2900, 5pm-10pm daily, sandwiches and burgers $7-9, entrées $15-23) opened in 2010, it changed the face of the town's main street, introducing a two-floor restaurant whose main concern was the atmosphere and taste rather than packing in the crowds. While the menu is sprinkled with Italian options—an elk parmigiana meatball appetizer, shrimp risotto, and cannoli—it introduced a Montana twist into its specialties of grilled Tuscan flatiron steak from local free-range antibiotic-free beef and Caesar salad with smoked rainbow trout. Make reservations for weekends and in summer.

When locals crave greasy barbecue, they head for **The Back Room Restaurant** (522 9th St. W., 406/892-3131, www.niteowlbackroom.com, 4pm-9pm daily, $7-15). The restaurant serves old-time gooey ribs and broasted chicken. Order the ribs country, spare, or baby back, or if you can't decide, get a gigantic combo plate accompanied by homemade sauces. Fry bread with honey, coleslaw, and homemade french fries overflow the plate. A server may call you "hon" as she delivers a roll of paper towels instead of napkins to handle the colossal mess. Abandon all concerns about calories or cholesterol; dig in, and when you're done, lick your fingers.

Kalispell Lodging, Camping, and Food

Kalispell—which lacks the resort atmosphere of Bigfork and Whitefish—has a variety of hotels and a changing array of restaurants downtown, along the access highways, and near strip malls. Most of the hotels and restaurants are located 15 minutes south of Glacier Park International Airport (on U.S. 2), the opposite direction from Glacier National Park and almost one hour from West Glacier.

KALISPELL ACCOMMODATIONS

Kalispell has several chain hotels sprawled on the outskirts of downtown, including hotels around the mall and strip mall areas. You can find them online (www.kalispellchamber.com). Other than chain hotels, the pickings are slim. Rates will be highest in summer, with lower prices fall-spring.

Hotels

Right in downtown Kalispell's shopping district, the historic **Kalispell Grand Hotel** (100 Main St., 406/755-8100 or 800/858-7422, www.kalispellgrand.com, $80-150) feels like it's a century back in time. Walking into the lobby, you're greeted by a tin ceiling, an ornate pump organ, and the original wide oak-banister stairway. Renovated guest rooms have smaller baths with showers rather than tubs. Although the ambience harks back to 1912, when the hotel opened with room rates at $2, its modern amenities now include an elevator, high-speed Internet access, air-conditioning, and TVs. In the afternoon, pick up home-baked cookies in the lobby.

Kalispell Camping

Quite a few year-round commercial campgrounds are scattered around Kalispell, all within 30-40 minutes of Glacier and 15-20 minutes to Flathead Lake or golf courses. They have comparable rates for tent sites ($15-25), sites for RVs ($25-32) with hookups, and the additional 7 percent state bed tax. Standard amenities include flush toilets, hot showers, dump stations, laundries, playgrounds, cable TV hookups, wireless Internet access, picnic tables, and fire rings.

The nearest to Glacier, **Rocky Mountain "Hi" RV Park and Campground** (825 Helena Flats, 406/755-9573 or 800/968-5637, www.glaciercamping.com) is adjacent to a spring-fed creek with 98 grassy sites tucked between large fir trees—a few with Swan Mountain views. Set back from the highway, you'll hear no road noise. With swimming, fishing, and canoeing in a wide creek, it's a good campground for kids.

Nearer to downtown Kalispell, two RV parks are adjacent to the noisy Highway 35 truck route. Each has something more to recommend it. **Glacier Pines RV Park** (1850 Hwy. 35, 406/752-2760 or 800/533-4029, www.glacierpines.com) has a seasonal outdoor heated swimming pool and grassy sites under large trees. **Spruce Park on the River** (1985 Hwy. 35, 406/752-6321 or 888/752-6321, www.spruceparkrv.com) accommodates 100 RVs and 60 tents in shaded sites. With its location on the Flathead River, you can fish from the campground.

KALISPELL DINING

Kalispell has common national chain restaurants along U.S. 93, but not in the few blocks of the downtown area. For a 1950s soda fountain throwback—huge scoops of ice cream, candy racks, and hot dogs—drop in at **Norm's News** (34 Main St., 406/756-5466). **Sweet Peaks** (343 Main St., 406/257-1102, www.sweetpeaksicecream.com), which has its first shop in Whitefish, rotates flavors of homemade ice cream.

Cafés

Using locally-sourced ingredients, the **Rising Sun Bistro** (25 2nd Ave. W.,

406/755-7510, www.risingsunbistro.com, 11am-9pm Tues.-Fri., 9am-9pm Sat., 9am-3pm Sun., $7-23) delivers homespun French food. The restaurant was revamped by Restaurant: Impossible in 2012, but it still serves up luscious eggs Benedict, crepes, quiche, soups, international burgers, signature sandwiches, and classic bistro-style dinners. French wines and six types of mimosas top off the meals.

Hit **Split Rock Cafe** (30 2nd St. E., 7:30am-2:30pm and 4pm-8pm Tues.-Sat., 4pm-8pm Sun.-Mon., 406/755-7577, $6-13) for homemade family-friendly American food that includes hand-cut fries and onion rings. Daily breakfast, lunch, and dinner specials put yummy spins on traditional foods. Music livens up happy hour.

Pizza

For old-style Montana atmosphere, visit **Moose's Saloon** (173 N. Main St., 406/755-2337, www.moosessaloon.com, 11am-1:30am daily, $5-19), where peanut shells and sawdust cover the floor in this funky old-time bar that has been a valley staple since 1957. It will be just what you imagine a Montana bar to be—dark and loud. But the pizza crust ranks highly with locals, and beer prices are cheap. Takeout is also available.

A chef-owned restaurant, the new **Hop's Downtown Grill** (121 Main St., 406/755-7687, www.hopsmontana.com, from 4:30pm Mon.-Sat.) quickly became a local favorite with wood-fired pizza. Dinner ($7-27) features gourmet Montana Angus beef burgers with homemade buns and made-to-order potato chips.

Fine Dining

North Bay Grille (139 1st Ave. W., 406/755-4441, www.nbgrille.com, lunch 11:30am Mon.-Fri., dinner 5pm daily) fills its fine dining menu ($15-30) with seafood and steak specialties. But many locals come for lighter meals ($9-15) of upscale sandwiches, pizzas, burgers, salads, small plates, and pasta. The bar serves up domestic and imported wines as well as a long list of imaginative martinis and margaritas.

Whitefish Lodging, Camping, and Food

Bustling in summer with Whitefish Lake and in winter with Whitefish Mountain Ski Resort, Whitefish is a resort town loaded with lodging and restaurants. It is 15-20 minutes west of Glacier Park International Airport (on U.S. 2) and 45 minutes west of Glacier National Park.

WHITEFISH ACCOMMODATIONS

If you're searching for upscale, Whitefish is the only Flathead Valley town that offers luxury lodging, but it also has a myriad of less pricey lodging options, including chain and independent hotels. Find a full listing of choices at www.explorewhitefish.com. You can also locate vacation homes and cabins to rent through Lakeshore Rentals (406/863-9337 or 877/312-8017, www.lakeshorerentals.us) or from individual owners through **VRBO** (www.vrbo.com). The highest rates for lodging properties are in summer, except for Whitefish Mountain Resort, and the second highest rates are in winter. Find off-season deals in the spring and fall. A 7 percent state bed tax will be added to the rates.

Hotels

In Whitefish, one mile from downtown restaurants and nightlife, **Grouse Mountain Lodge** (2 Fairway Dr., 406/892-2525 or 877/862-1505, front desk 406/862-3000, www.grousemountainlodge.com, $110-300) is right on a 36-hole golf course that becomes groomed cross-country

© BECKY LOMAX

The Lodge at Whitefish Lake offers luxury lodging.

skiing trails in winter. It has an indoor pool and outdoor hot tubs, a restaurant, and DSL and wireless Internet access; the lobby has a huge river-rock fireplace. Its 143 guest rooms, renovated in 2012, come in seven configurations, from a basic hotel room to more upscale accommodations with oversize showers with multiple showerheads. A complimentary shuttle accesses the town, Glacier Park International Airport, and the ski resort. As part of Glacier Park Inc. (www.glacierparkinc.com), the company that runs Glacier's lodges, you can also get one-stop reservations inside the park.

With a two-story lobby draped with a giant wrought-iron chandelier and a river-rock fireplace, **The Lodge at Whitefish Lake** (1380 Wisconsin Ave., 406/863-4000 or 877/887-4026, www.lodgeatwhitefishlake.com, $155-1,000) is more upscale than other valley hotels. Spacious 2-3-bedroom suites and condos vary in size and have balconies, fireplaces, slate floors, granite countertops, fridges, tubs and walk-in showers, and high-speed Internet access. The premier guest rooms overlook the lake, facing the sunset; upstairs north guest rooms have mountain views. Viking Lodge rooms are across the street adjacent to the parking lot. The lodge has a private beachfront on Whitefish Lake, an outdoor pool and a hot tub, a full-service marina, boat rentals, a day spa, a restaurant, and a lounge. Golf and skiing are both within 7-10 minutes' drive.

Bed-and-Breakfasts

A short walk to restaurants and nightlife in downtown Whitefish, the circa-1920 **Garden Wall Inn** (504 Spokane Ave., 406/862-3440 or 888/530-1700, www.gardenwallinn.com, $155-195, suite $275) is furnished with antiques inside, while a perennial garden blooms outside. It's an extension of Glacier Park, with historic photos and picture books in the living room, and if the weather deteriorates, you can curl up in front of a real fire in the glazed-brick fireplace. Five guest rooms each have private baths—some with oversize claw-foot tubs. In the morning, awake to a coffee or tea tray delivered to your room before heading to the dining room for a breakfast of treats like huckleberry-pear crepes.

A five-minute drive from downtown and 10 minutes from the ski resort, **Hidden Moose Lodge** (1735 E. Lakeshore Dr., 406/862-6516 or 888/733-6667, www.hiddenmooselodge.com, $100-200) provides three styles of upscale Montana-outdoors themed guest rooms with private decks and baths: lodge rooms, Jacuzzi rooms, and a suite. The great room curves around a large river-rock fireplace, and decks face the woods. Amenities include an outdoor hot tub, wireless Internet access, air-conditioning, cable TV, mini fridges, and complimentary evening beverages. Breakfast is big, with the house chorizo quiche being one of the favorites.

Resort

Located six miles above town, **Whitefish Mountain Resort** (406/862-2900 or 800/858-5439, www.skiwhitefish.com) has a range of lodging options—motels and condos ($60-699) and vacation homes ($100-2,100). Winter sees the highest room rates when restaurants, shops, and lifts open for the ski and snowboard season. Summer has moderate prices. Fall and spring are very inexpensive, but no lifts, shops, or restaurants are open. Kandahar Lodge has the best reputation for upscale accommodations with an outstanding gourmet restaurant; for budget lodging, ask about the Hibernation House. When Whitefish rooms fill in summer, you can find lodging at the resort.

Guest Ranch

The **Bar W Guest Ranch** (2875 U.S. 93 W., Whitefish, 409/863-9099 or 866/828-2900, www.thebarw.com) houses guests in a 6,200-square-foot Western lodge and cabin suites adjacent to a small lake and Spencer Mountain. Ranch activities pile on trail rides, rodeos, cookouts, boating, archery, hiking, fishing, and campfires. Three- and six-night packages include meals, lodging, and ranch activities (adults $850-3,090, children $450-1,380). Fall-spring rates run lower.

WHITEFISH CAMPING

Whitefish offers several private campgrounds; all will add a 2 percent tax on top of the 7 percent state bed tax.

Set in deep woods right on Whitefish Lake, **Whitefish Lake State Park** (U.S. 93, 1 mile west of Whitefish, then 1 mile north following signs, 406/862-3991, www.fwp.state.mt.us, year-round, $15-23) is perfect for swimming and launching boats but not for sleeping, as trains frequently rumble on the tracks crossing the park. With a good set of earplugs, you can survive the night. Amenities include flush toilets, picnic tables, fire rings with grills, firewood, running water, and a biker-hiker site.

Two miles south of town, **Whitefish KOA** (5121 U.S. 93 S., 406/862-4242 or 800/562-8734, www.glacierparkkoa.com, mid-Apr.-mid-Oct., RV hookups $30-60, tents $20-36) sits on 33 acres shielded from the highway by thick forest. The outdoor pool attracts kids, while oldsters gravitate to the adults-only hot tub. Amenities include flush toilets, showers, picnic tables, fire rings, cabins, hookups, laundry, a dump station, a camp store, wireless Internet access, free mini golf, free breakfast, and a restaurant serving nightly barbecues, sandwiches, and pizza.

WHITEFISH DINING

As a resort town, Whitefish is overloaded with outstanding restaurants. Because of the crowds, make reservations to avoid long waits in summer or winter. In spring and fall, a few restaurants alter their hours or close for a month on a whim to go fishing; call ahead to be sure they are open.

For burgers, head to the **Bulldog Saloon** (144 Central Ave., 406/862-5601), but keep the kids out of the X-rated-decorated bathroom stalls. The downtown bar-hopping scene heats up on summer weekends with **Crush Wine Bar** (124 Central Ave., 406/730-1030), a post-theater favorite. For homemade flavors of ice cream, stop at **Sweet Peaks** (419 3rd St., 406/862-4668, www.sweetpeaksicecream.com).

The newest sensation in town is the renovated **Casey's Bar** (101 Central Ave., 406/862-8150). The dive bar moved upscale into a three-story restaurant, bar, casino, and dance hall with a third-floor rooftop with views of Big Mountain.

Cafés

For breakfast and lunch, you might have to arm wrestle a local's claim to a daily seat at **The Buffalo Cafe** (514 E. 3rd St., 406/862-2833, www.buffalocafewhitefish.com, breakfast and lunch 7am-2pm Mon.-Sat., 8am-2pm Sun., dinner 5pm-9pm Mon.-Sat., breakfast and lunch $5-9, dinner $8-16) to order the house Buffalo Pie, with hash browns, ham, and cheese and topped with two poached eggs. **Loula's** (300 2nd St. E., 406/862-5614, www.whitefishrestaurant.com, 7am-3pm daily, $6-10) is the place for lemon-stuffed french toast with raspberry sauce, or a portobello mushroom, roasted red pepper, and cream cheese sandwich. Before leaving, pick up one of the trademark fresh-baked fruit pies ($18-24) to go.

Italian

A budding chain, **Ciao Mambo** (234 E. 2nd St., 406/863-9600, www.ciaomambo.com, 5pm-10pm daily, $11-23) transports you beyond the Flathead to Italy with its cramped noisy dining room lilting to tunes of Frank Sinatra and Andrea Bocelli. You can also enjoy a view of Big Mountain from the upstairs deck. Start with the Tootsie Roll appetizer, a ricotta-cheese-stuffed phyllo on marinara. Feast on house pasta like fettuccine alla Lulubella, a carbonara to knock your cholesterol through the roof. The Mambo Red house wine, served only by the glass, is surprisingly good and inexpensive.

For pizza, Montana's homegrown chain **MacKenzie River Pizza** (9 Central Ave., 406/862-6601, www.mackenzieriverpizza.com, 11am-9pm Mon.-Thurs., noon-10pm Fri.-Sat., noon-9pm Sun., $8-20) is a great family restaurant with traditional and eclectic (chicken fajita, Thai) pizzas with sourdough or natural-grain crusts. You'll also find giant salads, sandwiches, and pasta on the menu and local microbrews on tap.

Asian

Although most people don't see sushi and Montana as going together, the sushi at **Wasabi Sushi Bar and Ginger Grill** (419 2nd St., 406/863-9283, www.wasabimt.com, from 5pm daily summer, from 5pm Mon.-Sat. fall-spring, $9-25) has gained a large clientele. Fusion rolls, *nigiri,* sashimi, sake, and grilled

© BECKY LOMAX

Wasabi Sushi Bar and Ginger Grill whips up fusion rolls and sushi.

Asian specialties are served in a relaxed, bright atmosphere surrounded by wasabi-green walls. Large mirrors reflect the deft fingers of the sushi chefs in action as they make your rolls. Try the Black Widow, a peppered albacore topped with hot Sriracha sauce. You can also get rolls to go. Grill fare includes specialties such as wasabi pad thai.

Cajun and Creole

At **Tupelo Grille** (17 Central Ave., 406/862-6136, www.tupelogrille.com, from 5:30pm daily, $16-36), the flavors come from New Orleans. Start with a duck, chicken, and andouille gumbo followed by a tasty version of shrimp and grits, in which grilled shrimp doused in a spicy tasso cream sauce smothers grilled grits. If you can't decide between the Louisiana flavors, order the Cajun creole combo plate, which piles up a platter of crawfish étouffée, shrimp creole, and chicken and sausage jambalaya. Don't leave without your dessert: The bread pudding is scrumptious without being overly sweet.

Mexican

Pescado Blanco (235 1st St., 406/862-3290, www.pescadoblanco.com, 5pm-9pm daily, $15-21) is more than a cute variation on the name of Whitefish; their chefs excel at mountain Mexican cuisine, such as the bison enchilada. They also fly in fish twice a week for dishes such as halibut tacos with orange sauce and seared scallops with sauces appearing in the colors of the Mexican flag. Their signature margaritas are made with fresh lime and a 14 percent distilled agave wine, and they serve a full range of south-of-the-border beers and local microbrews.

Fine Dining

Whitefish also has more than its share of fine restaurants that specialize in Montana game, fish, and high-end steaks accompanied by extensive wine lists. At Whitefish Lake Golf Course, **Whitefish Lake Restaurant** (1200 U.S. 93 N., 406/862-5285, www.whitefishlakerestaurant.com, lunch 11am-3pm daily summer, dinner from 5:30pm daily year-round, lunch $8-12, dinner $19-40) offers historic ambience in a renovated 1937 log building. For an appetizer, try the New Zealand mussels followed by one of the restaurant's fish favorites, a halibut baked in phyllo with feta, roasted garlic, and spinach. The house specialty is roasted rack of lamb topped with a three-onion demi-glace.

The Lodge At Whitefish Lake Boat Club (1380 Wisconsin Ave., 406/863-4040, www.lodgeatwhitefishlake.com, lunch 11am-3pm daily, dinner from 5pm daily, lunch $9-15, dinner $19-39) is the only restaurant overlooking Whitefish Lake, with the romance of watching the sunset across the water. Dining is available inside or on the deck. Lunch features salads, sandwiches, and specialty pizzas. Dinner entrées dress up beef, fish, pasta, and vegetarian dishes. You can go for drinks and appetizers to try the sweet-potato chips with blue-cheese cream.

BACKGROUND

The Land

GEOLOGY

Glacier's mountains tell a long story—approximately 1.6 billion years of geologic history. Three geologic events sculpted Glacier and Waterton's scenery into its characteristic jagged parapets with swooping valleys: First, sediments layered on top of each other in an ancient sea; then, mountains moved; and most recently, an ice age gouged formations. Ever since, relentless erosion continues to shape the landscape. Wind and water chip away at peaks. Freeze-melt cycles wreak havoc on cliffs, prying off slabs of rock. Over time, weather leaves its mark on the land.

Ancient Belt Sea

Approximately 1.6 billion to 800 million years ago, a shallow lake covered parts of what is now Washington, Idaho, Montana, and British Columbia. The lake, known as the Belt Sea, accumulated sands washing down from adjacent highlands. Through pressure and heat, dolomites, limestone, argillites, siltites, and quartzites made layers like a colorful cake, one on

© BECKY LOMAX

ANCIENT ROCKS

Glacier contains some of the oldest exposed rock in North America.

ARGILLITES

Of Glacier's colorful rock formations, the most striking is the argillite, an iron-rich mudstone formed in layers on the floor of the shallow ancient Belt Sea 800 million-1.6 billion years ago. Its blue-green and purple-red hues leap off mountainsides and intensify under water. This clay and silt contains iron, which changes to red hematite when exposed to oxygen, thus giving Grinnell argillite its burgundy color. The Appekunney argillite did not oxidize, remaining green. Spot the red colors on Red Eagle Mountain when driving down the east side of Going-to-the-Sun Road. Find both argillites on the Grinnell Glacier Trail, the Iceberg Trail, at Red Rocks Falls, and while rafting on the Middle Fork of the Flathead.

RIPPLE ROCK AND MUD CRACKS

Raindrop impressions, water ripples, and mud cracks remain etched in stone—all evidence of their origins in ancient seas. Ripple rocks, found most often in red, blue, or beige layers, look like sands on a beach where waves left their marks. As the sea dried up, sediments compacted and cracked, similar to a mud puddle drying up in a driveway. Large blocks show webs of cracks filled in with other sediments—an effect that looks like dull maroon or turquoise tiles. Look for slabs with ripple marks and mud cracks along the Many Glacier Valley trails.

MAGMA INTRUSIONS

Don't be fooled: Yes, Granite Park and its namesake chalet are dubbed for the igneous rock; however, Glacier has no granite. When early prospectors found Purcell lava or pillow lava—rounded blue-gray formations—they mistakenly called it granite. This lava intruded up through sediment layers, billowing out in ropey coils and bubbles. See this lava on the Highline Trail between Granite Park Chalet and Ahern Pass.

One of the most visible magma intrusions is the diorite or Purcell sill. It appears from a distance as a 100-foot-thick horizontal black line sandwiched between thinner whitish layers. When magma boiled up between limestone layers 800 million years ago, it superheated the limestone, turning it white. You can see the diorite sill from Many Glacier Road, visible as a thick dark line on Mount Gould and Mount Wilbur. Hikers see it as black jagged teeth above Iceberg Lake or the solid line above Grinnell Glacier. The Highline Trail passes through the sill approximately one mile beyond Haystack Saddle. Look for a crystallized green sheen covering deep black. Your footing changes abruptly when you step onto the sill; instead of a broken scree bed, you'll find something more solid and volcanic.

STROMATOLITES

The Belt Sea became habitat for blue-green algae. Six species of this petite primitive lifeform lived in the sea, doing what algae does best—removing carbon dioxide from the water and giving off oxygen. During this process, calcium carbonate formed into stromatolites, a round rock formation 6-15 inches in diameter that looks like Van Gogh's *Starry Night* swirls. They grew in colonies that made 30-foot columns up to three miles wide. Find stromatolites along Going-to-the-Sun Road and trails such as the Highline and Piegan Pass. The presence of these algal forms in the Belt Sea produced an oxygen-rich atmosphere that allowed other life forms to develop—yes, including humans.

top of the other. Over eons, the layers piled up thousands of feet thick.

You can see these layers today in the mountains of Glacier. In a geologic feat found in very few places in North America, Glacier retained its sedimentary rock instead of seeing it metamorphose. Find these colorful layers in the mountainsides around Logan Pass, where multihued sediments stripe Mount Clements. You can also find layering on trails to Iceberg Lake, Grinnell Glacier, Gunsight Pass, and Colbalt Lake. Most of Glacier's lakes and rivers collect

© BECKY LOMAX

Grinnell Glacier is the most accessible icefield in the park.

a rainbow of rocks from higher elevations, compliments of the Belt Sea layers.

Uplift of Mountains

Between 150 and 60 million years ago, major tectonic movement along massive faults created the northern Rocky Mountains. The Pacific and Continental Plates pushed against each other until the ancient Precambrian rocks of the Pacific Plate slid atop the much younger dinosaur-age rock of the Continental Plate. During this uplift, a several-mile-thick Belt Sea chunk sidled 50 miles east and higher in elevation, where it is exposed today for visitors to see. This movement is known as the **Lewis Overthrust Fault.** Look for its evidence where geologists originally discovered the fault in 1890: on the side of Summit Mountain north of Marias Pass on U.S. 2.

During the uplift, rock heated and became pliable like bread dough. Sometimes it simply folded due to the pressure and heat. Find folds on Waterton Lake's east shore, above the Ptarmigan Tunnel trail, and between Josephine and Bullhead Lakes on the Swiftcurrent Trail.

Glaciation

More recently, glaciers carved the landscape. Two million years ago the Pleistocene ice age engraved the park's topography via huge advancing and retreating glaciers. Only the tops of Glacier's highest peaks poked out as nunataks, a summit completely surrounded by ice. Glaciers—thousands of feet deep—gouged out huge valleys, leaving a 5,000-foot variation in elevations from valley floors to peaks.

These ancient ice rivers bit into the landscape. Some valleys, like St. Mary Valley and Lake McDonald Valley, contain long finger-like lakes that sit where a large glacier once was. In other valleys, such as the Swiftcurrent Valley, the large glacier receded in a series of melts, leaving a series of smaller lakes instead of one large one. These huge rivers of ice also left U-shaped valleys, such as the broad Two Medicine Valley. These rounded valley floors stand in contrast to V-shaped river-carved valleys such as the Grand Canyon.

Glaciers are what molded the rugged peaks in the park. When three or more glaciers gnawed away on a peak, a horn resulted, such as Mount Reynolds or Triple Divide. Sometimes two glaciers chewed ridges paper thin into arêtes (French for "fish bone"), such as the ragged Iceberg-Ptarmigan Wall or the Garden Wall on the Continental Divide. The upper ends of glaciers often carved out cirques, steep-walled round basins such as Avalanche Lake basin.

As glaciers retreated, they left large piles of debris—rocks, sand, and gravel—in the form of moraines, like a big pile of dirty laundry. Large moraines, such as Howe and Snyder ridges flanking Lake McDonald, remain from Pleistocene ice, whereas smaller rubble piles in Grinnell or Sperry Glacier basin date to the last century.

While ancient Pleistocene ice melted in Glacier about 12,000 years ago, several miniature ice ages since then have shaped the land. The glaciers currently in the park are products of the last 8,000 years. During the **Little Ice Age** (1500-1850), most glaciers grew. Park tree-ring studies show evidence that there were more than 150 glaciers in the early 1900s. These are the smaller alpine glaciers in the upper basins of peaks. Some of these glaciers plummeted off cliffs, forming hanging valleys: The 492-foot Bird Woman Falls dives from a hanging valley suspended between Mount Oberlin and Mount Cannon that was once home to a large glacier.

Less than 17 percent of those alpine glaciers remain today, the largest of which is Harrison Glacier, at 0.7 square miles. Climatologists expect the 25 glaciers that remain in 2012 to melt sometime before 2030. Waterton no longer has any active glaciers. At Cameron Lake, you can look across the border to the icy remnants of Herbst Glacier, now too small to be classified as an active glacier.

Glaciers and Snow Fields

It's often hard to tell the difference between a glacier and a snow field. In early summer, they look the same, covered with fresh snow from winter. But they are distinctly different. It's simple math: When more snow adds than melts annually, glaciers form. The snow transforms into icy grains through freeze-thaw cycles. Snow builds up on the upper end of glaciers and pushes down, compressing ice crystals. Over years, the ice compacts in layers, mounting into a huge mass with a rigid surface and a supple base.

Glaciers are slow-moving ice. Aided by gravity, the ice presses down, forming a thin elastic barrier that carries the mass toward the glacier's toe, where it may calve off in chunks. Sperry Glacier moves about 12-20 feet per year, while Grinnell moves much more—30-50 feet per year. When the ice travels over convex ground features, its surface cracks, forming crevasses sometimes hundreds of feet thick. Hidden crevasses make glaciers deadly for travel, so do not walk out on them without appropriate rescue gear.

For a glacier to move, a certain amount of ice is needed—usually a surface of at least 25 acres and a minimum depth of 100 feet. Less than that and the ice becomes static—a permanent snow field. Moving glaciers behave similarly to a bulldozer, gouging out troughs and picking up rocks from the surrounding mountain. Once the winter season's snow melts, you can recognize glaciers by their telltale debris bands—lines of rocks on the surface.

Glacier After the Glaciers Melt

Locals often joke about Glacier Park's name: What should the park be called after its glaciers all melt? Of course, the name will remain the same. Despite the disappearance of the glaciers in the next two decades, evidence of the large ice age glaciers and smaller alpine glaciers will remain. The U-shaped valleys, horns, arêtes, hanging valleys, and moraines retain their formations thanks to glaciers. You can also find smaller evidence of glaciers. On the Avalanche Lake or Hidden Lake trails, look for glacial striations, or large scratches, on rocks where ice abraded the surface. Also, on the Avalanche Trail, you'll see erratics, large boulders strewn about from receding ice.

CLIMATE

Glacier and Waterton live on a collision course for both arctic continental and Pacific maritime weather. Wet weather races in from the Pacific with moderate temperatures. Near West Glacier, precipitation results in an annual average 29 inches of rainfall and 157 inches of snow. Waterton also sees more precipitation than the rest of Alberta.

Although the east side of the Continental Divide equals the west in terms of precipitation, wind produces more extremes. Winter winds blow snow from slopes, providing forage for ungulates. Winds also blow trains off their tracks. Several east-side high passes are notorious for raging unpredictable winds causing hikers to crawl on all fours. **Chinook winds**—warm winds with speeds that can exceed 90 mph—occur any time of year, but mostly in winter. Native Americans called them "snow eaters" for the snow they rapidly melted. When a Chinook descends the Continental Divide's east side, it blows warm and dry, fooling trees into thinking it's spring and catapulting their cells into spring water absorption. When temperatures plummet again, the cold freezes the water in their cells, killing the trees. This "winter kill" accounts for the number of dead silver trunks dotting east-side forests, especially visible in Two Medicine and Waterton.

Glacier is a land of weather extremes. Its maximum high hit 99°F, while its low was -36°F. Elevation makes a huge difference too: While Lake McDonald beckons swimmers to sunny beaches, frigid winds can rage across Logan Pass. Sometimes you'll experience four seasons in one day, so always dress in layers and carry extra clothing, no matter what the weather looks like in the morning. Rains move in fast, and snow can fall any month of the year.

Spring

While March-May are appealing off-season months to travel, in Glacier they are wet and cold, still clinging to winter. Snow buries the high country and much of the lowlands until late spring. May is moody, alternating between warm days and rainstorms or frequent late snows that can cause avalanches in the high country.

Summer

During summer months, June habitually monsoons, but July-August usher in warmer, drier skies. Higher elevations are often substantially cooler—up to 15 degrees chillier than valley floors. While cool breezes are welcome on baking summer days, they can also bring snows in August.

Fall

Autumn begets lovely bug-free warm days and cool nights. While aspen and larch trees turn gold, temperatures bounce through extremes—from highs of 75-80°F during the day to below freezing at night. The weather is seemingly schizophrenic as rains and snows descend for a few days, followed by clearing and warming trends.

Winter

Winter temperatures in Glacier vary depending on elevation, but mostly hang in the 10-25°F range, and snowfall is voluminous. Logan Pass is buried under 350-700 inches of snow per year. Temperatures can spike above freezing, with accompanying rain, or below 0°F with an arctic front. Because Chinooks visit Waterton more than the rest of Alberta, it is one of the warmest places in the province in winter. While the Canadian prairies suffer below-freezing temperatures, Waterton may be reveling in 30-50°F weather.

PRECIPITATION AND TEMPERATURES

Taken from West Glacier.

Month	Average number rainy/snowy days	Average snowfall (inches)	Average temperature (low-high)
Jan.	17	40	12-28°F
Feb.	13	23	18-34°F
Mar.	13	15	22-41°F
Apr.	11	4	29-52°F
May	13	0.4	37-64°F
June	13	0.2	44-71°F
July	9	0	47-79°F
Aug.	9	0	46-78°F
Sept.	9	0.1	39-67°F
Oct.	11	2	32-53°F
Nov.	15	17	25-37°F
Dec.	17	38	18-30°F

Daylight

Given Glacier's latitude and placement on the mountain time zone's western edge, hours of daylight fluctuate wildly during the year. In June, more than 16 hours of sun leave lots of time to play outdoors. First light appears around 5am, and dark doesn't descend until almost 11pm. By late August, dark descends at 9pm, with daylight shortening through autumn. At the winter solstice, the sun rises at 8am and sets at 4:30pm.

FLORA

Glacier and Waterton parks have rich floral diversity—one of the reasons the parks are UNESCO Biosphere Reserves. Forests, prairies, and peaks have different vegetation specific to elevation, habitat, and weather. Five different floral habitats flank the park's mountains, yielding a rich broad spectrum of plantlife that goes from rainforest to arid alpine tundra.

Glacier is home to 46 rare Montana plants; four are found only in the park. The flora includes 1,150 vascular plants, 400 mosses, and 275 lichens with species at the edges of their distribution: Great Plains flowers to arctic bulbs. The Lake McDonald Valley has nearly 100 Pacific Coast species.

For a small park, Waterton has a lot of rare

plants: 30 grow only within its borders, including the rarest plant, the Waterton moonwort. Waterton can also boast a total of 970 vascular plants, 190 mosses, and 220 lichens, ironically chalking up more diversity than its much larger national park sisters to the north, Banff and Jasper.

Grasslands

More than 100 grass species proliferate across the Glacier-Waterton prairies, which poke into valley drainages on the Continental Divide's east side and have been preserved by natural fires in the North Fork Valley. Waterton has 13 square miles of prairie—one of two prairie lands in the Canadian national park system and one of North America's last places where grizzly bears range into their historic grassland habitat. Grassland prairies sprout wildflowers that adapt to dry, shadeless, windy, and warm conditions.

Aspen Parklands

Aspens dominate east-side slopes, populating the valleys of Many Glacier, Belly River, Two Medicine, St. Mary, and Waterton. Harboring elk herds in winter and broken by wildflower meadows of arrowleaf balsamroot and sticky geranium, groves of quaking aspen shake their leaves in the slightest breeze—hence their name. They mark the transition between grasslands and coniferous forests. Mountain death camas, paintbrush, pasqueflower, lupine, stonecrop, and horse mint span the rainbow.

Montane Forests

In low to mid-elevations, dense forests mix poplars and firs, which vary substantially depending on moisture and winds. Cedar-hemlock forests with birch dominate wetter western valleys, while drier slopes yield limber pine, Douglas fir, white spruce, and lodgepole pine. The western larch, a conifer that loses its needles each winter, also inhabits lower-elevation forests. Below the shade-producing canopy, tiny pale cream-colored wildflowers hide for protection from the sun's drying rays; find fragile twinflower, foamflower, and orchids. Juniper, Pacific yew, thimbleberry, and serviceberry also have their niche.

Subalpine Zone

Between 5,000 and 7,000 feet in elevation, stately forests surrender to subalpine firs, dwarfed and gnarled in their struggle to survive in a short growing season, brutal winds, frigid temperatures, and heavy snows. For survival, trees develop a bent, stunted krummholz, forming a protective mat rather than growing upright. Whitebark pine and Englemann spruce also sneak into the subalpine. Between tree islands, lush mountain meadows bloom with a colorful array of columbine, bog gentian, valerian, fleabane, and beargrass. Flowers must do their business fast in the subalpine zone; yellow glacier lilies and spring beauties force their blooms through the snow.

Alpine Tundra

Nearly 25 percent of Glacier and Waterton is alpine tundra. Above the tree line, the land appears to be barren rock, but a host of miniature plants adapt to the harsh conditions of high winds, drying altitude, short summers, cold temperatures, and rocky soil that lacks organic matter. The miniature wildflowers survive by hugging the ground, blooming during their short few-week season. Hairy leaves provide protection from winds and the sun's high-elevation intensity. Mats of pink moss campion, delicate spotted saxifrage, purple butterwort, and Jones columbine fling their energy into showy flowers.

Huckleberries

Of all Glacier's flora, the huckleberry draws the most attention. While several varieties grow throughout the park, from lowlands to subalpine, they all have one thing in common: a sweet berry. Look for a low-growing shrub with

© BECKY LOMAX

Hikers like picking huckleberries.

small green to reddish leaves. About the size of a small blueberry, huckleberries ripen into a rich dark purple-blue. Find lowland berries in late July, but mid-August-early September is known as huck season. Grizzly bears carbo-load on hucks to survive winter.

Wildflowers

Glacier's wildflowers peak late June-early August, depending on snowmelt and elevation. Early summer brings on fields of yellow glacier lilies and white spring beauties poking buds through the snowpack. At lower elevations, the large white heads of cow parsnip bloom alongside roads and continue into higher elevations as summer progresses. Some years, beargrass—a tall white lily—blooms so thickly in July on subalpine slopes that the hillsides look snow-covered. Paintbrush spews fields in yellow, red, fuchsia, white, salmon, and orange. Just a reminder: Picking flowers in national parks is prohibited. Use your camera instead.

Poisonous Plants

Very few plants in Glacier are poisonous. Several can be toxic if eaten, so avoid eating plants or mushrooms. Most of Glacier is inhospitable for poison ivy, poison oak, and poison sumac, but watch for stinging nettles: Although not poisonous, they leave an obnoxious itchy residue on contact. A few people have allergic reactions to cow parsnip: If you have sensitive skin, wear long sleeves and long pants to avoid contact with the plant.

FAUNA

Glacier and Waterton teem with wildlife; there are 24 fish species, 63 mammals, and 272 birds. The diversity of animal life is one reason the parks have been designated Biosphere Reserves by UNESCO. The Crown of the Continent remains a North American bastion of an intact ecosystem, with many animals present that were here before the massive impact of human activity over the past 150 years. In the

SPECTACULAR WILDFLOWER SPOTS

Wildflowers do not bloom park-wide at once. When spring hits lower elevations, popping open buds around Lake McDonald and St. Mary, big Logan Pass alpine meadows cower under snow. As summer progresses, like a mist lifting, higher and higher habitats spread out floral displays. To identify wildflowers, pick up a field guide from the **Glacier National Park Conservancy** (406/888-5756, www.glaciernationalparkconservancy.org) in the St. Mary Visitors Center.

Here are some top places to see Glacier's wildflowers on display:

FROM THE CAR

- **Logan Pass:** Yellow glacier lilies bloom as the snow melts in early July, but they give way to pink alpine laurel, pale yellow paintbrush, and blue penstemon by late July.
- **Going-To-The-Sun Road:** Lower elevations bloom with huge white cow parsnip heads in early July. In late July-early August, wildflowers along the road's alpine section bloom with orange paintbrush, purple shrubby penstemon, and yellow columbine. In some years, high meadows slopes will look snow-covered in mid-July when three-foot-tall creamy beargrass blooms prolifically. July also brings on the big sunflower-like arrowleaf balsamroots and dusty pink prairie smoke in Two Dog Flats on the east side of the road along St. Mary Lake.
- **Two Medicine Road:** Blue camas blooms in early July.
- **Many Glacier Road:** Late May-early June brings tiny pink shooting stars, followed in July by hot-pink sticky geraniums, purple lupine, and sometimes tall light-pink hollyhock.
- **Chief Mountain International Highway:** In June, meadows pop with pink shooting stars while the few miles between the overlook and Highway 5 are lined with tiger lilies in early July.

ON THE TRAIL

- **Trail of the Cedars:** Delicate queen's cup and fairybell in July followed by pipsissewa in August in the rainforest.
- **Quartz Lakes Loop Trail:** In the North Fork, find fairy-slipper orchids in the rich forest duff in late June.
- **Highline Trail:** Color bursts everywhere along the Garden Wall in late July-early August with yellow arnica, deep blue gentians, creamy death camas, white valerian, and fuchsia monkeyflowers. More than 30 varieties of wildflowers speckle meadows.
- **Preston Park:** Hikers on the **Piegan Pass** and **Siyeh Pass** trails revel in the show of purple fleabane, fuchsia paintbrush, and fuzzy-headed western anemones spread thick across meadows. In early July, rare Jones columbine blooms on the switchbacks north of Siyeh Pass.
- **Scenic Point:** In early July, see several-hundred-year-old mats of pink moss campion, small bluebells, and red king's crown, the miniature plants of the alpine tundra.
- **Fifty Mountain:** Meadows that stretch about 1.5 miles yield big floral displays, starting with yellow glacier lilies and white spring beauties in early July. Late July-early August brings on a rich palette of wildflowers.

late 1980s, wolves migrated from Canada, adding more original members to Glacier's wildlife family. Only mountain bison and woodland caribou remain extirpated.

Bears

Two bear species roam Glacier's mountains: the black bear and the grizzly bear. Omnivores and opportunistic feeders, bears will eat anything that is easy pickings. Spending most of their waking time eating to gain 100-150 pounds before winter, Glacier's bears feed on a diet heavy in plant matter: bulbs, roots, berries, shoots, and flowers. Ants, insects, carrion, and ground squirrels fill in

EXPLORING THE ECOSYSTEM

One of the best ways to become intimate with Glacier's wildlife, geology, birds, and cultural history is to join the regionally and nationally recognized experts from the **Glacier Institute** (406/756-1211, www.glacierinstitute.org). Offered year-round, the courses blend in-the-field experiences with hands-on learning at Big Creek Camp in the North Fork or Glacier Field Camp near Apgar. You can learn to bird, watch bears, track animals on snowshoes, photograph wildlife, find herbs and mushrooms, and identify wildflowers. College credit is available for some of the workshops and classes. Adult seminars include wilderness first aid, art, photography, science, and ecology. Youth camps for ages 7-16 emphasize outdoor science. Most single-day courses cost $65-75; most multiple-day courses range $170-475, including lodging and meals.

For those looking for an intimate experience in Glacier, **Glacier National Park Associates** (406/387-4299, www.glaciernationalparkassociates.org) looks for volunteers each summer for backcountry projects. Some tasks restore historic log structures, reconstruct damaged trails and backcountry campsites, and transplant seedlings from the park's native-plant nursery. Past projects have included work at Sperry Chalet and backcountry patrol cabins. Led by a backcountry ranger intern, participants work on one project during a 3-5-day stay in the backcountry. No special skills are required—just a desire to help.

For those itching to contribute to scientific research in Glacier, the **Crown of the Continent Research Learning Center** (406/888-7800, www.nps.gov/glac) conducts citizen science projects every summer. For several years, they have run field studies on common loons, invasive weeds, and high-country species of concern such as mountain goats, pikas, and Clark's nutcrackers. Some training is necessary but is available through the center.

proteins. Contrary to popular opinion, humans are not on their menu of favorite foods.

Because bears learn fast, they adapt quickly to new food sources, be it a pack dropped by the side of the trail or dog food left out in a campground. For this reason, Glacier imposes strict rules for handling food and garbage in picnic sites, campgrounds, and backcountry areas. All garbage cans and dumpsters are bear resistant. Bears that eat human foods and garbage find themselves moved to a new habitat, or worse, destroyed.

Because grizzly and black bears are integral to Glacier's ecosystem, the National Park Service employs several bear rangers whose jobs entail monitoring and deterring bears from trouble. For bruins who linger near roadways and front country campgrounds, the bear team uses hazing methods—loud noises, gunshots, pellet beanbags, and sometimes Karelian bear dogs—in an attempt to teach bears to stay away. Nuisance bears are transplanted to remote park drainages or destroyed if their offenses warrant. "A fed bear is a dead bear," the truism goes. A bear that dabbles in human food often aggressively seeks more.

Bears are one of the least fertile mammals, giving birth once every two or three years. While black bears have a gestation of 220 days, for grizzlies spring mating season is followed by delayed implantation, in which the fertilized eggs are simply stored until winter. Pending the sow's health, the egg or eggs implant, resulting in 1-3 cubs born during winter's deep sleep. If her health is severely threatened, she may abort the egg instead.

Bears don't actually hibernate, as their respiration and pulse remain close to normal. Instead, they enter a deep sleep in which the body temperature drops slightly. Before crawling into their dens, they scarf down mountain ash berries, rough grasses, and twigs to form an anal plug,

© BECKY LOMAX

a grizzly sow and two cubs

which inhibits eating, urinating, or defecating during winter. Bears emerge in the spring ravenously hungry, heading straight for avalanche chutes to rummage for snow-buried carcasses.

Megafauna

Megafauna, the big animals like bears that everyone wants to see, populate Glacier and Waterton. They include three elusive members of the cat family: mountain lions, bobcats, and Canadian lynx. Quiet hunters and mostly nocturnal, cats may see you while you have no idea that they linger nearby. For mountain lions, deer tops the menu, while lynx favor snowshoe hares. Both cat populations rise and fall with their prey populations. With keen eyesight and hearing, these three cats stalk their prey, the lynx with the help of large snowshoe-shaped feet.

Gray wolf packs inhabit fairly large ranges of 100-300 square miles, so chances of seeing a wolf are fairly rare despite their relatively high reproductive potential of 4-7 pups per year. Coyotes, foxes, wolverines, and badgers round out the list of large carnivores. Although wolverines are the most elusive creatures, Glacier provides prime habitat for them with remote terrain, snow fields, and plentiful ground squirrels. Many hikers spot them along the Highline Trail.

Ungulates crowd Glacier's high and low country. Moose browse in streambeds and lakes. Find them in Swiftcurrent Valley, especially around bogs and willow thickets. Elk, mule deer, and white-tailed deer live throughout the park at the tree line and below, while mountain goats and bighorn sheep cling to rocky alpine slopes. During late spring, goats congregate at the Goat Lick on U.S. 2, seeking minerals for their depleted systems. They are also a regal staple at Logan Pass.

In Waterton, a small bison herd grazes in a paddock—a tiny remnant of what once roamed the prairies by the thousands. Visitors may drive the viewing road and hike a short overlook trail to see the bison.

BEAR COUNTRY

GRIZZLY BEARS VERSUS BLACK BEARS

Even though colors are used to name the bears, black and grizzly bears display a variety of fur hues. For instance, a reddish-black bear can give birth to three cubs of different colors: blond, black, and brown. Grizzly bears, while their name evokes silver hair, appear in all colors of the spectrum. Don't be fooled by color; look instead for body size and shape.

Grizzlies are bigger than black bears, standing on all fours at 3-4 feet tall and weighing in at 300-600 pounds. Black bears average 12-18 inches shorter on all fours. Adult females weigh around 140 pounds, while males bulk up to 220 pounds.

In profile, the grizzly has one notable feature: a hump on its shoulders. The solid muscle mass provides the grizzly's forelegs with power for digging and running. Black bears lack this hump. Their face profiles are also different. On the grizzly, look for a scooped or dished forehead-to-nose silhouette; the black bear's nose will appear straighter in line with its forehead. Note the ears, as the grizzly's will look a little too small for its head while a black bear's ears seem big, standing straight up. Paw prints in mud reveal a difference in their claws and foot structure. Grizzly claws are four inches long with pads in a relatively straight line, while black bear claws are 1.5 inches long with pads arced across the top of the foot.

Although both bears have mediocre vision, they are fast runners. In three seconds, a grizzly bear can cover 180 feet.

HIKING IN BEAR COUNTRY

With a few precautions, you can eliminate the scares.

- **Make noise.** To avoid surprising a bear, use your voice—sing loudly, hoot, or holler—and clap your hands. Bears tend to recognize human sounds as ones to avoid; they'll usually wander off if they hear people approaching. Make loud noise in thick brushy areas, around blind corners, near babbling streams, and against the wind.
- **Hike with other people.** Avoid hiking alone. Keep children near. Very few bear attacks happen to groups of four or more.
- **Avoid bear feeding areas.** If you stumble across an animal carcass, leave the area immediately and notify a ranger. Toward summer's end, huckleberry patches provide high sugars.
- **Hike in broad daylight.** Avoid early morning, late evening, and night.
- **Never approach a bear.** Head swaying, teeth clacking, laid-back ears, a lowered head, and huffing or woofing are signs of agitation: Clear out slowly.
- **If you do surprise a bear, back away.** Contrary to all inclinations, do not run. Instead, back away slowly, talking quietly and turning sideways or bending your knees to appear smaller and nonthreatening. Avoid direct eye contact. Leave your pack on; it can protect you if the bear attacks.
- **Use pepper spray or play dead.** If you surprise a bear that attacks in defense, aim pepper spray at the bear's eyes. Protect yourself and your vulnerable parts by assuming a fetal position on the ground with your hands around the back of your neck. Play dead. Move again only when you are sure the bear has vacated the area.
- **If a bear stalks you as food, or attacks at night, fight back.** While bears stalking humans as prey is extremely rare, use any means at hand—pepper spray, shouting, sticks, or rocks—to tell the bear you are not an easy food source. Try to escape up something, like a building or a tree.
- **Pay attention to trail signage.** Special bear signage is used at trailheads to inform hikers of concerns. Yellow **bear warning** signs indicate bears are frequenting the trail; use extra caution and make noise. Orange **bear closure** signs indicate a trail is closed, usually because one has been aggressive or is defending a carcass.
- Two books have accurate information on bears: Bill Schneider's *Bear Aware* and Stephen Herrero's *Bear Attacks: Their Causes and Avoidances*.

© BECKY LOMAX

a bighorn sheep ram

Small Mammals

Members of the weasel family—fishers, pine martens, minks, and weasels—inhabit forests and waterways. The short-tailed weasel changes color in winter: Its fur becomes white, except for the small black tip of its tail. Snowshoe hares also change to white in winter, their large feet providing extra flotation on snow. In subalpine country, a chorus of eeks, screams, and squeaks bounce through rockfalls. The noisemakers are pikas, which look like big-eared tailless mice, and the ubiquitous Columbian ground squirrel, recognized by its reddish tint. Looking like fat house cat-size fur balls, hoary marmots splay on rocks, sunning themselves. Scampering between high alpine rocks, golden-mantled ground squirrels look like oversize chipmunks with their telltale gold stripes.

Fish

With 750 lakes and 1,500 miles of streams, Glacier provides abundant habitat for both native and nonnative species of fish. Bull trout, westslope cutthroat trout, and whitefish are among the 17 native species. To promote recreational fishing, lakes were once stocked with nonnative fish such as rainbow trout, arctic grayling, and kokanee salmon. Introduced species flourished, threatening native fish, whose populations are now waning. Since the 1970s fish are no longer stocked in Glacier or Waterton.

Fish in Waterton Lakes feed on a tiny crustacean, the opossum shrimp—a relic species that inhabited the area prior to the Pleistocene ice age. As glaciers melted, the tiny shrimp returned through the Missouri-Mississippi watersheds. Spending its entire life in darkness, it lingers on the lake bottom during the day, surfacing only at night.

Birds

More than 200 species of birds mean every park visitor can see wildlife. Bird checklists are available at visitors centers in both parks

Ptarmigan turn white in winter for camouflage in the snow.

to assist with identification. In summer, trees teem with songbirds—cedar waxwings, thrushes, chickadees, vireos, sparrows, dark-eyed juncos, and finches. Brilliant-colored western tanagers and striking mountain bluebirds flit between treetops. Sightings of rufous and calliope hummingbirds are common. Woodpeckers, including the large red-capped pileated woodpecker, pound at bark in search of bugs. Ground birds such as the chicken-size grouse surprise hikers on trails, while smaller ptarmigans—whose plumage turns white in winter—blend with summer coloration into rocks. Steller's jays and Clark's nutcrackers add to the cacophony.

Because of Glacier's profuse rivers, streams, and lakes, waterfowl find plentiful habitat. Loons, grebes, mergansers, and goldeneyes fill almost every lake, while harlequin ducks migrate to rapidly flowing streams in spring for nesting. Tundra swans use Glacier's lakes as a stopping place during their annual migration to and from their arctic breeding grounds. American dippers, or water ouzels, nest near waterfalls: The dark bird's obvious bobbing action is a dead giveaway of the species.

Raptors

Nothing is more dramatic than sighting a golden eagle soaring along the Continental Divide. Commonly nesting in remote spots, goldens often return yearly to the same location. Glacier also boasts about 10 nesting pairs of bald eagles, seen along waterways year-round. Above lakes, ospreys dive for fish from impressive heights, while red-tailed hawks and American kestrels hover over field mice. Listen carefully, for nights are haunted by the small pygmy owl's "whew" call and the great horned owl's six deep hoots.

Snakes and Spiders

For the most part, Glacier and Waterton are devoid of poisonous snakes and spiders. The climate is too harsh for rattlesnakes. However, you will find garter and bull snakes on some trails. Due to colder conditions, native spiders are small, although a bite may produce swelling or an allergic reaction.

ENVIRONMENTAL ISSUES

Climate Change

The current increase in global temperatures affects Glacier Park like nowhere else. Changes seem to be happening faster here than elsewhere, which is why Glacier serves as a living laboratory for studying climate change. While glaciers have shrunk since 1850, ecologists predict that the park's namesakes will all melt before 2030—producing not just a loss of ice but a shift in flora and fauna. As temperatures warm, the tree line advances upward in elevation, encroaching on alpine zones. Glacier's tree line was once 3,200 feet lower than it is today; how far up it will climb is unknown.

A rising tree line will cause basins scoured clean by ice and blooming with wildflower meadows to succumb to heavy forests of spruce, fir, pines, shrubs, and bushes. Photographs have already recorded significant changes in vegetation in some locations in the park. Plants at the fringes of their distribution may disappear entirely.

Shifts in floral habitat may force wildlife to change elevation or latitude in search of food sources. Species such as the heat-intolerant **pika** may suffer extinction, and animals adapted to cold winters such as mountain goats and wolverines may suffer if they can't adapt.

Because of Glacier's easily accessed alpine areas, scientists are monitoring melt rates of Grinnell and Sperry Glaciers to help predict future impacts on the park's biodiversity. The Northern Rocky Mountain Science Center has produced a series of repeat photography collections showing changes in glaciers and forest growth, comparing photographs from the last

© BECKY LOMAX

Due to its fast-melting glaciers, the park serves as a living laboratory for studying climate change.

century to present day. You can see these at www.nrmsc.usgs.gov and at Many Glacier Hotel.

Endangered Species

In the 1800s, more than 100,000 **grizzly bears** roamed grasslands and foothills in the Lower 48. Today, in less than 1 percent of their historic range, fewer than 1,500 grizzlies forage for food. Greater Glacier's grizzly bears are currently listed as threatened on the Endangered Species List, but thanks to bear management efforts assisting their recovery, that may not be for long.

In an effort to count the grizzly population, the U.S. Geological Survey conducted two major studies around Glacier and continues with monitoring today. Collecting scat and bear hair via barbwire stapled to rub trees and surrounding scent lures, scientists used tweezers to bag the hairs for DNA genotyping of species, sex, and individual. You may find barbwire on trees along trails where biologists are still gathering samples. The study found a healthy grizzly population, with 765 bears spread across 7.8 million acres in northwest Montana. Glacier houses the densest populations. A continuing Montana Fish, Wildlife, and Parks study radio-collars female grizzlies to track reproduction and mortality. It found that the grizzly population in the Northern Continental Divide Ecosystem, which includes Glacier, is growing at three percent per year. Both studies have shown that grizzlies have exceeded federal recovery levels, so the government machinery is moving toward delisting the grizzly bear.

Grizzlies require a large range; many travel outside the park and across international boundaries. Human pressures from road and house building, agriculture and livestock, timber harvesting, and mineral, oil, and gas mining impact their habitat. Just outside Waterton, legal Canadian hunting and predator-control programs subject bears to high mortality rates. In northwest Montana, poaching, management actions, and private landowners account for the deaths of 20-30 grizzlies per year. While bad berry crops and encroaching rural development contribute to bears getting into trouble, inappropriate attractants—garbage, livestock grain, and bird feeders—lead to many of the deaths.

Recorded sightings of the **Canada lynx** have declined substantially in the past 40 years, prompting it to be listed as threatened in 2000. In coniferous forests, the lynx follows its primary prey, the snowshoe hare, and the cat's cyclical population rise and fall mirrors hare numbers. Park studies have followed tracks in the snow to ascertain the lynx's status.

Two indigenous trout descended from ice-age lakes that formed as the glaciers retreated: **westslope cutthroat trout** and **bull trout.** Glacier provides a stronghold for these fish. Bull trout populations have declined 90 percent, forcing it to be listed as an endangered species in 1998, but pure westslope cutthroat have yet to be placed on the list. While habitat degradation and overfishing contributed to the demise, another menace came from nonnative lake trout stocked for recreational fishing, turning them into easy prey. But the biggest threat comes from hybridization with other trout such as rainbows. Removing nonnative species is impractical; the park uses fishing regulations to protect pure populations.

Other species not officially listed as endangered also suffer threats to their survival. Of all the ungulates, **bighorn sheep** face the greatest risk. Once widely scattered across most western mountain ranges, the sheep today live in fragmented pockets. Hunting, disease, agriculture, mining, competition for food, fire-suppression policies, and habitat destruction forced this grassland forager into the more rugged fringes of its historic range. Today, 400-600 bighorn sheep graze in Glacier, with an additional population in Waterton. Recent studies used GPS radio collars to track the sheep, and

© BECKY LOMAX

Pikas are being monitored due to the growing threat of climate change.

DNA samples revealed two genetically different populations in northern and southern Glacier.

Climate change poses a threat to alpine species that rely on cooler temperatures. In the past several years, citizen science programs have aided the National Park Service in collecting population data on **pikas** and **mountain goats,** two animals that could be threatened with the change in their habitat. Baseline population counts are being gathered to assist in monitoring what happens to these animals as the climate warms.

Current research is also monitoring other species of concern. Annual counts of waterbirds, such as **loons** and **harlequin ducks,** are keeping tabs on these small populations. A winter-hair snag study is tracking the number of **wolverines,** as Glacier appears to be one of the few strongholds in the Lower 48 for the gluttonous weasel.

While other animals are in danger, **gray wolves** have seen a recovery. Once ranging throughout most of North America, gray wolves disappeared from Glacier-Waterton by 1920 due to predator-control programs. In the 1970s they were placed on the Endangered Species List. In 1986, following the natural migration of the Magic Pack from Canada, Glacier saw its first litter of pups born in over 50 years. By 2009 numbers in the Northern Rockies rebounded to the point where the federal government delisted the wolf, and Montana permitted hunting and trapping wolves. While no hunting is permitted inside the park, wolves cross the boundaries to go outside the park.

North Fork of the Flathead

Currently, Glacier's northern boundary is twice as long as the joint boundary with Waterton—the area is one ecosystem, but it lacks protection. Threats include proposed mining operations that could alter the unique North Fork ecology. A coalition of U.S. and Canadian organizations has joined forces to lobby for Akamina-Kishinena Provincial Park in British

Columbia to become protected as a national park wilderness area in order to protect the North Fork of the Flathead River. That change would match the two national park boundaries in length, offering more protection for the shared watershed, wildlife, and air. Find more information at www.flathead.ca.

Fire

Following decades of heavy fire-suppression policies, forest fuels built up to high levels in Glacier. An average summer sees 13 fires across 5,000 acres; some summers spike higher, like 2003, when 15 percent of the park blazed. Despite the smoke, inconvenience to visitors, and area closures, lightning-caused fires are a natural process and are healthy for the ecosystem. They remove bug infestations, reduce deadfall and nonnative plants, release nutrients into the soil as a good fertilizer, and maintain a natural mix of vegetation. Natural uneven burns create a mosaic of charred timber amid greenery, a patchwork that leads to greater diversity of vegetation and wildlife. In the natural process of regrowth, the burns flourish with wildflowers, birds, and animals.

Historical Protection

Glacier has many cultural and historical resources, but protecting archaeological and historic assets is difficult. At 50 years old, artifacts—even garbage dumps—are considered historic, according to federal law. To date, Glacier has identified 429 archaeological sites, and Waterton has 358. But many have not been cataloged. More funding is needed for adequate protection.

Non-Native Plants

Sometimes the prettiest flowers are the most noxious, as is the case with exotic weeds such as spotted knapweed, St. John's wort, and oxeye daisies, introduced via horses, cars, livestock, and railroads. Their broad roots, high seed production, and chemicals inhibit the growth of native plants, lessen diversity, and reduce wildlife habitat. Both Waterton and Glacier curb the spread of nonnative plants through roadside mowing, herbicides, or natural means.

History

Human use of the Crown of the Continent dates back at least 10,000 years. Evidence shows that the native people living near Glacier and Waterton today have ancestral roots fishing in Upper Waterton Lake and driving bison across the Blakiston Valley prairies.

Native Americans

Spanning what became the U.S.-Canadian border, the **Blackfeet,** or Niitsitapi ("original people"), included three nomadic groups who based much of their livelihood on hunting bison in the vast prairies on the Continental Divide's east side. The most northerly group, the Siksika, or Blackfoot, were the first to meet European traders. (To refer to the group, *Blackfoot* is used in Canada, and *Blackfeet* is used in the United States.) The other two—the Blood (or Kainai) and Piegan (or Piikani)—made up the southern groups. For thousands of years, according to the Blackfeet, their lands were between the Saskatchewan and Yellowstone Rivers.

During the summer, Blackfeet groups convened for the sun dance, a ceremony held on the plains, but during the rest of the spring and summer, efforts focused individually on stocking food: hunting, digging roots, and collecting berries. As bison moved northwest to their wintering ranges, groups met again to hunt—sometimes at buffalo jumps, where hunters funneled bison over a cliff to slaughter them

© BECKY LOMAX

Native Americans celebrate their heritage during the annual North American Indian Days.

for food, hides, and bones. Afterward, they returned to their winter camps, sheltered in deep mountain forests.

For the Blackfeet, the Glacier Park area was known as the "Backbone of the World." Used for spiritual sanctuary, the mountains provided places for prayer and sacred ceremonies. A place to gather guidance, the mountains also yielded holy plants and roots used for their healing properties. Some of Glacier's peaks, lakes, and rivers still use Blackfeet names today: Going-to-the-Sun Mountain, Two Medicine Lake, Pitamakin Pass, and Running Eagle Falls.

On the Continental Divide's west side, the **Salish** and **Kootenai** hunted, trapped, and fished, ranging east over the mountains on annual bison hunts. Known as the Ktunaxa, the Kootenai (in Canada *Kootenay*) comprised seven bands spanning the western Rockies from southern Alberta to Missoula, Montana. The Kootenai typically used mountain passes like Marias, Cut Bank, Red Eagle, and Brown to cross through Glacier and Waterton to hunt, and the Blackfeet used the same passes for raiding parties. For the Kootenai, the Lake McDonald area was a place for sacred dances, hence its original name of Sacred Dancing Waters.

Two other nations lived in the Glacier-Waterton vicinity: the Assiniboines or Stoney people, and the Gros Ventres people. Both of these groups find namesakes in the park, with a lake, a pass, and three peaks named for the Stoney. In the park's northeast corner, the Gros Ventres, which means "big belly," left their name on the Belly River and Mokowanis drainages with Gros Ventre Falls. Little evidence remains in the park of the presence of the Flathead and Kalispel people.

As westward expansion brought more nonnatives, Native Americans were moved into government-planned reservation boundaries: The Siksika were settled near Calgary, the Blood were moved onto a reserve adjacent to Waterton, and the Piegans, the largest of the three Blackfeet groups, split in two, with the North Piikani settling near Pincher Creek in Alberta and the South Piikani in Montana. Their reservation included Glacier Park's eastern slopes up to the Continental Divide. The Salish and Kootenai were moved to the Flathead Reservation southwest of Glacier. Smallpox and social problems took their toll on all of these indigenous groups.

Explorers, Trappers, and Miners

In 1803, when **Lewis and Clark** came west, they bypassed Glacier. At Camp Disappointment, located today on the Blackfeet Reservation, they came within 25 miles of Marias Pass—one of the lowest passes through the treacherous Rocky Mountains—but never found it.

Soon, French, Spanish, and English fur trappers entered the Glacier-Waterton area, but the land between the Continental Divide and the plains belonged to the Blackfeet. In 1895 the federal government negotiated a settlement with the Blackfeet to purchase the portion of their reservation that makes up Glacier's eastern slopes today. Starving and in dire need of money, the Blackfeet agreed to the terms of the sale, and Glacier became a public **forest reserve.**

Miners arrived, looking for copper and gold. At the turn of the 20th century, mining boomed in Many Glacier and Rising Sun. Western Canada's first oil well spewed at Waterton, and Montana's first was at Kintla Lake. Neither oil nor mining paid off, both supplanted by burgeoning tourism.

Building a Park

Pressure to find rail passages through the northern Rockies began in the mid-1800s. When the Great Northern Railway finally succeeded in 1891 to lay track over the Continental Divide, the face of Glacier changed. The railroad company needed a destination for its wealthy passengers. The railroad's economic needs and preservationists spawned the idea of **Glacier National Park,** which became a reality on May 11, 1910.

William Logan—for whom Logan Pass is named—took the reins as the first superintendent of the nation's 10th park. Charged with building a headquarters, hiring rangers, constructing trails, and surveying for a road through the park's interior, Logan did little his first year but put out fires—literally: More than 10 percent of the park flamed during one of the West's biggest fire seasons. His second summer finally saw steps toward readying Glacier for visitors.

In order to provide travelers with places to stay and go, the **Great Northern Railway** created many of the park's facilities: hotels, tent camps, chalets, roads, trails, and boats. Competing for travel time and dollars from wealthy Americans taking steamships to Europe, the railroad pitched the slogan "See America First" to lure vacationers to Glacier, which became known as "America's Switzerland." Large hotels such as Many Glacier and Glacier Park Lodge were built to impress and touted the high-end amenities of the era, such as steam heat.

Horse concessionaires operating from every hotel and chalet in the park merged into the Park Saddle Horse Company. By the mid-1920s the way to see the park was on horseback. At its peak, the Park Saddle Horse Company operated more than 1,000 horses and led more than 10,000 visitors through the park each summer.

As the country's infatuation with the automobile grew, the demand for a road bisecting Glacier's interior increased, and the **Transmountain Highway,** named later after Going-to-the-Sun Mountain, altered how visitors toured the park. Although building the western portion of the Sun Road began in 1919, the 50-mile project was not completed until 1932. The opening of Going-to-the-Sun Road ushered in a new era of park visitation. A fleet of red buses hit Glacier's roads for touring. With increased motorized travel, camping gained in popularity, and the Great Northern Railway added budget motor inns to its property collection. With the popularity of Going-to-the-Sun Road, saddle trips and the pricey chalets began to meet their demise.

During the Great Depression and World War II, travel restrictions and fuel conservation made park visitation plummet, forcing hotels and chalets to close. Several chalets fell into disrepair and had to be razed. As bus-tour business usurped rail travel and private car travel grew, the Park Saddle Horse Company folded. The railroad's hotel business suffered, losing $500,000 annually. Finally, in 1954, the Great Northern Railway sold Many Glacier Hotel and Lake McDonald Lodge to the National Park Service and unloaded the two remaining chalets for $1. In 1957 the railroad sold the hotel concession business and remaining Glacier Park Lodge and Prince of Wales Hotel to a Minneapolis corporation, which subsequently sold three years later to Glacier Park Inc. (GPI), which has in turn been purchased and sold by several parent companies but continues to operate the park lodges today.

Of the remaining park lodges and chalets, six are listed as **National Historic Landmarks.** Going-to-the-Sun Road was recognized as the first road in the United States to become a National Historic Landmark. It also is the only road in the country to be a National Historic Landmark and a National Civil Engineering Landmark.

Saving Park Attributes

In the past two decades, ailing park facilities have received facelifts and rehabilitation. Sperry and Granite backcountry chalets saw restoration after they were both closed in the 1990s. Today, they offer rustic places for hikers to overnight, much like they did in their heyday. Glacier's red jammer buses were also sidelined in the 1990s, but Glacier Park Inc., the National Park Fund, and Ford Motor Company collaborated on getting them back on the road.

Currently, two major rehabilitation projects are still underway. Going-to-the-Sun Road is in the midst of a 10-year $270 million reconstruction to shore up the road against vehicle wear and tear, torrential rains, mudslides, and avalanches. Many Glacier Hotel has been undergoing a multiyear $30 million upgrade to straighten the building and restore the dining room to its original look.

International Peace Park

In 1932, Glacier and Waterton made front-page headlines as the world's first **International Peace Park.** The brainchild and work of Rotary International chapters from Alberta

© BECKY LOMAX

A shrine to peace stands at the International Peace Park, in Waterton.

and Montana, their lobbying efforts paid off as the Canadian Parliament and U.S. Congress officially recognized the continuity of the parks. With credit to the longest undefended border in the world, the U.S. and Canadian governments dedicated the parks together as **Waterton-Glacier International Peace Park.**

Biosphere Reserve

In 1976, the United Nations Educational, Scientific, and Cultural Organization (UNESCO) designated Glacier Park as a **Biosphere Reserve.** Three years later, Waterton Lakes received the same recognition. As a Biosphere Reserve, the parks are recognized for their huge diversity of wildlife and plants. Part of the designation is also due to the parks functioning as living laboratories for significant scientific research into fire ecology and climate change.

World Heritage Site

In 1995 UNESCO declared both Waterton and Glacier a **World Heritage Site.** This designation was assigned for the parks' natural beauty and unique geological features. Their beauty is attributed to the dramatic topography created by sedimentation in the Belt Sea, the Lewis Overthrust, and glaciation. Those three actions exposed some of the oldest sedimentary rock in North America and created unique geological features, such as Triple Divide Peak, from which water flows to the Pacific, the Gulf of Mexico, and Hudson Bay.

ESSENTIALS

Tips for Travelers

FOREIGN TRAVELERS

Entering the United States

Except Canadians, international travelers entering the United States must have passports and a current I-94 form ($6). Travelers from countries in the Western Hemisphere Travel Initiative, such as Canada, must have a passport, U.S. passport card, enhanced driver's license, or NEXUS card. Visas may also be required for some countries. For the list of visa waivers and visa applications, check www.state.travel.gov.

Entering Canada

For international travelers entering Canada, passports are required. Travelers from the United States and Western Hemisphere Travel Initiative countries may enter Canada with passports, U.S. passport cards, enhanced driver's licenses, or NEXUS cards. Visas are not required for visitors from about 50 countries, including the United States. All others must apply for visas. Find the list of visa-exempt countries and visa requirements at www.cic.gc.ca.

© BECKY LOMAX

Road Ports of Entry

Chief Mountain Border Crossing (7am-10pm daily June-Labor Day, 9am-6pm daily May 15-May 31 and Labor Day-Sept. 30) is a seasonal port of entry on Chief Mountain International Highway. A year-round port of entry on Waterton-Glacier's east side, **Piegan-Carway** (7am-11pm daily) is on U.S. 89 and Alberta U.S. 2. Due to flooding damage in the North Fork Valley, the only west-side port of entry now is **Roosville,** on U.S. 93 and British Columbia Highway 93 north of Eureka. It's open 24 hours daily year-round, but it is also 90 miles from West Glacier.

Goat Haunt

Even though Goat Haunt, USA, is accessible only by boat or on foot, tightening border policies have affected the small seasonal port of entry at the south end of Waterton Lake. Because of the International Peace Park status, special regulations are in effect. For visitors in Canada traveling down Waterton Lake in private boats or on the tour boat, clearing U.S. immigration is not required, even though you cross the Canadian-U.S. border. At Goat Haunt, you can debark and wander around freely along the beach and walkway between the International Peace Park Pavilion and the boat docks without going through immigration control. However, hikers going beyond Goat Haunt must show a valid passport or passport card at the immigration office (11am-5pm daily June-mid-Sept.). Visitors from countries other than Canada and the United States must have a current I-94 form or I-94W status to hike beyond Goat Haunt. The forms ($6) are not available at Goat Haunt immigration office but are available at the Chief Mountain, Piegan-Carway, or Roosville border crossings. For further information on crossing from Canada into the United States, call the Roosville Port of Entry (406/889-3865).

For day hikers returning to Canada, immigration inspection is not required; however, backpackers hiking into Canada must phone the Canada Border Services Agency (403/653-3535) when they reach the Waterton Townsite. You can also phone the agency for information in advance of your trip. People taking the Waterton boat will be given immigration forms to fill out.

Customs

In general, Canada and the United States have similar customs laws: no plants, drugs, firewood, or live bait can cross the border. Some fresh meats, poultry products, fruits, and vegetables are restricted, as are firearms in Canada. Pets are permitted to cross the border with a certificate of rabies vaccination dated within 30 days prior to crossing. Bear sprays are considered firearms in Canada; they must have a U.S. Environmental Protection Agency-approved label to go across the border. For clarification, call the Roosville Canadian customs office (250/887-3413). If you purchase Cuban cigars in Waterton, they are not permitted into the United States.

Money and Currency Exchange

If you travel to Waterton for a day or two, you don't need to exchange money. Waterton has no bank, but the **Tamarack Village** (214 Mount View Rd., 403/859-2378, www.hikewaterton.com, May-mid-Oct.) does offer money-exchange services for Canadian and U.S. currency only. Most stores and businesses in Waterton accept U.S. currency but give Canadian currency as change. Exchange rates vary by store; to receive the best exchange rates, use credit cards.

For Canadians visiting Glacier or Flathead Valley, some businesses accept Canadian currency. They are used to converting it, but credit cards will receive the most accurate exchange rate. On Glacier's east side, you'll find no banks to exchange currency; the closest banks are in Flathead Valley.

For both Canada and the United States, traveler's checks in smaller denominations ($20 and under) work best for short trips on either side of the border. International travelers should exchange currency at their major port of entry (Seattle, Vancouver, or Calgary).

TRAVELING BY RV

RVing is a great way to travel, but in Glacier it has its limitations. Roads are narrow, curvy, and shoulderless, and some campsites cannot fit larger RVs.

Road Restrictions

Going-to-the-Sun Road restricts RVs and trailers. From bumper to bumper, vehicles must be 21 feet or shorter to drive the road over Logan Pass between Avalanche Campground on the west and Rising Sun on the east. A truck-trailer or car-trailer combination must also be under 21 feet. The maximum width allowed, including mirrors, is 8 feet; maximum height is 10 feet. Despite meeting width and height requirements, camper drivers still feel pinched as they navigate the skinny lanes hemmed in by a 1,000-foot vertical wall and oncoming traffic inches away.

Don't lose heart just because you travel by RV. You can still see the famed Going-to-the-Sun Road via Glacier Park Inc.'s red-bus tours, Sun Tours, and free park shuttles, or rent a car in West Glacier, East Glacier, or St. Mary.

Camping

Not all campgrounds in Glacier can accommodate larger RVs. Apgar can handle the largest RVs, up to 40 feet. Fish Creek, Many Glacier, and St. Mary can fit RVs up to 35 feet. Two Medicine can accommodate RVs up to 32 feet. Only the shorter RVs can fit into sites at Rising Sun (up to 25 feet), Avalanche (up to 26 feet), and Sprague Creek (up to 21 feet, but towed units are not allowed). Large units are

© BECKY LOMAX

Large RVs will find limited campsites and are not allowed up to Logan Pass.

not recommended at Bowman Lake, Cut Bank, Kintla Lake, Logging Creek, and Quartz Creek.

Campgrounds inside the park do not have hookups, nor do campgrounds in adjacent national forests or the North Fork. For hookups, head outside Glacier Park to commercial campgrounds in West Glacier, East Glacier, St. Mary, Flathead Valley, outside Waterton Park, and along U.S. 2. Waterton Lakes National Park, however, is an exception: the Townsite Campground has hookups.

Generator use is also restricted in campgrounds inside Glacier by hours and campsite location. Find details on generator hours and permitted locations online (www.nps.gov/glac).

Disposal Stations

Seven locations inside Glacier Park have disposal stations: Apgar, Fish Creek, Many Glacier, Rising Sun, St. Mary, Two Medicine, and Waterton. Many private campgrounds at West Glacier, St. Mary, and East Glacier have disposal stations as well, but the North Fork has none. In Waterton National Park, you'll find dump stations at the Townsite and Crandell campgrounds and at commercial campgrounds outside the park.

Repairs

Should you need repair services, drive to the **Pierce RV Supercenter** (3138 U.S. 2, Kalispell, 888/896-0889 or 406/752-8050, Mon.-Sat.) just south of the airport in Flathead Valley. Call ahead for an appointment; in summer their schedule is often full. If you cannot drive to the Flathead, **Mike's Mobile RV Services** (406/261-7684) can come to you. He can repair many things where you are, but you'll pay a lot for him to come to Glacier. In Waterton, **Pat's Gas Station** (224 Mount View Rd., 403/859-2266) can do minor repairs.

TRAVELING WITH BOATS, CANOES, AND KAYAKS

Glacier poses unique issues for those traveling with boats. Trailers are not allowed over Going-to-the-Sun Road, so those towing boats are required to drive around U.S. 2 to get from one side of the park to the other. Due to overhangs on the Sun Road, rigs also can be no higher than 10 feet, so truck-camper combinations with kayaks, canoes, or rafts on top may be too tall.

Regulations in both Glacier and Waterton require all boats, including kayaks and canoes, to obtain free permits. Boats must be cleaned, drained, and dried to avoid infesting the pristine park lakes with aquatic invasive species. In Glacier, permits are available at park headquarters in West Glacier, St. Mary Visitors Center, Two Medicine, and Many Glacier Ranger Stations as well as at Polebridge entrance station. For Waterton, permits are available at the park entrance and at the visitors center. Pick up park boating regulations at all locations; some lakes restrict the use of motorboats.

Outside Glacier, out-of-state boats over 12 feet in length must have a home-state registration; they can be used in Montana for up to 90 consecutive days. In-state boats must have Montana registration and decals on the boat. For a complete list of Montana boating regulations, see www.fwp.mt.gov. For boating on Blackfeet Reservation lakes, you'll need a conservation permit (406/338-7207, www.blackfeetfishandwildlife.com, $20), available in St. Mary, Browning, and East Glacier.

Motorboaters head most often to **Lake McDonald,** as it sees less gusty winds than **St. Mary Lake.** Smaller **Bowman Lake** and **Two Medicine Lake** are also fun. Most larger boats and water-skiers prefer Flathead Valley's larger and warmer lakes.

Canoers and kayakers paddle Glacier's lakes for the stunning scenery and quiet ambiance. While paddlers can tour any lake that offers a launch spot, some adventures rank more highly. In **Many Glacier,** paddle across **Swiftcurrent Lake** and up the slow-moving **Cataract Creek** to **Lake Josephine** for bear watching and views of the Continental Divide. In the **North Fork,**

© BECKY LOMAX

Kayakers can access seven lakes in Glacier.

take in the remoteness of **Kintla Lake** and **Bowman Lake** with an overnight trip.

River rafters and kayakers gravitate to the **Middle Fork** and **North Fork of the Flathead River,** which form Glacier's boundaries. Designated Wild and Scenic Rivers, they bounce between float sections and white water. Check with the Flathead National Forest's Hungry Horse Ranger Station (406/387-3800, www.fs.fed.us/r1/flathead) for regulations, float guides, and flow levels.

TRAVELING BY BICYCLE

Glacier is a tough place to cycle. There are no shoulders, roads are narrow and curvy, and drivers gawk at scenery instead of the road, all putting the cyclist in precarious positions. With that caveat, for a dedicated cyclist, nothing compares with bicycling Going-to-the-Sun Road, one of the country's premier cycling routes. Other roads surrounding Glacier also make good rides, particularly the 142-mile loop linking Going-to-the-Sun Road and U.S. 89, Highway 49, and U.S. 2. Roadies do it in one day; tourers ride the loop in two or three days. Those riding the loop need to be prepared for large trucks and RVs whizzing by their elbows.

Rental bikes are available at several locations in Flathead Valley. If you fly in, you can ship your bike to **Glacier Cyclery** (406/862-6446, www.glaciercyclery.com) in Whitefish for storage ($9) until you arrive. The shop will also reassemble it for you and provide return shipping services (rates vary).

Bike Trails

Designated bike trails are few and far between in Waterton-Glacier. In fact, Glacier has only two trails, both in the Apgar area—one paved, one dirt. No bicycles are allowed on any other backcountry trails in Glacier. In Waterton, a paved bike trail and four backcountry paths permit bicycles.

Campsites

Several of Glacier's campgrounds maintain campsites specifically for cyclists and hikers: Apgar, Fish Creek, Sprague Creek, Avalanche, Rising Sun, St. Mary, Many Glacier, and Two

Medicine. Held until 9pm, the sites are shared, holding up to eight people, who pay $5 pp. If these sites are full, you must find a regular designated unoccupied tent site, which is impossible in midsummer late at night. Hiker-biker sites have special bear-resistant food storage containers.

Safety

Because of the narrow shoulderless roads, cyclists should have some riding ability before hitting Glacier's roads. Drainage grates, ice, and debris can quickly throw bikes off balance, adding to the challenge. Although cyclists on Going-to-the-Sun Road are fairly common, many drivers are so agog at the view that they may not be fully aware of your presence—which is a good reason to wear a helmet and bright colors. Skinny shoulderless roads demand riding in single file. For added protection, be sure your bike has reflectors on both ends, and use lights in fog and at dawn, dusk, or at night.

Restrictions

Because of high traffic volume and narrow lanes, Glacier enforces bicycling restrictions on Going-to-the-Sun Road's west side. Two sections of the road are closed 11am-4pm daily June 15-Labor Day: between Apgar Loop Road and Sprague Creek Campground; and eastbound (uphill) from Logan Creek to Logan Pass. The ride from Sprague to Logan Creek takes about 45 minutes; the climb from Logan Creek to Logan Pass usually takes about three hours.

Repairs

Bring spare tubes and brake pads, a pump, and equipment to make minor repairs yourself. The park doesn't have any bike shops to bail you out. For major repairs, head to the bike shops in Flathead Valley.

TRAVELING BY MOTORCYCLE

Motorcyclists relish riding Going-to-the-Sun Road. On sunny days, the ride is unparalleled; on inclement days, it's bone-chilling. The alpine wonderland attracts scads of decked-out Harleys and Goldwings as well as motorcycle clubs who come just to tour Going-to-the-Sun Road.

Many motorcyclists gravitate to Montana because the state requires helmets only for those under age 18. However, since most drivers on Going-to-the-Sun Road find their attention severely divided between the scenery and the road, you may want to consider head protection in case you get hit. In Canada, helmets are required.

Motorcyclists are allowed to use the shared biker-hiker campsites ($5 pp) at the park's major campgrounds. These are first come, first served and are held until 9pm.

Rental motorcycles are available in Flathead Valley from **Harley-Davidson** (866/927-0973, www.mtharley.com). If you need repairs, the Flathead Valley has several motorcycle shops. Some specialize in one brand over another. Your best bet is to check business listings to pick the appropriate service for your machine.

TRAVELING SOLO

Plenty of people travel solo to Glacier, but hiking alone in the park is not recommended due to bears and mountain lions. Nevertheless, some hikers still venture into the backcountry alone. If you're one of them, make lots of noise while hiking and brush up on your bear skills. Solo travelers looking for trail companions can join park naturalist hikes. For times and dates, check the *Ranger-led Activities* brochure or www.nps.gov/glac. Solo travelers can also join commercially guided day hikes and backpacking trips with **Glacier Guides** (406/387-5555 or 800/521-7238, www.glacierguides.com).

TRAVELING WITH CHILDREN

Children can find plenty of fun in Glacier and Waterton. The lakes, albeit chilly, offer lots of water play, and both parks have child-friendly trails.

Junior Ranger Program

In Glacier, kids can earn a Junior Ranger

Badge by completing self-guided activities in the *Junior Ranger Activity Guide,* available at all visitors centers. Most activities target ages 6-12 and coincide with a trip over Going-to-the-Sun Road. When kids return the completed newspaper to a visitors center, they are sworn in as Junior Rangers and receive Glacier Park badges.

Discovery Cabin

The Discovery Cabin in Apgar serves up educational kid fun during summer. Hands-on activities guided by interpretive rangers teach children about wildlife, geology, and habitats. Check with Apgar Visitors Center for directions and hours.

Hikes

For young kids, short hikes of 2-4 miles roundtrip work best. On Going-to-the-Sun Road, go for Avalanche Lake, Hidden Lake Overlook, and St. Mary and Virginia Falls. In Many Glacier, hike to Red Rocks Lake or take the boat across Swiftcurrent and Josephine Lakes to hike to Grinnell Lake. In Two Medicine, take the boat up-lake to hike to Twin Falls or Upper Two Medicine Lake. In Waterton, walk to Grizzly Gardens at Cameron Lake or Blakiston Falls at Red Rocks. When hiking with children, always take snacks and water along. If toting a little one who still needs to be carried, Glacier Outdoor Center (11957 U.S. 2 E., West Glacier, 406/888-5454 or 800/235-6781, www.glacierraftco.com) rents kiddie packs.

© BECKY LOMAX

Families can backpack to many locations in Glacier.

TRAVELING WITH PETS

Pets are allowed in Glacier Park, but only in limited areas: campgrounds, parking lots, and roadsides. They are not allowed on trails, beaches, off-trail in the backcountry, or at any park lodges or motor inns. When outside a vehicle or in a campground, pets must be on a leash or caged. Be kind enough to avoid leaving them unattended in a car anywhere. Be considerate of wildlife and other visitors by keeping your pet under control and disposing of waste in garbage cans.

Pets are not allowed on Glacier Park trails. Protection of fragile vegetation and preventing conflicts with wildlife are two main reasons; bears provide their own class of reasons. For walking the pooch, the paved 2.6-mile Apgar Bike Trail allows pets on leashes (pedestrians are also allowed on the trail). To hike with Fido, head to the surrounding Flathead National Forest, where pets are permitted. Contrary to Glacier, Waterton does permit dogs on leashes on its trails.

Overnight kenneling is only available at kennels in Flathead Valley. The closest is in Columbia Falls—**Triple R Kennels** (636 Kelley Rd., 406/892-3695, www.triplerkennels.com)—but check business listings for more choices in Kalispell, Whitefish, and Bigfork.

SENIORS

National parks, as well as lands run by the U.S. Fish and Wildlife Service, U.S. Forest Service, and Bureau of Land Management, offer a great bargain for U.S. citizens or permanent residents over age 61: $10 buys the National Parks and Federal Recreational Lands Pass, valid for life. To purchase one, bring proof of your age (a state driver's license, birth certificate, or passport) in person to any national park entrance station. In a private vehicle, the card admits four adults in the vehicle, plus all children under age 16. This pass is not valid in Waterton.

The lifetime park pass also grants 50 percent discounts on fees for federally run tours and campgrounds; however, discounts do not apply to park concessionaire services like hotels, boat tours, and bus tours. Glacier's historic hotels do not give discounts to seniors, but some private lodging establishments surrounding the park do; ask to be sure.

ACCESSIBILITY

Visitors with special needs should pick up an *Accessible Facilities and Services* brochure to see a list of services and accessible facilities. You can get these at visitors centers and entrance stations. The information is also available online (www.nps.gov/glac). The **Disabled Traveler's Companion** (www.tdtcompanion.com) gives comprehensive information for traveling in Glacier. Park information is available also by TDD (406/888-7806). Special programs and sign-language interpretation may be available with two weeks' notice; call 406/888-7930 to set it up.

Park Entrance

Blind or permanently disabled U.S. citizens or permanent residents can get a free lifetime National Parks and Federal Recreational Lands Access Pass for access to all national parks and other federal sites. The pass admits the pass holder plus three other adults in the same vehicle; children under age 16 are free. Pass holders also get 50 percent discounts on federally run tours and campgrounds. Get these passes in person at entrance stations with proof of medical disability or eligibility for receiving federal benefits.

Park Facilities

Five campgrounds in Glacier reserve 1-2 sites each for wheelchair needs: Apgar, Fish Creek, Rising Sun, Sprague Creek, and Two Medicine. Picnic Areas at Apgar, Rising Sun, and Sun Point also have wheelchair access, as do all lodges within the park boundaries, although they have a limited number of guest rooms that conform to Americans with Disabilities Act Accessibility Guidelines. Other wheelchair-accessible sites include boat docks at Lake McDonald, Many Glacier, and Two Medicine as well as evening naturalist programs in Apgar Amphitheater, Lake McDonald Lodge Auditorium, Many Glacier Hotel Auditorium, Rising Sun Campground, and Two Medicine Campground. Most parking lots offer designated parking.

Trails

Glacier and Waterton both offer wheelchair-accessible trails. In Glacier, the Apgar Bike Trail, Trail of the Cedars at Avalanche, Running Eagle Falls Nature Trail in Two Medicine, Goat Lick Overlook, Oberlin Bend Trail, the International Peace Park Pavilion at Goat Haunt, and the Many Glacier Trail from the picnic area are wheelchair accessible. Some surfaces are rough in places; just be prepared for it. In Waterton, wheelchairs can access Linnet Lake Trail, Waterton Townsite Trail, and Cameron Lake Day Use Area.

While pet dogs are not permitted on Glacier's backcountry trails, service dogs are allowed—although due to bears, they are discouraged. With service dogs, be safe by sticking to well-traveled trails during midday.

HEALTH AND SAFETY

Bears

Safe behavior can deter bear attacks. Glacier has the highest density of grizzly bears in the

© BECKY LOMAX

Bears are permanent residents in Glacier and Waterton.

Lower 48, and black bears find likable habitat here too. Food is the biggest bear attractant. Proper use, storage, and handling of food and garbage prevents bears from being conditioned and turning aggressive. With strict food and garbage rules, Glacier has minimized aggressive bear encounters, attacks, and deaths—for both humans and bears.

Bears are dangerous around food, be it a carcass in the woods, a pack left on a trail, or a cooler left in a campsite. Protecting bears and protecting yourself starts with being conscious of food—including wrappers and crumbs. Trail-mix tidbits dropped along the trail attract wildlife, as do "biodegradable" apple cores chucked into the forest. Pick up what you drop and pack out all your garbage; don't leave a Hansel-and-Gretel trail for the bears.

Camp safely: Use low-odor foods, keep food and cooking gear out of sleeping sites in the backcountry, and store it inside your vehicle in front country campgrounds. In front country campgrounds, you'll find detailed explanations of how to camp safely in bear country stapled to your picnic table. For information on camping in bear country, pick up a copy of the *Waterton-Glacier Guide* and Glacier's *Backcountry Guide* at entrance stations, visitors centers, ranger stations, permit offices, or online (www.nps.gov/glac).

Hike safely: On trails, you'll hear jingle bells, sold in gift shops as **bear bells.** Locals call them "dinner bells," and many hikers hate them. While making noise best prevents surprising a bear, bells fail to carry sound the way a human voice does. To check their minimal effectiveness, see how close you get to hikers before you hear the ringing. Bear bells are best as a souvenir, not as a substitute for human noise on the trail in the form of talking, singing, hooting, and hollering. You may feel silly at first, but everyone does it.

As of 2010 federal law allows people that can legally carry **firearms** under federal, state, and local laws to bring their guns into Glacier. However, federal law prohibits firearms in certain facilities—government offices, visitors centers, ranger stations, fee-collection buildings, and maintenance facilities. Those places are marked with signs at all public entrances. Discharging firearms in the park is illegal except when presented with "imminent danger."

Most hikers use **pepper spray** with a capsicum derivative. These deter bear attacks without injuring the bears or humans. Unlike insect repellents, do not use bear sprays on your body, in tents, or on gear; it is to be sprayed directly into a bear's face, aiming for the eyes and nose. Wind and rain may reduce its effectiveness. Small purse-size pepper sprays are too small to deter bears; buy an eight-ounce can. Practice how to use it, but still make noise on the trail. Pepper spray is not allowed on airplanes unless it's in checked luggage, and only brands with U.S. Environmental Protection Agency labels can be carried into Canada.

Mountain Lion Encounters

These large cats rarely prey on humans, but they can, especially small kids. Making antibear noise will also help you avoid surprising a lion. Hike with others, and keep kids close. If you stumble on a lion, above all, do not run. Be calm, and group together to appear bigger. Look at the cat with peripheral vision rather than staring straight on, and back away slowly. If the lion attacks, fight back with everything: rocks, sticks, or kicking.

Water Hazards

Contrary to popular belief, bears are not the number-one cause of death in Glacier; rather it is drowning from falling. Be extremely cautious around lakes, fast-moving streams, and waterfalls, where slick moss and algae cover the rocks. Waters are swift, frigid, clogged with submerged obstacles, unforgiving, and sometimes lethal.

Giardia

Lakes and streams can carry parasites like *Giardia lamblia*. If ingested, it causes cramping, nausea, and severe diarrhea for up to six weeks. Avoid giardia by boiling water (for one minute, plus one minute for each 1,000 feet of elevation above sea level) or using a one-micron filter. Bleach also works (add two drops per quart and wait 30 minutes). Tap water in campgrounds, hotels, and picnic areas has been treated; you'll taste the chlorine.

Dehydration

Many first-time hikers to Glacier are surprised to find they drink more water than at home. Glacier's winds, altitude, and lower humidity can add up to a fast case of dehydration—which often manifests first as a headache. While hiking, drink lots of water—more than you normally would. With children, monitor their fluid intake.

Glacier's water requires filtering before drinking.

Altitude

Some visitors from sea level locales feel the effects of altitude—lightheadedness, headaches, or shortness of breath—at high elevations like Logan Pass. To acclimatize, slow down the pace of hiking and drink lots of fluids. If symptoms spike, descend in elevation as soon as possible. Altitude also increases UV radiation exposure: To prevent sunburn, use a strong sunscreen and wear sunglasses and a hat.

Ice and Snow

While glacial ice often looks solid to step on, it harbors unseen caverns beneath. Buried crevasses (large vertical cracks) are difficult to see, and snow bridges can collapse as a person crosses. Be safe by staying off the ice; even Glacier's tiny ice fields have caused fatalities. Steep angled snowfields also pose a danger from falling. Use an ice ax and caution, or stay off them. If you want to slide on the snow for fun, slide only where you have a safe run out away from rocks and trees.

Hypothermia

Insidious and subtle, exhausted and physically unprepared hikers are at risk for hypothermia. The body's inner core loses heat, reducing mental and physical functions. Watch for uncontrolled shivering, incoherence, poor judgment, fumbling, mumbling, and slurred speech. Avoid becoming hypothermic by staying dry, avoiding cotton clothing, and donning rain gear and warm moisture-wicking layers. Get hypothermic hikers into dry clothing and shelter. Give warm nonalcoholic and noncaffeinated liquids. If the victim cannot regain body heat, get into a sleeping bag with the victim, both stripped for skin-to-skin contact.

Blisters

Incorrect socks and ill-fitting shoes cause most blisters. Cotton socks absorb water from the feet while you're hiking and hold onto it, providing a surface for friction. Synthetic or wool-blend socks wick water away from the skin. To prevent blisters, recognize "hot spots" or rubs, applying moleskin or New-Skin to sensitive areas. In a pinch, slap duct tape on trouble spots. Once a blister occurs, apply blister bandages or Second Skin, a product developed for burns that cools blisters and cushions them. Cover Second Skin with moleskin to absorb future rubbing and secure the Second Skin.

Hantavirus

Hantavirus infection, with flu-like symptoms, is contracted by inhaling dust from deer mice droppings. Avoid burrows and woodpiles thick with rodents. Store all food in rodent-proof containers. If you find rodent dust in your gear, disinfect it with water and bleach (1.5 cups bleach to one gallon water). If you contract the virus, get immediate medical attention.

Mosquitoes and Ticks

Bugs can carry diseases such as West Nile virus and Rocky Mountain spotted fever. Protect yourself by wearing long sleeves and pants as well as using insect repellents in spring-summer, when mosquitoes and ticks are common. If you are bitten by a tick, remove it, disinfect the bite, and see a doctor if lesions or a rash appears.

Hospitals and Emergencies

For emergencies inside the park, call 406/888-7800. For emergencies outside the park, call 911. On Glacier's west side, the nearest hospitals are in Flathead Valley. **Kalispell Regional Medical Center** (310 Sunny View Lane, Kalispell, 406/752-5111) and the **North Valley Hospital** (1600 Hospital Way, Whitefish, 406/863-3500) are 35 minutes from West Glacier and can be up to 90 minutes from Logan Pass, depending on traffic. On Glacier's east side, **Northern Rockies Medical Center** (802 2nd St. E., Cut Bank, 406/873-2251) is approximately one hour from East Glacier and just under two hours from St. Mary.

Getting There

ORIENTATION

Getting your bearings in Glacier is not difficult; the park is split along the Continental Divide into an east side and a west side, each with several entrances following valley drainages. Two Medicine, St. Mary, and Many Glacier are on the east, while Lake McDonald and the North Fork cover the west. Although U.S. 2 passes briefly through the park's southern tip between East Glacier and West Glacier, southern entrances into the park's core are all via foot or on horseback trails. On the north side, Waterton Lakes National Park provides access via boat, on foot, or on horseback across the Canadian-U.S. border into Glacier's interior.

Only one route bisects the entire park: Going-to-the-Sun Road. Rush hour in Glacier is on this road 11am-4pm seven days a week mid-July-mid-August.

Most summer visitors love the park's expansive east-side views. Tiny seasonal towns fall away into miles of broad prairie. On a clear day, not much obstructs the view to Ohio. By autumn, not many services remain open to take the Rocky Mountain Front's brutal winds.

The park's heavily forested west side balances remote corners of the North Fork with the busy hub of West Glacier. Mountain snows feed large rivers that drain through the Flathead Valley into Flathead Lake. Mixed with farmland, rural pockets, and resort towns, the fast-growing valley—anchored in winter by recreational skiing—is a year-round enclave for 90,000 people.

SUGGESTED DRIVING ROUTES

From Western Montana

From I-90 just west of Missoula, take exit 96 onto U.S. 93 north, which leads 103 miles to Flathead Valley. This scenic route passes below the craggy Mission Mountains and along Flathead Lake, the largest freshwater lake west of the Mississippi. Drivers coming from Spokane can cut off miles by exiting I-90 at St. Regis and following the signs to Glacier Park (north on Highway 135, northwest on Highway 200, and east on Highway 28). You'll pass the funky little towns of Paradise and Hot Springs, harking back several decades, before joining U.S. 93 heading north at Flathead Lake.

In Kalispell, a confusing highway maze jogs through Flathead Valley. Follow signs to the park or West Glacier. In downtown Kalispell, turn right onto U.S. 2 east, which is also East Idaho Street. Travel for two miles, and turn left with U.S. 2, traveling north 12 miles toward Columbia Falls. At the intersection with Highway 40, turn right; follow the highway through Columbia Falls, continuing another 16 miles on U.S. 2 to West Glacier. The total mileage from I-90 to West Glacier is 145 miles; driving time on the mostly two-lane highway is usually less than 3.5 hours, but it can be four hours or more with heavy traffic, snow, or road-construction delays. Spokane to West Glacier (271 miles) is a 4.5-hour drive.

From Eastern Montana or Yellowstone

This long but extremely scenic approach follows the Rocky Mountain Front, a highway for golden eagle migrations and the buttress for the Bob Marshall Wilderness Complex. Those stitching together a Yellowstone National Park and Glacier vacation will need an entire day (7-10 hours) to drive from one park to the other. From I-90 in **Butte,** turn north toward Helena onto I-15 (exit 129/227) and drive 101 miles to exit 228, two miles north of Wolf Creek. Turn north onto U.S. 287.

North along U.S. 287, strong side winds can slow travel with gusts strong enough to

rock RVs and trailers. Follow narrow two-lane U.S. 287 north 66 miles through Augusta to Choteau ("SHOW-toe"), the epitome of a Rocky Mountain Front town, with 1,700 residents, grain elevators, and hunting. In Choteau, the road turns left for a bit onto U.S. 89 (Main St.). From Choteau, head north 72 miles to Browning. Again, narrow curves slow driving time, but you will soon see Glacier's peaks jutting up from the plains. Just before Browning, you'll join U.S. 2. At Browning's west end, turn left as U.S. 2 leaves town. It leads 13 miles to East Glacier. The total driving time to cover the 253 miles from I-90 to East Glacier is about five hours. High winds and traffic may slow travel, but the scenery is worth the drive.

From **Great Falls,** two routes lead to East Glacier, both with spectacular views of the Rocky Mountain Front as it pops up off the plains. For easy interstate and highway driving, take I-15 heading north to Shelby and then U.S. 2 west to East Glacier (143 miles). Folks who want to get to Glacier quickly take this 2.5-hour route.

A much more interesting approach with a few less miles, however, strikes off through small rural Rocky Mountain Front towns. From Great Falls, head 10 miles north on I-15 to catch U.S. 89 north toward Browning. The route travels past Freezeout Lake, known for its snow goose migration. Connect with the Butte route in Choteau. While this 139-mile route is a few miles shorter, the narrow road makes for slower driving, taking 2.75 hours to get to East Glacier—longer if you stop for explorations.

From the Canadian Rockies

Many travelers link Glacier with a trip in the national parks of the Canadian Rockies—Jasper, Banff, Yoho, and Kootenay. The Flathead Valley connects directly to the Canadian Rockies via U.S. 93 and British Columbia Highway 93, which runs north-south to Banff. To get to Glacier, travel south on Highway 93 through British Columbia toward Cranbrook. Six kilometers (4 miles) before Cranbrook, merge with Highway 3 heading 58 kilometers (36 miles) east toward Elko, where you can continue east to Waterton and Glacier's east side or south toward West Glacier.

To head to Waterton, stay on Highway 3 for 96 kilometers (60 miles) through Crowsnest Pass and turn south onto Highway 6 at Pincher Creek. Drive 32 kilometers (20 miles) to Waterton Lakes National Park, where the seasonal Chief Mountain Highway connects with Glacier Park's east side.

To head to West Glacier, take Highway 93 south at Elko for 39 kilometers (24 miles)

PARK ENTRANCE FEES

National parks survive in part on entrance fees. Glacier is no different. Entrance fees are collected at Two Medicine, St. Mary, Many Glacier, West Glacier, Polebridge, and Camas. When stations are unstaffed, self-pay kiosks allow you to purchase passes.

No single-day passes are sold, only seven-day passes:

- Single vehicle: May-Nov. $25, Dec.-Apr. $15 (admits all persons in vehicle)
- Single person: May-Nov. $12, Dec.-Apr. $10 (on foot, bicycle, or motorcycle)

Two annual passes are also available but can only be purchased when entrance stations are staffed. Use of these nontransferable passes also requires showing photo ID, but they admit all people in a single vehicle for seven days.

- Glacier National Park Pass ($35): grants unlimited entry for one year; must be purchased in person at entrance stations
- National Park and Federal Recreation Lands Pass ($80): can be purchased at entrance stations, online (www.store.usgs.gov), or by phone (888/ASK-USGS–888/275-8747, ext. 1); admits a maximum of four adults in the vehicle; children under age 16 enter free

In addition, lifetime passes to all national parks are available for U.S. citizens and residents over age 61 ($10) and U.S. citizens with permanent disabilities (free). These must be purchased in person with appropriate documentation at a park entrance station. This pass admits a maximum of four adults in the vehicle; children under age 16 enter free.

Glacier and U.S. public lands passes are not valid for entrance to Waterton Lakes National Park in Canada.

Glacier offers free entrance on Martin Luther King weekend in January, National Park Week in April, Get Outdoors Day in June, Public Lands Day in September, and Veterans Day (Nov. 11).

toward Roosville on the Canadian-U.S. border. After crossing through the border station, continue south 63 miles on U.S. 93 through Eureka to Whitefish. Drive with caution: Deer frequent the road between Eureka and Whitefish, earning it the nickname "Deer Alley." In downtown Whitefish, 25 miles from Glacier, U.S. 93 turns south again at the third stoplight. Drive two miles to the junction with Highway 40; you'll see signs for Glacier Park. Turn left toward Columbia Falls. Along the way, Highway 40 becomes U.S. 2. Follow the signs to Glacier Park. Expect six hours total driving time from Banff to West Glacier.

From Calgary

From Calgary, head south for 181 kilometers (113 miles) on Highway 2 toward Fort Macleod. A detour to Head-smashed-in Buffalo Jump (403/553-2731, www.head-smashed-in.com), a World Heritage Site, is worth a few extra hours. Just before Fort Macleod, Highway 2 merges with Highway 3 for a few miles heading east.

If you are starting your Glacier adventure in Waterton Lakes National Park, turn west onto Highway 3 and drive 27 kilometers (17 miles) to Pincher Creek. At Pincher Creek, turn south onto Highway 6 for 32 kilometers (20 miles) to the park entrance. From Calgary to Waterton is 240 kilometers (149 miles) via Pincher Creek. The distance can be covered in less than three hours.

To head straight to Glacier from Calgary, continue from Fort Macleod south through Cardston to the Carway-Piegan border crossing. The 266 kilometers (165 miles) from Calgary to the border at Carway should take about three hours. As a general rule, speed limits in Alberta tend to be little lower than in Montana, especially compared to Montana's rural narrow two-lane highways, which can be posted at 70 mph.

Speed limits in Canada are posted in kilometers; 80 km/h is 50 mph. From Carway, cross the Canadian-U.S. border onto U.S. 89. Drive 19 miles to St. Mary for Going-to-the-Sun Road's east entrance, 25 minutes from the border. To enter the park at Many Glacier instead, turn right at Babb, 10 miles south of the border, and drive 12 miles to Many Glacier Hotel and Swiftcurrent (40 minutes total).

TRAIN ROUTES

In the U.S., Glacier is one of the rare national parks actually serviced by train. In fact, much of the park's development came from Great Northern Railway, and Amtrak offers an updated way to reach the park on a historic rail line.

Amtrak

Amtrak's daily ***Empire Builder*** (800/USA-RAIL—800/872-7245, www.amtrak.com) stops at several locations at Glacier Park. The route originates in Chicago, stopping at Milwaukee, St. Paul-Minneapolis, and Fargo as well as smaller towns on its way to Glacier. It's about 29 hours' ride from Chicago to East Glacier. On the west side, trains from Seattle and Portland join in Spokane and stop in Whitefish before reaching West Glacier in a little more than 15 hours. Skirting the southern edge of the park, the train stops in West Glacier and Essex year-round and at East Glacier in summer, making for an easy arrival, with lodging available adjacent to the depots. Between Seattle and Shelby, Montana, National Park Service guides offer educational services on board.

From Seattle or Portland, the eastbound train lands riders conveniently in Glacier by morning. Eastbound trains hit Whitefish at 7:26am, West Glacier at 8:16am, Essex at 8:55am, and East Glacier at 9:54am. From Chicago, westbound arrivals reach East Glacier at 6:45pm, Essex at 7:41pm, West Glacier at 8:23pm, and Whitefish at 8:56pm. Check with Amtrak for changes to schedules and service. The down side of rail travel is that the train has a reputation for running late, especially in winter when avalanches can disrupt the schedule, or during spring flooding; on the westbound train, be prepared to arrive in the middle of the night.

Special Amtrak deals are available. Kids ages 2-15 pay half price. Seniors, veterans, AAA and NARP members, military personnel, and students can also get 10-15 percent discounts; check Amtrak's website for details. High summer travel volumes make reservations imperative.

VIA Rail Canada

If you're traveling across Canada by **VIA Rail** (800/VIA-RAIL—800/842-7245, www.viarail.ca), you'll have a difficult time getting to Waterton and Glacier. Between Winnipeg and Vancouver, the route jogs far north of Waterton. The closest you can get to Waterton is Edmonton, 534 kilometers (332 miles) away. Most train travelers switch to air or bus travel to Calgary and then rent a car.

TRAVEL HUB: FLATHEAD VALLEY

The closest and easiest access to Glacier National Park is Flathead Valley. If your flight arrives before evening, you can catch a shuttle and be at Lake McDonald inside Glacier Park in time to catch the sunset. Because Glacier Park International Airport has no lodging in its immediate vicinity, if you come in on a late flight or want to explore Flathead Valley a bit, you will have to stay in one of four towns. Columbia Falls is closest, between the airport and Glacier, but Whitefish is more attractive, with its resort-town atmosphere of shopping, nightlife, a lake, golf, and the ski resort. Kalispell and Bigfork are farthest from Glacier.

Airports

The closest airport to Glacier National Park, **Glacier Park International Airport** (FCA, U.S. 2, Kalispell, www.iflyglacier.com), is served

© BECKY LOMAX

Amtrak connects Whitefish with three stops on Glacier's southern boundary.

by Alaska/Horizon, Allegiant, Delta, United, and SkyWest, with nonstop flights from Minneapolis, Chicago, Denver, Salt Lake City, Las Vegas, Oakland, and Seattle. Even though the airport is called Glacier International Airport, its only international connections are charter flights. With only three gates, it's easy to meet up with groups at this tiny airport, walk to the baggage claim just a few hundred feet from your gate, or find the car-rental desk. In the terminal, **The Glacier Grille** serves cafeteria food, espresso, beer, and wine. Hotel and prearranged shuttles are right outside.

Although the airport is within Kalispell city limits, many visitors are surprised to find the Kalispell hotels 10-15 minutes away in the opposite direction of the park. In fact, the airport is almost equidistant between downtown Kalispell, Whitefish, and Columbia Falls. Because the airport is only 25 miles from West Glacier, you can sit on the beach at Lake McDonald the day you arrive if you want to maximize your park time.

Although Spokane is an alternative airport, it requires a five-hour drive to reach the park.

Train

Amtrak's ***Empire Builder*** (800/USA-RAIL—800/872-7245, www.amtrak.com) stops in Whitefish twice daily, once eastbound and once westbound. From Seattle and Portland, the eastbound train hits Whitefish at 7:26am, departing for Glacier Park 20 minutes later. You'll arrive at West Glacier at 8:16am, Essex at 8:55am, and East Glacier at 9:54am. From Glacier, the westbound train arrives in Whitefish at 8:56pm and departs at 9:16pm for Spokane. Reservations are a must in summer.

Bus

No bus routes connect to Glacier; the closest you can get is Whitefish. Trailways's **Rimrock Stages** (800/255-7655, www.rimrocktrailways.com) runs one bus daily between Missoula and Whitefish ($26 one-way). It leaves Missoula at 8:15am, arriving at 11:40am in Whitefish, where you have to find a place to stay overnight until the train to West Glacier departs the next morning. Similarly, with your return connection, the westbound train arrives in Whitefish in the evening, but you won't be able to catch the bus to Missoula until 11:55am the next day. On the upside, if you have to hang out, Whitefish is a nice place to be.

Taxis and Shuttles

Flathead-Glacier Transportation (406/892-3390 or 800/829-7039, www.glaciertransportation.com) provides shuttles and taxis to all east-side and west-side hubs in Glacier, all towns in Flathead Valley, and Whitefish Mountain Resort. Drivers will meet any flight as well as pick you up at any park lodge, trailhead, or surrounding town to transport you back to the airport. They even accommodate the early morning and late-night flights. Trips from the airport run to West Glacier (one person $40 one-way), Lake McDonald Lodge ($55), East Glacier ($140), Whitefish ($23), downtown Kalispell ($23), and Bigfork ($40). Each additional person costs $3; call ahead for reservations.

Taxi companies come and go in the region, but usually Whitefish and Kalispell have taxi service. Check business listings for current operators.

Tours

Most Glacier Park tours originate inside the park or in towns that border the park. However, the **Glacier Park Inc.** (406/892-2525, www.glacierparkinc.com) Great Lodges of Glacier and Glacier Adventure tours includes transfers to and from Amtrak and Flathead Valley's Glacier Park International Airport.

Car Rental

The Glacier Park International Airport terminal has four rental-car agencies with desks in the airport: **Hertz** (406/758-2220 or 800/654-3131, www.hertz.com), **National-Alamo** (406/257-7144 or 800/CAR-RENT—800/227-7368, www.nationalcar.com), **Avis** (406/257-2727 or 800/230-4898, www.avis.com), and **Budget** (406/755-7500 or 800/527-0700, www.budget.com). Kalispell and Whitefish also have rental-car agencies, listed at www.iflyglacier.com; they will deliver a car to the airport for you or pick you up.

RV Rental

The closest RV rentals are located near Glacier Park International Airport, a 20-minute drive from Glacier. **J & L RV Rentals** (1805 U.S. 2 W., Columbia Falls, 406/892-7666, www.jandl-rvrentals.com) has motor homes and trailers. Although somewhat expensive (from around $150 per day), RVing is an easy way to tour national parks with the good parts of camping but without the hassle of tents. Be aware, however, of Going-to-the-Sun Road's vehicle length restrictions (21 feet). Only the smallest RVs will be able to drive the highway. With larger RVs, you must use park and shuttles or bus tours to see the historic road, or rent a car.

Equipment Rental

In West Glacier, **Glacier Outdoor Center** (11957 U.S. 2 E., 406/888-5454 or 800/235-6781, www.glacierraftco.com) has the most comprehensive collection of rental gear for rafting, camping, backpacking, and fishing. They have a complete list of rental gear available and rates online. Reservations are recommended, and you'll need a valid ID to rent.

Other recreational rental gear—skis, kayaks, boats, and bicycles—is available through specialty outdoor shops and marinas in Flathead Valley.

Food and Accommodations

Because Glacier National Park is so close to Glacier Park International Airport, many travelers go directly into the park the day they arrive; likewise with flying out. However, for those adding Flathead Valley explorations to their itineraries, lodging varies from dirt-cheap to high-end, and many hotels offer complimentary airport shuttles. There is no lodging or dining in the immediate vicinity of the airport; find options in Columbia Falls, downtown Kalispell, and Whitefish.

TRAVEL HUB: GREAT FALLS

Straddling the mighty Missouri River, Great Falls, Montana, is an east-side gateway to Glacier. But the additional distance to Glacier and lack of easy connections with Amtrak and buses make renting a car preferable to drive the 143 miles to the park. With a flight arriving by late afternoon, you can be in East Glacier to watch the sunset that same day.

For travelers who are fairly well prepared, Great Falls can work as a travel hub, but for those requiring camping equipment or RV rentals, none are available. The nearest gear and RV rentals are on the park's west side in West Glacier and Flathead Valley, both a convoluted detour out of the way from Great Falls.

If you have time to spend in Great Falls, two things are worth exploring. The **Lewis and Clark National Historic Trail Interpretive Center** (4201 Giant Springs Rd., 406/727-8733, year-round, call for hours, adults $8, under age 16 free) is a museum with historical displays, live demonstrations, hands-on activities, and multimedia shows. The **C. M. Russell Museum** (400 13th St. N., 406/727-8787, www.cmrussell.org, year-round, call for hours, $4-9) celebrates the work of the famous Western painter Charlie Russell (1864-1926), who summered in his cabin on Glacier's Lake McDonald and is known for his early West scenes—depictions of cowboys, mountains, hunters, and horses.

Airport

Great Falls International Airport (GTF, on I-15 south of Great Falls, 406/727-3404, www.gtfairport.com) is served by Alaska/Horizon, Allegiant, Delta/Sky West, Frontier, and United airlines with nonstop flights from Denver, Salt Lake City, Minneapolis, Las Vegas, Phoenix, and Seattle. Like the airport at Kalispell, its international label comes from a couple of charter flights from Canada. Located outside town, the airport is convenient for picking up on-site rental cars but requires hotel-provided shuttles or a taxi ride to access hotels and restaurants in town, 10 minutes away.

Trains and Buses

You can get to Great Falls by bus, but not further to Glacier. Trailways's **Rimrock Stages** (800/255-7655, www.rimrocktrailways.com) connect Montana locales with Great Falls. From Great Falls, the closest westbound Amtrak depot is Shelby, 87 miles north, but it's difficult to get there. A free county van (Northern Transit Interlocal, 406/470-0727, www.toolecountymt.gov) makes the connection twice a week, but not in time to prevent needing to spend a night in Shelby, and you're better off renting a car to drive to Glacier rather than renting a car to catch the train.

Taxis

Some hotels provide airport shuttle service. Otherwise, **Diamond Cab** (406/453-3241) is the only option to get into town from the airport.

Car Rental

Great Falls has most national rental car chains. **Alamo** (406/727-0273 or 800/462-5266, www.alamo.com), **Hertz** (406/761-6641 or 800/654-3131, www.hertz.com), **Dollar** (406/453-3535 or 800/800-4000, www.dollar.com), **National** (406/453-4386 or 800/227-7368, www.nationalcar.com), and **Avis** (406/761-7610 or 800/230-4898, www.avis.com) are located in the airport terminal.

Food and Accommodations

Great Falls has hotels and motels ranging from low-end to moderately priced accommodations but nothing too upscale. Most national hotel chains are downtown. For hotels offering airport shuttles, check with the **Great Falls Airport** (www.gtfairport.com) or the **Great Falls Convention and Visitors Bureau** (800/735-8535, www.greatfallscvb.visitmt.com).

For a filling meal at a reasonable price and a view overlooking the Missouri River, head for **MacKenzie River Pizza Company** (500 River Dr. S., 406/761-0085, 11am-9pm Sun.-Thurs., 11am-10pm Fri.-Sat., $7-20), Montana's creative answer to pizza chains. The restaurant serves cowboy nachos, giant salads and sandwiches, eclectic pizzas, and Montana microbrews.

TRAVEL HUB: CALGARY

Calgary is the closest metropolitan city to Glacier. If you schedule your trip in mid-July, you can take in one of the biggest rodeos in the world—the **Calgary Stampede** (403/269-9822 or 800/661-1767, www.calgarystampede.com). However, travel from Calgary to Glacier or Waterton can be a challenge. No train connection is available. No bus route goes all the way to Waterton or Glacier. Most visitors traveling from Calgary rent a vehicle. With an early afternoon flight arrival, you can be walking the beach at Waterton Lake in the evening.

Airport

Calgary International Airport (YYC, 403/735-1200, www.calgaryairport.com) bustles with flights from Tokyo, London, and Frankfurt. It has restaurants, shopping, and service from more than 25 airlines. Airport shuttles connect with downtown, hotels, rental-car agencies, and the Greyhound Bus Terminal. Because Calgary is still 240 kilometers (149 miles) from Waterton, most visitors heading to the park rent a car. Others chop off part of the distance by flying south to **Lethbridge** (YQL, www.lethbridgecountyairport.com) via **Air Canada** (888/247-2262, www.aircanada.com), where they rent a car to drive the 140 kilometers (87 miles) to Waterton.

Bus and Shuttle

You cannot reach Waterton or Glacier traveling by **Greyhound Canada** (403/265-9111 or 800/661-8747, www.greyhound.ca). Daily buses run from Calgary International Airport to Pincher Creek, but no farther: From Pincher Creek, you could hire a taxi with **Crystal Cabs** (403/627-4262, C$70 one-way) to get the 50 kilometers (31 miles) to Waterton. Reservations are strongly advised.

The **Airport Shuttle Express** (403/509-1570, www.airportshuttleexpress.com) runs charter vans from the Calgary airport or downtown Calgary to Waterton. A charter van can be economical for small groups to split the fare (roughly C$400) and the tip for the driver. Service is also available to Chief Mountain border crossing to connect with Glacier's east side shuttle or to hotels in East Glacier, Browning, and all Amtrak stations around Glacier (C$550-800).

Car Rental

Most major car-rental chains have desks inside the Calgary Airport terminals or within a shuttle ride down the road. Vehicles can be booked from home through American sister companies: **Alamo** (800/462-5266, www.alamo.com), **Hertz** (800/654-3131, www.hertz.com), **Dollar** (800/800-4000, www.dollar.com), **National** (800/227-7368, www.nationalcar.com), **Budget** (800/472-3325, www.budget.com), and **Avis** (800/230-4898, www.avis.com).

RV Rental

Two RV-rental companies are within three kilometers (2 miles) of the Calgary Airport: **Canada RV Rentals** (250/999-2734 or 866/672-3572, www.canada-rv-rentals.com) and **CanaDream** (403/291-1000 or 800/461-7368, www.canadream.com). RVing is a fun but somewhat pricey (small rigs start at C$150 per day) way to tour national parks without having to put tents up and down each day; however, be aware of Going-to-the-Sun Road's vehicle-length restrictions (21 feet). You may have to supplement your RV tour with shuttles or red-bus tours to see the historic landmark, as only the smallest RVs are permitted to drive on the highway.

Equipment Rental

If you need outdoor gear, **Calgary Outdoor Centre** (2500 University Dr. NW, 403/220-5038, www.calgaryoutdoorcentre.ca) rents equipment for reasonable rates. It has gear for camping, backpacking, boating, bicycling, fishing, snowshoeing, climbing, and skiing. Per-day rates ($4-13 per item) are charged for tents, backpacks, GPS units, stoves, sleeping bags, clothing, hiking boots, climbing gear, and rain gear. They also rent rafts, kayaks, skis, canoes, mountain bikes, and car racks. A complete list of rental gear and rates is available on the website. Call to reserve equipment ahead of time, a must during midsummer; a nonrefundable deposit by credit card is required. When you pick up your gear, try it on to be sure it fits, and have the staff demonstrate how to use unfamiliar equipment. You'll also need a driver's license or photo ID to rent gear.

Food and Accommodations

The airport terminal houses the extremely convenient **Delta Calgary Airport Hotel** (403/250-8722 or 877/814-7706, www.deltahotels.com, C$170-400). Within a few miles of the airport, major chain hotels start at $110; some offer airport shuttles. For additional hotel information and reservations, check http://calgary.airporthotelguide.com or contact **Tourism Calgary** (403/263-8510, www.tourismcalgary.com).

Budget-minded travelers may want to head for a hostel. The **HI-Calgary City Centre Hostel** (403/670-7580, www.hihostels.ca, und C$36) has dorm beds. If you are planning on staying in hostels across Canada as part of your trip, purchase a Hostelling International membership ($35), which gives 10 percent discounts on nightly rates.

Canadian cuisine is somewhat bland, but a few Alberta specialties merit a taste. Calgary is in the heart of cattle country; grass-fed Alberta beef graces menus in all forms, as does buffalo. At the high end, it's amazingly tender and sweet; at the lower end, it's still decent. The doctored-up Canadian french-fry dish called *poutine* can be served with a variety of toppings, but the traditional version include cheese curds and gravy. Contrary to many towns east of the Rocky Mountains where steak-and-potato fare reigns, Calgary is much more cosmopolitan, with a good share of international restaurants. Canada's 5 percent Goods and Services Tax (GST) will be added to lodging and food bills.

Getting Around

DRIVING

Driving in Glacier National Park is not easy. Narrow roads built for cars in the 1930s barely fit today's SUVs, much less RVs and trailers. With no shoulders and sharp curves, roads require reduced speeds and shifting into second gear on extended descents to avoid the fumes of burning brakes. Two roads cross the Continental Divide: Going-to-the-Sun Road bisects the park, while U.S. 2 hugs Glacier's southern border. Both are two-lane roads; however, Going-to-the-Sun Road is the more difficult drive, climbing 1,500 feet higher on a skinnier, snakier road than U.S. 2. It's also currently undergoing a decade of reconstruction. Going-to-the-Sun Road is open mid-June-mid-September, while U.S. 2 is open year-round. Going-to-the-Sun Road does not permit RVs and trailer-combos over 21 feet long.

Paved two-lane roads also lead to Two Medicine, St. Mary, Many Glacier, and Waterton. But don't be deluded: Just because roads are paved doesn't mean that they are smooth. Frost heaves and sinkholes pockmark them, bouncing passengers and slowing travel. Montana is also the land of dusty, potholed dirt roads: On the west side, two notorious bumpy roads lead up the North Fork Valley; on the east side, a dirt road leads into the Cut Bank Valley. In some places they are decent; in others they are as bad as they can be without requiring a 4WD vehicle. Larger RVs and those with trailers will not be comfortable on some dirt roads.

Gas

Gas up before you go: You won't find service stations on every corner. Gas is available in

© BECKY LOMAX

Short guard rails provide some safety on the cliffs of Going-to-the-Sun Road.

West Glacier, East Glacier, St. Mary, Babb, and Waterton, but few of the stations can repair severely broken-down vehicles. For big vehicle work, you'll need to hit Browning or Flathead Valley in Montana or Pincher Creek in Canada.

MAPS AND PLANNERS

Park maps that include both Glacier and Waterton are available at entrance stations, visitors centers, ranger stations, and online (www.nps.gov/glac). These maps are perfect for driving tours and perhaps a short walk or two. However, for those heading into the backcountry on day hikes and backpacking trips, pick up a topographic map. Four *Trails Illustrated* maps ($10-12) are available: the large Glacier that includes Waterton, and the more detailed Many Glacier, North Fork, and Two Medicine maps. The *USGS Glacier Park* map does not include Waterton. Buy these topographic maps through **Glacier National Park Conservancy** (406/888-5756, www.glaciernationalparkconservancy.org). For more detailed maps, USGS maps are available in the 7.5-minute series at Flathead Valley sporting goods stores or through the **U.S. Geological Survey** (888/ASK-USGS—888/275-8747, http://store.usgs.gov). For hiking Waterton, you'll find the best topographic map at the **Waterton Lakes Visitor Information Centre** (403/859-5133). You can also order it online (www.gemtrek.com). The Gem Trek map (C$10) shows roads, trails, and bike routes, and it adds trail descriptions for easy, moderate, and strenuous hikes. It also includes the eastern end of Akamina-Kishinena Provincial Park and the Goat Haunt area of Glacier.

For hiking trails, small area brochure-type maps (Many Glacier, Lake McDonald, Two Medicine, Logan Pass, and St. Mary) are available at ranger stations, visitors centers, hotel activity desks, and online. These do not have as much detail as topographic

DRIVING TIMES

Instead of using miles to plan your trip, use driving times that reflect the real road conditions around Glacier. From the following hubs, you can plan a trip from Whitefish to Many Glacier, for instance, by adding up the times between each of the hubs for your chosen route. Plan to add more time for photo stops, sightseeing, traffic delays, entrance station lineups, border crossings, or construction.

FROM WEST GLACIER TO:

- Apgar: 0:08
- Polebridge via Outside North Fork Road: 1
- Polebridge via Inside North Fork Road: 2:30
- Essex: 0:35
- East Glacier: 1:10
- Logan Pass: 1-1:30
- St. Mary: 1:15-2

FROM POLEBRIDGE TO:

- Bowman Lake: 0:35
- Kintla Lake: 1:10

FROM EAST GLACIER TO:

- Essex: 0:35
- West Glacier: 1:10
- Two Medicine: 0:25
- Browning: 0:15
- St. Mary via Highway 49 and U.S. 89: 0:50
- St. Mary via Browning and Duck Lake Road: 1:05

FROM ST. MARY TO:

- East Glacier via U.S. 89 and Highway 49: 0:50
- East Glacier via Duck Lake Road: 1:05
- Browning via U.S. 89: 0:40
- Browning via Duck Lake Road: 0:45
- Logan Pass: 0:35
- Many Glacier: 0:35
- Chief Mountain border crossing: 0:35
- Waterton: 0:75

FROM MANY GLACIER TO:

- St. Mary: 0:35
- Waterton: 1:30

TO WEST GLACIER FROM:

- Columbia Falls: 0:25
- Glacier Park airport in Kalispell: 0:40
- Whitefish: 0:45
- Kalispell: 0:50
- Bigfork: 1:10

FROM GREAT FALLS TO:

- East Glacier: 2:30

FROM CALGARY TO:

- Waterton: 3:20
- St. Mary: 3:30
- Many Glacier: 3:45

maps but can work in a pinch for day hikes on well-signed trails.

River floaters can find river maps in the *Three Forks of the Flathead Float Guide* ($13) at **Glacier National Park Conservancy** (406/888-5756, www.glaciernationalparkconservancy.org) bookstores.

Each year the National Park Service updates its *Glacier Vacation Planner,* a newspaper listing current information on campgrounds, roads, the park, visitors centers, border crossings, trails, and safety. Call the park (406/888-7800) for a mailed copy; the current edition is also online (www.nps.gov/glac).

For maps and information about national forests and the Bob Marshall Wilderness adjacent to the park, contact the **Hungry Horse Ranger Station** (10 Hungry Horse Dr.,

CELL PHONES AND INTERNET ACCESS

CELL PHONES

One of the best inventions for emergencies, cell phones allow immediate access to help. However, in an area as mountainous as Glacier, they do not always work.

Flathead Valley has comprehensive cell-phone coverage, but Glacier gets intermittent service. Dealing with a flat tire may require more than a cell phone call to AAA. Along much of Going-to-the-Sun Road and U.S. 2, cell-phone reception is nonexistent. You can get service in St. Mary, East Glacier, West Glacier, Apgar, and Waterton, but not in the North Fork, Goat Haunt, Many Glacier, Two Medicine, or Logan Pass.

Hikers and backpackers should carry a cell phone for emergencies, but do not rely on it as the sole means of rescue. High mountains and deep valleys prevent reception in most locations. Be prepared to deal with emergencies and self-rescue.

When phones do work in Glacier, use of cell phones in the park requires etiquette:

- Turn off ringers, because phone noise catapults hikers and campers from a natural experience back into the hubbub of modern life.
- If you must make a call, and the phone does work, move away from campsites and other hikers to avoid disrupting their experience.
- In backcountry chalets, go outside and away from people.
- On trails, refrain from using phones in the presence of other hikers.
- Be considerate of other people in the backcountry and their desire to get away from it all.

INTERNET ACCESS

In general, Internet connections are not available in Glacier. Visitors centers, lodges, and ranger stations do not have wireless connectivity available. Wireless Internet access is available at a few lodging properties and commercial campgrounds in St. Mary, East Glacier, and West Glacier. Wi-Fi is widely available in Flathead Valley hotels, campgrounds, cafés, and libraries.

Hungry Horse, 406/387-3800, www.fs.fed.us/r1/flathead). For Lewis and Clark National Forest, call the **Rocky Mountain Ranger Station** (1102 Main Ave. NW, Choteau, 406/466-5341, www.fs.fed.us/r1/lewisclark).

COMMUNICATIONS

While you will find cell-phone service and Internet connectivity in the small towns surrounding Glacier, it's a different story at park lodges and campgrounds. You won't find cell-phone service and Internet in the North Fork, Goat Haunt, Many Glacier, Two Medicine, Logan Pass, parts of U.S. 2, Glacier's backcountry, ranger stations, or visitors centers. High mountains block reception on remote trails and many of the roads surrounding the park. Sometimes you can't even get a GPS signal with peaks blocking reception.

SHUTTLES

Bus Shuttles

Inside Glacier, the National Park Service runs **free shuttles** July 1-Labor Day. These are shuttles, not guided tours. Between Apgar and St. Mary, they stop at 17 points on **Going-to-the-Sun Road,** including Logan Pass and trailheads. Get on or off at any of the stops denoted by interpretive signs. No tickets are needed, and no reservations are taken. Departing every 15-30 minutes, these extremely popular shuttles enable point-to-point hiking on some of Glacier's most spectacular trails. All routes begin uphill service at 7am daily, with the last departures from Logan Pass at 7pm. On the west side, destinations may vary with each shuttle; confirm your destination when you board to be sure you have the right one.

Glacier Park Inc. (406/892-2525, www.

glacierparkinc.com, $10-50 one-way) runs a van service (daily early June-late Sept.) north-south on the park's east side. It links East Glacier, Two Medicine, Cut Bank Creek, St. Mary, Many Glacier, Chief Mountain border crossing, and Waterton. No reservations are taken, and you pay in cash when you board. Additional shuttles run from Many Glacier to St. Mary (July-Labor Day) to accommodate hikers on the Highline-Swiftcurrent and Piegan Trail; call or check the website for current schedules.

By reservation, **Sun Tours** (406/226-9220 or 800/786-9220, www.glaciersuntours.com, June-Sept.) can shuttle hikers from St. Mary or East Glacier to east-side trailheads. Costs vary with the number of passengers, gear, time, and location.

Running shuttles year-round by reservation, **Flathead-Glacier Transportation** (406/892-3390 or 800/829-7039, www.glaciertransportation.com, $23-280 one-way, each additional person $3) picks up travelers and backpackers at Glacier International Airport and transports them to Chief Mountain border crossing, Many Glacier, St. Mary, Two Medicine, East Glacier, Essex, West Glacier, Apgar, Lake McDonald Lodge, Polebridge, and U.S. 2 trailheads. They also run shuttles to Flathead Valley towns: Whitefish, Columbia Falls, Kalispell, and Bigfork.

In Waterton, **Tamarack Outdoor Outfitters** (Tamarack Village Square, 214 Mount View Rd., 403/859-2378, www.hikewaterton.com, summer, C$13-120) shuttles hikers to the popular Carthew-Alderson trailhead or to Chief Mountain border crossing to catch Glacier Park Inc.'s east-side Glacier shuttle.

Boat Shuttles

Hikers and backpackers also use tour boats as hiking shuttles to reduce foot miles. In Glacier, **Glacier Park Boat Company** (406/257-2426, www.glacierparkboats.com, June-Sept., adults $6-12 one-way, children $3-6) carts hikers across Two Medicine Lake and in Many Glacier across Swiftcurrent and Josephine Lakes. Both add early morning Hiker Express shuttles in July-August. Pay at the docks; you do not need reservations to catch a return boat. If the last boat back is full, the boat company continues to run shuttles until all hikers are accommodated. Reservations are accepted with pre-payment.

In Waterton, **Waterton Shoreline Cruises** (403/859-2362, www.watertoncruise.com) runs boat shuttles to the Crypt Lake Trailhead (late May-early Oct., C$10-20 round-trip), and the tour boat to Goat Haunt, USA, functions as a hiker shuttle June-mid-September for round-trip (C$12-40) or one-way (C$9-25) rides.

TOURS

Bus Tours

Two bus-tour companies operate in Glacier Park, both traveling the scenic Going-to-the-Sun Road. You'll get the "inside story" on the park from both companies' guides. Neither include park entrance fees or meals.

Departing from East Glacier, Browning, St. Mary, and West Glacier, **Sun Tours** (406/226-9220 or 800/786-9220, www.glaciersuntours.com, June-Sept., adults $35-70, children $20-25) leads four- and seven-hour daily tours over Going-to-the-Sun Road in 25-passenger air-conditioned buses with huge windows. Interpretation is steeped in Blackfeet cultural history and park lore.

The **red jammer buses** with roll-back canvas tops are operated by Glacier Park Inc. (406/892-2525, www.glacierparkinc.com, late May-late Sept., adults $40-85, children $20-43). Daily tours depart from all the park lodges for Going-to-the-Sun Road, Waterton, and other destinations in the park environs. The company also guides the popular **Great Lodges of Glacier** tour (late June-mid-Sept., $2,069 pp d), a six-day romp through four of the park's historic lodges. The tour begins and ends in East Glacier, but pickups are available from Glacier Park International Airport in Flathead Valley as well as from Amtrak stations. Traveling by historic red jammer buses, the tour stays at four historic park lodges. Their **Great Glacier Adventure** tour ($2,229 pp) ups the activity by adding hiking, fly fishing, and rafting. Rates include lodging, meals, transportation around Glacier, boat cruises, and short walks. All of these tours sell out, so make reservations early.

Boat Tours

Five glacier-carved lakes in Waterton-Glacier International Peace Park have scenic boat tours. In Glacier, **Glacier Park Boat Company** (406/257-2426, www.glacierparkboats.com, daily June-Sept., $12-24, children $6-12) operates daily boat tours on Lake McDonald, Two Medicine Lake, St. Mary Lake, and in Many Glacier on Swiftcurrent and Josephine Lakes. Departure times vary; buy tickets at the docks or pre-pay by phone. In Waterton, scenic boat tours travel down Waterton Lake across the international border. **Waterton Shoreline Cruises** (403/859-2362, www.watertoncruise.com, daily May-early Oct., adults C$40, teens C$18, ages 4-12 C$12, under age 4 free) departs several times per day, with a stop at Goat Haunt, USA (late May-mid-Sept.). Purchase tickets at the dock.

© BECKY LOMAX

Two boats on two lakes in Many Glacier provide tours and hiker shuttles.

WALKING TRAILS

Trail Status

Conditions on Glacier's trails vary significantly depending on the season, elevation, recent severe weather, and bear closures. Swinging and plank bridges across rivers and creeks are not installed until late May-June. Some years, bridges are installed and then removed a few weeks later to wait for rivers swollen with runoff to subside. Most years, higher passes are snowbound until early July, and steep snow fields often inhibit hiking on the Highline Trail until mid-July or so. Ptarmigan Tunnel's doors are usually open mid-July-early October. To find out about trail conditions before hiking, you can stop at ranger stations and visitors centers for updates or consult Trail Status Reports (usually only updated June-Sept.) on the park's website (www.nps.gov/glac).

Signage

All park trailheads and junctions have excellent signage. Be prepared, however, to convert kilometers to miles in your head to understand distances. Some signs show both kilometers and miles, others simply kilometers. This is, after all, the International Peace Park, and kilometers are more international. If you hike in Waterton, all trail sign distances use kilometers. Pull out your math skills: To convert kilometers to miles, multiply the kilometers listed by 0.6 (example: multiply 3 kilometers by 0.6 to get 1.8 miles). To convert miles to kilometers, multiply the miles by 1.6 (example: multiply 2 miles by 1.6 to get 3.2 kilometers). These

TRAVEL GREEN IN GLACIER

Montana may not be up to par with big cities for recycling infrastructure, but Glacier is making advances. Because the park is located at the apex of three continental watersheds, it is a prime place to practice green habits.

CUTTING EMISSIONS

- Park your car to take shuttles. Free shuttles run July-Labor Day on Going-to-the-Sun Road, and other paid shuttles link points on Glacier's east side, including Waterton.
- Consider a guided tour. The historic red-bus fleet converted to a dual-fuel system that allows the buses to run on propane as well as gasoline.
- Many park restaurant menus now include local products–wine, beer, meats, and veggies–to reduce excessive transportation.

RECYCLING

- All campgrounds, picnic areas, and visitors centers are equipped with recycling bins adjacent to bear-resistant garbage cans. Please recycle aluminum and plastic. Glacier Park Inc., operator of most of the park lodges, provides blue containers for recycling collection in the guest rooms of each hotel.
- Glass is problematic in Montana, as the state has no recycling infrastructure for it yet. If you are driving, consider carrying your glass containers home with you to recycle. Glacier Park Inc. converted its beer to kegs in its bars and to cans in its stores to eliminate the waste from glass bottles. You can even buy Montana microbrews in aluminum cans. The company is also phasing out the use and sale of all plastic beverage bottles.

ECOCONSCIOUSNESS

- The Apgar Transit Center was built with LEED principles in lighting, water, waster, construction, and landscaping. Native plants, trees, and soils from the site were reused.
- Glacier Park Inc., operator of most of the park's historic lodges, achieved the ISO 14001 Certification for Environmental Management. Their lodges now use biodegradable products for carryout foods, compact fluorescent lightbulbs in guest rooms, ecofriendly cleaning products, bulk purchasing, and organic guest room amenities.

calculations are simple, easy approximations you can remember for the trail. Some hikers enjoy kilometers—the number is always higher, so the accomplishment feels greater. (For more precise conversions, multiply by 0.62 to convert kilometers to miles; to convert miles to kilometers, multiply by 1.61.)

Trailheads may also display yellow **bear warnings** or orange **bear closure** signs to alert hikers to frequent bear activity. Heavily trampled areas may have a **footprint with a red slash**—universally recognized as "don't walk here." Obey these signs: They protect fragile alpine meadows from abuse and protect area replanted with native plants.

Backpacking

Glacier National Park's backpacking is unrivaled. Sixty-six designated backcountry campgrounds spread campers out, so you never feel crowded, and the permit system guarantees you'll find solitude. You can hit the popular trails—the Highline, the Belly, and Gunsight Pass—or head for something really remote, like the Nyack-Coal Loop or Goat Haunt to Kintla. Backpacking information, permit applications, advance reservations, trail status reports, and backcountry campsite availability are online (www.nps.gov/glac). Call the park (406/888-7800) to speak with someone in person regarding conditions and routes. Use hiker shuttles to create easy point-to-point routes. While you can

ICEBERG / PTARMIGAN TRAIL
MI. KM.
PTARMIGAN FALLS 2.6 4.2
ICEBERG LAKE 4.9 7.9
PTARMIGAN TUNNEL 5.3 8.5
ELIZABETH LAKE CG. 10.1 16.3
BELLY RIVER R.S. 13.5 21.7
RESPECT ALL REGULATIONS
BACKCOUNTRY CAMPING PERMIT REQUIRED
© BECKY LOMAX

Many of Glacier's trail signs include both kilometers and miles.

get permits and information at ranger stations (Two Medicine, Many Glacier, Polebridge) and visitors centers (Logan Pass, St. Mary), the main place to pick up permits is Apgar Backcountry Office (406/888-7859, May-Oct.).

Guides

National Park Service naturalists guide free hikes during summer in Glacier and snowshoe excursions in winter. Consult schedules in the current *Ranger-led Activities* newspaper, available online at www.nps.gov/glac under "Brochures" or in visitors centers. Parks Canada naturalists guide free summer hikes in Waterton. Check for the current schedule in the visitors center or online (www.pc.gc.ca). Naturalists from both parks lead the International Peace Park hike twice weekly in July-August.

Commercial guide services are provided by one company in Glacier and one in Waterton, with reservations required. **Glacier Guides** (406/387-5555 or 800/521-7238, www.glacierguides.com) leads day hikes, chalet overnights, and backpacking trips that depart weekly for three, four, and six days. Sherpa services are also available if you don't want to carry your own gear. One of the most popular trips packages hiking to both backcountry chalets for two nights each. **Waterton Outdoor Adventures** at Tamarack Outdoor Outfitters (214 Mount View Rd., 403/859-2379, www.hikewaterton.com) leads day hikes in Waterton Lakes National Park.

Climbing

Glacier's peaks and off-trail scrambles are irresistible; the park's crumbly sedimentary rock, however, makes climbing risky. Loose handholds, wobbly footholds, rockfall, and unstable scree and talus slopes are hazardous. Safety while climbing is imperative. Each year, accidents and sometimes fatalities occur from falling while climbing. Only venture off-trail for climbing if you know the terrain and inherent risks. Do not attempt climbing in Glacier

GETTING INTO THE BACKCOUNTRY

Miles of well-marked scenic trails make Glacier rate high with backpackers. **Backcountry camping** is allowed in designated locations. Each campground has 2-7 sites, with four people allowed per site. All backcountry campgrounds have pit toilets (some with great views), community cook sites, and separate tent sites. No food, garbage, toiletries, or cookware should be kept in the tent sites. A bear pole, bar, or bear-proof food storage boxes are available.

Many backcountry campsites do not allow fires; carry a lightweight stove for cooking. Take low-odor foods to avoid attracting bears, and practice Leave No Trace principles religiously.

Bring backpacking gear (a tent, a sleeping bag, a pad, clothing, rain gear, topographic maps, a compass or GPS device, a first-aid kit, insect repellent, sunscreen, fuel, cooking gear, and a stove) plus a 25-foot rope for hanging food, a small screen or strainer for sifting food particles out of gray water, a one-micron or smaller filter for purifying water (tablets and boiling can also do the job), and a small trowel for emergency human waste disposal when a pit toilet is unavailable.

Permits are required (adults $5 pp per night, ages 8-15 $2.50, under age 8 free). By mail, a limited number of sites may be reserved ($30 extra). In person, stop by a permit office no more than 24 hours in advance to get permits at Apgar Permit Office (406/888-7859), St. Mary Visitors Center (406/732-7751), Many Glacier Ranger Station (406/732-7740), Two Medicine Ranger Station (406/226-4484), and Polebridge Ranger Station (406/888-7742). Hours generally run 8am-4:30pm daily May-November. In winter, call 406/888-7800.

SUGGESTED 3-4-DAY ROUTES

- **Gunsight Pass Trail:** This 20-mile trail between Jackson Overlook and Lake McDonald Lodge crosses two passes and connects with Sperry Chalet. Stay at Gunsight Lake, Lake Ellen Wilson, and Sperry, but add on the spur trail to Sperry Glacier.
- **Highline Trail:** For an international hike, begin at Logan Pass and finish 30 miles later at Goat Haunt to catch the boat across Waterton Lake into Canada. Camp at Granite Park, Fifty Mountain, and Kootenai Lakes.
- **St. Mary to Two Medicine:** A 35-mile trail links prime fishing lakes along several high passes in bighorn sheep country. Camp at Old Man Lake, Morningstar Lake, and Red Eagle Lake.

SUGGESTED 5-10-DAY ROUTES

- **Northern Traverse:** Between Chief Mountain border crossing and Kintla Lake, the 58-mile trail crosses three passes as it wanders just south of the Canadian border. Camp at Cosley Lake, Glenn's Lake, Stoney Indian Lake, Lake Francis, Boulder Pass, Upper Kintla, and Kintla Lake.
- **North Circle Tour:** Following in the footsteps of the historic horseback tours through Glacier, this 54-mile loop connects Many Glacier via Ptarmigan Tunnel with the Belly and the northern Highline. Camp at Elizabeth, Cosley, Glenn's, and Stoney Indian Lakes; Fifty Mountain; and Granite Park.
- **Continental Divide National Scenic Trail:** The trail runs 110 miles from Marias Pass to Waterton in a stunning conclusion to the 3,100-mile trail. For this route, connect front-country and backcountry campgrounds.

alone or without experience. Most ascents are actually scrambles, but still not for the inexperienced. For routes, J. Gordon Edwards's *A Climber's Guide to Glacier National Park* has been the undisputed bible, but Blake Passmore's new *Climb Glacier Park* gives more detailed information for climbing around Logan Pass.

Begin all off-trail adventures by registering at a ranger station or visitors center, and go prepared. Be aware of closures for bears and fragile vegetation, especially around Logan Pass. Check with visitors centers or ranger stations for the status, or call 406/888-7800. Always practice Leave No Trace principles. For emergencies, carry a cell phone along, but don't depend on its ability to work everywhere in the park. Instead, be ready to self-rescue.

No commercial guiding outfitters operate climbing trips in Glacier. To hook up with climbers, **Glacier Mountaineering Society** (www.glaciermountaineers.com) offers volunteer-led climbs for members, usually on weekends, and each summer they pack one week in July full of climbs for Mountaineering Week. Annual memberships cost $25. The website is also loaded with climbing info.

RESOURCES

Suggested Reading

DRIVING GUIDES

Guthrie, C. W., Martha Cheney, and Diane Krage. *Glacier National Park Legends and Lore: Along Going-to-the-Sun Road.* Helena, MT: Farcountry Press, 2002. An 88-page mile-by-mile tour of the historic road with Native American tales from Hugh Monroe, known as Rising Wolf of the Blackfeet.

Schmidt, Thomas. *National Geographic Road Guide to Glacier and Waterton Lakes National Park.* Washington DC: National Geographic, 2004. A handy 93-page guide to driving the park's roads. Each section is complete with a map, nature notes, landscape features, and stops.

GEOLOGY

Alt, David, and Donald W. Hyndman. *Roadside Geology of Montana.* Missoula, MT: Mountain Press, 1986. Although Glacier's roads are treated minimally, the diagrams and descriptions are useful even to nongeologists. It is the best resource for geology on roads outside the park.

Raup, Omar B., Robert L. Earhart, James W. Whipple, and Paul E. Carrara. *Geology Along Going-to-the-Sun Road.* West Glacier, MT: Glacier Natural History Association, 1983. An easy-to-read 63-page geology guide for folks with no science background. Maps, 21 stops, and diagrams describe the geologic phenomena on the historic highway, along with great photos showing rock formations.

Ahlenslager, Kathleen. *Glacier: The Story Behind the Scenery.* Wickenburg, AZ: KC Publications, 1988. Color photos and text tell the natural history of Glacier in this 48-page book with emphasis on geology.

GRIZZLY BEARS

Chadwick, Doug. *True Griz.* San Francisco: Sierra Club Books, 2003. True stories of four grizzly bears—their survival and deaths. Chadwick is a reputable bear biologist.

Herrero, Stephen. *Bear Attacks: Their Causes and Avoidance.* Guilford, CT: The Lyons Press, 2002. Somewhat sensationalized with attention to gory detail, Herrero's book paints a picture of the myriad reasons for bear attacks while also covering safety and how to avoid attacks. Not for light sleepers who plan to go into the backcountry. Herrero is one of the leading authorities on bear research.

McMillion, Scott. *Mark of the Grizzly.* Helena, MT: Falcon Press, 1998. McMillion tells the stories behind 18 different grizzly bear attacks. He doesn't shy away from the gore, nor does he become preachy or judgmental, but he does examine each attack in detail to determine what we can learn about bears.

Olsen, Jack. *Night of the Grizzlies.* Moose, WY: Homestead Publishing, 1996. A true story of one night in 1968 when grizzlies killed two women in two different locations in Glacier's backcountry. This event altered park policies regarding food and garbage as well as bear management practices.

Schneider, Bill. *Bear Aware.* Helena, MT: Falcon Press, 2004. This handy little 96-page book is packed with advice on how to hike safely in bear country. One section tackles bear myths, debunking them with facts.

WILDLIFE

Chadwick, Doug. *The Wolverine Way.* Ventura, CA: Patagonia Inc., 2010. Stories of the gluttonous creatures that epitomize wilderness, gleaned from research in Glacier.

Fisher, Chris. *Birds of the Rocky Mountains.* Edmonton, Canada: Lone Pine Publishing, 1997. A Lone Pine Field Guide for birds found in the Rocky Mountains—every species from raptors to waterfowl, songbirds to woodpeckers. Large drawings help with identification, and descriptions include details on size, range, habitat, nesting, and feeding. Details point out differences between similar species.

Fisher, Chris, Don Pattie, and Tamara Hartson. *Mammals of the Rocky Mountains.* Edmonton, Canada: Lone Pine Publishing, 2000. A Lone Pine Field Guide for 91 species of animals found in the Rocky Mountains—a breeze to use. Each animal has details on physical description, behavior, habitat, food, denning, range, and young. Similar species are described to point out differences for identification.

Harada, Sumio, and Karen Yale. *Mountain Goats of Glacier National Park.* Helena, MT: Farcountry Press, 2008. Harada has photographed mountain goats in Glacier for the past two decades; Yale chronicles their behavior.

Wilkinson, Todd, and Michael H. Francis. *Watching Glacier's Wildlife.* Helena, MT: Riverbend Publishing, 2002. A 96-page guide to when, where, and how to see Glacier's wildlife.

HISTORY

Djuff, Ray, and Chris Morrison. *Glacier's Historic Hotels and Chalets: View with a Room.* Helena, MT: Farcountry Press, 2001. Loaded with historical photos, this quasi-coffee-table book tells the story behind each of Glacier Park's lodges and chalets, including the chalets that no longer exist. A great background read for anyone who falls in love with Glacier's historic lodges.

Glacier Centennial Program Committee, ed. *A View Inside Glacier National Park.* Glacier National Park, 2010. This collection of 100 stories about Glacier's 100 years celebrated the park's centennial in 2010.

Guthrie, Carol. *All Aboard for Glacier: The Great Northern Railway and Glacier National Park.* Helena, MT: Farcountry Press, 2004. For train buffs, the history of the Great Northern Railway building up Glacier as a destination for its passengers.

Guthrie, C. W. *Glacier National Park: The First 100 Years.* Helena, MT: Farcountry Press, 2008. The official centennial book contains rich color and historic photos in its decade-by-decade waltz through Glacier's history.

Guthrie, C. W. *Going-to-the-Sun Road: Highway to the Sky.* Helena, MT: Farcountry Press, 2006. With historic photos and maps, Going-to-the-Sun Road takes shape in this chronicle of the 20-year building of the National Historic Landmark.

Holterman, Jack. *Place Names of Glacier National Park.* Helena, MT: Riverbend

Publishing, 2006. A list of 663 park names—how peaks, passes, lakes, rivers, and valleys in Glacier acquired their monikers.

Lawrence, Tom. *Pictures, a Park, and a Pulitzer: Mel Ruder and the Hungry Horse News.* Helena, MT: Farcountry Press, 2000. Photos and stories from Lawrence, a Pulitzer Prize-winning journalist and editor for 32 years at the *Hungry Horse News.* Much of the history covers Glacier.

NATIVE AMERICANS

Grinnell, George Bird. *Blackfoot Lodge Tales.* Whitefish, MT: Kessinger Publishing, 2007. Grinnell, who negotiated the purchase of reservation land for the park, chronicles Blackfeet stories from his days in Glacier in the late 1800s.

Schultz, James Willard. *Blackfeet Tales of Glacier National Park.* Helena, MT: Riverbend Publishing, 1916. Original Blackfeet stories collected by Schultz in the late 1800s, including the history of Two Medicine, Cut Bank, St. Mary, Swiftcurrent, and Chief Mountain.

NATURAL HISTORY

DeSanto, Jerry. *Logan Pass: Alpine Splendor.* Guilford, CT: Globe Pequot Press, 1995. Gorgeous photos and short easy-to-read descriptions of the Logan Pass environment, including grizzly bears, red buses, hiking, climbing, winter, wildflowers, and geology.

Kershaw, Linda, Andy MacKinnon, and Jim Pojar. *Plants of the Rocky Mountains.* Edmonton, Canada: Lone Pine Publishing, 1998. A Lone Pine Field Guide for eight types of flora found in the Rocky Mountains: trees, shrubs, wildflowers, aquatics, grasses, ferns, mosses, and lichens. Although the pictures are small, the detailed descriptions of appearance, season, and habitat help in identification. Notes on each of the 1,300 species given include fun tidbits on the origin of names and Native American uses.

Kimball, Shannon Fitzpatrick, and Peter Lesica. *Wildflowers of Glacier National Park and Surrounding Areas.* Kalispell, MT: Trillium Press, 2005. One of the best regional flower guides. Flowers are categorized by color, with big sharp photos allowing easy identification. Includes entries for trees, ferns, and grasses.

Rockwell, David. *Exploring Glacier National Park: A Natural History Guide.* Helena, MT: Falcon Press, 2002. Contrary to the title, this is not a guide book but a description of Glacier Park's natural history. Rockwell covers geology, glaciers, flora, fauna, fires, and human impact on the ecosystem in the best available in-depth natural history book on the park.

OUTDOOR RECREATION

Arthur, Jean. *Montana Winter Trails: The Best Cross-country Ski and Snowshoe Trails.* Guilford, CT: Globe Pequot Press, 2001. Trail descriptions include five detailed trips for Glacier and several more for Flathead Valley.

Duckworth, Carolyn, ed. *Hiker's Guide to Glacier National Park* and *Short Hikes and Strolls in Glacier National Park.* West Glacier, MT: Glacier Natural History Association, 1996. Two books covering Glacier only, not Waterton. The hiker's guide contains 110 pages describing popular trails. *Short Hikes* is a 46-page book covering 16 favorite 1- to 4-mile walks.

Edwards, J. Gordon. *A Climber's Guide to Glacier Park.* Helena, MT: Falcon Press, 1995. The definitive guide to mountaineering in Glacier National Park. Edwards pioneered many of the routes up Glacier's peaks and is considered the park's patron saint of climbing. Routes cover technical climbs and off-trail scrambles.

Good, Stormy R. *Day Hikes Around the Flathead.* Whitefish, MT: Flathead

Guidebooks, 2011. A self-published book covering 99 day hikes with maps, route descriptions, distances, difficulty, and special emphasis on identifying dog-friendly trails. Available only through local bookstores and outdoor shops.

Meador, Mike, and Lee Stanley. *Mountain Bike Rides of the Flathead Valley.* Whitefish, MT: self-published, 2005. A 60-page roundup of the Flathead's best fat-tire rides, with maps, directions, and elevation profiles. Available only at Glacier Cyclery in Whitefish.

Molvar, Erik. *Best Easy Day Hikes in Glacier and Waterton Lakes.* Helena, MT: Falcon Press, 2001. A roundup of day hikes in both Glacier and Waterton. At half the size of his hiking guidebook, this focuses only on day hikes, with emphasis on well-signed, less-strenuous trails.

Molvar, Erik. *Hiking Glacier and Waterton Lakes National Parks.* Helena, MT: Falcon Press, 2012. The most definitive trail guide for Glacier and Waterton Parks. Molvar gives detailed trail descriptions, including maps, for all the popular trails inside the parks. Routes cover day hikes, overnights, and extended backpacking trips. Hiker safety, campsite details, and fishing information are also included.

Molvar, Erik. *Hiking Montana's Bob Marshall Wilderness.* Helena, MT: Falcon Press, 2001. A detailed trail guide covering the Great Bear, Bob Marshall, and Scapegoat Wilderness Areas. Trail descriptions include maps, elevation charts, and accurate information on how to find even the more difficult-to-locate trailheads.

Passmore, Blake. *Climb Glacier National Park,* vols. 1 and 2. Stevensville, MT: Stoneydale Press, 2011. This illustrated guide provides climbing routes for 16 peaks in the Logan Pass, Siyeh Bend, and Highline Trail region in Volume 1. The second volume covers Two Medicine and Firebrand Pass areas. Color photos, maps, and GPS points identify routes.

Sande, Nathan. *Instant Gratification: Selected One-day Ski Trips in the Flathead Backcountry.* Kalispell, MT: self-published. A 66-page guide with maps and route descriptions for backcountry telemark and *randonnée* ski trips in the Swan Mountains, Flathead Range, and Glacier Park. Available only at Rocky Mountain Outfitter in Kalispell.

Schneider, Russ. *Fishing Glacier National Park.* Helena, MT: Falcon Press, 2002. The most definitive fishing guide to Glacier. Schneider explains what flies to use to catch certain fish, where you'll catch arctic grayling or westslope cutthroat trout, and where you'll find nothing.

Internet Resources

GLACIER PARK

Glacier National Park
www.nps.gov/glac
The official website for Glacier National Park. It provides information on park conditions, roads, campsites, trails, history, and more. Six webcams are updated every few minutes. In addition to trip planning information, the site includes downloadable maps, publications, and backcountry permit applications as well as a Going-to-the-Sun Road status report, updated daily.

Glacier Natural History Association
www.glacierassociation.org
The best resource for books, maps, posters, and cards on Glacier Park. A portion of the proceeds from book sales are donated to the park.

Northern Rocky Mountain Research Center
www.nrmrc.usgs.gov
The research center works under the U.S. Geological Survey. The website contains current research in Glacier on grizzly bears, glaciers, climate change, bighorn sheep, avalanches, and amphibians.

The Glacier Institute
www.glacierinstitute.org
An educational nonprofit park partner, the Glacier Institute presents programs for kids and adults in field settings taught by expert instructors. Field classes take place in Glacier as well as surrounding ecosystems.

Glacier National Park Associates
www.nps.gov/gla/partners/gnpa.htm
This volunteer nonprofit assists with historic preservation and trail work and is always looking for volunteers to help on projects for a few days.

National Park Service Reservation Center
www.recreation.gov
Two campgrounds in Glacier—Fish Creek and St. Mary—take reservations using this service.

Trail photos, videos, and blogs
www.hike734.com
Jake Bramante documented all of Glacier's 734 miles of trail in 2011. You can look up specific trails by map to see photos, video, and blogs.

Glacier Park Chat Room
www.glacier.nationalparkschat.com/phpBB3/
Locals moderate a chat room about hiking, camping, eating, lodging, climbing, and traveling in Glacier.

WATERTON PARK

Waterton Lakes National Park
www.pc.gc.ca/waterton
The official website for Waterton. It contains most of the basic park information on camping, hiking, and Parks Canada-operated services, but not the commercial services in Waterton Townsite.

National Park Service Reservation Center
www.pccamping.ca
Log on to make reservations at Waterton's Townsite campground and other Canadian national parks.

Waterton Chamber of Commerce
www.mywaterton.ca
This website offers the most complete dining, lodging, recreation, visitor services, and camping information for Waterton. Some services adjacent to the park are also included.

FLATHEAD VALLEY

Flathead Valley Convention and Visitors Bureau
www.fcvb.org
The Flathead Valley's tourism board covers

info on Kalispell, Columbia Falls, Whitefish, Bigfork, Lakeside, Flathead Lake, and ski resorts. You'll find recreation, lodging, dining, and special events.

MONTANA TRAVEL

Glacier Country
www.glaciermt.com
The official state travel website for northwest Montana. You can find lodging, dining, and activity information, and it's easy to navigate by activity or location.

Montana Travel
www.visitmt.com
The official travel website for Montana. You'll find access to the state's activities, lodging, dining, and recreation by location or activity.

Montana Department of Transportation
www.mdt.mt.gov
Travel advisories and road conditions for Montana. Glacier's interior roads are not yet included on the website; information on Going-to-the-Sun Road is sporadic. Check the park's website for the most accurate information.

Lewis and Clark National Forest
www.fs.fed.us/r1/lewisclark/
Information on campgrounds, trails, fishing, cabin rentals, and other recreation, particularly for the Bob Marshall Wilderness.

Flathead National Forest
www.fs.fed.us/r1/flathead
At this official website, find info on campgrounds, fishing, rafting, wilderness areas, cabin rentals, ski areas, trails, and other recreation. However, the recreation section is limited to specifics for trails.

Montana Fish, Wildlife, and Parks
http://fwp.mt.gov
Up-to-date fishing and hunting information, licenses, state park, and wildlife refuge details for Montana.

CANADIAN TRAVEL

Travel Alberta Canada
www.travelalberta.com
The province's official portal to Alberta resorts, parks, ski areas, festivals, events, cities, outdoor recreation, and touring. It's easy to navigate by location or activity to find what you want.

Alberta Road Reports
www.ama.ab.ca/road-reports
Check this site for road construction, advisories, and closures from the Alberta Motor Association.

British Columbia Transportation
www.gov.bc.ca/tran
Road reports update travel information, closures, construction, and weather for British Columbia. Webcams will give you a firsthand look.

Akamina-Kishinena Provincial Park
www.gov.bc.ca/bcparks
Information on recreation, camping, and hiking in Akamina-Kishinena Provincial Park adjacent to Waterton and Glacier. There are also maps.

Index

H

I

U

V

WXYZ

List of Maps

MAP SYMBOLS

Expressway	Highlight	Airfield	Golf Course
Primary Road	City/Town	Airport	Parking Area
Secondary Road	State Capital	Mountain	Archaeological Site
Unpaved Road	National Capital	Unique Natural Feature	Church
Trail	Point of Interest	Waterfall	Gas Station
Ferry	Accommodation	Park	Glacier
Railroad	Restaurant/Bar	Trailhead	Mangrove
Pedestrian Walkway	Other Location	Skiing Area	Reef
Stairs	Campground		Swamp

CONVERSION TABLES

°C = (°F - 32) / 1.8
°F = (°C x 1.8) + 32
1 inch = 2.54 centimeters (cm)
1 foot = 0.304 meters (m)
1 yard = 0.914 meters
1 mile = 1.6093 kilometers (km)
1 km = 0.6214 miles
1 fathom = 1.8288 m
1 chain = 20.1168 m
1 furlong = 201.168 m
1 acre = 0.4047 hectares
1 sq km = 100 hectares
1 sq mile = 2.59 square km
1 ounce = 28.35 grams
1 pound = 0.4536 kilograms
1 short ton = 0.90718 metric ton
1 short ton = 2,000 pounds
1 long ton = 1.016 metric tons
1 long ton = 2,240 pounds
1 metric ton = 1,000 kilograms
1 quart = 0.94635 liters
1 US gallon = 3.7854 liters
1 Imperial gallon = 4.5459 liters
1 nautical mile = 1.852 km

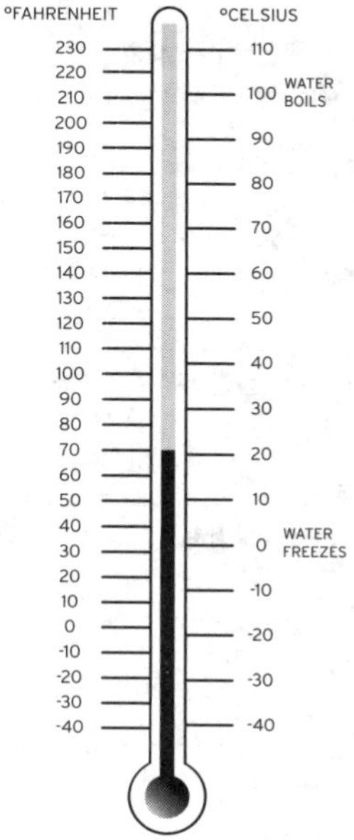

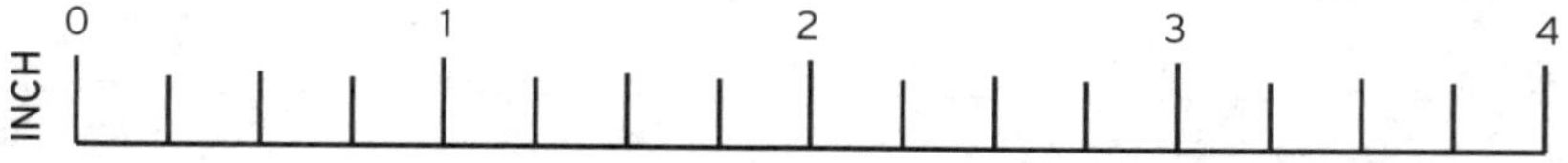

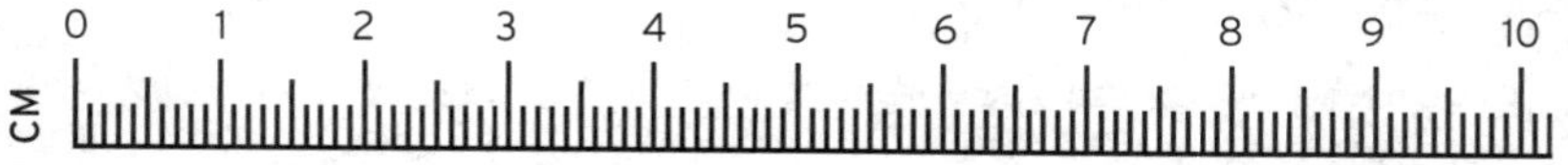

MOON GLACIER NATIONAL PARK
Avalon Travel
a member of the Perseus Books Group
1700 Fourth Street
Berkeley, CA 94710, USA
www.moon.com

Editor: Elizabeth Hollis Hansen
Series Manager: Sabrina Young
Copy Editor: Christopher Church
Production Coordinator: Domini Dragoone
Graphics Coordinator: Kathryn Osgood
Cover Designer: Domini Dragoone
Map Editor: Kat Bennett
Cartographers: Kat Bennett and Chris Henrick
Indexer: Deana Shields

ISBN-13: 978-1-61238-324-8
ISSN: 1557-6299

Printing History
1st Edition – 2006
4th Edition – May 2013
5 4 3 2 1

Front cover photo: September sunrise at wild Goose Island Overlook at Glacier National Park, © Scott Pudwell Photography/Flickr/Getty Images
Title page photo: Highline Trail, Becky Lomax
Front color photos: all Becky Lomax, except pg. 10 Snehit/123RF, and pg. 19 Jason Ross/123RF.

Printed in Canada by Friesens

KEEPING CURRENT

If you have a favorite gem you'd like to see included in the next edition, or see anything that needs updating, clarification, or correction, please drop us a line. Send your comments via email to feedback@moon.com, or use the address above.